Organizational Behavior
Real Research for Real Managers

Third Edition

Jone L. Pearce
University of California, Irvine

Melvin & Leigh, Publishers Irvine, California

Melvin & Leigh, Publishers
6 Curie Court
Irvine, CA 92617
orders.melvinleigh@cox.net
www.melvinleigh.com

Cover design by Heather Kern

Printed in the United States of America

Organizational Behavior Real Research for Real Managers / Jone L. Pearce

Includes bibliographical references and index.

ISBN-13: 978-0-9786638-2-7

1. Organizational behavior. 2. Management I. Pearce, Jone L. 1952-

HD58.7.P43 2012

This publication is designed to provide accurate and authoritative information with regard to the subject matter covered. It is sold with the understanding that the publisher is not engaged in rendering legal, accounting, or other professional advice. If legal advice or other expert assistance is required, the services of a competent professional person should be sought.

Printed in the United States of America on mixed recycled paper

Visit our home page at www.melvinleigh.com

Organizational Behavior Real Research for Real Managers

To my students

Contents

Preface

This is a different kind of textbook. *Organizational Behavior Real Research for Real Managers* addresses those practical problems managers face in doing their organizational work. It looks to systematic organizational behavior research seeking to discover which organizational actions and practices actually do and do not work. Unlike other organizational behavior textbooks, *Organizational Behavior Real Research for Real Managers* actually translates this scholarly research for real managers seeking to understand and control organizations. Other textbooks in the field of organizational behavior have failed to do this. One reflection of that failure is Ohio State's Organizational Behavior faculty's finding that 80% of the top-50 MBA programs in the country did not use textbooks in their introductory organizational behavior classes. Why is this so?

- Existing organizational textbooks are targeted to large undergraduate courses where the students have little practical experience of organizations. These textbooks are chasing the largest classes: more students, more book sales. There is no need for these textbooks to address practical management problems because their readers have not yet faced these challenges.

- Other textbooks contain too many "facts" that have long been discredited by scholars. Too many organizational behavior textbooks review familiar but discredited theories, after which the most honest of them will note that the ideas are "controversial." Doesn't controversy require someone arguing for the other side? When all evidence points to the contrary, who is arguing for movement up and down a Maslovian hierarchy of needs, or for Herzberg's Two Factor Theory of Motivators? These old ideas are long discredited, so why waste a reader's time by explaining them? Other organizational behavior textbooks are a disservice to students, as well as to those scholars who have worked so hard to produce new knowledge.

- With a need to keep the attention of young people, other textbooks resort to long lists of this month's trendy topics and cartoons. Rather than this straining-too-obviously for relevance, *Organizational Behavior Real Research for Real Managers* helps readers with their own practical organizational problems.

- Other textbooks often do contain practical advice but make no pretense that it is based in research, usually just reprinting advice from popular management books.

With increasing numbers of experienced professionals and managers taking part-time and Executive MBA courses and enrolling in university-based non-degree executive education courses in organizational behavior, there is a need for a book that clearly, honestly and accurately conveys what the field of organizational behavior can say to experienced managers. These students have no patience for dull lists of seemingly unconnected facts, and those trained in organizational behavior want to be able to share the knowledge from their field, not assign well packaged consultant's anecdotes and advice. This book was written to fill that need.

The book is organized by managers' practical organizational problems, but care is taken to draw on the most careful research. Readers will see extensive endnotes to that scholarly research. Because most of those works are difficult scholarly studies, student readers are not expected to consult these sources. However, their instructors may find them useful, particularly in subfields outside their own specialties. Because this book is intended to be useful to practicing managers and experienced professionals, practical advice is developed from the scholarly research; however, these generalizations are clearly identified as generalizations from research as boxed *Applications*.

Instructor support is available from the author at jlpearce@uci.edu.

I am indebted to those who helped and supported me in this project. First, my students: it is from them that I learned so much about the practical problems managers face and became dissatisfied with the ill service they received from our textbooks. They are my inspiration and motivation. I want to thank the University of Washington's Business School, which supported me with their Hansen Chair in the early stages of this project, and Karl Vesper who provided crucial advice. I received invaluable editorial assistance from Eric Oberg, Boris Groysberg, Lisa Barron, James O'Brien, Samara Larson, and Steve Sommer, and library research assistance from Ann Clark. Any coherence this book has is due to them; the errors are all mine. Most importantly, Harry Briggs has been a wonder; he has applied his considerable editorial skills to many earlier versions of this draft and has provided invaluable professional advice on textbooks and the business of textbooks. His infinite patience and good cheer are the miracle that sustains me.

1

Why Organizational Behavior

This is a book for people who want to understand organizations so they can take charge of the organizations in their lives. Those who have set ambitious goals for themselves will need to harness organizations. Whether they want to make a million dollars, see their new technology conquer the marketplace, or save the planet from global warming, they will need organizations. Even those with more modest aims, such as accomplishing project team objectives without doing all of the work alone, winning that promotion, or getting through staff meetings without suffering a stroke will find this book useful.

This book is based on the premise that real research can be useful to managers' real problems. Because organizations are so complex, much of our common sense about them is of little use. Opinions differ, and our own experiences with organizations are necessarily limited. Here real social science research is used to inform our popular opinions and received wisdom. It addresses the question: What does the evidence say about what really works?

This is a book covering what research in the field of organizational behavior can usefully tell us about managers' real organizational challenges, but it is different from standard textbooks in that field. Textbooks are encyclopedic lists of bits of research findings, enlivened with cartoons and color photographs. If the bits of information in textbooks are organized at all, they are grouped by academic topic. This approach makes it difficult for people who want to take action in organizations to make sense of the material and act based on it. This book is organized by the real organizational challenges faced by those who must work with and through organizations. Its focus is on managers, because it is their work to manage people in organizations, but a practical understanding of how to master organizations can be useful to many others. One reflection of this focus on the real organizational challenges faced by real managers is the questions addressed by the chapters:

- What do managers need to do to be effective and successful? (Chapter 2)
- How can managers hire the best employees? (Chapter 3)
- How do feelings affect organizational work? (Chapter 4)
- What is the most effective way to manage employee performance? (Chapter 5)
- What makes leaders successful? (Chapter 10)
- If it doesn't work out, how do you terminate employees in ways that minimize damage to the employee and the organization? (Chapter 11)

THE CHALLENGE OF ORGANIZATIONAL MASTERY

Management exists for those problems too complex for either markets or common sense.[1] The very complexity of organizations can overwhelm common sense, making this boxed popular opinion false. Common sense is developed in face-to-face relationships, ones where we have enough time to get to know one another. These common sense understandings are usually enough for most of our social challenges. However, organizations put people into complicated relationships requiring knowledge that goes beyond common sense.

> ***True or False?***
>
> *Isn't management just common sense?*

- Organizations are very large systems of interdependence, and no one person has all of the information about what is going on everywhere. Those who try to solve their organizational problems by trying to know everyone and understand everything that every one is doing quickly burn themselves out.
- Common sense is not enough for organizational mastery because of the uncertainty that comes from changing technologies, competitors' new moves, and shifting financial and market conditions. These require organizations to change continuously and some times to become different organizations altogether. So, even those who have successfully mastered one organization may find that it

needs to change into a different one that they may not understand at all.

- Successful management requires more than technical knowledge of how organizations work. Organizations exist to get work done, and our personal feelings about other people can interfere with getting that work done. We may take a job or start an enterprise for some practical purpose, but we find that some of the people we work with are helpful, others are talented or clever, others may see you as the person who can help them get what they want, and some will see you as the boulder blocking the road to their dreams. Some people make mistakes that cause you serious harm, others are lazy or resentful or just rub you the wrong way. We all have differing feelings about the people we encounter in organizations, and those feelings matter. No amount of training in rational decision making or management techniques will make these feelings go away.

Organizational mastery is a challenge. Organizations undertake work too complex for markets or any one person to fully comprehend. They attempt such work with people who all have their own agendas and antipathies, using highly complex management systems, all under continuous pressure to change. The more you want to get done in life, the more likely you are to face challenging, complex and difficult organizational problems. Making organizations work for you is very hard, often counter intuitive, and requires a sophisticated understanding of what organizations are and how they function. Common sense is not enough.

TESTING OUR MANAGEMENT OPINIONS

Because the challenge of organizational mastery is so difficult and can never be solved once-and-for-all, there are many books offering popular advice on leadership and management. These are usually well-written, and readers often can find good advice from any one of them. However, they are all based on the writer's personal experiences, and the problem with personal experience is that people have had many differing organizational experiences and so give contradictory or uselessly vague advice. One example of this contradictory advice: Britain's wealthiest entrepreneur, Richard Branson, had this to say about the celebrity American real-estate developer Donald Trump: "*He has a list of the most important things you need in order to be successful in business, and I don't agree with any of them.*"[2]

A look into the book shelves of your local bookstore for management advice will reveal thousands of opinions, anecdotes and bullet-point lists. Some may spur a useful idea, but many are contradictory, some are cryptic, and others just silly. Your organizational success is important, and this hodgepodge of opinions and advice can be misleading, paralyzing and dysfunctional.

And it gets worse. All of us already know something about how to succeed in organizations. Even the very youngest of readers will have mastered the art of figuring out how to get their teachers to give them the grades they need to pursue their goals, probably have struggled with tyrannical bosses, or, as volunteers had "friends" who "forgot" and left them to clean up after the club fair. But even though we all have mastered some organizational skills, as we develop ever more demanding goals or face new problems, our old organizational skills can fail us. Successful organizational mastery means succeeding in differing organizations. Morgan McCall and David Lombardo[3] found that one of the best predictors of which promising young managers actually rose to the top of their companies was the ability of the more successful managers to recognize that each new job had different demands requiring new approaches. Those aspiring young managers who could not cope with difficult bosses or the more complex political demands of a new assignment failed.

Because all of us already have mastered some organizational skills and have read some of those popular leadership and management advice books, we all carry around with us many **management opinions** about the management and leadership of organizations. Management opinions are those assumptions, ideas and theories that we no longer question, but just assume, like the one about common sense in the box above.

A further challenge to organizational mastery is that no matter how much we might understand about organizations intellectually, we are all emotionally involved. As the personal consequences for organizational incompetence become more important, our anxiety and distress impede our ability to analyze and make careful decisions.[4] It doesn't matter how much any of us may know about succeeding in organizations; if we are furious, it is hard to apply that knowledge effectively. And there is plenty to infuriate when doing organizational work. Other people are careless and make mistakes that make you look bad, or team members don't deliver by deadline. And, of course, the people around us also become angry, bored, envious, and complacent. No one should ever assume that just a few extra facts, or repeated advice to be more analytical, are all that is needed to succeed. Here we will explicitly face the reality that our organizational success depends on learning how to manage our own and others' emotions.

> In his 2001 Presidential Address to the American Sociological Association, Douglas Massey noted that the social conditions for human rationality have existed for only about 100 years, whereas we have had 6 million years to refine and develop our emotional intelligence. He says that we "have unwisely elevated the rational over the emotional in attempting to understand and explain human behavior. It is not that human beings are not rational — we are. The point is we are not *only* rational. What makes us human is the addition of a rational mind to a pre-existing emotional base.

Because organizations are so complex, can defy common sense, and certainly are frustrating, many of our personal organizational and management opinions are limited. This book addresses the most common management opinions by holding them up to eight decades of research in organizational behavior to see if (or when) they are actually supported by the evidence. Many of our personal management opinions, as well as that bookshelf of practical advice, is often just wrong.

Each opinion appears in a box throughout the book. These opinions have been organized into chapters focused on practical organizational problems we face in trying to work successfully through organizations. These problems have come from executives and experienced MBA students who have been asked to describe their biggest organizational challenges, and from the problems addressed in popular leadership and management self-help books.

This book addresses organizational challenges that are useful to both non-managerial participants and to managers. However, the focus is on managers' organizational challenges. Because managers' jobs are to run organizations, more of their challenges are organizational challenges. But those who are not experienced managers can still gain much practical organizational knowledge. Most of the information — how to get what you want from organizations — is useful for anyone working in and through organizations. We all want something from organizations, and the things we want to accomplish make us dependent on knowledge about organizational behavior. Knowing what your boss's problems are is useful to your own organizational success, and at the end of each chapter several implications for non-managers are made explicit in the sections titled, *Implications for Managing Managers.*

WHY ORGANIZATIONAL BEHAVIOR

There have been thousands of studies over the past eighty years seeking to discover which organizational actions and practices actually do and do not work. This branch of the social sciences is called **organizational behavior**. Much research in organizational behavior is designed to answer questions about why people do what they do in organizations, how they can be more influential, to identify which management practices are most effective, and to explain how norms, feelings and cultures affect organizational functioning. Organizational behavior research identifies and tests popular management opinions, as well as more complex explanations. This research uses a wide range of social science methods such as experiments, surveys, interviews, observations and archival studies to test theories and popular management opinions. Over the decades, organizational behavior researchers working around the world have produced a wealth of systematic and reliable organizational understandings that are as useful as the best personal management opinions. Unfortunately, it is rarely worth a normal person's time to try to dig through this vast academic literature to find the useful bits. This is because most of the research is either inaccessible to an untrained reader or addresses problems far removed from their needs. This is so for several reasons.

First, much organizational behavior research addresses an academically trained audience, and so untrained readers often cannot understand the work. The statistics and tables can be difficult to try to decode without training. Also, large numbers of organizational behavior studies focus on ferreting out errors. Scholars are schooled to be very skeptical, and although this is a virtue, it can make for very dull reading, even for those who care deeply about such errors. Finally, a lot of this research addresses scholarly debates and disputes that have no interest to those concerned with the challenges of practical organizational problems. Again, these debates are useful to scholarship because researchers need to come to agreement on how-we-know in order to conduct useful research. However, it serves no purpose to drag those wanting practical organizational knowledge into these disputes. When there is no practical application for a line of research, it isn't mentioned here.

In addition, some older research addressed management ideas that were popular at the time but have since been thoroughly discredited by the research. Unless that discredited idea still surfaces as a popular management opinion, there is no reason to waste the readers' time with it. This book is not a history of organizational behavior scholarship, but an extraction of what is practically useful today from this large body of research.

It is for all of these reasons that too often, "That's academic," has come to popularly mean, "That's useless." But research in organizational behavior is not useless: you cannot have thousands of smart people thinking carefully and sifting evidence for so long trying to learn what does and does not work in organizations without producing something of value, actually quite a lot that is valuable.

Nevertheless, it is important to note that organizational behavior research, like all social science research, has limitations. For one thing, it is hard to know whether or not particular management programs or practices will really work in your own organization because the situations in which these practices must be implemented can vary so much, and in ways we do not fully understand. For example, a new performance management system may solve one organization's accountability problem, but in another undermine its existing system of accountability.

What is worse, what one company calls, say, a "quality circle program," can be very different in reality from the policies and practices another calls by the same name. As a practical matter, such limitations mean that a well-designed study can find some circumstances in which a particular management opinion is not true, but no one study can ever be the last word. This doesn't mean we need to give up: just because social science is incomplete does not mean that we need to reject all of it in favor of our own personal management opinions. Organizational behavior research is useful in alerting us to some of the circumstances in which an opinion does not apply, and it is useful in fostering a critical stance toward all sweeping statements about organizations and management. If you can learn to suspect and critically evaluate your own management opinions, assumptions, and academic theories from reading this book, that alone will provide a strong basis for your organizational success.

Finally, although organizational behavior research, like all the social sciences, tends to have a narrow focus on what is wrong or does not work, it can provide the basis for developing practical advice: where to look, what to anticipate, and what to avoid. To encourage this active diagnostic work, practical applications based on the research are offered to help avoid the paralysis that can come from a sole focus on what is wrong and does not work. While finding out which opinions are wrong is an important responsibility of academic research, we all still need to take action to be successful in organizations. So, action implications based on the research are offered in the boxed sections titled, *Applications*. They are intended to spur your own thoughtful analysis and actions.

PUTTING ORGANIZATIONAL KNOWLEDGE TO PRACTICAL USE

The Importance of Organizational Diagnosis

Because organizational behavior research is not supposed to provide replacement opinions, it is no substitute for a careful analysis of your own unique set of organizational circumstances. For example, although we have learned that many pay-for-performance systems can create more motivational problems than they cure, this does not mean that pay should never be tied to job performance. Rather, readers will learn where and why most pay-for-performance programs come to grief and how to design ones that avoid dysfunctions (or where to anticipate problems, if they cannot be avoided). The key is to combine your own knowledge with insights from research through your own **organizational diagnosis**.

An accurate diagnosis depends on a careful analysis of an organization, its environmental pressures and the people doing the work. Contrary to the boxed opinion there are not many managers who fear doing anything until they have conducted yet one more analysis. Most organizational participants don't spend enough time analyzing their organizational situations. This boxed opinion is intended for those whose fear of the consequences of a bad business decision leads them to want to continue to conduct studies seeking information about a future that is unknowable. However, in most organizations, procrastination is pretty quickly self-punishing unless the proposed action isn't really necessary to organizational performance anyway. That is, those stuck in analysis-paralysis usually are responding to their observation that making mistakes will be punished in their organizations. If organizations are actually rewarding procrastination when they really want to see decisive action, there is an incentives problem (see Chapter 6), and clever word play will not get people to do something they expect will be punished. The more important practical challenge is to take the time to understand our own organizations and those who work there. Organizations are very complex social settings, where the reasons for practices and actions often are obscured by long chains of policy-practice-personality interactions. Most managers need to spend more time seeking understanding of their complex organizational worlds, not less.

> ***True or False?***
>
> *Don't get trapped in analysis paralysis*

The never-ending popularity of quick-fix solutions[6] reflects the desire all of us have to find a way to get rid of our messy organizational problems as fast as possible, so we can get on with the more interesting work. Yet, recall what Morgan McCall and David Lombardo showed us: those managers who took the time to diagnose and understand each new situation were the ones who succeeded. Others also have found that managers who had more accurate diagnosis of their organizational environments were more successful: Susan Ashford and Anne Tsui found that the highest performing managers had a more accurate understanding of how others viewed them,[7] and higher performing managers were more aware of their own managerial strengths and weaknesses than were average performing managers.[8]

There is no short cut. To be effective in any particular organization you need an accurate understanding of its own pressures and its unique players, in all of their nuance and complexity. Although the rest of the book will provide guidance on where to look, organizational mastery requires a commitment to lifelong organizational diagnostic work.

Application — Organizational Diagnosis

- Remember the cliché: "When you assume you make an ass of you and me." Become aware of your assumptions and test them.
- Find out how others view the situation. Take them to lunch, and pick their brains. Don't just rely on the same few people, but try to find out how many different people see the situation. Social scientists call this **triangulation**.
- Develop alternative explanations. This is called **counter-factual thinking**: seeing things as they might have been or developing multiple different explanations for what happened. Those more adept at counter-factual thinking are more effective.[9]
- Know the difference between **theory** and **data**. Theory is an explanation ("Why" something happened), and data are what actually happened. Too many jump to explanations so quickly that they have forgotten the data their theory was supposed to explain. Learn to differentiate between 1) what you actually saw, 2) what people really said, and 3) why you think it happened. This is hard to do and will require practice.
- Do not forget that successful managers need to take action. For help getting started try http://ww.mindtools.com/pages/article/newHTE_04.htm

Understanding What Drives Success

Odds are that today's media darlings, those "excellent" and "innovative" companies, will almost certainly be tomorrow's failures.[10] The business press knows that readers enjoy reading about the latest new ideas as much as they later like to read articles condemning the child-like excitement and mass conformity their own articles helped to foster. For example, five years later, the once praised "excellent companies" were found to have paid so much attention to their customers that they didn't notice that those customers were disappearing.[11] Today's management favorites too quickly will be denounced as tomorrow's foolish fads. Eric Abrahamson has documented the rise and fall of management fads over the decades, proposing that this seemingly silly behavior actually reflects the anxiety managers have about the great difficulty and ambiguity of their work.[12] This book cannot make managerial work any less difficult, but it, and disciplined continuous organizational diagnoses, can make it less ambiguous.

A slavish chasing of each new trend as recommended in the box is damaging to organizations, not least because it leads organizational participants to lose confidence in their managers' intelligence as they are jerked from one partially implemented fad to another. Worship of the latest media-crowned "best companies" is a dangerous habit and one that is hard to break; everybody loves celebrities, and organizational work based on careful diagnoses and persistent implementation is really hard. So to help in the stern determination needed to eliminate this worship of false gods, this book provides no anecdotes about this month's trendy companies, no bullet-pointed advice from last week's business press cover-boy. These omissions will help to free us from this perilous slavishness to fads and also allow examples that can be more honest because lawyers have not screened them. It is much more useful to have a clear understanding of the organizations and people who are critical to your own personal success than it is to have a superficial understanding of some air-brushed ideal.

> ***True or False?***
>
> *Today's successful companies have the secrets to your success.*

Finally, the success of some organizations is dependent on the quality and focus of their people, but there are other organizations that succeed despite shockingly poor management of employees. Here the opinions are contradictory: despite the popularity of the opinion that success depends on people, those steeped in economics claim an opposite opinion, that people are interchangeable and only incentives matter, not the particular personalities.[13] This people-don't-matter opinion has a steep financial cost to its adherents: companies that did not value their employees did not suffer in their initial public offering prices, but they were less likely to survive than those initially offered companies that did value their employees.[14] Such ideology is risky for employees: those who viewed themselves as free agents (no commitments to anyone or anything but themselves) were rated as poorer performers.[15] That is, it seems that the economically trained true believers in people-don't-matter were more likely to lose money on their investment choices: a stock tip for the organizationally astute.

There is plenty of additional evidence that people can matter to organizational success:

- People who feel fairly treated are less likely to steal from their employers.[16]

- American companies with employees who report that their workplaces are friendly, that they have job security, are paid fairly and have opportunities are twice as profitable as the average Standard & Poor's 500 Largest American companies.[17]

- A study of Canadian corporate bankruptcies found that the most common reason for the failure of new companies was their managers' deficient knowledge of how to manage.[18]

If people can be so important to organizational success, why have most of us seen organizations that somehow seemed to succeed despite (or because?) they made life miserable for the employees who worked there? While people can be important to an organization's competitive success, we all have seen situations in which the opinion expressed in this box is not true. How can we account for these conflicting observations?

> ***True or False?***
>
> *Competitive success is attained through people.*

This is because, although organizations are composed of people, they are not mere collections of people. Organizations provide products and services to customers and clients, and sometimes a particular organization is the only place customers or clients can get the product or service they want. No matter how frustrated those customers and clients may be with shoddy products or services, they have no other real choice. An organization may have a product so much in demand that it can survive the disruptions of rapid employee turnover and can attract employees willing to suffer for higher pay than they could get anyplace else. Many hedge funds and leveraged buyout firms exist to find those companies — attractive products or services but poor management — and make the management changes needed to increase their value. Similarly, sometimes there really is only one employer available in a particular region, and monopsonies (only one buyer of labor) can mistreat their employees with impunity because employees have no place else to go. Other times, failing large organizations can take a long time to die, and their slow decay can be painful to everyone. These are examples of the circumstances in which attracting competent workers, making sure they are working effectively, and responding to product and technology changes do not matter to organizational success. In those circumstances, employees who are trying to do a good job or make the innovations and changes needed to help their organizations will not matter. We all want to think we are important to our organizations, but our future depends on a brutally honest diagnosis of how important our work can ever be to our organizations.

Application — Diagnose Whether or not Employees Are Critical to an Organization's Success

- Is much of the work designed around interchangeable employees who are easily trained? This occurs in many factories in low wage countries. People are not critical to these organizations' success.

- Is the organization's success determined by events completely outside the control of the people working in them? This is the case for many governmental organizations, with tasks, goals and budgets set by politicians to serve their political needs.

Your answers to these questions imply two possible courses of action: If people are interchangeable and success is controlled by outsiders, *and* if the organization has resources to burn, authority is nonexistent, and you enjoy emotionally engaging struggles over status symbols, then you might as well stay and enjoy yourself; or if people are interchangeable and success is controlled by outsiders *and* if the organization has financial problems, other people have real power over you, or you would rather put your energy into productive activities, then you should leave.

Understanding Irrationality

> ***True or False?***
>
> *People are irrational.*

The false boxed opinion is a very popular one that is dangerous for anyone wishing to be successful in organizations. This belief is a result of a misunderstanding of the interplay between rationality and emotionality. Because we all can tell tales of outlandishly self-damaging acts we have seen at work, it is easy to believe that some people in organizations are just plain crazy, and nothing can be done about it. But think: the large psychoanalytic and clinical psychology industries exist to find the rational in seemingly irrational actions. This is because what can appear to an observer as **irrational** (or dysfunctional to the actor) may be quite functional from the perspective of the person engaging in the act.[19] Sometimes the person may not be fully conscious of his or her motives, or may be unwilling to acknowledge them, but that does not mean that there is no reason for the action at all.[20] At work, some may irrationally insult others, and so damage their own career prospects, but it could be that their need to express anger and frustration, at that time, overwhelmed any long-term calculations. If you think those around you are acting irrationally, you need to stop using a label that halts diagnosis and start to work at discovering what rewards they may see in their actions. Calling someone at work crazy may feel good, but it does not help to more effectively manage the situation. People do those crazy things for a reason, and when we call them crazy, we stop looking for that reason.

How to find that reason? The lesson of a hundred years of research in clinical psychology suggests that it doesn't matter that you might be correct that the behavior actually is dysfunctional and the other person is hurting him or herself. If you want to change the behavior, or work around it, you need to discover what its reward is to the person doing it.

Application — Why Are They Doing That?

- Ask the seemingly irrational person what his or her reasons are. Sometimes it is as simple as the person having a wrong theory about how to get things done in your organization. Sometimes people have mistaken theories about what is rewarded and punished in their organizations, and so they can be helped with more accurate information.

- Of course, people are not always willing to admit to themselves (let alone to others) why they do certain things. If they are unaware, it could be that their actions serve as **defense mechanisms**, helping them to avoid facing something even more painful.[21] If the problem is persistent in the face of clear, accurate information about organizational rewards and punishments, don't assume you can change rigidly defensive behavior on your own; professional help is needed. However, there are mild, everyday versions of such ego defensive actions at work. For example, a person might be unwilling to admit that his aggressive behavior toward colleagues in meetings stems from his resentment at their perceived disdain of him. These behaviors are not compulsively driven, but emotions are involved. If you find that someone's actions have a significant emotional component, do not treat it as a wrong-theory problem (first point above). That is, don't keep repetitively providing information or lecturing the person about the dysfunctions of the behavior; if information didn't work the first time, why would it work the fifth time? If emotion is involved in the behavior, the behavior will not change until the emotion is addressed. Some tips for working with emotionally driven actions appear in Chapters 4 and 5.

- If you do not know what the perceived reward is for the actions, find out. Make an effort. "Crazy people" can cause a lot of trouble if you do not understand why they are acting this way. And remember the next time you hear someone declare that someone else is crazy or irrational, what they are really saying is, "I don't want to bother understanding this person."

Understanding Organizations

Understanding others' motives, perceptions, hopes, and fears is not enough by itself for organizational success, and a myopic focus on it can be a dangerous distraction. The boxed opinion is false. Understanding your organization is at least as important as understanding the people who work there. Clinical psychologists have a great deal of insight, but it is insight designed to help those who are unhappy or seriously debilitated regain personal control or peace of mind.[22] Organizations are full of people who are more or less psychologically functional, but who find themselves frustrated by complex environments in which people depend on others in ways they do not understand. Organizations are settings in which actions that would normally be commonsensical (like, "be nice") can have negative consequences (if a manager values being nice so much that employees exploit this by working on the tasks they think are interesting, ignoring critical tasks, and so forcing the company into bankruptcy).

> ***True or False?***
>
> *If I can just figure out these people, I will be successful.*

Our organizational actions are heavily influenced by our organizational circumstances. What is rewarded in this organization? What is measured and carefully monitored? What kinds of people does the organization hire? After all, selection systems, incentives and controls are all designed to get people to do organizationally useful things. If it were only a question of the individual psychology of people, none of these incentive systems, policies and controls would be needed. Clinical psychology developed to treat people who find that their psychological problems overwhelm the specifics of their settings, and so psychologists have focused on understanding individuals' thoughts and feelings. But most people working in organizations are not psychologically overwhelmed all of the time; rather, they respond to the expectations, rewards and punishments they find in their organizational work.

Organizations are constructed settings designed to produce certain desired actions in others. People with particular skills, attitudes and values are selected; incentive systems are created to encourage some actions while discouraging others; sophisticated accountability systems and cultures are developed to ensure that the people in organizations do not go astray, and people are shunned or expelled if their actions fall short. Organizations are carefully crafted and constantly adjusted, staffed by people who are expected to best respond to the incentives the particular organization can provide. Those who delight in trying to psychoanalyze everyone they meet, while ignoring what is selected, measured, rewarded, and punished in that organization, are not going to be successful managers. Although insights into others' thoughts and feelings can be useful (and is always entertaining), those insights should never dominate organizational diagnoses. Organizations are difficult and cannot be ignored. The following chapters will provide frameworks that can help with this challenge.

Key Words

Management opinions

Organizational behavior

Organizational diagnosis

Triangulation

Counter-factual thinking

Theory and data

Irrational

Defense mechanisms

2

Why Managers?

Organizations are managers' work, yet there seems to be great confusion about what the manager's job involves, even among those who have been doing it for years. We know that engineers design new machines, accountants compile accounts, and waiters wait on tables, but what do managers do? Without an understanding of what managers should be doing, we cannot judge whether or not they are doing it well. In this chapter, we will see what those who have studied managerial work have to say about what managers do and about what the most successful managers seem to be doing that makes them better than others. It concludes by looking at a few common misperceptions about management.

ORGANIZATIONAL DEMANDS

Organizations are very demanding, and too few really ever master them. While the boxed popular opinion is charming, it is not true for managers; kindergarten is a wonderful place to learn personal hygiene and simple cooperation skills, but these are insufficient for the challenges of doing organizational work. Even clever fifty-year olds find organizational mastery daunting. Organizations are complex and make demands that are not always obvious. A brief summary of those demands follows.

> ***True or False?***
>
> *Everything I need to know I learned in kindergarten.*

Performance Pressures

Organizations exist to get something done for others, and this creates performance pressures. Whether it is a quality product that must be delivered on time or a needed medicine kept in stock so a patient won't die waiting for its delivery, performance matters. These performance pressures cannot be eliminated by good manners and wishful thinking. Even, when everyone understands what is required, agrees on what needs to be done and when every single person works with good will and the best of intentions, organizational work is hard. These pressures create stress.[1] When people are under stress, they are more likely to be irritable, rude, and to perform poorly.[2] All of us deal with performance pressures in different ways, but we must all work together to achieve the performance necessary for organizational survival.

Divided Perceptions

Organizations gain great efficiencies from division of labor, but division of labor creates its own challenges. **Division of labor** is the breaking of tasks into smaller components. For example, in a fashion house, there are different specialists to create a single garment: designers, pattern makers, textile designers, pattern cutters, sewers, and so on. Virtually all organizations divide tasks because this division allows individuals to develop specialized expertise (and so better performance) as well as allowing the more efficient use of materials and equipment (and so reducing costs).[3] But divided tasks mean divided information and differing perceptions of goals and priorities. Increasing division of labor leads to diverging incentives for those doing the work and increasingly disparate cultures over time. Any one of those can create organizational dysfunctions severe enough to swamp the efficiencies gained from division of labor. All of them require active management to prevent organizations from collapsing in disarray.

Dependence of All on Each One

Division of labor also has the effect of creating greater **systemic interdependence**, or the dependence of all on any one. Without division of labor, each person could work independently, so that if a few could not perform their tasks, the rest could still do theirs and the organization would still produce. However, when an organization's work is divided into separate tasks, with everyone dependent on others, a failure in any one component makes organization (or system) failure more likely. For example, if one group of programmers develops a new software program together, any one of them could de-bug it, reducing the group's dependence on any one programmer. However, if each programmer has specialized on only one part of the program and one of them leaves the company, it could put the entire program at risk. As organizations grow to take advantages of economies of scale and market power, division of labor and specialization increase, thus increasing systemic interdependence. Systemic interdependence makes the management of those interdependent components critical to organizational survival.

As organizations succeed and grow, they create divisions and specializations that must be coordinated across the organization and must adjust to changes from new technologies and markets. Different organizational designs can reduce the dysfunctions arising from divided information, goals, incentives, and cultures and interdependence despite differing needs for innovation, speed, and quality. However, organization design alone is never sufficient, nor can it be designed once and for all. Managers are needed to cope with the unexpected — someone calls in sick, a competitor's new product is more attractive to customers, interest rates have increased — all these and more require organizations to adjust. Managers are the crucial means by which the organizational left hand can know what the right hand is doing. And the knowledge, skills and stamina needed to manage others in divided performance–pressed organizations is not something that can be learned in kindergarten. Graduate MBA programs struggle to impart such skills.

MANAGERS' WORK

Managers take responsibility for the performance of their groups or organizations, as well as coordinate with other groups, organizations, and the environment. They make sure that the organization continues to produce what is needed as technologies, markets and governments change. So the boxed popular opinion is false — managerial work is very real. The **managerial job** is not as concrete as hammering a nail, removing an appendix, or floating a bond issue, but very few concrete tasks could be done without the organizational infrastructure managers create and maintain. How exactly do managers do that? We now have several decades of research on what it is, exactly, that managers really do and why.

> ***True or False?***
>
> *I don't do any real work; I'm a manager.*

Constant Communication about What Is Happening Now

How do managers keep organizations together? First, we know that managers spend most of their time doing this in face-to-face communication with other people.[4] All who have studied managerial activities in a wide variety of industries and countries have found that managers prefer the current and immediate to the old. They want face-to-face communication rather than telephone conversations, the telephone over meetings, and meetings over written reports. As Henry Mintzberg noted, managerial preference is for the most current, immediate information, and that usually comes from direct personal contact. This makes sense. If managers are to adjust and coordinate, they need to gather current information from many different sources, and the most current information comes from other people reporting on what is happening now. If they are to make sure their organizations anticipate and respond to rapidly changing events, they need to constantly monitor what is going on. Anything unexpected or important in a formal report should have been communicated long before its publication date.

Never-ending Demands

Henry Mintzberg[5] and others emphasize that managers work at an unrelenting pace. It is not so much that they work long hours, but that they do so many different things, very quickly, one after the other. Even chief executive officers, who are assumed to spend more time taking the long view, were found to never have a break — the brief times before formal meetings were consumed with informal exchanges of information, and the few times that these executives were not scheduled, their subordinate executives would swoop in with crises and problems. There is always more information to gather, more people to consult, or another fire that must be put out. Because managers' work is never done, they are always trying to squeeze in one more meeting, another consultation, or a quick email.

Bewildering Variety

Managerial work consists of hundreds of different kinds of tasks, each usually taking only a few minutes, coming in throughout the day in no particular order. Robert Guest found that the factory foremen he studied did between 237 and 1073 different tasks each day![6] Henry Mintzberg's chief executives' phone calls averaged only six minutes, unscheduled meetings twelve minutes, with half of their observed activities completed in less than nine minutes. A study of 160 British managers observed over a four week period found that these managers had only nine periods at work when they went a half-hour without being interrupted.[7] Managers' days are filled with countless different tasks, each one on the heels of the other. Managers could go from a tough budgetary battle to a party thanking a retiring employee, and there be grabbed by two other people who wanted to provide a brief update or warn of a looming problem. Because managers are responsible for knowing anything that might affect their organizations, they cannot easily place limits on their jobs. Furthermore, they are constantly learning of things that may have strategic implications or affect their peers and employees. This means they not only receive a lot of current information, they need to pass along information, tips and rumors to others who might need to act on it.

There is some variation in managerial work at differing hierarchical levels and in differing industrial sectors. Evidence suggests that the larger the organization, the less time chief executives spend on the formal managerial activities involved in operational control; instead they spend more time in formal meetings and with a wide ranging network of external contacts.[8] Because the chief executives of larger organizations are farther away from operational and sales revenue responsibilities, they exercise more of their control via other managers in meetings. In addition, larger organizations are more visible and more economically important to outsiders, and so their executives are more likely to be concerned with community and political matters, whether executives welcome these tasks or not.[9] Similarly, managers in governmental organizations face complex interest group pressures, and so their decisions must be made cautiously. This means governmental managers must be more focused on outside activities than their private-sector counterparts.[10]

The Method in this Madness

Despite the variations, all managerial jobs can look a lot like chaos, and there is a long history of those from the sedate and measured worlds of professional work who take managerial jobs only to get blind-sided by this torrent[11]. Far too many new managers assume that the fragmentation, pace and constant interruptions are a result of faulty management or disorganization, and that if only things were planned better, job descriptions made clearer, and everyone around them a little more disciplined, this "incompetence" would disappear, and they could get on with their real jobs. Although their frustration and exhaustion are understandable, this diagnosis is seriously amiss.

Managers exist to gather information and adjust their organizations (upward, laterally, and downward) in response to that information. Managers' work is to meet with peers, supervising managers, and outsiders to gather information that may suggest a change needed in their own group or organization. They must gather information from their own employees that might suggest a change with larger strategic significance, and they will need to persuasively relay all of this to those who can make such decisions. What is more, managers must spend the time necessary to earn the trust of the many others from whom they might learn the subtle, informal information that no sensible person would ever put in a formal report. Managers need to spend a lot of time with other people, sometimes doing things that don't look like real work but that are necessary to keeping vital information flowing. The work is not orderly and structured, but that doesn't mean it cannot be competent and thoughtful.

The managerial job is to put the pieces back together again, with the pieces themselves ambiguous and constantly changing. Such work requires constant attention, seeking to get information that is partial, biased and confused from other people. And anytime a disruption occurs — a key employee quits, a new product is placing unexpected strain on the accounting department, or a machine has broken down causing a delay for the customer who generates 60% of your revenue — everything else must be dropped to make sure the emergency is addressed. Certainly, some of these emergencies may have been avoided, and managers need to be constantly searching for organizational or policy solutions that will routinize those tasks that can be routinized. Nevertheless, the work of managers is to constantly gather any and all information that may help the organization and to manage the unexpected. No systems or amount of planning can remove the unexpected, and managing the unexpected is managers' work.

Application — Will I Be Happy as a Manager?

- Do interruptions drive you crazy? Because managers are responsible for taking care of unexpected problems and emergencies, they can never plan their days; handling interruptions is the manager's job.

- Do you like to spend time with people? A manager's job is to gather and distribute the new and informal information that is not available in written reports. Managers have to invest most of their time building relationships with a lot of people, and if you get impatient with others, it will show. This doesn't mean managers have to be gregarious people persons; sincerity is important to building trust, and a little well-meaning social awkwardness can be charming.

- Is it important that everyone like you? Those with a high **need for affiliation**, or the desire to be with others in a setting of fellowship and friendship, were not found to be successful managers.[12] Managers are responsible for the organization's performance, and sometimes that requires them to be unpleasant to people who are weak performers. This is difficult for anyone to do but particularly for those who really value being part of a warm friendly group.

- Do you like a sense of completion? Does unfinished business get under your skin? Those who have studied the personalities of successful managers have found that those with a high **need for achievement**, or a strong desire to succeed at difficult tasks, were less successful managers.[13] It seems that the managerial job is too open ended to provide satisfaction to those who have a strong need for a concrete sense of achievement.

- Do you like to make things happen? A strong **need for power** is a good predictor of managerial success.[14] Influencing others is what managers need to do if they are to do their jobs well. Those who enjoy making things happen will enjoy doing managerial work.

- Can you control your temper? Those with high **activity inhibition**, or a strong capacity for self-control, have been the most successful managers.[15] Managers must represent their group or organization, and so the job is one of inherent conflict with others. Those who can make their own best case and help others to change their behavior without losing their tempers will be more successful managers than those who cannot.

WHAT *EFFECTIVE* MANAGERS DO

There has long been interest in describing what managers actually do. The box lists Henri Fayol's 1916 managerial tasks. In the years since then, hundreds of books have further refined his original list, adding and subtracting — usually adding — managerial tasks. But as was noted long ago, these really are just the vague objectives of managerial work, ways of naming what needs to be explained.[16] Because these lists do not tell managers what to do to be effective as a manager, they really are not very useful. For example, managers certainly must **control**, that is, make sure that the required products or services expected from their groups or organizations are delivered. But there are many different ways to do that, some more effective than others. Should managers require daily (or hourly) reports? Should managers manage by walking around[17] and personally inspecting the work? Should managers hold weekly staff meetings? Keep up informal channels of communication? Or some combination of those? Those are just some of the many ways managers might control, and depending on the work and the people doing it, some combinations of them will be more effective than others. As a practical matter, managers do not really need labels for their tasks as much as they need to know exactly what actions they should take to be effective.

> ***True or False?***
>
> *Effective managers plan, organize, coordinate, and control.*

Fortunately, Fred Luthans and his colleagues set out to discover just what more effective managers did differently than the less effective ones.[18] They conducted an extensive study of hundreds of different managers in a diverse sample of American organizations in manufacturing, retailing, hospitals, financial institutions and government agencies. Managers' tasks were divided into twelve more-specific activity categories, and the researchers found some interesting differences between the effective managers in their sample and the ineffective ones. Their activities and examples of high-level managerial performance in each of the activities are listed in the following table.[19]

Managerial Activities from the Most to Least Important to Managerial Effectiveness

Activity	Highly Effective Examples
1.Exchanging Routine Information	Every week has a scheduled meeting with subordinates, shares ideas and leads a discussion of new methods and procedures
2. Handling Paperwork	Prepares daily, weekly, and monthly reports, which include cost reports and comparisons with past records and activities
3. Motivating/Reinforcing	Immediately compliments a subordinate who handles an irate customer/client very well
4. Disciplining/Punishing	Writes a reprimand, sends copies to the employee and the personnel file, and uses this information in determining the employee's annual wage increase
5. Managing Conflict	Talks face-to-face with two employees whose functions overlap when one of them believes the other receives too much recognition or salary, listens to both, and sorts out the facts
6. Staffing	When filling a position, considers in-house personnel for promotion, reviews outside applications, holds interviews, reviews information and makes the selection decision
7. Training & Developing	Coaches the staff on necessary work processes, organizes presentations of procedures through slides and transparencies, and involves the staff in practical training exercises

8. Planning	Sets goals and then holds face-to-face meetings with workers, giving specific instructions, review dates, and deadlines
9. Decision-making	Reads all facts related to a problem or issue and discusses the facts with others involved.
10. Controlling	Makes personal visits to work areas in different departments or units on a scheduled basis to check on work progress and compares summaries or employees' performance to standards
11. Interacts with Outsiders	Handles customer/client relations with other organizations in the industry and meets with members of clubs important to the organization
12. Socializing/Politicking	Entertains top-level managers in the organization, such as playing tennis or going fishing with them

The activities are listed in their order of importance from those done by the most effective managers down to those done by the least effective managers. As can be seen, exchanging routine information, particularly with their employees, was the activity that best characterized the most effective managers. Second in importance was the completion of paperwork that is so critical to organizations' control and accountability systems. Next in importance are the activities of motivating, disciplining, managing conflict, staffing and training. Planning, decision-making, and controlling trailed, with the activities of socializing with outsiders being the least characteristic of effective managers in these studies. In another study, Ben Schneider found that those managers who made sure their employees had the facilities, tools, and training needed to do their jobs well produced better organizational performance.[20]

Given that managers must put the pieces back together again, deal with unexpected emergencies and scan the environment for information that might suggest their organization should change, it isn't surprising that the most effective managers spent much of their time exchanging information with others. If it is the managerial job to gather and disperse information, then those who do more of that will be more effective. Similarly, if managers must manage emergencies and adjust their organizations to enhance performance, they will need to spend time working with their employees making sure that performance targets are clear, staff openings are quickly filled, and the inevitable conflicts that occur are managed before they blow up into crises. Effective managing means taking the time to adjust the organization and address its glitches before they grow to organization-destroying catastrophes.

Application — Become a More Effective Manager

- Set aside regular times for informal information exchange. These can be lunches or coffee breaks, but they should be regular and frequent enough to make everyone feel comfortable about speaking up.

- Set aside regular times for formal information exchange (for example, staff or project meetings). These will become more frequent as new information that affects others' work and priorities is generated more quickly. Organizations facing rapid changes might have daily meetings, but even the most sedate workplaces should have informational meetings at least several times a year.

- Do your paperwork on time. Paperwork seems like a waste of time because it is not done for the person completing it. Nevertheless, reports and forms are part of the organization's control system, and so are often the only way a manager is visible to other important people in the organization. Anything important to your bosses and their staff should be a priority to you: effective managers know that making other people's jobs more difficult is not the way to win friends, and company accountants and budget officers can be valuable friends. Remember, paperwork is necessary to higher level executives' own accountability, and you will be judged by how reliably and completely you do it.

WHAT *SUCCESSFUL* MANAGERS DO

One of the most important contributions of the research of Fred Luthans and his colleagues was its contrast between the tasks that **effective managers** (those who have satisfied, committed subordinates producing good organizational results) do and the tasks that **successful managers** (those who were promoted more quickly) do. They found that the widely held opinion in this box is a perilous misdiagnosis of what successful managers actually are doing.[21] Yet, they found that, the most successful managers allocated their time among their tasks differently than the most effective managers.

> ***True or False?***
>
> *To be a successful manager, it is more important to kiss up to your bosses than it is to produce good results.*

Networking

The biggest difference was in the two least effective managerial activities of interacting with outsiders and socializing/politicking. By contrast, these were the dominant activities of the most successful managers. The most successful mangers spent 48% of their time on networking activities whereas the most effective managers spent only 11% of their time with outsiders, peers and their bosses. Does this mean that kissing up really does matter more to managerial success than producing results?

Not necessarily. First, let's look more closely at what **networking** activities are. These include joking around, chit chat, discussing rumors, complaining, and seeking to influence. In other words, networking activities are nurturing personal relationships with others, and if those others are important to the organization, this work can be critical. These relationships can help the manager's group or organization in several ways. First, this is how managers hear about those informal matters that cannot be put into reports. Examples include pending changes, who is really influential, and what important people like and dislike. This kind of information can be invaluable in helping an organization to adjust to change. For example, hearing informally of a coming 4% budget cut could give departmental managers the time to analyze their budgets and propose cutting the 4% in ways that do the least damage to their own departments' performance.

Networking and Power

In addition, this kind of informal interaction is how **power** is built. Power is the ability to get others to do things they otherwise would not do. Managers need power to protect their groups or organizations, to get the resources they need to complete their tasks, and protect them from disruptive demands. Power is critical to managerial success, and the higher the managerial level in large organizations, the more amassing power and informal influence becomes the critical managerial activity.[22] This is why the successful accumulation and use of power becomes one of the most important skills evaluated for promotions. The higher the managerial level, the more the job requires persuading and influencing different kinds of people — customers, clients, bankers and politicians, among many others. Those who can competently supervise technical work but cannot build alliances and the trust of those outside their own group are signaling that they are not going to be able to perform the tasks required in higher-level managerial jobs (power is covered in more detail in Chapter 9). Networking is doing the job required of high-level executives, and successful managerial networking is demonstrating a necessary skill for these high-level executive jobs. Of course, socializing and politicking can be used for self-aggrandizement at the expense of others or the organization, but because these managerial skills are so necessary to organizational performance, their demonstration tends to attract attention.

BEING BOTH EFFECTIVE *AND* SUCCESSFUL

But can't managers be both effective and successful? In Fred Luthans's study, only 8% of managers could be classified as both effective and successful. Because effective and successful managers did different things, what did these stars do? The researchers found that this small group of both effective and successful managers tended to mix the two styles, balancing their time between exchanging information, managing subordinates, and networking activities. So it certainly can be done. Fred Luthans and his colleagues just found that it rarely was done in the organizations they studied. Is it really this bad? Can so few managers be both effective and successful? Although the importance of networking to executives' managerial performance is clear, do all organizations place such a low value on the performance-critical managerial activities of exchanging information and managing employees? The answer to this question seems to depend on the differing demands on differing organizations, and so the demands on the managers responsible for their organizations. There are some grounds for thinking that some organizations value managerial effectiveness more (and some value it less) than the organizations in the study.

DEMANDS FOR ORGANIZATIONAL EFFECTIVENESS AND MANAGERIAL SUCCESS

We know that this study's organizations were large and that executives in large organizations may find it particularly difficult to differentiate between effective and ineffective networkers. What could account for their neglect of the more effective managers? We certainly find popular accounts of ineffective networkers being promoted. Two famous accounts can illustrate: John De Lorean's description of his superiors in General Motors from the 1970s[23] and the description of Chief Executive Officer Ross Johnson's personally disastrous loss of control of RJR Nabisco in 1988.[24] John De Lorean describes an organization in which promotions were given to the **least-obvious-choice** (the manager whose previous performance would lead observers to name any number of better qualified and prepared alternatives). He suggested that this was because the obvious choices for promotion (the more effective manager) would believe that they earned the promotion by their own performance and so would not feel beholden to anyone else. By contrast, the least-obvious-choice knew to whom (not to what) they owed their success and so would act as a loyal servant of the one who promoted them. De Lorean reported that only rarely would an effective manager be promoted in the General Motors he knew. Similarly, RJR Nabisco's Ross Johnson was described as someone who always focused on keeping his superiors (and immediate subordinates) jolly through extensive socializing, corporate-jet supported golf excursions, and the like. He was so confident in his networking skills that he could not recognize his own ineffectiveness in the very different business of contested leveraged buy-outs that cost him his job.

What did General Motors and RJR Nabisco share that would seem to make managerial effectiveness so unimportant to career success? One obvious answer is their lack of competitive pressures. At that time, both companies were very large oligopolies, meaning that they were the dominant players among a few companies, in industries with a built-in demand from millions of consumers, who either had few other options for necessary transportation or were addicted to tobacco. Companies in oligopolies do not seek to aggressively compete because larger profits are available for all through forbearance and (however implicit) coordination.[25] And, of course, ownership was dispersed among many thousands of shareholders for both companies, so there was no single owner with enough power over management to compel these executives to maximize profits. If there are not compelling demands on organizations to more effectively compete or maximize profits, we can hardly expect their managers, or anyone else, to voluntarily put themselves under unforgiving pressure to be effective. What is valued in managers' organizations without tough performance pressure will vary. In any case, without harsh, unrelenting demands on the organizations to be effective, we would not expect to see managerial effectiveness rewarded. Organizational demands differ, and an accurate diagnosis of our own organization's demands are a useful guide to which managerial activities will really be valued.

Application — Will Effective Managerial Performance Be Appreciated in this Organization?

All managers in every organization think they are pressured to perform, but such pressures are really a matter of degree. Below are just a few of the signs that effective organizational performance may not be the real priority for a particular organization.

- Do clients wait in long lines, or do customers have to wait for back ordered items? For example, poor client service is common in state agencies and schools because the elected officials like to promise more services than they like to raise taxes to pay for. Many political officials welcome the opportunity to shift blame to "ineffective bureaucrats."

- Are expenses lavish? Examples include publicly traded firms with company jets, winter meetings held in Caribbean resorts, or expensive art on the walls. If you work for such a company and think these are required motivators, please visit any technology company with eighteen-month product life-cycles. You will see many brilliant, highly motivated people working punishing hours in crowded open offices.

- Do managers find it easier to work around problem employees and departments rather than solve the performance problem? Additional employees and a proliferation of committees and departments are not as much fun as art and jets, but they are just as wasteful.

COMMON MANAGERIAL MISCONCEPTIONS

One of the most insulting common managerial misconceptions is the distinction between managers and leaders. It is insulting because attempts to distinguish the two use contrasting lists of positive things (that leaders do) and negative things (that mere managers do). These pernicious distinctions are illustrated with the presumed differences in the time perspectives of managers and leaders.

The Importance of Crisis Management

Managers manage the unexpected, which makes effective crisis management an important responsibility. This boxed popular opinion disparages managers by implication; mere managers just respond to their immediate pressures. This is manipulating with words: leaders are good, they have vision and inspire; managers are bad, they just focus on operations. Actually, in some other languages the meanings are reversed, with leader as the old-fashioned autocrat with a corruption of the English word, manager, applied to those who are forward looking and modern.[26] So, rather than manipulation-by-name-calling, what do we really know about the time perspectives of managers?

> ***True or False?***
>
> *Leaders have a long-range perspective.*

Managers' time perspective varies by organizational level.[27] There is evidence that managers at higher organizational levels work on problems with longer time horizons.[28] Managers at lower organizational levels have more responsibility for maintenance of workflow, "chief executives negotiated acquisitions, while first-line supervisors negotiated delivery dates."[29] Yet in small companies and those operating in the fastest-paced environments, lower level managers have extensive strategic — that is, long range — responsibilities.[30] In conclusion, having a long-range perspective is a responsibility of some managerial jobs but not all.

Nevertheless, all managers face a crush of events impinging on their attention. All managers must drop other tasks to resolve crises that can be critical to organizational survival. For example, the Chief Executive Officer of Johnson and Johnson was widely praised for his direct management of the Tylenol poisoning crisis in the late 1980's, and his actions are now taught in business cases.[31] Running as fast as you can and fighting fires effectively is the critical contribution that managers make to their organizations. No beautiful long range vision ever amounted to anything without someone to manage the endeavor.

Application — More Effective Crisis Management[32]

- Have crisis plans in place so that rapid decisions can be made and quickly communicated to the affected parties.
- Don't try to minimize a bad situation; communicate all the bad news at once, rather than let it continue to come out in pieces.
- Conduct regular audits to identify vulnerabilities. Benchmark your practices against peers.
- If crises seem to be repetitive, for example, arising because the same employees are repeatedly ineffective, then this is a performance problem that must be addressed.
- If crises seem to be repetitive, arising because other people in the organization do not consider how their actions will affect your group, then this is a problem of insufficient managerial influence.

The Importance of the Work

Managers' most important job is to assume responsibility for the performance of their group or organization and to obtain and transmit accurate information about it. So this false boxed opinion is the wishful thinking of narcissistic employees. People know that their bosses are not their mothers. For example, employees know that if they do not have the resources they need to do their work, their manager's most important job is to make sure that those who control those resources provide them. That is why one study found that managers influence in the organization was a much better predictor of their employees' satisfaction with them than whether or not the supervisor was considerate of their needs and feelings.[33] It is not that anyone likes an inconsiderate boss; it is just that most employees are smart enough to prefer someone who can get them what they need to do their jobs and fend off unreasonable demands from others. Their manager is an employees' only legitimate point of contact with the rest of the organization, and a boss who commiserates with employees and complains about the rest of the organization without getting them the resources they need to do their work is nobody's friend.

> ***True or False?***
>
> *Managers' most important job is to be sensitive to their employees' needs.*

The critical importance of managers' ability to get resources for their group or organization is reflected in the importance of power motivation in predicting managerial success. In a study tracking managers at American Telephone and

Telegraph over sixteen years, those managers with higher needs for power consistently outperformed other managers.[34] If one of the most important jobs of managers is to obtain resources and support from others, then those who enjoy influencing others will welcome, rather than shrink from, those necessary tasks. Again, employees appreciate and value influential managers, reporting better team spirit and a clearer understanding of organizational demands when working for managers who had higher personal needs for power.[35]

Finally, it isn't just that being hyper-responsive to employees' needs can distract from important priorities, managers who see their jobs as responding to their employees' needs can find themselves exploited, to the detriment of their own and their organization's performance. After all, employees have status needs, and everyone enjoys interacting with those with higher status.[36] There are always those employees who are happy to take every daily complaint to a willing ear, especially if that willing ear has higher status. Advising managers that their most important task is to be sensitive to employees' needs does not help managers distinguish between subordinates' work-relevant needs and the needs some have for attention and status. Trying to meet these latter needs can consume managers' valuable time without doing anything to support the group or organization's performance. There are only so many hours in a day, and managers have an infinite set of demands on their time. **Role overload** (responsible for too much work) and its attendant stress and exhaustion are very real threats for all managers.[37] Those who also try to take the very considerable time necessary to listen to all complaints and strive to meet all of their employees' personal as well professional needs are probably not spending the time they should in networking with all of those others on whom the performance of their group depends. Although building trust and confidence requires spending time listening to others' gossip and complaints, judgments must be made about when this becomes so time consuming that performance suffers. A few ideas that might help to sustain relationships while investing less in them follow.

Application — Manage Your Time with Employees

- Set aside specific times for chit chat, gossip and listening to complaints. Explicitly social settings are best; Japanese managers have perfected the after-work drinking party as a place where honest feedback and complaints can be spoken under the shield of drunkenness. Settings that allow brief stops and provide the ability to leave when you want are ideal.

- If you are invited to company farewells, birthdays, and other occasions, try to stop by, even if it is only for a brief congratulations. It takes very little time to honor and respect others, and it is easy to leave these events after a brief time.

- Put a clock you can see directly behind the shoulder of guests seated in your office. If a guest begins a long-winded complaint, apologize, say you promised to get back to someone at [whatever time it is right now], and apologize the person out of your office.

- When you are listening to someone, give that person your full attention. You will be better appreciated if you give people your full attention for only a couple of minutes than if you give them more time but then fidget, look at your watch, and in other ways signal that you are not interested in what they are saying. In the workplace it really is quality time, not quantity, that matters.

The Importance of Accountability

Employees need to be accountable; however, too many managers assume that the only way to achieve accountability is through close personal surveillance. Contrary to the boxed popular management opinion, closely watching employees can become a self-fulfilling prophecy of ever-escalating perfunctory effort, resentment and hostility. Research confirms that when employees were expected to be successful, they had greater motivation and better performance.[38] Those managers who expected their employees to perform poorly produced poorer performing employees. When we recognize that time spent watching other people is time not spent on those information exchanges and networking activities that make managers more effective and successful, we can see

> ***True or False?***
>
> *Employees will slack off if they are not watched.*

that the costs of constant surveillance are high indeed.

The important distinction is between **surveillance** and **accountability**. Every person doing organizational work must be accountable, and there must always be some way of assessing performance. But this does not need to be through direct personal surveillance. Employees would much rather receive feedback on their performance impersonally, through reports, than personally from anyone.[39] Managers are responsible for control, but large formal organizations staffed by professional managers were developed because they are a more effective means of control than standing over someone's shoulder watching every move. Professional management means using formal controls such as tracking reports, status reports, and output information sent via email rather than orally. The forms will vary with the tasks to be performed, the management of employee accountability is discussed in more detail in Chapter 5.

Managing Is Good for Your Health

So far, this chapter has been a long catalogue of cautions and warnings about the very challenging, fast-paced managerial job of unrelenting interruptions, crises and frustrations. Now for some good news for a change: Managerial responsibilities may be stressful for many, but contrary to the boxed opinion, this job is actually good for your health.[40] Research covering many different industries and countries strongly supports the claim that the higher you are in an organizational hierarchy, the better your health. Supervisors have better cardiovascular health and live longer than those doing front-line work; middle managers live longer than supervisors, and chief executive officers live the longest of all. This does not seem to be a matter of access to better health care, but is the result of the greater autonomy and control over their working lives that come with increasing managerial responsibilities.[41] And apparently the greater social status and esteem that go with more important jobs also lead to better health and longer lives. The managerial job may be difficult and frustrating, but once mastered, it provides more opportunities to pick your assignments, accomplish your work in the ways you would prefer, and bask in all of the advantages of higher status. The more you succeed at managerial work, and so assume ever better managerial positions, the higher your odds for a long and happy life. So mastering organizations not only helps you achieve your ambitious goals, it is good for you.

True or False?

Managerial stress leads to heart attacks.

Implications for Managing Managers

✓ Don't be a pest to your boss. Managers are overloaded and time pressured. Whenever you talk to a manager, make it short and to the point.

✓ In the North American cultural context, when you bring a problem to a manager, also be sure to bring one or two possible solutions. Of course, you may lack critical information, and so your own solutions may not be the best ones, but they will initiate a problem-solving discussion. In any case, you will not be guilty of **upward delegation** (washing your hands of a problem once you have told your boss about it). Other cultures expect other behavior with bosses: know before you go.

✓ Even if your manager does not ask you for written reports of milestones and objectives achieved, provide them at least once a year. This will help you to remember all that you have accomplished and can provide an early opportunity to learn if you and your boss do not agree on your objectives.

✓ If your organization does provide formal milestones and objectives for your job, do not submit reports on different objectives (that you think should be considered in your evaluation). This is a strong signal to everyone that you are stubbornly refusing to do the job you were hired to do or are trying to avoid accountability for poor performance, and it throws away any chance you might have had to later plead misunderstanding.

✓ Many managers have a high need to exercise power. Don't let your own desire to feel in control lead you to unnecessarily rob managers of one of their few pleasures. Remember that those who are better at activity inhibition are more successful in organizations.[42] Let a manager tell you what to do every now and then; you won't regret it.

Key Words

Division of labor	Effective managers
Systematic interdependence	Successful managers
The managerial job	Networking
Need for affiliation	Power
Need for achievement	The least-obvious-choice
Need for power	Role overload
Activity inhibition	Surveillance
Managerial tasks	Accountability
Control	Upward delegation

3

How to Hire

Anyone who has hired the wrong person will tell you that hiring is one of the most important decisions a manager can face. The wrong person in a job can be devastating. It is hard to imagine anything more costly: for the employee it can be an overwhelming career derailment; co-workers resent having to carry the extra work, and managers become frustrated with the countless hours of performance counseling and paperwork needed to remove an employee.

Hiring the right people is one of the most important things a manager does, and yet it is also the one that managers are the most likely to neglect. It seems that just when it is most important to spend the time it will take to find the right person, too many managers, swamped with the extra work a vacancy has created, just grab the first person who looks acceptable. This is called **satisficing**: doing the minimum necessary to get through a task, rather than **maximizing**: seeking the best performance possible.[1] Fortunately, there is extensive research addressing these organizational challenges, and this chapter will introduce these ideas.

IDENTIFYING THE BEST PERSON FOR YOUR JOB

> ***True or False?***
>
> *Hire the best.*

We all want to hire the best person for the job; the difficulty is in identifying the best at what. This boxed opinion is fine in the abstract, but it is useless as practical advice. Some successful companies, such as Microsoft Corporation, state that they try to hire the smartest people they can find,[2] whereas a leading American airline, Southwestern Airlines, proclaims that it seeks employees who share its values and attitudes.[3] Others advocate matching job requirements to skills (e.g., self-confident people in sales). There are as many theories about what makes the best employee as there are company leaders who have been asked the secret of their success. Systematic organizational behavior research can help us sort out these conflicts.

Hiring for Organizational Fit

We do know that those who are hired for their **fit with the organization** (common values and attitudes) are happier at work and less likely to leave for another job than those hired for other reasons.[4] This is because working with others who have the same outlook and experience is enjoyable for most people. However, this does not mean that these happy comfortable employees are better performers: we also know that employees hired for their fit with the existing organization are *not* better performers than those hired with no regard for how they would fit with the organization.[5] That is, hiring for fit with the organization makes for happier employees, but it does not necessarily produce the best performers. This makes fit a particularly dangerous temptation for hiring managers. We are all attracted to people who are like ourselves[6] and feel more comfortable surrounded by people like us. But selecting people like yourself is selecting people who make you comfortable, not people who are better performers, a dangerous practice that will be explored in more detail later in the chapter.

Hiring the Right Personality

If fit is not the best determinant of performance, then do the better performing employees have certain character traits or personalities that we could discover during hiring? We know that those who are hiring do seem to be looking for certain personalities. They will say they are looking for "people who aren't afraid of hard work," or "team players," or an employee "with a positive attitude." These are informal ways of describing differences in personality. Are there some personality traits that make for better performing employees? To answer this question we need to be more precise.

Personality is an individual's unique and relatively stable pattern of behavior, thoughts, and emotions. A person's personality is more or less the same, no matter what the situation, but not in a rigid sense. For example, a person may be talkative and highly sociable in most situations, but can sometimes be quiet and withdrawn, say on the first day of a new and frightening assignment or due to jet-lag induced exhaustion. People have personality differences that tend to be apparent in many different situations, and there has been a great deal of research seeking to learn which personalities tend to be found in the best performing employees.

For our practical purposes, the important information to take from the tens of thousands of studies of personality over the past decades is that there are five stable and reliable dimensions of personality.[7] These dimensions have been called **The Big Five**, and recent research on the effects of employee personality and their job performance has focused on them.

Big Five Personality Dimensions

***Conscientiousness* ranges from**

Lazy, Disorganized, Unreliable	to	Hard Working, Organized, Dependable, Persistent

***Emotional Stability* ranges from**

Insecure, Anxious, Depressed, Emotional	to	Self-confident, Calm, Secure

***Agreeableness* ranges from**

Cold, Belligerent	to	Warm, Cooperative

***Extraversion* ranges from**

Reserved, Timid, Quiet	to	Gregarious, Assertive, Sociable

***Openness to Experience* ranges from**

Practical, Narrow Interests	to	Creative, Curious, Cultured

To select just the highlights from this large body of research: it will surprise no one that employees higher in conscientiousness also tend to have higher performance.[8] **Conscientious** employees are hard working, persistent, reliable and want to achieve. These characteristics lead to more effort and persistence, and so to better job performance, all else being equal. The dimension of **emotional stability** also predicts better employee job performance, although it is a weaker predictor of performance than conscientiousness.[9] Calm and self-confident employees cope more effectively with the interruptions and crises that are inevitable at work.

So, when it comes to hiring the best performers, the important practical problem is to accurately assess potential employees' conscientiousness and emotional stability. Reliable and valid written tests to do this exist.[10] However, not all managers can persuade their human resources departments to use such tests. Lacking those, what can managers do to hire the conscientious and emotionally stable? It may seem obvious that everyone would want to hire employees who are hard working, organized, dependable, who persevere, are calm, self-confident, and secure. But how many of those making hiring decisions ask themselves how they will learn these things about applicants before they begin recruiting? Any hiring manager can use references and the selection interview to assess these and other personality dimensions. Ideas for making better use of such hiring tools are described later in the chapter.

Of course, there are many studies of the personality predictors of employee job performance in particular jobs. For example, although applicants' **extraversion** is not a good predictor of their job performance in all jobs, it is a good predictor of their performance in jobs requiring social confidence.[11] One of the more interesting examples of personality predictors of performance in specific jobs is the finding that a high need for achievement, although not a good predictor of a manager's job performance in large organizations (as we saw in Chapter 2), is a good predictor of success among entrepreneurs.[12]

In addition to the big five personality dimensions, there is another difference among applicants that studies show predicts better employee job performance. This is our relatively stable tendency to have positive or negative feelings about the world around us.[13] Those with **positive affectivity** tend to have positive feelings across different situations, and those with **negative affectivity** tend to have negative feelings. Those with positive affectivity tend to interpret events in a positive light and have a better sense of well being, while those with negative affectivity tend to interpret events, themselves and others in a negative light and have more negative moods such as sadness or anger. As would not be surprising, those with higher negative affectivity have lower job performance,[14] lower performance on decision-making tasks,[15] and interestingly, were more likely to report that they were themselves victimized at work.[16] Because employees with positive affectivity are willing to tackle problems and interpret ambiguous situations more positively, they seem to be better performers across a wide range of jobs. Reliable and valid paper and pencil measures of applicant affectivity, such as the Multidimensional Personality Questionnaire,[17] are available, and like conscientiousness and emotional stability, hiring managers can seek to assess these informally during reference checks and job interviews.

Hiring for the Job

It should go without saying that effective employees must have the particular knowledge, skills and abilities required by the job they will be doing. Nevertheless, many managers are not as clear as they could be about exactly what job knowledge, skills and abilities are needed before hiring. Clarity about job requirements doesn't take much time and is important for three reasons.

First, the research reminds us that if you don't know what you want, you aren't likely to get it. Carefully analyzing and describing the kinds of job knowledge, skills, and abilities needed for successful job performance before beginning a search is invaluable. Well-managed organizations have **job descriptions** for a reason. Job descriptions are written descriptions of the purpose of a job, how it fits with other jobs in the organization (e.g., to whom it reports in the hierarchy), its major duties, the tasks to be performed, responsibilities, and the training or education required to perform it. Writing down exactly what someone is supposed to do in a job helps by providing a preliminary list of the knowledge, skills and abilities that a hiring manager will want to assess before making a hiring decision. Clarity about what is needed to succeed in particular jobs helps keep decision makers focused on gathering the actual information they need without jumping to conclusions.

Job descriptions are also helpful in establishing your **job-related criteria** for hiring. These are the qualifications, knowledge, skills and abilities needed to successfully perform the job. The emphasis is job-related so, for example, the criteria cannot include height or weight requirements unless those are necessary for the successful performance of the job. In the United States and many other countries, managers are required to use job-relevant criteria for hiring employees, and the research cited above helps to establish legal job relevance. It isn't just your hunch that conscientious, more emotionally stable employees free of neuroticism and negativity are better at their jobs; studies have established that it is so.

Application — Write Job Descriptions

- Know the uses of the job description. Job descriptions can be used for many different things: developing criteria for making hiring decisions, setting pay levels, developing performance appraisals, and the like. Practical managers need to be very clear about exactly what job descriptions are used for in their own organizations. If job descriptions are used for important decisions elsewhere in the organization, successful managers learn how write descriptions that will enable them to attract, retain, and reward the best employees. They never leave this important task to human resources professionals.

- If an organization does not have a formal process for writing job descriptions, managers still benefit from writing their own. They help managers be sure they remember to consider all the job-relevant criteria when hiring as well as provide the basis for successfully managing employee performance.

- If you need to develop your own job description without professional help, get a copy of one from a previous job or a friend to use as a template. But remember: job descriptions are used for many different kinds of things, so don't be afraid to eliminate bureaucratic jargon and anything else that does not accurately describe the knowledge, skills and abilities needed for the job.

Hiring the Smartest

When seeking to hire the best, there is another easily measured personal characteristic that has been established as a powerful predictor of job performance: intelligence, or what is today more fashionably called, **cognitive ability**. This is the ability to understand abstract concepts and ideas, to reason accurately, and to solve problems. Some have summarized it as the ability to learn.[18] There is no question that cognitive ability is the best general predictor of job performance across all jobs and that it can predict job performance more than twice as well as conscientiousness, the best personality predictor of job performance.[19] What is more, the more important the job (the higher the management level or more demanding the professional requirements) the better job performance is predicted by an applicant's cognitive ability. Again, this should not be surprising: To do any job well, employees must be able to evaluate new information and make judgments. If no judgments were needed, rules could be written and machines could carry out the tasks. Certainly, the more a job demands that employees skillfully evaluate new information, make judgments, and accurately analyze ambiguous and conflicting reports, the more we would expect, and do in fact find, that those better in cognitive ability perform their jobs better.

Hiring employees based on cognitive ability not only produces the better, more flexible job performance that managers and co-workers value, it saves much time and trouble. It has been calculated that if the United States Federal Government used rank-ordered cognitive ability scores to hire employees rather than selecting from among all of those in the top 20%, it would have saved US$13 billion.[20] Furthermore, assessing job applicants' cognitive ability is very easy: Wonderlic and Hexaco produce simple tests of cognitive ability that can be completed by applicants in a few minutes, and it is more difficult to fake than personality.[21] And it gets even easier: because intelligence tests were originally developed to predict school achievement, school achievement is a good substitute way to assess cognitive ability. Although not perfect, school grade point average is a better measure of an applicant's cognitive ability than any hunch developed during an interview.

Because applicant cognitive ability is such a good predictor of job performance and it is so easy to assess, why don't we see cognitive ability tests given to every job applicant? There are two reasons: discomfort and legal. First, as Sara Rynes and her colleagues so persuasively argue, many human resources management professionals are uncomfortable with these tests.[22] This is because, in the United States at least, many people hold negative stereotypes about highly intelligent people: that they are impractical, socially inept, arrogant, and brilliant on occasion but under-perform the slow-but-steady over time.[23] Many of us just do not want to believe that smarter people are better performers in virtually all jobs, but the evidence from many careful studies demonstrates that those with better cognitive ability tend to outperform others at work. This does not mean that cognitive ability is a perfect predictor of job performance. No one predictor of job applicants' future job performance ever is. Motivation and the performance management system count, of course, as do conscientiousness, emotional stability, and the particular knowledge, skills and abilities needed for that job.

Hiring and the Law

Sara Rynes and her colleagues suggest a second reason for resistance to more widespread use of formal measures of cognitive ability in hiring decisions: when there are a large number of applicants for only a few jobs, the test will often eliminate applicants from **protected groups**.[24] In the United States, as in many other countries seeking to counter employment discrimination, laws exist that make it a crime to discriminate. In the United States, the legally protected groups are based on race, national origin, sex, and religion; in India certain castes are protected, and so on, with different countries having different protected groups based on their own history and present circumstances. In the United States, the implementation of this law for hiring decisions has focused on requirements that selection procedures be job relevant. As a practical matter, if a selection method produces **adverse impact** on a protected group, the employer is obligated to establish that the selection procedure is job relevant.[25] A selection procedure has adverse impact when it disproportionately excludes protected group members, and many human resources professionals fear that when there are many applicants for very few jobs, as often occurs for attractive and well-paid positions, cognitive ability tests might produce an adverse impact. If that happened, the employer might face legal proceedings and be obligated to demonstrate the cognitive ability test's job relevance. Similarly, an employer could inadvertently cause adverse impact with a rigid reliance on tests of conscientiousness and emotional stability, in which women score slightly higher than men.[26] One of the reasons so much research has been done on the predictive power of applicant cognitive ability has been that so many employers have had to demonstrate that these formal measures to select among applicants are job relevant, even when they have demonstrated adverse impact.

One final note: this U. S. legal requirement that selection procedures be job relevant if they produce an adverse impact on protected groups applies to all procedures used to make hiring decisions. That means that anything at all used to making hiring decisions — reference checks, informal interviews, previous work experience, hunches, and gut feelings — must be job relevant. Given the dread most Americans who make hiring decisions (and their bosses) have of discrimination lawsuits, it is not surprising that many managers will just fudge their hiring to make sure that whatever procedures they use produce job offers to protected group members in their proportion to the applicant pool. This informal practice fuels backlash and exacerbates prejudice.[27] How to escape from this trap? James Camion and Richard Arvey reviewed U. S. legal cases on the subject of adverse impact and determined that the actions described below have helped employers establish the legal defensibility of their hiring procedures.

Application — Legally Defensible U. S. Hiring Procedures

The U. S. courts have found that selection procedures with the following characteristics were legally defensible, even if they had an adverse impact on protected group members:[28]

- Develop job descriptions. You can hardly hire the best person for the job if you are unclear about exactly what the person will be doing. Discussing and writing down exactly what the job involves and what knowledge and skills it uses will help all parties involved in the hiring decision to be clear about what is required.
- Select and train multi-racial interviewers of both genders. There is evidence that interviewers tend to give higher scores to candidates from their own race,[29] so careful attention to balance helps.
- Conduct reviews of recruiter behaviors and decisions.
- Keep good records of interviews.
- Monitor job interview outcomes for adverse impact.

Finally, most countries have quite detailed employment laws, and any organization large enough to be locally visible (and so likely to become a symbol for political interests or a deep-pocket target of plaintiffs' attorneys) should always get local legal advice on hiring policies and practices.

AVOIDING ERRORS IN PERCEIVING OTHERS

Mistaken perceptions of others are very common, and so this boxed popular opinion certainly is false when it comes to hiring. Managers need to make important judgments based on very little information, and one way to reduce hiring mistakes is to better manage errors in their perceptions of others. Although seeing may be believing, decades of research in **person perception** suggest that believing all too often determines what is seen. We all make errors in our perceptions of others. When

> ***True or False?***
>
> *I'll know it when I see it.*

left implicit, these misperceptions can have serious consequences for our own performance at work. Problems from misperceptions are often exacerbated in managerial jobs with their many assessments of others based on ambiguous cues. Managers need to diagnose and make judgments based on what other people do and say, and so a more explicit understanding of their person-perception biases is critical to their effectiveness. Perceptual biases can affect many managerial judgments at work, and we will return to this subject when discussing performance management. But because hiring decisions are made on such brief and often impressionistic information, perceptual errors can be particularly damaging in decisions to hire.

Implicit Personality Theories

We all depend on our perceptions of others; we make judgments about why someone did something, and we form impressions of others. These impressions affect how we perceive, evaluate and weigh future information about them. These inferences about others often are based on the most limited data. For example, it is long established that we tend to assume that physically attractive people have positive personality characteristics.[30] Clearly, pretty people are not necessarily smarter, more conscientious, or kinder than others.

Many of our **implicit personality theories** are incorrect.[31] Long ago, psychologists discovered that we all tend to develop implicit personality theories about others; that is, unawares, we assume that people will have some certain characteristics from knowing something else about them. So, for example, if I observe that an applicant is talkative, I tend to assume that she is friendly and popular, even though I know nothing about her friendliness or popularity.

We make quick extrapolations because knowing why a person did something provides valuable information about what that person might do in the future. For example, if your boss loses her temper and yells at one of your co-workers during a meeting, you reasonably want to know why. Is it because she is generally disagreeable and emotionally unstable? If her actions resulted from these relatively stable personality traits, you would learn to expect such outbursts and plan accordingly. Or did this co-worker make an error that will place the entire department in jeopardy of cutbacks the boss just learned of earlier in the day? In that case, you would want to learn what set her off and avoid making the same mistake yourself. How do you decide which of your theories about the incident is correct? Harold Kelley developed what he called the **theory of causal attribution**.[32]

Attributing the Causes of Another's Actions

Harold Kelley established that when observing others' actions we will attribute it to either **internal causes** or **external causes**. Internal causes are ones the actors can control; they are causes internal to the person. They include the person's motivation to engage in the act (yelling at these subordinates is the only way to get their attention) and personality (disagreeableness and emotional instability). External causes of another's actions are ones they do not control: the person took the action because particular circumstances compelled it (overwhelming distress at pending cuts or direct instructions from her boss to get tougher with employees). If others' actions are internally caused, we will perceive and evaluate new information about them differently than if we judge the actions to be externally caused. We all ask ourselves three questions about others' actions in trying to determine whether they were internally or externally caused:

- Does the person act this way at other times? This is the **consistency** of the act. The more consistent the behavior, the more likely we are to judge it as internally caused.

- Does the person act this way in different places? If the act is unique to that one place, it is more distinctive, and the greater its **distinctiveness** the more likely we are to judge it as externally caused by the circumstances of that particular place.

- Do other people act the same way? If others are doing the same thing, there is high **consensus**, and we are more likely to judge the act as externally caused by the shared circumstances they all experienced.

If we observed that this boss tended to scream at one employee or another at every meeting (high consistency, low distinctiveness), we would probably attribute her behavior to an internal cause, like disagreeableness or emotional instability. If, however, she had never raised her voice at anyone before and we noticed that all of the managers coming out of that morning meeting seemed to be upset (low consistency, high distinctiveness, high consensus), we might ascribe her actions to external causes, perhaps information she received at that morning meeting.

How is this relevant to hiring the best employees? When hiring people, we usually make important decisions based on very little information. In the yelling-boss example, the employees would have worked with that boss and so have had many opportunities determine the consistency, distinctiveness and consensus of her actions. By contrast, when hiring, it is rare to have the luxury of watching the applicant interact with others in many different settings. We all want to be accurate in our attributions of internal or external causes of others' actions, and so understanding our implicit rules for attributing causality can help prevent unthinkingly false causal attributions about another. The fewer the opportunities to check our initial causal attributions against new observations, the more likely we are to be mistaken. Some of these common perceptual biases include:

Fundamental-attribution Error

In practice people have a bias toward attributing internal causes to other people, while attributing external causes to their own actions.[33] We do this because if we attribute internal causes to others, we believe we can better predict their behavior in the future. After all, dispositions are relatively stable, and so if we can characterize another person as disagreeable, rather than temporarily upset about an event that happened that morning, we feel like our social world is more predictable. In contrast, we have more information about our own internal states, and have seen ourselves acting differently in many different situations. We do not have direct access to others' internal states, and so are more likely to assume the actions we observed are typical, and so due to internal states.[34] So, for example, a job applicant may have been awake the night before a job interview caring for a sick family member, but his slow responses during the interview are falsely attributed to an internal state (low cognitive ability) by the interviewer. Hiring managers are particularly motivated to understand who an applicant is (internal state) and so need to take particular care not to fall prey to the fundamental attribution error.

Similarity-attraction Bias

People tend to be attracted to and to perceive more favorably those who are similar to themselves.[35] We saw that interviewers tend to rate applicants from their own race more favorably. Whether trying to create a better fit between themselves and co-workers (creating a more pleasant personal work environment) or unconsciously projecting their own positive self-regard onto similar others, the bias toward hiring people similar to themselves is well-established. But there is no evidence that people similar to those making hiring decisions are better performers. Similarity-attraction bias in hiring is obviously unfair and needs be guarded against. What is worse: because the results of this kind of bias are obvious to those who do not share the similarity, those who hire using this bias develop reputations as people who cannot be trusted to hire the best performers.

First-impression Error

We form elaborate and holistic implicit personality theories of others very quickly, and then those first impressions bias our perceptions of any new information we receive.[36] For example, one study found that job candidates who initially made more favorable impressions (more attractive application forms and test scores) were treated more favorably during their job interviews.[37] They were asked easier questions and treated more warmly. This treatment helped the interviewees relax and project more warmth (positive affectivity). Making a good first impression in interviews is a better predictor of getting a job offer than similarity.[38] Although job applicants will want to remember that first impressions do indeed count, hiring managers should be on guard that their first impressions do not distort the subsequent information they collect.

MANAGING A MORE EFFECTIVE HIRING PROCESS

More Effective Use of References

The best predictor of employees' future job performance is their past job performance.[39] Applicants who were chronically late to work in previous jobs are unlikely to be punctual in their next jobs. If the applicant was in frequent conflict with coworkers in his last two jobs, you should expect more of the same in your workplace. This means that the boxed opinion may reflect a common practice, but it is an uncommonly foolish one. The most valuable predictor of what kind of employees applicants will be is the kind of employees they were before. And who knows the most about an applicant's past job performance? The people you will call for **references**. Employment references are the written or oral descriptions of an applicant's past performance. References provide hiring managers with their best opportunities to assess an applicant's future performance. The effective use of references is the single most valuable hiring tool a manager has; the ineffective use of references is possibly the single biggest mistake that managers make.

> ***True or False?***
>
> *Call references only when you are ready to make a job offer.*

What managers glean from those who have had a chance to observe an applicant for more than a brief job interview is probably the most critical information they can collect about an applicant. This is why managers should not wait until they are ready to make an offer before calling references. Why? By the time managers are ready to make an offer, they want to hire the person and have already formed a holistic impression of the applicant. We are all subject to **confirmation bias**.[40] After we have already formed a positive or negative impression of someone, we tend to notice and attend to information that will confirm that initial decision. This can be particularly dangerous when calling references. Reference checkers who have already decided to hire someone are not as sensitive to pregnant pauses and subtle hints as they need to be.

Most references are uncomfortable telling flat-out lies, even to strangers,[41] and so they will often provide subtle cues if the applicant/former employee has had performance problems. The reference might pause for a lengthy period of time or repeat obviously rigid scripts as if by rote. Or the reference might provide a telling hint, "I'm sure she will do well in your organization, we have a very challenging group". It is critical in successful hiring to draw on all of your best social skills and be alert to a reference's inner conflicts and pregnant pauses. Just as psychoanalysts find much telling information in Freudian slips, so those speaking with applicant references can learn a great deal about an applicant's past job performance by being hyper-vigilant about references' hesitations and cautious phrasings.

This also is why managers should never, ever delegate reference checks to someone working for recruiting firms or in their human resources departments.

These time-pressed employees will just work through their scripts as quickly as possible. They will not be as quick to explore pregnant pauses because any uncovered problems will mean more work and explanations for them, and any problematic hires will be your problem not theirs. Certainly, they can confirm educational credentials, previous employment and salaries, but only you, the person who will bear the burden of hiring the wrong person for the job, should ever check with those who have observed the applicant at work.

In fact, the common observation that most people get their jobs from personal contacts[42] probably comes from a lack of faith in the willingness of strangers to provide honest assessments of employees. Many of those who are all too aware of the costs of the wrong hiring decision believe they cannot get an accurate assessment of applicants' past job performance and so will not hire strangers. Rather, they will rely on personal referrals and internal promotions.[43] Too many managers give up before really trying to get accurate descriptions of applicants' past job performance.

Application — Get an Honest Assessment of an Applicant's Performance from Others

- Inoculate yourself for confirmation bias before the call by reminding yourself that your first impressions could be wrong and by dwelling on the pain and difficulty of hiring the wrong person.

- Call references before deciding who to bring in for interviews. If applicants do not want a current employer to know they are job hunting, ask to call someone they had worked with in a previous job or someone they trust to keep the search confidential.

- Ask the reference to describe behavior, not the applicant's personal characteristics. Suggest specifics scenarios: "Last time 'X' occurred, could you please describe what happened." You want accurate descriptions, not ill-considered theories.

- Ask questions focused on what successful employees actually do. For example, to assess conscientiousness you might ask, "Has [name] ever missed a deadline?, stayed late to complete an important assignment?, not delivered on what was promised?" Be sure to ask for specific examples.

- **Snowball references**. Ask each reference to suggest someone else who has worked with the person and so can describe the applicant's performance. If applicants try to restrict you to a narrow list of references, ask why. Persistent managers who ask specific questions about applicants' prior performance can get a lot of information.

- If applicants do not give permission to contact any references until you are about to make them an offer, or if they want to restrict your contacts to a narrow list of people, let them know that this will eliminate them from consideration. Explain that it is your policy to use reference descriptions of past performance in deciding whom to interview for all hiring decisions, and stick to this policy. Good employees will be confident in what you will learn, and poor employees will be eliminated before you have wasted too much time on them

More Effective Use of Selection Interviews

Selection interviews are the least accurate way to predict an applicant's future job performance. Given all of the person-perception errors we've discussed, it isn't surprising that selection interviews are much worse predictors of later job performance than is information coded from a biographical job application.[44] Interviewers are very motivated to discover stable internal causes because they are trying to make quick judgments about an applicant's personality, affectivity and cognitive abilities. Interviewers have to make important hiring decisions based on limited information, and the pressures created by an unfilled position motivate them to get the position filled as quickly as possible. For these reasons, selection interviews have a very bad reputation among professional industrial-organizational psychologists,[45] and the boxed popular opinion is false.

> ***True or False?***
>
> *Selection interviews are the best way to pick employees.*

Despite the demonstrated problems with biased selection interviews, no one is going to abandon them. Why? One reason is that interviews allow hiring managers to assess characteristics that, if they were able to be more articulate about it, they might describe as cognitive ability, conscientiousness, emotional stability, and positive affectivity: characteristics we all have good reason to believe make better performing employees and a more collaborative workplace. They may also try to assess other complex personal traits or qualities of judgment that are believed to be job relevant in that organization — such as an ability to address aggressively hostile criticism without losing your temper. Interviews of job applicants also provide opportunities to clarify ambiguities in work histories. Questions can be asked about past experience, and job knowledge can be explored. Interviews provide opportunities for informal **job samples**, or opportunities for the applicant to demonstrate a sample of actual job performance. Job samples are often used for simple jobs (e.g., a typing test for a typist job). Interviews allow pseudo-job-samples for more complex tasks. For example, a hiring manager might ask questions such as, "Last time you had an angry customer, describe the circumstances and what happened." Finally, the systematic research that allows us to get definitive answers about predictors of employee success requires a precise measure of job performance, a measure that many would see as too narrow. Only recently have scholars developed better measures of the subtle behaviors that may help to improve the performance of an entire work group and organization but would not show up on narrow measures of productivity.[46] Those can include helping others, making constructive suggestions, pitching in to get a deadline met, and the like. Research using those more complete measures of employee performance has shown that selection interviews can be accurate predictors of employee job performance.[47]

Applicant interviews can be improved. Interviewer training helps, but this only works with extensive practice and feedback.[48] Although adding another untrained interviewer does not improve accuracy,[49] training multiple interviewers and combining interviews with other sources of information does.[50]

Application — Get More Accurate Information from Selection Interviews[51]

- Develop an accurate job description and use it as the basis for the interview questions.
- Outline the topics to be covered. This is enough structure to make sure you cover everything with all interviewees. Contrary to what you may have been told, rigidly asking the same questions of all interviewees does not make interviews more reliable. Certainly it is disliked by applicants and is done only because it is believed (but not demonstrated) to reduce legal liability. An outline of topics is sufficient structure.
- Take notes during the interview. This helps ensure a more accurate recall of the interview.
- Ask unexpected questions, these are harder to fake.
- Do not conduct panel interviews. Panel interviews are *not* more reliable and feel like a stressful inquisition to many applicants. Have different interviewers speak with applicants separately and then meet to discuss.
- Guard against common interviewer biases: favoring candidates that talk more during the interview, making decisions in the first few minutes and then going easier on favored applicants, favoring prettier people, and preferring those who are similar to themselves.

Even with your best effort, selection interviews will always be error-prone. However, managers do have a better hiring tool, **assessment centers**. In assessment centers, several trained raters evaluate job applicants on a number of different tasks and exercises. Assessment centers are the employee-selection gold standard. In an assessment center, applicants complete many different assessment tests and perform group and individual tasks, all of which are rated by all of the trained raters. Assessment center ratings have accurately predicted employee job performance and promotions decades later.[52] They reduce similarity-attraction bias and first impression error because they provide a larger sample of applicant behaviors in different settings and because the raters develop an overall rating after discussions. However, assessment centers are expensive and require a professional staff to train raters and manage the centers. Nevertheless, hiring managers can mimic some of the best features of assessment centers, improving their chances of accurately predicting which applicants will be the better performers.

Application — A Practical Manager's Quick-and-Dirty Assessment Center

- It cannot be said too many times: Develop a job description for the position. Before evaluating applicants, you should ask yourself how you plan to learn whether or not applicants have all of the knowledge, skills and abilities required.

- Check your first impressions. After narrowing the pool to the finalists, articulate your first impressions of each one to alert yourself to possible first-impression errors at the next stage.

- Check your similarity-attraction bias. Are these finalists similar to you in ways that are not job relevant?

- Assess conscientiousness. This can be attempted in interviews, but sophisticated applicants understand that they need to present themselves as workaholic eager-beavers, so assessing conscientiousness in interviews may not be effective for many applicants. The best predictor of future conscientiousness is past conscientiousness, and this is best obtained from references.

- Assess cognitive ability. The best quick-and-dirty assessment of cognitive ability is school achievement. Some assessment of cognitive ability can be gained by discussing job experience and technical problems with applicants, but take care that you do not confuse cognitive ability with talkativeness.

- Have as many people as possible assess job finalists. **Triangulation** (or comparing the results of multiple measures) contributes to accuracy. The more interviewers in more kinds of settings, the better you will be able to compare and discuss individual assessments. This can be built into interviews by having applicants go to meals, take tours, look at housing, and so on, all with different assessors. All assessors should have read the job description and discussed ways to assess the desired characteristics, knowledge, skills, and abilities. Afterward, bring the interviewers together to explore discrepancies and behaviors; people will not really explore and elaborate if they have to write it down.

- Invest sufficient time to gather the applicant information you need. Attempting to maintain a false front is difficult to do over longer periods of time (two-day interviews with dinners late into the night are quite effective here). Remember: the more information from different sources, the better.

Attracting the Best Employees

Much of what it takes to attract the best applicants experienced managers already know: have the most attractive job. Having more applicants increases your chances of hiring better performing employees. Jobs are more attractive for any number of reasons: interesting work, promotion opportunities, attractive location, and of course, higher pay.[53] More applicants allow hiring managers to be picky and so reduce the chances of a bad hiring decision. However, even those making hiring decisions who can afford to be picky should be fair and respectful to all applicants. Those with jobs that attract hundreds of applications can sometimes feel crushed under a never-ending avalanche of aggressive networkers. However, building routinized systems that provide applicants with prompt and polite responses are an important public relations investment. Certainly, astute applicants are hyper alert to cues about what a job and employer are really like because taking a job is an important decision for anyone. Job applicants who think an organization is using fair selection procedures are more likely to accept offers.[54]

Attracting the best applicants to accept your job offers requires judgment and diplomacy. On the one hand, good employees have choices, and you want these employees to accept your job offers. On the other hand, the boxed opinion that applicants need to be sold on the job by emphasizing only the positive is not the best approach. There is strong evidence that **realistic job previews** produce more realistic job expectations, higher employee performance and lower turnover.[55] A realistic job preview provides applicants with both positive and negative information about the job. That is, when both accurate positive information and accurate negative information about a job were offered to applicants, those accepting the job offers had more positive initial expectations (now their confirmation biases would dispose them to interpret on-the-job information more favorably), they were better performing employees, and they were less likely to leave the job for any reason.

> ***True or False?***
>
> *When hiring employees, you need to sell them on the job.*

All of these positive effects of realistic job previews were increased if the positive-and-negative information was provided in person.[56] Apparently, people who are told information in person, rather than by written material or from a videotape, pay more attention to it and see it as more likely to be honest. Of course, one reason why realistic job previews are so effective is that some prospective employees who hear negative information do not accept the job offer. But isn't it better to have those employees decline while you still have other applicants and before you have hired and trained them? This is not to say that those recruiting employees should be insensitive to creating a positive impression; realistic job previews provide positive as well as negative information.

Application — Attractive Yet Realistic Employment Interviewing[57]

- Do not begin applicant interviews with negative information; this would be seen as so completely unexpected that applicants would think you were crazy. Negative information is better presented at subsequent interviews or near the end of a one- or two-day interview.
- Accurately describe the job environment; do not inundate the applicant with negative information. Remember, negative information at the interview stage is rare and so will probably be better remembered than positive information. A modest amount of negative information goes a long way.
- Decide in advance what you will say. Ask yourself what you would have wanted to know about this job before taking it. Also ask, "What do people in this job complain about?" Then ask yourself whether that is likely to be important to this applicant. Sharing that information with applicants has the added effect of helping to inoculate them from shock and disappointment when they first hear those complaints from fellow employees.
- Have those already holding the job provide positive and negative information because they will be more credible to applicants. Face-to-face communication is more effective, ideally in a context in which such information is usual, for example at the end of a long dinner or lunch.
- Remember that you are still speaking to organizational outsiders when speaking to applicants; take care not to reveal trade secrets or competitively damaging material.

Hiring the best employees is one of the most important tasks a manager undertakes. It is too often neglected because harassed managers are so time pressed, and yet coping with poorly performing employees takes much more time than attentive and thoughtful hiring. Time invested in hiring well is never wasted.

Implications for Managing Managers — Landing that Job

- ✓ Find opportunities to signal that you are conscientious, emotionally stable, and have positive affectivity. Come prepared with anecdotes that demonstrate these characteristics that you can insert at an appropriate time during the interview. Remember the importance of nuance and judgment, and that conveying your strengths with style and sophistication is a strong signal of cognitive ability.

- ✓ Try to put your interviewer at ease and create a positive mood. Emotions are contagious, so try to spread confidence and good will, not fear and anxiety.

- ✓ Interviewers will form an implicit personality theory of you very quickly, so try to convey an attractive one. The good news for job applicants is that faking during selection interviews can be successful.[57]

- ✓ What you will say and do in those first few days on the job will form the basis for everyone else's inferences about your motives and personality. Take care.

- ✓ Organizations in the same industry can be very different. For example, some encourage employees to have portable skills while others want employees to develop in ways that are valuable only to that organization. Be sure to get as much information as possible about how the job fits with your own skills and goals before accepting any offer.

Key Words

Satisficing

Maximizing

Fit with the organization

Personality

The Big Five

Conscientiousness

Emotional Stability

Agreeableness

Extraversion

Openness to experience

Positive and negative affectivity

Job descriptions

Job-related criteria

Cognitive ability

Protected groups

Adverse impact

Person perception

Implicit personality theories

Theory of causal attribution

Internal and external causes

Act consistency

Act distinctiveness

Act consensus

Fundamental Attribution Error

Similarity-attraction bias

First-impression error

References

Confirmation bias

Snowball references

Job samples

Assessment centers

Triangulation

Realistic job previews

4

Making Sense of Feelings at Work

Why would managers need to worry about squishy stuff like feelings? After all, work is work. But ignoring feelings is impossible. Emotions like rage, jealousy and resentment can lead people to abandon all concern for calculating which actions are in their own best interest, making organizational reward systems useless. People also develop likes and dislikes that can be impervious to any contradictory information. Our actions at work are driven as much by feelings as they are by rational calculations, and no attempt to understand what people do in organizations can ignore them. Nevertheless, as important as feelings are, many of us have developed a healthy trepidation about feelings at work. Feelings can be unpredictable, violent, irritating, and distracting. This leads to two extreme and equally unproductive reactions.

One extreme is to declare that all feelings should be banished from the workplace: demand a professionalism that requires we set our personal likes and dislikes aside. As the unrealistic inset box advises, good professional practice means we salute the uniform and not the person and flee the room at the first sign of a tear. This is exactly what the earliest scholar of modern organizations, Max Weber, advocated,

> ***True or False?***
>
> *Check your emotions at the door.*

> "*...the more bureaucracy is 'dehumanized' the more completely it succeeds in eliminating from official business love, hatred, and all purely personal, irrational and emotional elements which escape calculation. This is the specific nature of bureaucracy and it is appraised as its special value.*"[1]

Although no one has ever thought it was actually possible to completely dehumanize organizations, it remains an impossible ideal that drives policies in many organizations: objective examinations to select who will be promoted, impersonal seniority rules for who is let go, commands to "keep it professional," and the like.

> ***True or False?***
>
> *Employees should express their feelings at work.*

The opposite extreme is reflected in this dangerous boxed inset opinion: spend time discussing and analyzing feelings. In this other extreme ideal, every slight is explored for what it reveals about the other person's deepest emotions. These advocates claim the expression of everyone's feelings, thoughts and opinions should be received with deep respect and infinite patience.[2]

Although organizations have survived using both of these extreme approaches to feelings at work, neither one is optimal. Impersonal professionalism, of course, is an ideal that can never be achieved in practice. Feelings are always present. They are fundamental to who we are. As one illustration of their importance, many books have been written exploring the manipulation of emotion by history's great leaders.[3] Charismatic leaders explicitly influence and direct followers' emotions in order to achieve extraordinary things (see Chapter 10 for a discussion of charismatic leadership). Those who try to manage without emotion will find they can achieve only a shallow and limited organizational performance. At the other extreme, open discussion of feelings at work is based on the assumption that this is the best way to prevent feelings from interfering with work. For good or ill, feelings cannot be tamed by discussion, and open discussion has its own costs in heightened emotional contagion, manipulation, and play acting. This extreme is no more a panacea than rigid impersonal professionalism.

Emotions are central to who we are and how we understand the world around us and cannot be either successfully suppressed or exorcised. Rather, we can only hope to understand what they are, how they arise, and how they affect how organizations work. Feelings have a significant effect on individual employees' job performance, on whether they stay or leave their jobs, and on the collaboration necessary to organizational performance, and so understanding them has immense practical value to managers.

UNDERSTANDING FEELINGS

The expression of feelings in organizations is a complicated issue. In the first place, what we are feeling at work *is* usually already clear to others, whether we talk about our feelings or not. Apparently, most of us are quite poor at disguising our emotions.[4] Anat Rafaeli and Robert Sutton have observed that customers know when service employees are unhappy in their jobs, and when customers perceive that service employees are unhappy, they themselves become less happy with the organization's services.[5] The transparency of our emotions to others should not be surprising;

we all pride ourselves in being able to read others' emotions and moods. Throughout our lives, we read others' and our own feelings and react to what we perceive in organizations and elsewhere. In other words, we are already expressing our feelings to others. The question is, What do we know in particular about how these feelings affect the workplace?

We know that in many circumstances, expression of employees' feelings at work is seen as something that managers should manage. Because our emotions can be so visible to others, and so important to those observing them, managers in many organizations have required the expression of certain emotions while working. Through trial and error, those responsible for organizations have come to the conclusion that employees in some jobs will be more effective when they visibly express particular emotions. So, debt collectors are trained to express anger as a way to induce debt re-payment, and airline flight attendants are expected to express calm and pleasure when working with passengers. This is called **emotional labor**, or the job requirement to display particular emotions, whether actually feeling them or not.[6] Much has been written about the psychological toll a constant demand to express positive emotions employees are not actually feeling can have on their health, and under some circumstances, on their quit rates.[7]

So, many jobs require employee expression of certain emotions because their expression is good for business. Formally requiring particular emotional displays is normal business practice, but it is one that is not quite acceptable, and certainly not as legitimate as the professional suppression of emotional display. This confusion (and insincerity) about the role of emotions does not help us to understand them. Here the research in psychology and organizational behavior on feelings is reviewed for any possible clarity it can provide.

Defining Feelings

Although we are all, of course, familiar with emotions, in practice they can be difficult to define. But the different forms they take have differential organizational effects. So we begin by distinguishing between emotions, moods and temperament (or what we have been calling dispositions).[8]

- **Emotions** are short (lasting from half a second to five minutes) reactions to something in the environment. These are the familiar fear, joy, anger, sadness and the like. Emotions play an important role in survival, providing us with information and helping to direct our attention to what is important.

- Emotions should not be confused with **moods**, which are general, longer lasting summaries of how we are generally feeling at any point in time. Whereas emotions are high in intensity, moods usually are not so sharply experienced: they are the background feelings that we have throughout the day. Moods can be complex combinations of perceptions and emotions, but research on their effects in organizational settings has reliably grouped them into positive and negative moods. Like emotions, moods also direct our attention. For example, people are likely to pay attention to information that matches their current mood:[9] So, those in negative moods are more likely to pay attention to negative performance feedback.

- Temperaments or **dispositions** are stable traits that seem to be present at birth. So, for example someone may have an anxious temperament (neuroticism), but that does not mean that the person is always experiencing the emotion of anxiety. Similarly, someone dispositionally low in neuroticism might become anxious, say before an important job interview. In Chapter 2 we have already discussed one such disposition, negative affectivity.

Influencing Others' Feelings

Certainly, many believe that the management of emotions, moods and dispositions is important to organizational work. Those seeking to sell a product begin with a joke or a small gift because these can create more positive, and so more receptive, moods. Skilled interviewers begin by asking easy straightforward questions to increase interviewee comfort and confidence in answering questions because a comfortable interviewee will be more expansive and forthcoming. We all seek to manage our own and others emotions, although we may do so with little awareness of what we are doing and why.

In addition to trying to foster moods that we believe will help us achieve our goals, we also try to manage our own and others' feelings at work simply because emotions and moods are contagious in a way that rational analysis is not. We know that managers' moods affect their employees' moods,[10] and the reverse — that employees' moods affect their managers' moods.[11] Our moods affect nearly all others we come into contact with, and their moods affect our own. This is **emotional contagion** and has long been recognized as a workplace tool. This is why employees in direct contact with accused perpetrators, customers and clients are directed to display particular emotions. Police officers interrogating suspects fake anger or sympathy to influence suspects' own feelings, and salespeople have learned to display positive moods that they hope will be contagious. Occupational training for many jobs involves teaching the craft of emotional display and the discipline of avoiding contagion from those displaying disadvantageous emotions. Novices practice using differing scenarios to help them build their skills in directed emotional contagion. For example, those who must work with others who may be distraught, such as police officers, flight attendants and negotiators, are trained in techniques to help them avoid catching others' distress.

Even in settings without explicit professional emotional display requirements, people will informally, and sometimes unconsciously, seek to create and sustain desired emotions and moods via contagion. Those who perceive that another is anxious might try to calm or lighten that other's mood, not out of altruism, but simply because they do not want to catch the other's anxiety. Emotional contagion is why those who work together often develop distinctive department or team-level morale.[12] Emotions and moods are contagious, and we all tend to catch them from those we work alongside on a regular basis. Of course, the outcome of manipulation through directed emotional contagion is uncertain. It can be consciously resisted like all attempted manipulations: awareness of the manipulator's intent and technique can undermine its effectiveness.

The prevalence of emotional contagion means that we are continuously communicating our emotions and moods to others, whether we realize it or not. If people are already expressing their feelings so clearly and so actively in organizations, what can it mean to say that people should discuss their feelings at work? Many do advocate more active discussion of feelings than is typically seen in the workplace.[13] This could indicate a confusion of therapeutic discussion of emotions after a traumatic event (beneficial),[14] with emotional display rules for day-in-day-out work (various). Certainly, if such discussions are unusual in a particular organization, attempts to make them happen run the risk of creating anxiety. We do know that sharing intense emotions induces a strong emotional response in others in a wide variety of cultures. The contagiousness of such strong feelings can induce greater intimacy among the participants, but in the extreme, some more vulnerable participants may find such discussions unbearably distressing. Workplaces are not therapeutic environments, and many in those settings may be in direct competition for promotions or attractive assignments. In such settings, coercing open displays of thoughts and feelings can result in elaborately false games in which the sophisticated strategically reveal (real or feigned) emotions, and the unsophisticated and emotionally vulnerable are put at risk.[15]

Emotional Intelligence

Although we all seek to read others' emotions, moods, and dispositions, we are not all equally skilled at it. The ability to read others' emotions is now popularly called **emotional intelligence**.[16] Jack Mayer and Peter Salovey coined this term to describe four distinct skills:

- **Perceiving emotion**. This is the ability to accurately identify emotions and their causes in oneself, in others, and in stories.

- **Using emotion to facilitate thought**. This could involve something as simple as using a deadline (fear) to motivate oneself or others to complete a project. Or it could be more sophisticated. For example, drawing on knowledge that most employees perform better when in a positive mood, employees may consciously try to put themselves in a positive mood by reviewing events that improve their mood before beginning work.[17] Similarly, anxiety leads people to be more careful and systematic, and so drawing employees' attention to the importance of a task can raise their anxious attention to detail.[18]

- **Understanding emotions**. This skill involves knowing how emotions affect one another, how they are caused, and how they can change.

- **Managing emotions**. This is the skill of enhancing or creating certain moods in oneself or in others. There has long been dispute about whether or not thoughts alone can control emotions or whether they can only be changed by another emotion.[19] So we do not know whether talking one's self into a desired mood works as well as trying to evoke the mood by recalling events that evoked the desired mood.

Emotional Intelligence and Performance

The ability to perceive, understand and manage others' emotions would seem to be an important and valuable skill for managers. However, emotional intelligence seems to be a weak predictor of managerial effectiveness, contradicting the boxed popular management opinion. The ability to accurately interpret nonverbal emotional displays has been extensively studied.[20] Those who more accurately recognize nonverbal emotional expressions are rated as more charismatic and socially skilled,[21] warmer and more sympathetic,[22] are more positively evaluated by others,[23] and made more profitable investment decisions.[24] Because managerial work involves working with and through other people, we might expect that skill in reading nonverbal emotional displays would contribute to managerial effectiveness. However, apparently this is only the case for women. Women managers who were good at reading emotions from others' nonverbal behaviors had higher job performance than those who were not, but this skill was not a predictor of managerial job performance for men.[25] Kristin Byron proposed that this unexpected finding results from **gender-role incongruence**. Because, in general, women are expected to be interpersonally sensitive and nurturing, and to be better than men at decoding emotions from nonverbal behavior.[26] Better emotional intelligence is expected of women (at least in her American sample). However, those holding management roles in the United States are expected to be assertive and to take action, not necessarily to be socially sensitive to their employees. This produces role incongruence for women managers. For this reason, those women in management positions who can combine assertive authority with the gender-role expected skill of accurately perceiving others' emotions were judged by both their bosses and employees as more effective than other women in similar positions.

> ***True or False?***
>
> *Successful managers have high emotional intelligence.*

This contradicts the popular idea that all managers would be more effective if they were better at perceiving emotions.[27] It is unclear why American men in managerial jobs that require extensive work with others do not benefit from accurately perceiving others' emotions, a skill that has been shown to benefit men when they work in other occupations involving extensive work with others.

Nevertheless, this is still early research in the United States, a society known for valuing emotionally distant individualism. For example, in some non-American cultures, leaders are expected to be caring paternalists,[28] and so it is possible that more skilled reading of employees' emotions may be a better predictor of perceptions of performance in those cultures.

So emotions are on display at work, and they are actively manipulated by members of certain occupations to better manage those whom they must serve or try to control. Some of us are more skilled at reading, understanding and influencing feelings than others, and such emotional intelligence seems to lead to better managerial performance for some managers, but not all.

Application — Understand Emotions

One way to improve our emotional intelligence is to have a clearer understanding of why some important workplace emotions arise:[29]

- **Anger**. Anger is the reaction to a demeaning offense to yourself or your group. Anger is experienced when we believe we can overcome or defeat the offender, and so this is an emotion that leads to aggression. In workplaces, anger can be generated by demeaning treatment that implies the target lacks social significance. Most people who experience anger at work tend to express those feelings directly to the person who provoked it.

- **Anxiety**. Anxiety is provoked when we face a threat to our confidence in our ability to survive and prosper. Because we are constantly being evaluated at work and may be uncertain of our performance, anxiety is ever present in most workplaces. However, unlike anger, which spurs action, anxiety reflects a lack of confidence and so is rarely expressed to the source of anxiety. If it is expressed, it is to friends, co-workers or family members.

- **Guilt**. We feel guilty when we have violated a moral requirement. The guilty will usually try to remove or atone for the transgression by apologizing or making restitution. For example, this emotion can afflict a newly appointed supervisor who must now act for the organization but may feel guilt at treating former co-workers (and friends) in ways that can seem disloyal.

Application — Understand Emotions *cont.*

- **Shame**. We feel shame when we have not lived up to social standards of the right thing to do. Whereas guilt refers to universal moral standards, shame is a social failure. Thus, an accountant who testifies against his co-conspirators in an embezzlement fraud may feel shame at the betrayal of colleagues but no guilt about the theft. The experience of shame is more painful than guilt, and those feeling shame will try to hide the bad behavior or shift the blame to someone else.

- **Pride**. Pride is pleasure in enhanced status based on a personal or group achievement. It enhances our sense of our value as a person, and so is the opposite of shame. Although we all enjoy feeling pride, and it is often a major motivator of workplace performance, it can easily create a sense of superiority over others, leading us to denigrate those others and so make them angry. Possibly for this reason, most cultures frown on public displays of pride, such as bragging, and value displays of humility.

- **Envy**. This is a two-person emotion in which one person wants what another has unfairly obtained. Inherent in workplaces is competition for promotions, pay, and status, which provides fertile breeding grounds for envy. Envious people are likely to try to sabotage or damage the other person, and envious people will often form coalitions to act against the envied one.

Telling someone not to feel envy, anxiety or other emotions is not effective. If certain emotions seem to be causing dysfunctional actions, it would be better to address the cause of the emotion.

EMPLOYEE HAPPINESS AND ORGANIZATIONAL PERFORMANCE

The question of whether happy workers are more productive than unhappy ones has spawned decades of research exploring every kind of happiness and possible type of job performance. There are many reasons for the perennial popularity of what has been called the **happy-productive-worker thesis** (making workers happy will cause them to be more productive): it allows labor negotiators to claim that happier workers will be more productive (so deserving higher pay), it allows human resources professionals and researchers to be supportive of both labor and management, and it is common sense that happy employees would be better performers. If this boxed popular opinion were true, everybody would win.[30] Unfortunately, this thesis is either somewhat true or utterly false depending on the definitions used of both "productive workers" and "happy workers."

> ***True or False?***
>
> *Happy workers are more productive workers.*

Understanding Job Performance

Simple employee productivity or task performance does not capture all of the job performance that organizations need from employees. **Contextual performance** is the contribution people make in support of task performance.[31] It includes any voluntary act that facilitates organizational goal attainment. Examples include efforts such as working hard to meet a deadline, helping coworkers, taking the initiative to solve unexpected problems, making constructive suggestions, developing oneself and spreading good will. Contextual performance is important to most jobs, and it is critical to professional and managerial job performance. Organizational performance requires more than a narrow focus on doing as instructed; it requires employees who pitch in, help others, and use their best judgment to solve whatever problems they confront.

Using narrow measures of task performance or productivity that exclude contextual performance, literally hundreds of studies have established a very weak relationship between this part of job performance and all the different ways of looking at employee happiness. There is no evidence at all that making employees happy will lead them to become more productive on their tasks.[32] So there is no ambiguity here: none of the many ways we know to make employees happy — by paying them more, treating them with consideration, creating a just workplace[33] — will lead individuals to produce more, no matter what we all want to believe. Employee happiness does matter to organizational performance in other ways, but it does not — and this is probably the strongest, best established research finding in the field of organizational behavior — lead to greater worker task performance or productivity. Most organizations have worked hard to encourage task performance or productivity through training, having the necessary supplies available, and performance measurement and incentives. When all of those systems function as they should, employees' feelings matter little to narrow task performance. However, their happiness is important to employees' contextual performance.

Positive Moods and Performance

When job performance is defined more broadly to include the various aspects of contextual performance, the connection to feelings is more promising, but it varies somewhat based on the kind of worker happiness studied. First, when happiness is defined as a positive mood, the results are mixed. Although negative moods, such as fatigue, interfere with the performance of critical tasks in the military,[34] negative moods also lead to greater care and attention to immediate tasks and details and so to better performance on problem solving tasks.[35] In contrast, those in a positive mood will generate more ideas in a creativity task but seem less concerned about the quality of those ideas than those in negative moods.[36] It seems that positive moods signal that everything is fine, and so we pay less attention to the quality of arguments in persuasive appeals and are more likely to rely on stereotypes and other simplifying strategies rather than paying careful attention. For the kinds of organizational work requiring attention to detail and care to avoid errors, negative moods spur better performance. Good moods are relaxing; they signal that everything is fine just the way it is, and so they help with creative tasks.

Positive Dispositions and Performance

In addition, positive dispositions seem to lead to superior job performance among some professionals and managers.[37] Interestingly, positive affectivity is more important for better job performance for those employees with longer tenure, whereas negative affectivity leads to poor performance only among newer employees.[38] This doesn't seem to make sense. We know that those with positive dispositions have more positive moods and vice versa for negative dispositions,[39] so why would negative moods lead to more care and attention, but positive dispositions lead to better overall job performance? Don't care and attention matter to job performance?

It seems likely that the distinction between narrow task performance and contextual performance might account for these conflicting reports. Negative moods signal us to be alert to dangers and difficulties, so we are more attentive to the task at hand. Thus, we set deadlines for ourselves at least partly to create a self-induced mood of anxious attentiveness. However, for overall job performance, especially for managers with their pressing time demands and need to collaborate and gather information, positive affectivity is beneficial because it leads others to view them more positively and sympathetically. It could be that others are more willing to share information and in other ways collaborate with those who have positive dispositions because they are pleasant company. The support and cooperation of others aids in performance of the managerial job of information exchange and influence.

Job Satisfaction and Performance

Although the study of employee emotions, moods and dispositions is relatively new, there has been a great deal of research on an earlier understanding of employee happiness called job satisfaction. **Job satisfaction** is a pleasurable feeling resulting from an evaluation of one's job and job experiences.[40] Alert readers will have noticed that this older concept is really a combination of feeling (pleasurable) and rational analysis (evaluation). It combines both the outcome (feeling) and a possible cause of that feeling (appraisal of what this job offers compared to other alternatives). You don't have to be a trained social scientist to guess that such a complex definition can create confusion.[41] Fortunately, most employees who have been asked about their job satisfaction do not pay much attention to fine points, and so pretty reliably report themselves as satisfied, dissatisfied or something in between.

Job satisfaction is an **attitude**, that is a feeling, positive or negative, about something. Just as employees can have positive or negative attitudes about their jobs, they can have a range of positive and negative attitudes about any other aspect of work: their pay, their boss, their coworkers, top management, and so on. For this reason, the study of job satisfaction also involves the study of how employees' attitudes might influence their actions at work.

The attitude of job satisfaction does lead to better contextual job performance as reflected in more altruism, more consideration of others, and more helping behavior, as well as fewer dysfunctional behaviors, such as reluctant, perfunctory effort or problem drinking.[42] Those who have positive feelings about their jobs help out and are more supportive coworkers. Job satisfaction is *not*, however, very strongly correlated with narrow task performance. Similar results are found for the other workplace attitudes. As with mood and dispositions, workplace attitudes such as job satisfaction do seem to lead to higher employee contextual performance but not to more efficient performance of the task itself, whether that task is number of patients seen, arrests made, deadlines met, or policy manuals written. Why should worker happiness be more strongly associated with contextual performance than task performance?

Acting on Feelings

Although all of us have feelings and attitudes about many aspects of our organizational work, we do not always act on them. Whether we do, or do not act on our feelings and attitudes in a particular situation can be clarified by distinguishing between strong and weak settings.[43] **Strong settings** are those with powerful normative expectations and incentives to behave in certain constrained ways. **Weak settings** are ones in which the participants do not have clear expectations about how to behave. For example, when students walk into a college classroom, they know to sit in one of the audience chairs (not the chair facing the audience next to the podium), to speak quietly until the instructor begins speaking, and then to sit in a pose of calm, attentive listening (whether or not they feel calm or are actually listening). College classrooms are strong settings.

Most task performance takes place in strong settings. After all, organizations go to a great deal of expense and trouble to make sure that employees know what is expected of them on the job and to establish elaborate and sophisticated accountability systems to manage employee performance. If an organization's performance management and incentive systems are working properly, we should not find that emotions, moods, dispositions, or attitudes would have powerful effects on employee task performance.

However, contextual performance is more voluntary and cannot be mandated and controlled in advance. This means that contextual performance takes place in relatively weak settings, and that is why attitudes and feelings are better at predicting employee contextual performance. For example, Frank Smith found that those employees with positive attitudes about work were more likely to come into work after a large snow storm in Chicago but attitudes did not predict absenteeism on the same day in New York, which had no snow.[44] In weak settings, people have more choice about what to do, and so their feelings and attitudes will have a bigger impact on whether they choose to take the trouble to have high contextual performance.

Employee Absenteeism and Turnover

Employees cannot perform if they do not show up to work. This is another way in which employees' feelings and attitudes can affect team, departmental or organizational performance: whether or not employees come to work ready and willing to do their jobs. **Absenteeism** is when employees do not do their work at the scheduled time, whether they have called in sick or taken an unauthorized leave. **Turnover** is the voluntary departure of employees from their jobs. Certainly, high levels of absenteeism and turnover are costly to organizations: harassed co-workers must take on their absent colleague's work, substitutes must be hired, and new employees must be trained.[45] Unhappy workers are much more likely to quit, to be absent, or in other ways withdraw from organizations that make them unhappy.[46] These can be very costly, especially to managers' time. Happier employees find that their organization is attractive to them. Because the organization is attractive to happy employees, they are more likely to show up and less likely to leave. There is strong evidence that divisions with higher managerial, and especially employee, turnover have lower profits.[47] It is not the case that happier employees are necessarily more productive on their tasks, narrowly defined, but happier employees are more likely to go that extra mile and less likely to be absent and to leave. All of these actions directly contribute to organizational performance.

Although any number of different workplace attitudes can lead to employee withdrawal, the one we know the most about is **organizational commitment**, or the extent to which employees are committed to the organization. Organizational commitment consists of both **affective commitment** (commitment to the organizations' goals and values) and **continuance commitment** (a commitment to stay with the organization because there are no attractive alternatives). Whereas employees low in both forms of commitment are more likely to be absent or to quit,[48] only the more emotion-focused affective commitment is a good predictor of contextual performance behaviors like helping others.[49] Particularly noteworthy is evidence that affective commitment can counteract the highly problematic behaviors that are encouraged by pay-for-performance systems. The sales associates in a large nationwide company were less likely to engage in misleading potential customers and front loading sales if they felt an affective commitment to their organization.[50] The positive consequences of employee affective commitment have been found in numerous countries and for many diverse occupations, even for temporary workers.[51] Thus, this boxed popular management opinion is true.

> ***True or False?***
>
> *Committed employees are better employees.*

Employees have many potential commitments, not just to their organizations. For example, employees who are committed to their work group or coworkers are also less likely to be absent or quit.[52] For many employees, a pleasant work environment is more important than advancement. Good managers will be sure to have an accurate diagnosis of the feelings, attitudes and commitments of everyone they come into contact with at work. Just as employees may have positive or negative attitudes about many different aspects of work, so employees may be committed to the organization, or to their coworkers, or to the new product, or to their clients, and any of these can influence their contextual performance, their absenteeism, and whether or not they will leave.

Feelings, Attitudes, and Organizational Performance

Employee emotions, moods, dispositions and attitudes affect organizational performance in two additional ways. First, contextual performance is often helping others at work with their own performance, providing useful suggestions and the like, and so should result in higher levels of team, departmental or organizational performance. Research does show that the higher a team's average positive mood, the better the team's task performance.[53] Additional evidence that employee feelings matter for organizational performance comes from a study finding that the average job satisfaction of factory workers in different factories predicted those factories' performance: the higher the employee satisfaction, the higher the factory's output and efficiency.[54] So, although job satisfaction does not lead employees to perform better on their job tasks, which are driven by the organizations' performance management and incentive systems, organizational performance is more than the sum of individual employees' narrow task performances. Happier workers are more likely to show up at work, to stay, and to be willing to invest in contextual job performance: help coworkers, take the initiative to solve unexpected problems, and in many other ways engage in consummate effort. These actions improve aggregate group and organizational performance. Employee happiness does not make employees more productive in the narrow sense, but it does matter to team and organizational performance.

The second reason employee emotions affect organizational performance is because emotions are contagious. Employee emotions, moods, dispositions, and attitudes influence what others at work feel. The positive feelings reflected in helping co-workers can create a circle of support and assistance that has been reflected in team and organizational performance. Of course, such positive employee actions do not guarantee high organizational performance. Organizations staffed by enthusiastic and committed employees may fail because markets have shifted or technology has become obsolete. Contextual performance may not be enough to save every organization, but it never hurts.

What Makes Employees Happy

What do we know about what leads employees to have positive feelings about their organization, jobs, bosses and coworkers? First, as is not surprising, employees with more positive dispositions are more likely to have positive attitudes about their jobs, supervisors and organizations.[55] In addition, those employees who see a good fit between what they want from a job and what the job provides are more satisfied.[56] Those who believe that their workplace is fair and just feel more positively about it than those who do not,[57] and employees are happier with jobs that provide more autonomy and variety.[58] Interestingly, those who take jobs they do not expect to hold for long report more negative attitudes about the job than those who expect to work at their jobs for an indefinite time.[59] So expecting to be working temporarily reduces happiness with a job. Although those who are paid more are more satisfied with their jobs, women are not less satisfied than men, despite their lower relative pay.[60]

In conclusion, just as there are many things that employees may feel good (or bad) about at work and may be more (or less) committed to, so there are any number of things that can cause such feelings. Pay is only one among many. What is dangerous is that high pay is very effective at inducing employees to stay in their well-paid jobs. So, those well-paid employees who are unhappy — because of injustice or because they hate their jobs or because they received insulting treatment — may stay for the money and damage organizational performance. Such employees may act on their unhappiness in any way they can get away with — perfunctory effort, undermining others or anything else, limited only by their imaginations. Unhappy employees who do not leave because they have no attractive alternatives risk spreading their negative feelings and attitudes throughout the organization.[61]

Application — Make Employees Happy

Because most studies of employees' happiness have been based on a utilitarian understanding of happiness, most of this work has focused on employees' assessments that their current jobs are better than the alternatives. So what makes a job better than the alternatives?[62]

- Better pay than at other jobs the employee could get.
- Lack of alternative jobs: employee job satisfaction is highest in areas of high unemployment.
- Jobs higher in the organizational hierarchy.
- Jobs with more autonomy that use the employees' skills and knowledge and provide knowledge of results.
- Jobs that provide the particular satisfactions that the employee values (for example, congenial colleagues for those who value this or high pay for those who value that).
- Fair treatment.
- Co-workers with positive dispositions (because they create positive emotional contagion).
- Employees trained in more positive self-talk or positive interpretations of events.[63]

FEAR AND JOB PERFORMANCE

Fear is an emotion that leads to a desire to escape. But if escape is not possible (at least not immediately), it can lead to stress, and stress can lead to several dysfunctions. In Chapter 2, we saw that the image of the stressed executive succumbing to a heart attack is a false one. Rather, the opposite is true. Across a wide variety of countries and industries, the lower employees' rank in an organization, the higher their levels of stress and the worse their health.[64] The culprit seems to be job **autonomy**, or the degree of control over work, which usually increases with organizational rank. The less control civil servants,

True or False?

Stress kills.

nurses, and factory workers, among others, had over how to do their work and its pace, the higher their blood pressure and adrenaline levels, and those levels persisted outside of work, with more health care required for those employees years later.[65] So the boxed opinion is true.

But stress, takes a long time to kill; what are its effects on organizational behavior in the meantime? We experience **stress** when we judge that our environment is so demanding that it exceeds our ability to manage it or that it is dangerous to our well-being. We can ask people to tell us their levels of experienced stress, but stress also can be assessed by certain biological markers, as was done in the above-cited medical studies. The more a workplace challenge is new, unexpected, ambiguous, difficult or time-demanding, the more likely it is to be experienced as stressful. This is why autonomy and a sense of personal control are important. When people feel that they have sufficient control over their situation to allow them the time to learn about the problem, or the authority to sidestep or delegate it, they are less likely to experience stress.

Stress can have negative consequences for employee and organizational performance. When under stress, people revert to ingrained habits rather than gathering new information. A study of the deaths of firefighters in the Mann Gulch Fire found that this reversion to ingrained habits under stress led to needless deaths because the firefighters trapped behind a brush fire did not diagnose their situation.[66] Similar **threat-rigidity responses** have been found in other organizations.[67] When people are under stress, they narrow their search for alternatives, which leads to rigidity in decision making. When diagnosis and careful decision making are important to effective job performance, stress leads to poorer performance. Finally, when under high stress, those who are more intelligent perform more poorly than the less intelligent — smarter people give us their expected superior performance only when under low stress.[68]

Why then, do so many managers seem to believe that employees need the stress of fear to perform well? If stress kills, leads to rigid responses, and poorer job performance, why would so many hold this false boxed opinion? Perhaps they have learned from experience that their own employees are among the less intelligent, so stress does little to reduce their job performance. Or perhaps some managers believe this because they know that people can put more effort into familiar, habituated tasks when under stress, and they simply assume that the problems their employees face are routine ones that do not require much thought. So it is possible that this opinion is based on a clear understanding of the effects of stress on employees' performance, based on an accurate diagnosis of their employees and their tasks, unburdened by any concern for its consequences for employees' health. Alternatively, as we will see in the next chapter, *Managing Performance*, perhaps managers with this opinion are confusing the focus and discipline of having clear, challenging goals with the stress and anxiety of fear.

> ***True or False?***
>
> *Employees need to have a fire lit under them or they won't perform.*

Application — Reduce Employee Stress

The following are approaches to reducing stress-inducing workplace ambiguity, increasing employees' perceived control, and potentially useful coping strategies.[69]

- Reduce unnecessary uncertainty. The creation of artificial uncertainty by secrecy, changing performance standards or delaying information does nothing to motivate better performance.

- If uncertainty cannot be eliminated, explain and provide time lines for announcements when further information will be known. For example, management in an acquiring company can immediately let employees in an acquired company know which jobs are subject to reductions stemming from consolidated functions, what the process will be for making further decisions about layoffs, and the expected time line for those announcements.

- Increase control whenever possible. Employees should be given clear guidance on performance standards, practices and objectives and then be allowed to do their work without someone providing superfluous surveillance. One popular approach to increasing experienced autonomy in manufacturing is to group tasks into team responsibilities and then let the teams select team members and generate suggestions.[70]

- The opportunity to talk to others experiencing the same stressful conditions reduces stress. Talking can provide powerful buffers against stress at work.

- Stress management programs do not reduce stress in the long run, if employees must return to the same stressful workplace. However, when the stressful conditions can be reappraised or reframed, cognitive skills focused on learning how to reframe and interpret events in a more positive, controllable way can help. For example, instead of saying, "I always screw up," employees might learn to say, "Today did not go well, but I learned the following things from it..."

Implications for Managing Managers

- ✓ Be wary of jobs that require you to constantly display emotions you are not feeling. They are bad for your health.
- ✓ Managers catch their employees' emotions as readily as employees catch emotions from their managers. Do you only see your boss when you have a complaint, making yourself a source of frustration and anxiety?
- ✓ Develop your ability to read emotions from nonverbal behaviors. Any time you are sitting and waiting is an opportunity to improve your emotional intelligence. For example, meetings are particularly good places to observe and develop your understanding of how emotions affect others and combine in complex ways.
- ✓ If you were surprised by someone's emotional response, take the time to discover why your assumption was off the mark.
- ✓ If something upsetting or distressing happens to you at work, by all means do talk about it with someone else. But be cautious: the person standing next to you when you become upset is not always the person you should trust with your immediate reactions.

Key Words

- Emotional labor
- Emotions
- Moods
- Dispositions
- Emotional contagion
- Emotional Intelligence
- Perceiving emotion
- Using emotion to facilitate thought
- Understanding emotions
- Managing emotions
- Gender-role incongruence
- Anger
- Anxiety
- Guilt
- Shame
- Pride
- Envy
- Happy-productive-worker thesis
- Contextual performance
- Job satisfaction
- Attitude
- Strong settings
- Weak settings
- Absenteeism
- Turnover
- Organizational commitment
- Affective commitment
- Continuance commitment
- Autonomy
- Stress
- Threat-rigidity response

5

Managing Performance

Employee performance matters. Both common sense and substantial evidence[1] tell us that high performing organizations need high performing employees. For this reason, one of the most important responsibilities of managers is to encourage and direct the job performance of their employees. Because managing performance is so important, we find much popular advice — and thus inevitable contradictions and misconceptions — about managing employee performance. Fortunately, there is substantial research seeking to understand how to motivate, direct and sustain high levels of employee performance in organizations. This organizational behavior research does provide useful guidance about what does and does not work, as well as warning of traps common sense can create when it comes to trying to manage performance in organizations. This chapter is organized into four parts: employee motivation, establishing accountability, the challenge of measuring the performance you really want, and the challenges of formal performance appraisals.

THE NON-PROBLEM OF EMPLOYEE MOTIVATION

> ***True or False?***
>
> *Employees will not do something if there isn't anything in it for them.*

Decades ago, the challenge of managing performance was seen as one of motivating workers. **Motivation** is the why and how we work toward some objective and our persistence in trying to reach that objective. It involves intensity (how much effort), direction (what exactly the person is trying to do), and persistence in exerting that level of effort to accomplish the task.[2] However, although some managers continue to worry about employee motivation, they need not: we understand how to motivate. Creating and sustaining motivation can be diagnosed and straightforwardly addressed. This happy situation is largely due to the implementation of expectancy, self-efficacy, goal setting theories, and the theory of causal attribution. So, the boxed opinion is true. The challenge is making sure they believe their actions will lead to something they actually want.

Diagnosing Motivational Problems

In his **Expectancy Theory**,[3] Victor Vroom proposed that employees' motivation comes from their analysis of what performance they can expect from their efforts, what the costs and benefits will be from those efforts, and how much they personally like or dislike those particular costs and benefits. That is, before expending effort at work, employees ask themselves three different questions:

- What are the costs and benefits of my efforts? Can I *expect* any rewards from the organization (hence, the name Expectancy Theory)? Will I get that promotion? A pay raise? The esteem and admiration of my boss? And, what costs might I expect from that effort? Would I have to stay late and miss more dinners with my family? Incur the resentment and jealousy of my peers? In other words, before expending effort, individuals ask themselves: Do my benefits from this effort outweigh my costs? If the answer is, "No," Expectancy Theory predicts no effort, and so no motivation.

- How much do I, personally, value each of those possible benefits and costs? The theory emphasizes that it doesn't matter how much anyone else thinks the person *should* value those benefits and costs, it is how much the person considering expending the effort *actually* values them. If he or she doesn't personally value the expected benefits of the effort more than the costs, Expectancy Theory predicts no effort, and so no motivation.

- If I expend the effort, what is the chance that I can actually perform at a level that would result in the benefits I value? That is, it is not enough to expect benefits for the performance and to want those benefits; there will be no effort if the person does not believe he or she has the abilities or resources to attain the necessary performance. For example, someone might be uncomfortable around people, and become impatient at meetings. If she knows those characteristics will make her a poor manager, she will judge that she does not have the possibility to become an effective manager, and so Expectancy Theory predicts she'll expend no effort to become one.

If any one of these three elements is missing, we would not expect effort. If the costs of the effort outweigh the benefits, employees will not make the effort. If the benefits the organization offers are unattractive (or the costs are too personally odious), employees will not make the effort. If employees do not have the ability or resources to turn effort into the performance necessary to obtain the benefits, they will not make the effort.

Of course, Expectancy Theory is a highly rational theory, and we know that emotions often trump rationality. However, this theory has been a good predictor of effort for those actions important enough for individuals to take the time to analyze their options.[4] Certainly, emotions color how individuals make these assessments; for example, those with more positive affect are more likely to judge that the available rewards are more attractive, that the odds of achieving attractive rewards are higher, and that they have the ability and resources necessary to obtain those rewards.[5] That is further evidence that we all are better at rationalizing what feels right than we are at rationally weighing evidence. Nonetheless, for practical purposes, whether or not employees are sufficiently rational decision makers is not as important as Expectancy Theory's usefulness in diagnosing why people do what they do in organizations.

Application — Understand Motivational Problems

Motivational problems usually present themselves as others not doing what you want them to do. These could be employees, suppliers, colleagues, or your own boss. You need to ask yourself: Why is the person not motivated to take the action I want? Motivational problems require a careful diagnosis, and the following questions can help guide your analysis:

- Does the person have the ability and resources to do what you want? It does no good to pile on the incentives (or threats of punishment) if the person does not believe it is possible to do what you want. If the motivation problem results from this perceived **ability or resources deficit**, it can only be remedied by making sure the person believes the task can be done. It is an all-to-common mistake to misdiagnose someone's belief that they cannot do something as an incentives problem, so always ask this question first.

- Does the person actually value the expected benefits being offered more than the expected costs? Everyone does not value the same things. For example, many see no real opportunity for any pay raise of significance or gain their greatest pleasures at work from a congenial relationship with coworkers. You cannot make people value what you think they should value or assume that everyone else values what you personally value. What is more, don't forget that many people value their sense of personal autonomy (and self respect) more than the small amount of additional money they might expect to get. An accurate diagnosis depends on understanding what others actually do value and then being sure to attach what they really do value to the actions you want.

- Are rewards really contingent on the effort required? This is the **incentives problem**: managers hope for "A" from their employees while actually rewarding "B."[6] Do you hope the person will be a team player but only reward for individual job performance? A corollary to this problem is assuming that the only reward that can and should be attached to effort is money. Money does matter to people, but it is not the only thing that does, and too many managers just assume that if they do not control much money they cannot motivate. People want many different things, so be creative. Addressing money's role in the incentive problem is complicated enough for a more detailed discussion in the following chapter.

Remember: Expectancy Theory's key lesson is that it is the other person's perceptions that count here, not any objective reality. It is always possible that the person misunderstands his or her capabilities or falsely does not believe that valued rewards will follow effort or does not understand what effort will be rewarded. If so, the problem is one of clarifying their apparently inaccurate expectations.

Enhancing Self-confidence

What if employees do not have confidence in their ability to perform? This boxed common management opinion may or may not be true because it assumes that the reason employees aren't doing what you want is because they need more painful punishments; in Expectancy Theory terms, the motivation problem has been diagnosed as an incentives problem. Some motivation problems are incentives problems, but not all. If a lack of confidence is the real cause, neither alluring incentives nor scary punishments will do any good.

> ***True or False?***
>
> *All they need is a kick in the pants.*

Employees' confidence in their own abilities has been widely studied through Self Efficacy Theory. **Self efficacy** is a person's belief that he or she is capable of producing desired actions or performance or capable of avoiding undesirable ones.[7] That is, how confident are they that they can do the work? Self efficacy is vital to action — we don't do things we don't think can be successfully done — and so it is important to employee performance. Employees with higher self efficacy take more initiative and generate more innovative ideas, invest more effort, and persevere in the face of obstacles.[8] They try harder, and so they get more done. People with low self efficacy are consumed by self doubt, dwell on obstacles, and are easily convinced that any action is futile.[9] Those higher in self efficacy experience less debilitating stress because they are less likely to see themselves as lacking in control.[10] However, self efficacy is not all good: it can lead to performance problems. Those with high self efficacy are more likely to persist with previously successful actions when they no longer work and to commit similar errors of over-confidence.[11] Because entrepreneurship requires so much persistence, successful entrepreneurs are higher in self efficacy than are others.[12] Overall, those high in self efficacy take action and are persistent. Because those high in self efficacy get more done at work, fostering high employee self efficacy, can improve employee performance.

How can high levels of employee performance self efficacy be fostered? One approach is to create a **Galatea Effect**, or the effective cultivation of others' sense that they can achieve high performance. This is named for the statue created by Pygmalion in the Greek myth. Programs to create a Galatea Effect among new sales people and established professionals at work have resulted in significant improvements in their job performance.[13] It can be done. Successful methods for increasing self efficacy include mastery experiences, observing those who have mastered the tasks, and persuasion.

Application — Build Employee Self Efficacy Through Guided Mastery[14]

- Break down complex jobs into components that can be modeled easily. Teach each of the components. For example, new managers can be trained in the separate tasks of hiring effective employees, setting performance expectations, providing performance feedback, running a meeting, and so on.
- Teach general rules and strategies for dealing with different situations rather than scripted routines.
- Use a variety of specific examples of the application of the general rules and strategies.
- Use examples similar to the employee's own job and challenges.
- Apply the new skills in a practice situation with informative feedback.
- Train resiliency by including skills and strategies for overcoming obstacles and frustrations.
- Provide an opportunity to apply the skills on the job, with an opportunity to evaluate what was effective and ineffective.

THE IMPORTANCE OF ACCOUNTABILITY

True or False?

Just hire the right people and get out of their way.

Employees often do not have clear and accurate performance expectations even in otherwise well-managed companies.[15] The problem with this boxed popular opinion is that it assumes employees know what they should do to be successful. In other words, it assumes they have clear and accurate expectations. Experienced managers know that even the most motivated employees can invest their effort in projects that are short-sighted, activities they enjoy doing (rather than activities they should be doing), or work that just isn't as important as projects they should have been doing instead. And if employees do not know what they are expected to do in their jobs, they certainly cannot be expected to do it. Getting employees to put forth effort is not very difficult; the more challenging managerial problem is ensuring that employees' efforts are directed toward the right objectives, rather than wasting that effort in unproductive ways. When people in organizations are left alone to do what they want whenever they want to do it, they might sometimes do what is needed, but they are more often going to waste their time and intelligence, producing little of value for the organization and producing frustration for themselves. Clarifying and then continuously managing expectations via **accountability** is a critical part of managing employee performance.

Employees can be held accountable in many different ways. In small owner-operated organizations, the owners might continuously watch employees and so may have no need for formal systems of performance accountability. Here employees are accountable for keeping the boss happy, and all but the most pig-headed will understand this. However, as organizations grow larger and more complex than any one person can personally monitor, formal performance goals and standards for divisions, departments, teams and individuals are necessary to create and sustain accountability.

Goal Setting

The power of clear accountability is best demonstrated by research on Goal Setting Theory. A **goal** is the conscious aim of action (not the action itself). For example, to design a semiconductor chip that is 50% faster but only 10% hotter and no larger than the existing chip by August 30th is a **performance goal**. Another performance goal might be to reduce surgical catheter infections by 80% this calendar year. An action, like moving sterile equipment within easy reach of the surgical nurses, is not, in itself, a goal, although it could be a means to the goal of reduced surgical infections. As a way of holding employees accountable, goal setting can powerfully motivate and direct effort; however its very power makes it something that must be carefully managed to avoid unintended consequences.

Goal Setting Theory predicts (and this prediction has been supported in countless studies) that setting performance goals that are specific and difficult results in higher job performance than either easier goals or just being told to "do your best."[16] Setting specific, difficult goals works in a wide variety of jobs from the simple to complex research and development work.[17] Specific, difficult goals can also help spur creative ways to achieve the goal. When employees, teams, divisions and organizations have specific difficult goals, they produce superior performance. Goal setting really does work. Goals are better predictors of high job performance than personality and preexisting motivation.[18] And it may surprise some readers to know that specific, difficult goals produce higher performance whether or not money is attached to achieving them.[19] Why do performance goals work even without some payoff attached to achieving them? Because if we accept a goal as our own and we see it as achievable, goal achievement itself is psychologically rewarding. We all gain satisfaction from reaching our goals, especially difficult ones. Goal setting works because goals direct attention and effort to goal-related actions; goals are energizing, and they lead to more persistence.[20]

It is important to emphasize that goal setting only works when the goals are accepted as the employees' own,[21] and they believe they are able to achieve the goal.[22] Goals can be assigned by managers or others (that is, they do not have to be self-set to be effective), but the level of commitment to the goal is important, especially for very difficult goals.[23] So managers must always take care to be sure that any employee performance goals are accepted, and employees are highly committed to them. If they can do that, goal setting can be a powerful support to performance accountability and organizational control.

It is not difficult to gain employees' commitment to specific, difficult goals. When they take jobs, employees expect to be assigned tasks and to be held accountable for job performance, and most welcome clear targets and goals. Knowing what is expected, and having a way to know that they have succeeded, helps employees avoid frustration and anxiety. For example, those in volunteer jobs who were not held accountable for their job performance reported that they were insulted by such neglect.[24] Employees also welcome clear performance goals because they protect them from arbitrary and capricious demands. Employees with specific goals can feel like professionals with responsibilities rather than servants at the beck and call of others. For those reasons, getting difficult, specific goals is welcomed by employees as long as they do not anticipate perilously negative consequences for failure to reach their difficult goals. In other words, goal setting motivates but not in a vacuum, and employees who have learned to distrust those setting their goals will not accept or be committed to those goals.

One common way performance is undermined by mismanaged goal setting is by ratcheting goals. **Ratcheting goals** is when every met goal is followed by a higher goal in the next time period. Some managers do this because they know that the higher the goal, the higher the performance.[25] Certainly, setting ever higher goals can spur increased performance when the initial goals are accepted as **proximal goals**. That is, if employees know that the ultimate performance goal is so uncertain that a series of proximal goals will be set to generate enough additional information to eventually set realistic difficult goals, upward adjustment of successive goals will not sabotage acceptance. If, however, goal achievement is greeted with an arbitrary ratcheting to a new higher goal, management has sent a clear signal that goal achievement will be punished with additional performance pressure. We have long known that employees who believe management will ratchet their performance goals and quotas upward when goals are met collaborate in enforcing lower job performance among coworkers to avoid the punishment of ever increasing performance pressures.[26] Clearly, a performance management system that rewards employees for limiting their performance is dysfunctional. Employees are not stupid, and when their goals are routinely ratcheted upward they learn that their real objective is to work just at, but not above, the management-set goal. Such management actions undermine employee trust and so can reduce employee contextual performance. These are the fabled sullen and adversarial workplaces that the discipline of organizational behavior arose to repair.

Finally, because goal setting is such a powerful motivator, great care must be taken to establish goals for the performance you really do want to motivate.
In practice, this can be messy and difficult for several reasons:

- Goal setting works best when well learned skills are needed. If employees don't know how to reach the goal, the stress can be debilitating.[27]

- Conflicting goals can lead to worse performance than no goals at all.[28] Many jobs in public-sector organizations have such conflicting objectives. For example, a nation's customs service must prevent illegal products from coming into the country, but actions to prevent all unauthorized entry lead to slower border crossings, something that is very costly in an increasingly globalized economy. Customs services must therefore meet two inherently incompatible goals: preventing unauthorized entry, which leads to slower border crossings, and speeding goods across the border, which leads to more unauthorized entries. Thus, customs services, like many other public services, can face see-saw pressures to emphasize one goal or the other, depending on the most recent scandal agitating their political overseers. Such performance problems are too often misdiagnosed as faults of employee effort or ability rather than a fault of organizations with fundamentally conflicting performance demands.

- In some organizations, goals are established only for those portions of job performance that are most easily measured, directing attention away from other critical responsibilities.

- There is strong evidence that goals that are very difficult can lead employees to lie and engage in other unethical actions.[29] If employees are held strictly accountable for performance goals they feel are impossible to meet, many will respond by covering up problems as long as possible, misleading potential customers to make the sale, or any other opportunity their job provides for meeting that goal, no matter what the cost to the organization's reputation and long-term performance.

- It is not always possible to specify in advance what needs to be done. When faced with complex new tasks, specific difficult goals can lead to performance anxiety and an unsystematic scramble to figure out what to do.[30] Because goal setting depends on absolute clarity about what performance is wanted, genuinely uncertain environments are unsuitable for goal setting.[31]

So when coping with new or uncertain problems, when a job has conflicting requirements, when goals are too difficult, or when spontaneous decision making is critical, setting difficult, specific employee performance goals can result in worse organizational performance than no goals at all. Goal setting is very good at directing employee attention to actions to achieve those goals, so if those goals do not represent all of the priority tasks for a job, you will find people powerfully motivated to do the wrong things. Setting specific, difficult goals is one way to clarify expectations and ensure accountability, but it is not appropriate for all jobs or all aspects of many jobs. Because they are such powerful motivators, goals must be set with care and continuously evaluated for unintended consequences.

Application — Set Clear Expectations

- You must begin by being honest with yourself about what accountability you actually want from employees. If you really want to hold them accountable for prompt responses to your changing requests and instructions, establishing specific performance goals and measures wastes time and undermines their faith in your honesty.

- Write down any goals, tasks, accomplishments, and activities. Writing it down ensures clear communication, increased understanding, and accountability.

- Hold employees strictly accountable for what is observable, measurable, and critical to performance.[32]

- If job descriptions exist, use them as the basis for establishing accountability. For each responsibility, you can ask yourself, what would good performance look like? For example, when you have seen excellent performance on "takes initiative," what exactly did the employee do? What is a specific example of poor taking of initiative? The more specific and clearer the expectations, the easier it is to establish accountability.

- Revise and develop these behavioral descriptions. Bringing in other knowledgeable people helps to clarify and to ensure you are covering all of the critical responsibilities.

- After expectations have been developed, establish a regular time to meet and discuss performance with each employee, and then actually do this. Make it a priority: accountability means actually holding employees accountable. If there is never a day of reckoning, there is no accountability. Well managed organizations always have regular reviews of performance whether or not specific goals are set. These reviews are opportunities to discuss how the performance goals and measures should be adjusted and to jointly address problems that occurred during the period.

Managing Accountability with Feedback

Given what we know about the fundamental attribution error (that we all have a bias to see our *own* actions as driven by environmental pressures and to see *others'* actions as driven by their own intentions), it isn't surprising that many managers falsely assume that employees view their own performance as the managers do. Those responsible for the difficult and often painful job of providing feedback might wish that poorly performing employees understood the nature of their performance problems. Managers might wish the boxed opinion was always true, but in reality it rarely is; most of us have unrealistically positive self-evaluations. For example, survey after survey finds that more than 80% of employees believe that their performance is "above average;" among the more educated, such as scientists and engineers, more than 90% believe that their own performance is above average.[33] Yes, when you do the math you can see that about a third of all employees have an inflated sense of their own job performance. Furthermore, few employees feel they get good, detailed feedback about their performance.[34] These troublesome reports suggest we should never assume employees have accurate views of their own performance. This is not only a problem for organizations that are not getting the best employee performance; it is harmful to all those who falsely think they are doing their jobs well and never have the opportunity to improve.

> ***True or False?***
> 
>
> *Employees usually know when they are performing poorly.*

The best way for managers to make sure expectations are clear and employees know what they need to do to improve is to provide clear feedback. Ambiguous communication amplifies any existing impressions, true or false.[35] Feedback is the most flexible way to ensure clarity. It is the knowledge of the results of your own actions; it is information that signals either that performance is fine or that corrective action is needed:[36] no feedback, no possibility for corrective action. Thus, it isn't surprising that numerous studies demonstrate that specific, clear feedback that is focused on performance leads to higher employee contextual and task performance.[37] Furthermore, those employees who actively seek feedback — especially negative feedback — have better job performance than those who do not.[38] Seeking feedback is especially important for more ambiguous, open-ended managerial jobs. Clear expectations are not established once-and-for-all by setting challenging performance goals or writing job descriptions; high employee job performance requires constant feedback and follow-through with corrective action.

If employee performance is so critical to effective organizational performance, and accurate feedback enhances that performance, why are so many employees not getting the feedback they need? The theory of causal attribution helps in understanding this breakdown. As we saw in Chapter 3, this theory explains how and why people make the causal attributions they do. People ask, Why did that happen? Their own answers to that question help us predict what they will do about it.[39] This theory proposes that our causal attributions are based on whether or not the performance is attributed to the employee (internal cause) or attributed to something in his or her environment (external cause). One of Edward Deming's most enduring contributions to management was his insistence that evaluators are biased to make internal attributions rather than looking first to such external causes of poor employee performance as lack of equipment, inadequate information, faulty training, and so forth.[40] Furthermore, even if performance was internally caused, was the employee's poor performance caused by a temporary situation or were the causes more stable (consistency)? Temporary or one-time incidents can be safely ignored; consistent internal causes need to be managed.

The actions a manager will take to manage an employee's poor performance will differ if different causes are diagnosed. Performance feedback works best when it is a conversation about causes — a conversation about how to fix the problems. Objective observers certainly can disagree about the different causes of an employee's poor performance, and those differences in attribution can be even more pronounced because neither managers nor employees are wholly objective observers of employees' job performance. Employees are biased to attribute their own less-than-stellar job performance to external or uncontrollable causes. In contrast, their managers are biased to perceive the causes as internal to the employee and therefore controllable by him or her. Given this fundamental attribution bias, we find that employees often do disagree with their managers' performance feedback.[41] Because a positive assessment by supervisors is so important to subordinates, they sometimes focus on selling their own perception of their job performance rather than listening to their supervisors' analysis.[42]

For all of these reasons, a conversation with others about their poor performance can be frustrating to most managers. So it isn't surprising that many of them stop trying to provide honest performance feedback to their employees. They are tempted to distort feedback to make it more positive[43] or just give up when employees are solid performers in other areas. There has been much speculation about why so many managers abandon giving performance feedback to resistant employees, with the consensus being that in many organizations those responsible for giving performance feedback have little to gain by being brutally honest and much to lose. If managers are not confident in their own abilities to give feedback or not confident that employees can or will improve, there is little benefit to counter-balance the undoubted costs of a hostile and painful conversation leading to resentful employees.

So, employees attribute any performance inadequacies to external and uncontrollable causes (and assume everyone else also does so), and their managers attribute the causes to the employees themselves and so assume that feedback will not change anything. Performance feedback that does not take place, or is done in a way that damages performance, limits opportunities to diagnose and correct performance problems. Performance suffers and employees become frustrated and angry. What can be done? The best approach is to help managers become more skilled and confident in giving performance feedback.

The problem of disappearing performance feedback is exacerbated by many managers' lack of knowledge about how to give feedback that is more likely to be heard and less likely to result in a hostile reaction from feedback recipients.[44]

The following guidelines might assist the manager whose job it is to provide this necessary performance information to defensive and resistant employees.

Application — Give Effective Performance Feedback[45]

- Base feedback on objective information if possible, such as weekly production reports, monthly revenue, or customer complaints. What might otherwise be interpreted as personal criticism can be replaced with a joint focus on how to improve those numbers.
- Describe specific actions, not personalities. Be factual. Don't ever tell someone, "You are..."
- Never use condescending language or tone.
- Describe the effects of the action. For example, "When you do [describe the action] it leads to [describe the negative consequences for the organization]..." Practice this; it works.
- If you gain agreement that the effects are unwelcome, begin joint problem solving. For example, "How can we prevent..."
- If you do not gain agreement that the action occurred, wait for its next appearance. Do not try to persuade.
- If after a second attempt to describe the action, the employee still does not acknowledge or perceive a problem when it has just occurred, there are no opportunities for behavior change. So either live with the problematic behavior or remove the employee.
- If you do not gain agreement on the negative effects of the action, this lack of agreement is now the problem. If the negative effects are personal for the employee, resistance means there are no opportunities for behavior change, so either live with it or remove the employee. If the action has negative effects for others or the organization and the employee refuses to acknowledge those effects, you have a very serious problem. Consider removing or isolating the employee.

Application — Give Effective Performance Feedback *cont.*

- If the person gets very emotional during feedback (or at any other time), try the following: If the employee is talking (or shouting), let him or her talk it out before trying to address the underlying problem. Do not interrupt very upset people with rational observations or analysis; this will just further enrage them.[46] If someone cries, hand her or him a tissue and wait it out before trying to address the underlying problem. Crying should never terminate an important conversation; wait it out. For those employees who are slow to re-gain control of their emotions, formally reschedule the discussion for the next day. Don't let it drop, and do not let emotional outbursts lead to an avoidance of accountability. Many employees are quite ready to analyze performance problems after they have had a day to absorb the news.

- Be sure to follow up and either congratulate employees on their successful changes or take action if no change has occurred.

- Finally, use good judgement. If you have experienced employees who already know what they need to do, don't irk them by robotically providing feedback. Better to use your time together to solve problems and discuss plans.

MEASURING THE PERFORMANCE YOU REALLY WANT

There is no doubt about the importance of accountability, but accountability for what exactly? The power of what is measured to drive performance is clear. The difficulty is not in understanding this but in knowing how to set up measures of job performance to gain the power of tools such as goal setting to motivate the performance you really do want. This challenge arises from the fact that perfect measurement of employee performance is very rare in practice. If perfect performance measurement were possible, then organizations could hire contractors rather than employees. This means the popular hope expressed in the inset box is nearly always a false hope. We have employees because we cannot precisely measure all of what we might want from them in advance, and we will always depend on their contextual performance. But we still want to make sure employees have clear expectations about what they

> ***True or False?***
>
> *We just need to design a better performance measurement system.*

should do and so can be accountable for their actions. This dilemma can be addressed in part by carefully avoiding the following impediments to measuring the employee performance we really do want.

Measuring Quality

The first challenge to performance measurement is that those actions and performance outcomes that can be measured are not always the actions and performance outcomes most needed. A rigid adherence to what is most measurable can result in goal displacement. Neglect of what you really want to achieve in favor of what is most easily measured, or **goal displacement**,[47] can lead to serious problems for organizational performance. One form of goal displacement is a sole focus on **performance quantity** because it is easily measured: sales volume, deadlines met, earnings targets exceeded, and the like. For most jobs, these outputs are important and should be measured. However, alone they are incomplete measures of most jobs because they say nothing about **performance quality**, something that usually requires someone's judgment after the fact. So, sales volume may be important, but not if it comes from front loading the orders and so robbing sales from the next reporting period; deadlines must be met, but not by producing incomplete and thoughtless reports; and earnings targets met by managing earnings can be very damaging to an organization's reputation.

Furthermore, the importance of contextual performance has already been discussed. If good job performance is defined solely as achieving numeric targets, then no one should be surprised if employees produce quantity without helping customers and co-workers, problem solving, and exercising good judgment. They are just doing what they have been told the organization really wants.

Goal displacement can be avoided by including assessments of performance quality and contextual performance along with quantity measures. So, for example, sales associates might also be judged on the number of calls to clients and client evaluations of the associates. Examples of good judgment and citizenship can be recorded and discussed during feedback sessions. However, quality and behavioral assessments can rarely be specified with the same precision as performance quantity measures. Assessments of work quality and employee effort often rely on someone's judgment, and so are subject to interpretation and dispute. This means that such measures will be contentious and never perfectly satisfactory to everyone. Also, such measurement systems will make performance management more complex, and the greater the complexity the more difficult it is to gain the power of clear expectations.[48] However, if quality is important to performance and there are no measures devoid of subjective judgment after the fact, some loss in motivational power is preferable to a powerful system motivating the wrong actions. In short, there can never be a perfect job performance measurement system, and recognition of this is fundamental to managerial maturity.

Application — Accountability for Performance Quality[49]

- Approach performance problems in the same way you would any other quality improvement problem: use process flow charts and cause-and-effect diagrams to identify wasteful practices, rework, sources of conflict, and opportunities for improvement.

- Performance problems should first be viewed for any possible problems in system design rather than rushing to blame individuals.

- Contextual performance should be identified as a necessary component of job performance, and examples of successful contextual performance should be identified and discussed during performance reviews.

- Employees should be held accountable for quality improvement suggestions as well as for quantitative performance goals.

Measuring Innovation

A focus on what is most easily measurable can be particularly costly for experimentation and innovation. Specific difficult goals encourage employees to meet those goals, but because innovation is inherently unpredictable and unknowable, it cannot be subject to strict accountability for goals met. Such goal accountability can be interpreted as high evaluation pressure, and such pressure leads to less experimentation, and so, less innovation. In practice, what happens is that employees are admonished to innovate, but innovation is never measured. For example, some years ago the Bank of America established a program to promote innovations in new products and customer service. However, because employees' performance was still measured as meeting routine targets such as number of new customer accounts, there was little innovation.[50] This bank's attempt to encourage innovation is all too common: because innovation could not be specified in advance with specific goals and measures, it was left completely outside the performance management system. Organizations that say they want innovation, but hold employees accountable for what is most easily measured, will not get innovation from their employees. Research indicates that having multiple performance measures (such as current job performance and innovation) does not impede experimentation as long as there was low evaluation pressure.[51] Just because innovation must be assessed after the fact does not mean it cannot be assessed as part of expected job performance.

What Is Really Important Will Change

Change is inevitable. All organizations face pressures to change in response to shifting customer, client, patient, competitor, constituent, or governmental demands. And change continuously undermines existing employee accountability systems. First, all measurement systems decay over time, something that Marshall Meyer has called the **performance paradox**.[52] He provides evidence from a wide variety of businesses, social services and sports to show that once a measure of performance is used to evaluate, those being evaluated will seek to improve their performance on that measure. Over time they either learn how to perform better on that measure or are removed for poor performance. That is, after a period of time, all who are being evaluated on that measure will do well on it, and so the measure losses its ability to differentiate (all are high performers). This means the performance measures lose their usefulness. This inevitable process leads organizations to continuously add new measures that can better differentiate performance. But again, performance inevitably improves on the new measures, and so other measures need to be added.

This performance paradox is the reason why we often find very baroque and complex measurement systems, as evaluators constantly seek to discover the better performers, and performers constantly seek to improve on their performance measures. So over time, measurement systems can become extremely elaborate and complex, with ever more time and resources devoted to maintaining them. The more performance measurement is used to differentiate employees, the more severe this decay will be. This **ratings inflation** often is not correctly attributed to the external cause of the performance paradox, but is falsely attributed to soft-hearted or lazy performance raters. This mistaken internal attribution has led to attempts to force dispersion (must have both high and low performers in a predetermined distribution) on a measure on which all employees are actually performing identically. Such strong-armed human resources policies are rightly decried as arbitrary and unfair by both the employees and the managers rating their performance. These **forced performance distributions** are all too frequent, and as Marshall Meyer has persuasively demonstrated, based on an ignorance of the inevitable decay of all measures used to differentiate performers. It is fairer and more credible to add new measures than to force a distribution of ratings on a performance measure with no actual differences between high and low performers.

Just as inevitably, attempts to change and adapt organizations are undermined by existing employee measurement systems. The more detailed the performance measurement system, and the more specific the goals, the greater the likelihood that existing accountability systems will undermine change. The more sophisticated and elaborate the measurement system, the more resistant everyone is to changing it. What is a fair measure of performance on the new responsibilities? How exactly will employees need to allocate their efforts on these new initiatives? Employees worry about how they will fare under new and uncertain systems. If the new performance measurement system is not yet calibrated correctly, will they still be judged fairly? Furthermore, change requires managers and employees to devote considerable time to redesigning performance measurement systems, and this takes time away from other job responsibilities. Certainly those undertaking organizational changes need to build changes in employee accountability systems into their planning, including recognizing the amount of time managers will need to re-develop new accountability systems for their employees.

MANAGING PERFORMANCE APPRAISAL SYSTEMS

Given the importance of clarifying expectations and accountability, it is no surprise that many organizations have instituted formal performance appraisal systems. In **formal performance appraisal systems**, managers commit their evaluations of their employees to writing and place the evaluations in the employees' personnel files, usually with the requirement that the evaluator has met with the employee for a performance discussion. Such appraisal systems can include numerical ratings scales (for example, 5 = superior performance, 4 = exceeds expectations, 3 = meets expectations, and so on) for all types of personal traits, behaviors or performance characteristics. These systems may include performance goals established specifically for each job with a narrative description of whether the goal was achieved, or they might include any combination of the above.

Performance appraisal systems are intended to achieve three sometimes conflicting goals: 1) compel managers to record each employee's performance so this evaluation can be the basis for granting salary increases, promotions, and terminations; 2) ensure that performance feedback and developmental coaching for employees is provided at least once a year; and 3) let employees know what their future prospects might be in the organization. Because there are so many problems with how performance appraisal systems function in real organizations, we find advice like that appearing in the inset box. However, although performance appraisals can create serious problems when used for comparison purposes (Use 1 above), they can be useful to performance feedback and expectations clarification (Uses 2 and 3 above).

> ***True or False?***
>
> *Performance appraisals should be abolished.*

We have already learned that many managers dread giving their employees feedback, and forcing managers to do something they do not want to do does not mean that it will be done well. So, it is no surprise that many organizations have found that performance appraisals have disappeared in practice.[53] If the forms must be officially filed, managers will send a completed form in inter-departmental mail asking for the employee's signature, or if compelled to meet face to face, hand a completed form to employees for their signature with unmistakable body language indicating that discussion is not welcome. Furthermore, after all of the anxiety and fear of performance appraisal, very few organizations actually review those written records when deciding whom to promote. The many problems with performance-appraisals-in-practice have been widely studied, with much insight generated and some useful advice for managers produced. A brief review of those problems follows.

Appraisal Accuracy

Performance appraisals are notoriously inaccurate. There is substantial research documenting the many biases in performance appraisal ratings. To cite just a few examples. In Chapter 3, we saw that interviewers tend to rate job applicants from their own race more favorably. Similarly, the more similarities managers share with their employees (e.g., work values, work experience, age, race, gender) the higher they rate the employees' performance.[54] There are other impediments to accurate performance ratings: more experienced managers are more likely to attribute performance problems to external causes, but new managers are more likely to suffer from the fundamental attribution error and blame the employee for performance problems.[55] Intelligence is no help either: smarter managers are as likely to make performance rating errors as their less gifted peers; however managers who believe that personality and ability are more changeable and flexible are more accurate appraisers of performance.[56] Attempts to improve accuracy have focused on developing more descriptive performance scales (it doesn't really help),[57] and on rater training (also not much help).[58] With such serious accuracy problems, it is no surprise that those organizations that are not constrained by political pressures for formal employee evaluations do not use their performance appraisal data to make important personnel decisions.

More Effective Use of Appraisal Ratings

The effectiveness of performance appraisals depends on how they are used. If they are not used for anything at all, then the problems they create for managers will lead to their disappearance-in-practice. Alternatively, if the ratings must be used for pay increases and promotions, the performance paradox says that employees will exert great effort to improve their numbers, leading to a rating inflation that makes these measures useless for comparative purposes. Nevertheless, formal performance appraisals can be useful to managers and their employees. They are more likely to contribute to clarifying expectations and performance feedback when they are confined to employee development and career planning. If performance appraisals are the basis for a problem-solving performance discussion, they can help support a performance conversation in which managers learn what their employees want and employees can better understand their managers' performance expectations. So most of the problems with formal performance appraisals come from their use to compare employees; when used to support accountability and problem solving they can be helpful. This begs the question: must employees be compared?

Forcing Employee Performance into a Number

Employee comparisons usually are done by assigning an overall score to employee performance. Accuracy and the use of appraisals to improve employee performance are undermined by a focus on assigning numbers to rank ordering employees. Organizations do need to make comparative judgments about employees, but reducing employees with complex performance strengths and weaknesses to a single number, or worse, forcing rank ordering on performance, undermines accuracy and makes feedback difficult. Such summary numbers provide no information about performance expectations and no useful performance feedback, and so they do not help improve employee performance. Furthermore, such rankings of current performance say nothing about who may be the best performer in a higher level job. Finally, how was employees' work compared in producing these numbers? Some employees have performance that is easily measured, whereas others make contributions that must be judged by someone else after the fact. What cannot be doubted is that such systems are very de-motivating for those so ranked and place unreasonable burdens on managers who have to justify and defend their rankings to their outraged employees.[59] These forced numbering systems make performance-improvement planning discussions virtually impossible as employees focus on their number and try to lobby and cajole for a better one. These degrading numbering systems substitute counting for thinking, do not contribute to innovative employee or organizational performance, and reflect a misunderstanding of performance accountability.

Self-appraisal

Unfortunately, adding self-appraisals does not improve the accuracy of performance appraisals or make them more useful in performance feedback.[60] Self-appraisals are deeply flawed in practice, making this inset boxed opinion false. Self-appraisals are more lenient in support of a positive self-image[61] and are even less accurate than inaccurate managers' ratings of the employees' job performance.[62] After all, we know that many employees have an overly inflated view of their own performance, and so asking them to rate themselves puts them in a bind. Should they rate their own performance a little lower than they really think it is, in the hope they will seem suitably modest and their manager will insist on a gratifyingly higher rating? Or should employees provide their own honest (and probably inflated) performance self-assessment at the risk of revealing themselves to be clueless? Peer ratings are even worse, with less-than-outstanding peer ratings leading to significantly lower employee job satisfaction, lower team cohesiveness, and co-worker retaliation by lowering other team members' ratings in subsequent reviews.[63] This is not to say that asking employees to describe their own performance cannot be useful. When employees describe their performance and bring that description to a developmental performance discussion, it can help managers understand how employees view

> ***True or False?***
>
> *Having employees engage in self-evaluation makes performance appraisal more democratic.*

their own performance, aiding in performance feedback. This is different from asking employees (or their peers) to assign a number to performance.

So, performance appraisals are inaccurate, their use to compare employees creates arbitrary misleading numerical scores, and self- and peer-ratings just make everything worse. What can be done? Certainly organizations need to be sure that employees are accountable for performance, and forcing managers to make time in their busy schedules to discuss each employee's performance once a year can aid in both performance accountability and better performance. An emphasis on clarifying expectations, establishing accountability, and descriptive feedback, rather than comparisons, can make for productive performance-focused conversations. Also, it is only fair that employees know where they really stand with their managers. Finally, when employees can present their own perceptions, when they feel that the discussion is focused on job relevant factors, and when they have a chance to discuss concrete plans for improvement, performance appraisals can be effective.[64]

Application — Make Any Performance Appraisal System Work

- If your organization has a system with vague ideals such as "provides leadership," define what those mean with specific actions. For example, provides leadership could be defined for your employees as, in part, holding regular meetings with their own subordinates to discuss how their work contributes to strategy. Send these translations-into-specifics in writing to all the people you will evaluate as early in the performance period as possible.

- If your organization has a purely objective or performance-targets system, add specific actions that describe *how* these targets should be met and include examples of unit-supporting contextual performance. Send this elaboration in writing to all the people you will evaluate as early in the performance period as possible.

- If your organization has no performance appraisal system, create your own annual review by writing down specific performance expectations. There is no need for rating scales or templates. Ideas for these could be developed in a group discussion. After developing these expectations, send them in writing to all the people you will evaluate as early in the performance period as possible. Excellent practical guidelines are available at www.shrm.org.

- Before the appraisal meeting, send a written notice of the time and date for the meeting, attach a copy of the written performance expectations they have already received, and ask employees to be prepared to discuss their own assessments of how they met each performance expectation.

- In preparation for the meeting, list specific actions to illustrate each of the evaluation criteria. This will be aided by keeping an **incident file** (a file in which notes are placed throughout the year describing exactly what each subordinate did well or poorly). This helps to avoid focusing only on the very recent past, and employees will appreciate that you remembered specifics about their performance; it shows that what they do is important to you.

- Begin the discussion by asking employees to describe their performance on each of the criteria. If you agree with their assessments, you can just add a few specific examples from your incident file and spend time working together to solve any problems and plan for the future.

- Plan to spend a proportionate amount of time discussing specifics that reflect the employee's overall performance. That is, if the employee has been an excellent overall performer, spend most of the time discussing the specific things he or she did so well. Do not dismissively rush through the good performance in order to spend most of the time on the problematic areas.

- If you disagree with an employee's diagnosis of the problem, state your own diagnosis as specifically and descriptively as possible. If the employee disagrees, this disagreement is now a problem that needs to be addressed, mutually if possible.

- Try to begin and end with areas of success.

- At no time during the discussion should you hand a completed evaluation form to the employee. That would signal that you really had made up your mind beforehand and the discussion was just a sham. Within one week after the meeting, submit whatever written form is required by your organization along with a narrative based on your elaborated performance expectations to employees for their signatures. If your organization has no formal form to complete, submit the summary of your discussion with any revised performance expectations in writing to each employee, keeping a copy for yourself.

- Unless you are forced to do so by your organization, do not assign numbers to any employee's overall job performance, ever. The only possible use of such numbers is to compare employees working in far flung corners of a large bureaucracy (on what we know to be inaccurate assessments). No one likes to be graded (unless it is an A+). Don't destroy a potentially productive conversation with gratuitous numbers.

- If you do have to assign numbers to performance, make sure you can defend them and plan to manage the disappointment among those employees who receive anything lower than the highest possible rating. While you might wish employees would think it obvious that they are solid but not outstanding performers, very few will see it this way (and even those realists would love to be flattered by the highest ratings).

- End the discussion with a specific set of action plans, which may include modifications to the performance expectations.

ACCOUNTABILITY AND AUTONOMY

As should now be clear, accountability is central to successful performance management. However, accountability, properly managed, does not have to destroy employees' sense of autonomy in their work. **Autonomy** is the sense employees have that they are free to determine how they do their jobs. Employees who feel they have more autonomy in their jobs produce better quality work, are absent less often, and are less likely to quit than employees who feel they have little autonomy at work.[65] Accountability begins with assessment, but assessments do not have to be rigidly tied to the narrow goals or outputs that create goal displacement and damage a sense of autonomy.

How to create accountability without destroying a sense of autonomy is best illustrated by the introduction of a measurement program by New York City's police chief, William Bratton.[66] Previously, New York police precincts were measured annually on the number of police cars and officers on the street, number of raids, arrests made, and so forth. The chief wanted to shift the focus to accountability for crime control, and so he began requiring precincts to compile daily information on the numbers of different types of crime in each precinct on their new computers. These data were fed back to the precinct commanders, who were required to meet periodically with a review board to present their precincts' crime statistics and their plans for reducing crime. Under this new assessment system, precinct commanders now had more accurate and timely feedback for the crime in their precincts; it was now clear they were accountable for crime reduction. As a result, precinct commanders developed and shared new approaches to reducing crime. This new system led crime to plummet in New York. These New York City precinct commanders did not have specific goals for crime reduction; they reduced crime via assessment and problem solving discussions. This example illustrates that as long as an organization is able to be clear about its mission, it can establish accountability for employees' contribution to that mission through measurement, even if the missions or jobs are too complex or uncertain for specific performance goals. This can be done by clearly articulating what is wanted and then developing **multiple performance measures** that can reflect that performance. Note that having multiple performance measures is not the same thing as goal conflict (one goal can only be achieved at the expense of another goal).

For example, the best research universities require that their faculty be among the handful of most important contributors to scholarship in their fields. They assess this performancc in a varicty of ways: numbers of papers or books in the most prestigious (and competitive) publishing outlets, the number of other scholars who have cited their scholarship, detailed written evaluations of the work by the leading scholars at other universities, the quality of the university jobs the faculty member's doctoral students obtain, and others. These criteria are clear (written in personnel guidelines), can be flexibly combined (an unambiguously important scientific breakthrough can be rewarded before it has been heavily cited by others), and are difficult (most faculty do not pass the performance hurdles to receive tenure at the best research universities). Faculty in the most demanding research universities are held accountable for meeting these scholarship standards. They are fired in their early career if they do not meet them, and they are denied salary increases and assigned additional administrative duties if they do not meet them after securing tenure.

For those universities, a specific goal (say, number of publications) could lead to goal displacement (publish many meaningless publications in obscure journals), rather than the real performance goal of intellectual leadership. The key to accountability is multiple performance measures with flexibility and judgment. Multiple measurement systems are inherently more subjective than objective performance goals, but that does not mean that expectations are unclear or performance expectations are not demanding. Too many people confuse subjectively assessed performance with favoritism and ambiguity and think that the only way to remove them is to eliminate all subjective judgments. Organizations will get the performance for which they hold employees, teams, divisions, and organizations accountable. The challenge is to find the combination of measures that really reflects superior performance.

Finally, too many managers confuse assessment for accountability with surveillance. Intrusive surveillance undermines employee performance. This is because many employees hate close monitoring of their performance.[67] Closely watching employees at work reduces their autonomy, and many will retaliate by narrowing their jobs and so producing poorer job performance.[68] For example, resentful employees can engage in **malicious obedience**, following every rule and instruction thoroughly in the sure knowledge that this obedience will produce catastrophic organizational performance. An example of malicious obedience is an air traffic controllers' slowdown (creating long flight delays by meticulously following every rule). Close monitoring of employee performance has produced vicious circles of withheld cooperation and perfunctory rather than contextual performance. This often leads in turn to stricter organizational surveillance, producing a death spiral of sullen resentment and deteriorating organizational performance.

Accountability and autonomy are not mutually exclusive: corporate chief executive officers can be held accountable for corporate earnings growth while retaining the autonomy to decide how to achieve those corporate earnings. Successful accountability depends on developing measures of the performance that is really wanted (not just the performance most easily measured) and should not be confused with heavy-handed personal surveillance. Organizations get the performance they assess, and they get the performance they reward: the focus of the next chapter.

Implications for Managing Managers

- ✓ Find out what performance is *really* expected of you. Start by asking. After completing a task or project, ask your manager what you could have done better. Then listen without disagreeing or defending your actions. Try to understand the others' assessments as dispassionately as you possibly can. Next, look around. Who is being rewarded, and who is being punished? Why? Resist the urge to explain these observations away with cynical accounts that emphasize non-performance causes. Begin with the assumption that those who are being rewarded are contributing something to someone's idea of good performance, and learn what that might be. Too often, cynicism is just a way of avoiding honest self-appraisals.

- ✓ Try to get accurate performance feedback. Remember that most managers have been punished for providing honest feedback and so will be reluctant to be brutally honest. You must encourage them in small steps. Many people will provide indirect hints or pregnant pauses. You should actively encourage others to elaborate and then reinforce their honesty by vigorously nodding and thanking them for the information. Ask their advice for how you might do it better next time. Again, nod and thank them for their helpful advice. Most people want to share their observations and advice as long as they will not be punished for doing so. If you persist in rewarding them for accurate feedback, eventually you will have trained them to provide it. Actively practice feedback seeking with supervisors, experienced co-workers, peers, and anyone else who might have a perspective on your performance.

- ✓ If you got a low performance appraisal rating, learn why. Your most important task is to understand why your manager views your performance in this way. If you understand that, you will be able to either improve your performance or get a more suitable job on your own time table. Do not argue with your supervisor about the rating. Disagreement will make your manager defensive and gives you no opportunity to learn. Under no circumstances should you append a written dispute or excuses to the formal performance appraisal on file. Remember, most appraisals on file are never looked at by anyone ever again (so why anger your boss for a momentary emotional gratification?). In those rare organizations in which formal ratings are used for personnel decisions, your note does not change the rating, it just provides a permanent written record of your misunderstanding of how organizations really work. Undertake formal appeals with great caution.

Key Words

Motivation

Expectancy Theory

Ability or resources deficit

Incentives problem

Galatea Effect

Self efficacy

Accountability

Performance goal

Goal Setting Theory

Ratcheting goals

Proximal goals

Feedback

Goal displacement

Performance quantity

Performance quality

Performance paradox

Ratings inflation

Forced performance distributions

Performance appraisal systems

Incident file

Autonomy

Multiple performance measures

Malicious obedience

6

Managing Incentives

Incentives matter. People come together to do organizational work because they believe they will gain something from their actions. Those gains might be a desire to contribute to an organization that is doing good works, a sense of personal fulfillment, a company car, or anything else imaginable. Slavery is rare in today's world: employees voluntarily join and work in organizations for what they can get out of it. People participate in organizations because they gain more enjoyment, more valuable experience, a shorter commute, more money — more of something — than they could get from any of their alternatives. Whatever it is that employees get for their organizational work are their **incentives**.

Effective managers do not leave incentives to chance. They try to manage incentives in order to coordinate, motivate and hold employees accountable and to coordinate their actions with others. The effective management of incentives is necessary to organizational performance, and it is difficult to get right. Everyone complains about the incentive systems in their organizations, and managers and human resources professionals are constantly tinkering with incentives trying to make them better. Why are organizational incentives for employees so difficult? An understanding of this can help managers to begin to gain control over a major source of organizational frustration and dysfunction.

This chapter explains what systematic organizational behavior research says about why organizational incentive systems can be so difficult to manage and what seems to work and what doesn't. It discusses the challenges of being clear about what actions really are rewarded, discovering which incentives employees actually do value, money as an employee incentive, and concludes with a discussion of how to more effectively manage incentives.

CLARITY ABOUT WHAT IS REWARDED

One of the most common ways incentive systems become dysfunctional is from employee uncertainty about what actions will be rewarded. This is the incentives problem identified in Chapter 5. All too often, incentives are attached to actions the organization does not want, and employee actions it would like to see are either ignored or punished.[1] A good place to start to understand and effectively manage employee incentives is to begin with a diagnosis of which actions *really are* rewarded in the organization, and which actions managers feel *should be* rewarded.

The Actions Organizations Need from Employees

The actions managers expect from employees certainly will vary by the job. Scientists are expected to develop patentable product innovations, accountants are expected to meet filing deadlines, and truck drivers must get their deliveries to the right destinations on time. For this reason, all employee incentive systems need to begin with a clear and comprehensive understanding of the particular work that the employees are expected to do. That is done with job descriptions. Beyond the particulars of individual jobs, we can group employee actions into some general categories that can be useful in understanding the design of incentive systems. These employee actions can be summarized as follows.[2]

- **Join the organization**. All organizational participants must be enticed to work for the organization. Because membership in the organization is easily assessed (you know if someone you wanted to recruit accepted your job offer or not), incentives for employees to join the organization are not particularly problematic for managers. Unsuccessful recruiters will find out if they are providing pay, benefits and working conditions that compare favorably with their competitors'.[3] If these are favorable, but recruits still reject their job offers, managers can find out what exactly it is that makes their jobs unattractive. Location? Poor reputation? It is not difficult to discover and develop the right incentives to attract employees to join the organization.

- **Remain with the organization**. Organizations need to keep employees on the job; turnover is costly.[4] These costs include not only recruiting and training new employees but damage to organizational performance while new recruits learn the job. But again, if the pay, benefits, and working conditions are better than the competition, too much turnover is a signal that there is some problem with employee unhappiness or commitment that is not being managed. So, incentives to remain are usually not managers' biggest challenge.

- **Reliably show up at work**. If employees do not do their work when expected to do so, the work cannot be done. Absenteeism can be quite costly.[5] It is also easily assessed: someone is either working or not working. No ambiguity there. So, like joining and remaining, attendance is easily measured — you know exactly what employee actions you want — and so it is a straightforward matter to attach incentives to these actions.

Application — Absenteeism Is a Problem Easily Solved

Chronic absenteeism in a department or division usually arises because absenteeism has been inadvertently rewarded. Some common ways this occurs:

- When employees see absenteeism as legitimate — just the normal expected behavior at work — they will be absent more.[6] Make sure absenteeism is not seen as normal practice.

- The more paid sick leave days employees have, the more they will be absent.[7]

- Employees who are unhappy with the work they are doing or with their co-workers will be absent more than those who are not.[8]

- Employees are held accountable for reliably showing up for work; if chronic violators do not get this clear and unambiguous message, they should be removed.

- Providing financial incentives for attendance significantly reduces absenteeism.[9] Because absenteeism has a direct and quantifiable cost, such "paying for attendance" can be cost-effective. Unfortunately, too many managers just do not like such programs, and when they are stopped, the absenteeism reverts to its old, higher levels.[10]

When attraction, retention, and reliable attendance are problematic, usually it is because whoever controls incentives cares less about attracting the best recruits, employee turnover, or absenteeism than they do about something else. That something else can be many different things, such as keeping costs low or protecting bosses who makes their employees unhappy but contribute something else of value to the organization. The real challenge of managing incentives is not with attraction, retention or attendance, but with incentives for job performance. Recall that job performance consists of narrow task performance (direct job duties) and contextual performance (helping others and going above and beyond direct job duties).

- **Task performance**. As we saw in Chapter 5, measuring task performance is not always straightforward — sometimes performance quality is too complex for specific, difficult goals, or significant employee innovation is wanted. Managers need to take care to communicate what task performance actions or outputs will earn incentives and be sure that the incentives have not been inadvertently attached to the wrong actions or to just a subset of the actions needed for effective employee task performance.

- **Contextual performance.** Contextual performance cannot be specified in detail in advance. It consists of employees' consummate effort to do their best, to help when needed, and to spontaneously solve unexpected problems. Examples of contextual performance can be given, and contextual performance can be assessed after the fact by describing good and poor examples of it. But such after-the-fact incentives introduce uncertainty, contributing to the incentives problem.

How can managers make sure that their incentive systems promote high levels of task and contextual performance? We begin the discussion by clarifying three common assumptions managers often get wrong.

Many Employees Want To Contribute

Employees will differ in their own personal desire to go above and beyond the minimum job requirements. Those who are inclined to do this can be identified and hired because they are more likely to pitch in and help. For example, those who are higher in conscientiousness and positive affect are more likely to want to contribute and so have higher job performance.[11] Also, those employees who give more generously to charity are more productive.[12] So, applicants who are more inclined to collaborate, earnestly try to do good work, and to help others can be hired (and more importantly, those who generally distrust others and are only out for themselves can be avoided). Hiring only those employees who are inclined to high levels of contextual performance is a good place to start.

However, as important as it is to select the right employees, it is also important to make sure their social environment supports contextual performance. Employees do not act in a vacuum, and if those around them believe that only fools pitch in and help out, they are much less likely to do this themselves.[13] Employees work in social settings, and because all groupings of people talk about what is important in their environment,[14] organizational incentive systems are usually an important topic of conversation at work. Such conversations lead to a shared consensus about what "is really rewarded," and if that shared consensus is that working harder to produce quality work or pitching in to help others will be punished, the organization has a conflicting incentive system. Employees are forced to choose between whatever incentives the organization might bestow for quality work, innovation and contextual performance and the sure scorn and ridicule of those they work with all day, every day. What to do? Managers do not completely control employees' social environments, but they can learn to understand whether they support or undermine employees' decisions to go that extra mile. Social environments that punish high levels of task or contextual performance need a thoughtful diagnosis to uncover the reasons and then actions to eliminate them. More information about how to diagnose and influence workplace social environments is found in Chapter 7, *Navigating the Social Scene.*

Avoid Punishing the Performance You Really Want

One of the reasons employees will come to a consensus that contextual performance will be punished is that some organizations actually do punish extra effort without realizing it. Research shows that tying incentives to performance will result in more of that performance. For example, those retail-store managers paid for retail sales will have higher store sales.[15] This boxed popular opinion is supported by research; you will get the behavior you reward.

> ***True or False?***
>
> *You will get the behavior you reward.*

The problem is not that incentives do not work; it is that for many jobs it is hard to anticipate and measure all of the different kinds of performance you really do want. For example, managers will say they want employees to contribute to a cross-departmental task force, but employees' performance appraisal ratings are based solely on their own departmental task performance. Should we be surprised that the task force project is a low priority? Managers are told to spend time training and developing their employees, but they are rewarded for meeting deadlines and financial targets. Wouldn't we expect them to do those things that the organization is rewarding? Production workers are paid by the piece, but if they exceed their monthly production quotas by more than 10%, their jobs will be re-timed so that they will receive less money per piece produced. Of course, they will work together to be sure that they all limit their production so they can keep the piece rates as high as possible: that is what is rewarded.[16] Too many organizations say they want quality work, innovation and contextual performance, but they do not reward it. All of these actions take time, and employee incentive systems that are rigidly based on what is easily measured will not reward quality, innovation or contextual performance.

Actions Can Be Rewarded After the Fact

Quality, innovation, and contextual performance can be rewarded after the fact. We might expect that those who went above and beyond narrow task duties would be seen as valuable in those jobs with more responsibility. In fact, these are often the actions that lead to promotions to managerial jobs.[17] In addition to promotions, there are many ways to reward quality work, innovation and contextual performance after the fact: praise, recognition, bonuses, and more. There is evidence that many managers try to reward contextual performance with higher performance appraisal ratings.[18] What is important to remember is proportion: if the incentives for easily-measured task performance are certain, very large and valuable whereas the rewards for quality, innovation and contextual performance are puny and uncertain, the incentive system speaks loud and clear about what is really valued. That is, too often organizations punish employees who contribute more to their coworkers' and organization's performance. While we will still find those few martyrs who will continue to try their hardest to do their best in the face of organizational incentive systems to the contrary, this is no way to manage an organization.

Application — Reasons for Contextual Performance[19]

- Employees who believe their organizations value their contributions and care about their well being (**organizational supportiveness**) contribute more.

- Employees who think their bosses are considerate, willing to listen to their problems, and can be trusted (**managerial supportiveness**) tend to have higher contextual performance.

- Employees who have higher job satisfaction will do more.

- Employees who feel their organization is fair and just will do more to help the organization and co-workers than those who feel their organization is unfair.

- Employees who want to make a good impression will do more.

- Employees have lower contextual performance when the compensation of their executives is very high, when the organization is performing poorly, and after seeing their coworkers get layed off in an insensitive way.[20]

WHAT DO EMPLOYEES ACTUALLY WANT?

While finding ways to attach incentives to work quality, innovation, and contextual performance is inherently challenging, discovering what incentives employees actually value is not. The confusion that does exist seems to come from ham-fisted applications of the work of a previous generation of psychologists and philosophers to employee incentives. The early decades of organizational behavior research focused on sorting out these confusions, and so a brief clarification might be necessary for those who may still believe these discredited ideas.

Intrinsic and Extrinsic Rewards

Intrinsic rewards are the rewards you give yourself. You might build a boat, try to exceed your sales targets by at least 10%, or complete one project before beginning another, all because you want to do those things, not because someone else will reward you for doing them. We find those actions we enjoy doing just because we enjoy doing them to be intrinsically rewarding. **Extrinsic rewards** are rewards you get from someone else: a promotion, a bonus, praise, and the like. Those rewards managers control to try to motivate employee actions are extrinsic rewards, by definition.

Many employees often will go to extraordinary lengths to get the extrinsic rewards someone else is offering. Organizations cannot rely solely on employees' intrinsic rewards because that would mean relying on employees doing whatever they find most enjoyable at that moment. Even organizational volunteers get extrinsic rewards like community recognition and job training for their work.[21] Contrary to this boxed popular opinion, extrinsic rewards at work do not destroy the fun and excitement of a job. In fact, those with more engaging professional and managerial jobs are both more highly paid and more likely to find their work intrinsically rewarding.[22] It is true that intrinsic rewards are more reliable: people will keep doing what they enjoy doing, whereas work done for an extrinsic reward often will stop once the extrinsic reward is removed. However, workplaces always have had, and always will need, extrinsic rewards to motivate and coordinate all of the work done for them.

> ***True or False?***
>
> *Extrinsic rewards reduce the intrinsic rewards employees get from their work.*

Although no managers would rely only on intrinsic rewards for their employees, there is evidence that employees who (also) work for intrinsic rewards produce work of higher quality, more reliably show up for work, and are less likely to quit.[23] The more rewards, of whatever kind, the more motivating the work. What can be done to make an employee's work more intrinsically motivating?

Application — Provide Opportunities for Intrinsic Motivation[24]

- Jobs that use a wider variety of employees' skills are more intrinsically rewarding than those that do not. It is no fun doing the same simple task day in, day out.
- Completing a project from beginning to end is more intrinsically rewarding than doing just a small piece of the task with little understanding of what is being accomplished.
- Doing work that has an important effect on others is intrinsically motivating. It is easier to care more about quality performance when people's lives are at stake than when you are just processing the paper to support regulations you think are dumb.
- Employees who have the autonomy to plan, schedule and complete their work are more intrinsically motivated than those who do not. We all care more about the work we are personally responsible for.
- Employees who receive feedback about their performance are more intrinsically motivated. Without knowledge about which actions are effective, employees have no opportunity to gain enjoyment from testing their skills or accomplishing their goals.

Hierarchies of Needs

People do work for very different reasons, and these reasons can vary from the obvious (a paycheck) to the creepy (in response to some deep-seated psychological compulsion to punish oneself). Because what employees seek from work is so complicated, some decades ago psychologists sought to try to make more sense of it by drawing on psychological **need theories**.[25] These are theories of motivation that posit that people have biological and psychological needs (e.g., for water, food, companionship, esteem) and they are motivated to do what will satisfy those needs. However, over time these theorists developed longer lists of needs, making their theories less and less helpful.[26] To make need theories more useful, early organizational psychologists drew on Abraham Maslow's theory that needs were arranged in a hierarchy. In theories of **need hierarchies**, as soon as one type of need is satisfied, the one just above it in the hierarchy is now activated and so now the higher need drives actions.[27]

These need-hierarchy theories are fine as far as the biological basics are concerned, but they break down when applied to organizational rewards. Think about it: money is an important incentive in most organizations, but is money satisfying lower level needs for food and water, or is it satisfying higher level needs for esteem (can buy that expensive sports car), or for personal growth (can retire early and devote your time to good works)? So which need (or needs) does money satisfy? Need hierarchies for organizational incentives and the statement in the box were thoroughly repudiated more than thirty years ago.[28] Observation of the behavior of successful investment bankers should be enough to convince anyone that many, many people will continue to work very hard for more money long after they have enough to meet their biological needs. There are no organizational needs or organizational incentives that are superior to others, and people who value one work incentive are in no way operating at lower or higher levels than those who value a different organizational incentive. The managers' task is to understand what each of their employees actually do value from their work and to avoid temptations to denigrate anyone who wants something different from what they personally want.

> ***True or False?***
>
> *Once employees are paid enough, they are no longer motivated by money.*

MONEY AND MOTIVATION

Perhaps people should be paid for their performance, but we rarely find that this is true in organizations. This inset boxed opinion is a hope for something that cannot exist for most jobs in most organizations. Edward Deming argued against piece rates and other forms of paying people for what they produce,[29] and many, many studies over the decades find that, in practice, neither corporate executives' pay, nor many others' pay is actually tied to their performance.[30]

> ***True or False?***
>
> *Employees should be paid for performance.*

If money is such a good incentive, why is it so rarely tied to individual job performance? To diagnose this conundrum, we need to see what systematic research can tell us about three questions: Does money motivate? Can money be tied to performance? Can managers identify the performance they will pay for? This popular opinion needs to be rephrased: it is not whether or not employees should be paid for their performance; it is whether or not they actually can be paid for the performance organizations want.

Does Money Motivate?

Yes, money does motivate.[31] This boxed popular opinion is the result of a mistaken focus on what people say, instead of what they actually do. In practice, employees will report that money is not a very important incentive to them personally, but they firmly believe that it is important to "someone

> ***True or False?***
>
> *Money doesn't motivate.*

like themselves."[32] Because people do not want to seem crass, they will deny money's importance to themselves as an incentive. However, research focused on what employees do, rather than what they say, finds that money can be a very powerful incentive in organizations, particularly in reducing turnover[32] Enough money really does motivate many employees, all else being equal. The challenge of money as an incentive in organizations is not that it is not powerful, but that it is so powerful it can create more incentive problems than it solves.

Money can be a powerful incentive because money can be so many different things to different people. Employees may want different things, but money is one of the few incentives that enables them to get more of many of the different things they value. For those who like adventure travel, more money allows them to tramp through more jungles; more money allows employees to pay for tutors for their children; higher pay lets the harried single mother hire a house cleaner so she can spend her nights sleeping; and art lovers who earn more can buy better materials and collect more of their favorite works. This is not to say that money matters more than anything else at work; people also value security, interesting problems to solve, enjoyable coworkers, and their self-respect. And as we already know, different people value different things. But to say that money is not the only workplace incentive is not the same as saying that it never matters.

Another reason money can be such a powerful incentive is because it is the one metric that allows employees to compare themselves to others.[33] These comparisons happen both within organizations and in society as a whole. Within organizations, an employee may not be strongly motivated by the additional things that can be bought with a 5% salary increase, compared to a 4% increase. However, virtually all employees who discover that a coworker who they believe to be a poorer performer than themselves received a 5% increase, while they got only 4%, will be unhappy. Those who receive comparatively less will want to know why they were seen as worse performers than their more generously compensated coworkers, and woe to those managers who do not have carefully documented reasons for making these distinctions.

What is more, money is not only used for within-organization comparisons; it is used by the larger society as a way of judging who is more successful. We often cannot know how much responsibility and influence someone working outside our own work group has or how interesting their work really is. But employees all have their pay in common, and that means that pay becomes the one universal indicator of social status. You may suspect that those red sports cars parked at the entrance to your high school reunion mask indebtedness and collapsing marriages, but those classmates' annual pay provides a precise measure of who is ahead of whom. And the more educated the employees, the more likely they are to compare their pay to the pay of someone outside the organization,[34] a further reminder of managers' limited personal control over this powerful incentive. Of course, there are jobs for which this particular comparative game does not apply: the clergy, interns, students. However, like it or not, especially for those working in business, money is often the way society keeps score, and whether or not you personally think this is right, we all know everyone else is using money in this way, making it hard to ignore.

For all of these reasons, money as an incentive can be too powerful. People will go to extraordinary lengths to obtain this particular incentive, both for what it will buy and for what it tells everyone else about the value of their work and their status. They pay a great deal of attention to who is getting paid what. Some people neglect other responsibilities to get that incentive, and others will lie, cheat and steal to get more money.[35] Because money is so powerful as an incentive, managers must take great care in managing it.

Can Money Be Tied to Job Performance?

When most people think of **pay for performance**, they think that those who have higher job performance will make more than those who have poorer performance. However, except in rare circumstances, organizations really cannot pay employees for their job performance. This is because pay is the price of labor set by the **labor market**.[36] Organizations pay employees to join and remain in their jobs, and the going rate for some jobs is much higher than for others. Clearly if many, many people have the knowledge and skills to do certain work, they will drive the price down, leaving a job with relatively low pay. Think of **internships**, those extraordinarily low paid jobs with a very large supply of potential labor because of their glamorous surroundings or entry-level experience for desirable occupations. Experienced managers know that pay is driven by labor-market supply and demand, but they do not always think through what this means for pay for performance.

If a job has a labor-market pay rate, a sensible employer might pay about 10% above the going rate in order to attract the best potential employees, but to pay much more than that would be a waste of the organization's resources. An organization can have a receptionist who is an outstanding performer, and an executive vice president of marketing who is a mediocre performer. But no organization is going to pay that outstanding receptionist more than the mediocre executive vice president, no matter what their respective job performances. To so do would be to pay much more than the going rate for receptionists, or much less than what it would take to attract and keep executive vice presidents of marketing, or both. What people really mean by pay for performance is that the receptionist with outstanding performance receives a 5% pay increase while the mediocre executive vice president receives only 2% (which is probably more actual money for the executive vice president for marketing because the labor-market pay rate for that job is so much more).

Organizations do not really have true pay for performance systems for most jobs because they cannot. What organizations really have are labor-market pay systems with, at most, tiny pay differentials for those doing the same jobs based on an assessment of job performance. Managers need to be honest with themselves and their employees about this. Confusion can be costly. For example, organizations that try to avoid overpaying when changing to a pay for performance system by reducing the base pay and putting more of employees' **pay-at-risk** (dependent on job performance) find that employees react very negatively to being paid below market value, that performance does not improve, and that managers are forced to return to paying market-competitive wages when hiring new employees.[37]

Given all of the difficulties in accurately assessing performance, and the inevitable resentments of employees with pay raises fractionally smaller than what their co-workers get, why would any sensible manager award large differential salary increases? Certainly managers should not award any salary increase to poor performers; they should remove poor performers. Why are poor performers getting paid at all? But except in rare circumstances, organizations are not going to allocate large amounts of money to pay for job performance because it will lead to wasteful overpaying for labor, and the amount by which managers really can differentiate pay increases needs to be small to avert all out war among employees who need to cooperate with one another. It is not that money is not valued by employees; it is just that paying for individual job performance usually creates more problems than it solves.[38] Merit pay systems do not work[39] and so we find that organizations do not, and will not, have real pay for individual job performance for most jobs.[40]

Identify the Performance That Gets Paid

The reason why pay for individual job performance usually does not work is that it relies on a flawed understanding of organizations.[41] First, it assumes we can specify exactly what we want from employees in advance. In practice, uncertainty about priorities and unexpected changes are the reasons why organizations hire employees rather than contract for labor or services. Second, it assumes employees work independently. In practice, most employees depend on support staff and collaborate on large projects in doing their jobs. If only those whose performance is easiest to measure have the opportunity to earn substantial financial incentives, those providing their support services can become resentful. Such **internal inequity** can damage collaboration. For example, the wider the pay disparities among members of executive teams in, the less likely they are to collaborate, and the lower the companies' performance.[42] The management challenge is to actually tie pay to the performance you really want to motivate, and this performance will often involve uncertainties and collaboration. Recall the discussion of the challenges of measuring performance quality, innovation and contextual performance. Now take all of the inherent ambiguities involved in assessing critical employee contributions, and then add money to it. Money draws employees' attention like nothing else. This means that the tiniest logical flaw or inconsistency in performance measurement or pay administration will receive immediate attention and lengthy analysis.

For these reasons, organizations that use money as a performance incentive usually find that they are driven to be extremely explicit about what, exactly, will earn more money.[43] If managers are not excruciatingly clear about exactly what employees need to do to get this powerful incentive, they quickly find that employees will make their best guesses about what really will be rewarded, and organizations will find that they are powerfully rewarding the wrong actions. If managers are going to attach money to actions, they better make sure those are really the actions they want.

What are those few circumstances in which employees really can be paid for individual job performance? Real pay for individual job performance is appropriate for those jobs that directly produce revenue for the organization, so that employees can be given a percentage of the revenue they generate. Here employee job performance is nearly perfectly aligned with the organization's performance. Thus, salespeople earn commissions on their sales, investment bankers get a percentage of the deals they complete, and hedge-fund managers are paid a percentage of their portfolios' gains. Pay for individual job performance can be, and usually is, used to powerfully motivate employee performance for such jobs.

Yet, even under these ideal circumstances, these pay for individual performance systems come at a cost. Because these pay systems only reward the sale made or deal closed, employees neglect any tasks that do not directly contribute to what is being so powerfully rewarded. This means that the more these employees must collaborate with others, the more these pay systems can be counterproductive. For example, investment firm star traders who changed firms found their performance dropped significantly without the support systems they enjoyed in their previous firms.[44] Because the sales territories each employee is allocated can vary a great deal in their potential, these systems also foster vicious jurisdictional disputes and "client stealing." Furthermore, if these employees' job performance depends on the effective delivery of support functions, managers need to make sure that those critical employees get their own cut of the action to prevent their resentment and withdrawal of critical support. Finally, employees in jobs with such a high proportion of their pay tied to performance are notorious for their mobility, always hopping to the job that promises slightly more pay for their performance. This threat of job hopping drives managers to pay ever more to be able to stay ahead of competitors who might steal their best producers. Real pay for individual employee job performance is wonderful for those employees who can perform in these pressured environments, but they are not easy for the managers who must try to manage these workplaces.

Paying for Organizational Performance

One approach to harnessing the power of money as an incentive without creating dysfunctional effects for organizational performance is to tie incentive pay to organizational (or business unit) performance.[45] It makes sense that pay should be attached to the performance that really does matter. Of course, it may be difficult for some individuals to see how they are personally contributing to the performance of very large organizations, but an open discussion of the ways their work contributes to organizational performance can be valuable. Such discussions also help all employees to understand what the critical milestones and tasks are, enabling them to apply their own best judgment in supporting these organization-critical functions. For example, if one software group is working on a product that must be ready in time for an important customer's new-product launch, human resources professionals can be sure to expedite this group's requests for new employees, and purchasing agents will make sure their equipment needs have the highest priority. When paying for organizational performance, incentives encourage collaboration and help focus everyone's attention on the performance that matters.

There are many different ways to pay for organizational performance. Employees might be given stock (or stock options) so their personal wealth will rise and fall with organizational shareholder wealth. Other possibilities include cash bonuses when the organization or business unit reaches predetermined performance targets. The measures of organization or business unit performance can be as simple as a single profit target or complicated formulas that combine scrap rates, costs, revenue, new products, and so forth. The key feature of such plans is that *all employees* receive a payment based on the organization's performance, not just the top executives. When all gain or lose money, the attention of all is directed to organizational performance.

One of the best known such systems is the **gainsharing** plan of Lincoln Electric Company based in Cleveland, Ohio.[46] That program combines pay for individual job performance with year-end bonuses based on the organization's annual profits. The organization has a generous retirement program (incentives for organizational commitment), guarantees at least 30 hours of full time work per week to employees with at least three years tenure (security as an incentive), and requires employees to work at any assignment at the pay rate for that job and accept overtime work (employees do whatever is needed). Many of the higher performing employees make double or more than the labor market rate for their jobs. Lincoln Electric has obtained extraordinary productivity and cooperation, prospering in the varied business conditions of its past one-hundred years. However, gainsharing plans are not universally successful and require broad consultation and careful early management to get the performance formula right.[49] As with any incentive system, paying for organizational performance will not work in isolation from the organization's hiring and performance management systems. Nevertheless, when carefully managed, these plans draw attention to the fact that all employees are dependent on the success of the organization and help reinforce the idea that their success is as dependent on how they support their colleagues' success as it is on their own actions.

Application — Pay for Unit and Organizational Performance

- All employees should receive money based on the organization or unit's performance.

- The performance needs to be established in advance. Organizations that do not specify the organizational performance measures before the review period are usually just seeking ways to hide very high compensation for certain employees under the guise of pay-for-performance, as is the case for so many Chief Executive compensation plans.[48]

- Small payouts are not an excuse to avoid paying for organizational performance. These still attract employee attention.

- Be prepared to manage the disappointment if there is poor organizational performance and thus smaller payouts than in previous years. As with all pay systems, people quickly see their current pay as an entitlement.

- If the organization is a non-profit or governmental agency, organization-level goals can be set and all employees treated to a picnic or some other celebration to mark the occasion. In a government agency, if all managers donated a modest sum into a "performance fund" that would pay some of the costs of the celebration, it would be a powerful gesture.

MORE EFFECTIVE MANAGEMENT OF INCENTIVES

Money as an incentive is expensive, difficult to attach to the performance managers really want, and creates problems as employees compare the money they receive for their performance with what others are receiving. However, money is far from the only valuable incentive organizations can offer. Expecting money to carry the entire employee incentive burden is like playing hockey with half your team sitting in the penalty box. As should now be clear, managers do not control all organizational incentives, but they usually control more than they assume. Here two powerful, if frequently misunderstood, employee incentives, security and status, are discussed. This section concludes with attention to how employee perceptions of justice and trust affect employee reactions to organizational incentive systems.

Security

No one today believes that they truly have **employment security**, or the expectation that if they perform well and are loyal the organization, it will in turn be loyal to them.[49] Employment insecurity has spread to the kind of managerial and professional work that once seemed to offer lifetime employment.[50] This matters because the offer of employment security to those who were good performers was once the foundation of (white collar) employee incentive systems.[51]

Employment security ties employees' fates to their organizations, fosters organizational commitment, and has been the primary incentive for the work quality, innovation and contextual performance that foster better organizational performance.[52] Organizations that provide employment security will invest in more training because they have no fear that their more skilled employees will walk out the door. In that way, such organizations improve the quality of their employees.[53] Employees who believe their employers are trying to provide employment security have higher job performance and more enthusiastic contextual performance and are more emotionally committed to their employer than those who work for employers who do not attempt to provide employment security.[54] Those employees who do not expect employment security have a smaller network of colleagues at work they can call on for assistance and have poorer job performance,[55] perhaps because they are spending more of their time polishing their resumes for that next employer. Furthermore, those who feel more insecure in their jobs can be more resistant to organizational changes.[56] This makes sense: one of the most powerful universal social rules is the **norm of reciprocity**, the belief that we should treat others as they are treating us.[57] The very real decline in employment security is making it ever more difficult for managers to be sure employees do quality work, innovate, and help solve problems as they arise. What can managers do to try to re-establish this important incentive?

Application — Security as an Incentive

Many managers are nervous about providing job security as an incentive because employment security is so commonly associated with non-responsive inefficient bureaucracies. However, attempts to provide security combined with stringent performance accountability can be very effective.

- Even though you cannot promise employment security, you can communicate that you will try to provide employment security for highly performing employees.
- Attempts to provide employment security must always come with strong job performance accountability.
- Security as an incentive needs to be combined with careful hiring systems to minimize hiring those who cannot perform or who are uncollaborative.
- Security as an incentive works best when supported by a high-performance, customer-focused, results-driven culture. As described in Chapter 8, *Understanding Cultures*.[58]
- Because employment security cannot be promised in most competitive environments, provide honest information about the future of your organization. Be explicit about plans to build employment security for high-performing employees (e.g., training to keep skills up-to-date).
- Always be aware that employees need to consider their long-term welfare and will leave if they find that it is best served elsewhere.

Status

Workplaces are social settings where employees compare their compensation to what others are getting, develop friends and enemies, and jockey for status. **Status** is one's standing with a particular group; those with high status have a respected position in that group. Status has long been used as an employee incentive in organizations: many who have no interest in the tasks managers do covet the corner office that comes with the job. Engineers gain status from the number of patents they have secured, police officers from the number of arrests they have made, attorneys for the number of cases they have won, and so on. Many employees devote much time and attention to gaining and defending their organizational or professional status.

There is no doubt that having higher status brings many desirable things to those who have it. Those with higher status are healthier,[59] receive disproportionately higher rewards,[60] have more influence over others,[61] and are assumed to be competent in all things.[62] Those with higher status do not have to work as hard, receive more, are able to get more of what they want from others, and live longer to enjoy it.[63] It is probably the only organizational incentive as powerful as money (maybe more so in organizations with limited money), and a careful diagnosis of most organizations will reveal many people deeply engaged in struggles for more of it.

Clearly, status is used as an employee incentive in many circumstances. For example, the job of manager is often a very difficult one — squeezed from above and below, no longer able to work every day with supportive coworkers, less sense of personal achievement, and in many organizations pay that is not much more than employees could receive from overtime work. For many managerial jobs, the higher status is the primary incentive. It is noteworthy that organizations in which employees already have high status (professors in universities and physicians in hospitals) find it difficult to recruit managers (department chairs and medical directors). Status is one of the primary incentives organizations use to recruit employees into management positions.

Does this mean this boxed popular opinion that workplaces should be egalitarian is wrong? No, it is just a bit misleading. Those advocating workplace egalitarianism are usually arguing against status differences with no basis in performance.[64] Elaborately hierarchical systems of dining rooms, status-based lavatories, and layers of assistants between differing categories of employees and managers do not contribute to information exchange or a sense that everyone is working together. Employee attention to status itself cannot be removed, but organizations will be more effective to the extent that everyone believes that status derives from contributions to organizational performance, not from credentials or job classifications.

> ***True or False?***
>
> *Make the workplace as egalitarian as possible.*

Managers can use status as an incentive in two ways. One is to use their own status as an incentive. Although no one person can ever completely control status, which is ultimately a judgment of the many, those in authority usually attain higher status with their positions, and those with high status can extend that status to others. The title of the old song, "I Danced with a Man who Danced with a Girl who Danced with the Prince of Wales," reminds us of the power of **status generalization**. Those with higher status can reward those with lower status with their time and attention. For example, Donald Petersen, then the Chief Executive of Ford Motor Company, wanted the plant mangers to make implementing Ford's new quality improvement program a higher priority.[65] One of the ways he did this was by asking to spend most of his time during his regular plant visits speaking with the person responsible for the plant's quality improvement program.

Initially, this responsibility was assigned to low-level staff members, but when plant managers realized they would get more time with Ford's chief executive if they were responsible for a successful quality program, they rushed to volunteer for this assignment. With the best and most ambitious managers in charge of the quality programs, they were much more likely to succeed.

Another way to use status as an incentive is through recognition programs. This boxed opinion reflects too many managers' neglect of recognition as an incentive. **Recognition** comes from formal programs such as employee of the month, plaques given at banquets, laudatory stories featuring employees in newsletters, and the like. Such programs can be very cost effective. **Social recognition** is more informal, in which anyone recognizes another's contributions, expertise or help. Both of these can be very powerful incentives; the management challenge is to make sure that formal and informal recognition are not in conflict with another.

> ***True or False?***
>
> *Your praise is in your paycheck.*

There can be no doubt that many value the esteem, status and respect of others who are themselves powerful or respected.[66] When recognition is combined with performance feedback, there are larger improvements in employee performance in both manufacturing and service industries than when either is used alone.[67] In fact, when recognition was combined with performance feedback, it had the same impact as making money contingent on performance improvements in manufacturing companies and had twice the motivating power of money in service industries.[68] Finally, those organizations having more employees reporting, "In the past seven days, I have received recognition or praise for doing good work," had significantly higher business-unit customer satisfaction and loyalty, profitability, and productivity than those that fewer employees reporting that.[69] Recognition is very powerful incentive, and it is virtually free.

However, like all other incentives systems, recognition programs can be mismanaged, usually by becoming forced and fake. The requirement for regular monthly recognitions can damage their value: the first recognitions may have been for the unambiguously praiseworthy, but as more and more recipients receive them, the choices become less clearly performance based. Similarly, because recognition seems to be free, it can be over-supplied. Frequent praise, administered on some arbitrary reinforcement schedule, soon becomes a workplace joke. Certainly, formal recognition programs need to be based on performance that all participants agree is valuable.

Because the esteem and respect of one's coworkers and professional colleagues can be a very powerful motivator for many, this powerful organizational incentive system should never be ignored. Interestingly, the informal recognition of a supervisor can be more powerful than a company's formal recognition program.[70] Because managers control many things employees value, because they have status, because they are usually technical experts in most settings, their honest praise can be important. What is important to remember is that those who are most respected by the employee, for whatever reason, will be the ones whose recognition is most valued.

Recognition can be a particularly useful motivator when you want to motivate learning. **Learning** is critical to organizations because it involves developing new skills, using new technologies, understanding potential new customers' needs, and all of the other things organizations need to adapt to their changing environments. In the workplace, it is difficult to tie many incentives directly to learning because most significant learning requires sequences of complex actions and many trials before it takes place successfully. It is simply too cumbersome to try to tie incentives to all of these different sequential behaviors, and it is too frustrating to learners to have the money removed from what they have mastered and now attached to something else. Recognition and praise, however, can be tied to the different steps, helping to sustain motivation during what might be a long process.

Application — Ways To Recognize Employees[71]

- Match the recognition to the achievement. The completion of a critical project should receive more recognition than a quick helping hand.

- Provide many different ways to recognize employees; different people value different things.

- Informal recognition is important, but it should not be the only recognition. Bob Nelson's rule of thumb is that for every four informal recognitions (e.g., a thank-you) there should be a more formal acknowledgement (e.g., recognition at a staff meeting), and for every four of these an even more formal recognition such as praise at a company meeting.

- Formal programs to recognize employees should be very public, reflect the organization's strategy and values, and should be changed frequently so they don't become stale.

- Blanket recognitions of everyone are not really recognitions of anyone. Recognize specific accomplishments and explain why they are important to the organization.

Fairness

Incentive systems that are seen as unfair severely damage employee retention and job performance. This boxed popular opinion is widely supported by research. Incentive systems that employees see as fair are much more likely to be accepted, to motivate better job performance, and to result in less employee theft.[72] Employees who feel fairly treated are more committed to their organizations and have lower turnover, and their organizations have higher customer satisfaction and performance.[73] Those who feel they have been unfairly treated, particularly those who feel promises were broken or they were in some other way betrayed, have extremely negative reactions, such as aggression and retaliation. Betrayal is a particularly strong feeling — it leads to indignation, contempt, and rage that can last long after the incident took place: people who describe betrayals that happened over fifty years ago do so with fresh, strongly felt anger.[74] For these reasons, managers should make every effort to treat employees fairly, and what is equally important, make sure they are believed to be fair.

> ***True or False?***
> *Reward employees fairly.*

However, treating employees fairly is not a simple matter of doing what a manager thinks is right. What one person believes is fair may appear unfair to another. This challenge can be addressed by distinguishing distributive justice from procedural justice. The perception that the distribution of assignments, incentives and promotions is fair is called **distributive justice**. But because what employees tend to think is fair is biased toward valuing their own contributions more, this creates a natural employee bias to believe their organizations are unfair. For example, blue collar employees believe that unpleasant physical conditions should play an important role in setting pay levels, whereas white collar employees tend to think pay should be based more on education and responsibility.[75] A pay system that one set of employees thinks is fair can be seen as unfair by the other.

Organizations will not be able to distribute valued things equally: the best assignments cannot go to everyone, labor market differences mean pay levels will differ, and few can obtain promotions. This creates a potential challenge for managers: employees who did not receive the best assignment, the most money, or the promotion may feel unfairly treated. That means a lot of aggrieved employees. How can managers distribute incentives and the other things employees might value to manage performance without their employees feeling unfairly treated?

Because organizational resources usually are distributed unequally, organizational behavior researchers have turned to the study of another type of justice: procedural justice. **Procedural justice** is the belief that although I may or may not have gotten what I wanted (distribution), I believe that the decision was made fairly (procedures).[76] If employees believe that the procedures used to make the decision allowed them some voice in the decision, some control over the process, that it can be corrected if erroneous, and is based on accurate information, they will see the decision as more procedurally fair or just. Employees who believe their workplaces are procedurally fair or just respond as positively as those who got what they felt they deserved.[77] More recently, the study of workplace justice has extended to a focus on **interactional justice**, or the feeling employees have that they were treated with respect and consideration. Being treated with respect and consideration in management decisions can be *more important* to employees than whether or not they got what they wanted.[78] A careful management of perceptions of procedural and interactional justice allows managers to unequally distribute incentives without damaging employees' belief in their fairness.

Application — Increase Employees' Perceptions of Fairness[79]

- Explain the reasons for the decision; these must be the actual reasons.
- Be sure to explain who you believe employees should compare themselves to and why; fairness judgments are based on comparisons with others.
- Give employees a chance to voice their views before a decision is made. This must be sincere.
- Provide other attractive things for the good performer who did not get the promotion. Can you offer more interesting work? Or a reclassification to a higher pay grade?
- Provide opportunities to correct errors. We all make mistakes, and providing a system for appeals and corrections leads employees to judge their organizations as fairer. For example, employee drug testing is judged as fairer by employees when they have an opportunity to request a retest.[80]
- Always treat employees with respect and consideration for their feelings.
- If the decision really was out of your hands, say so.
- Always assume that information about differential pay raises and private deals will become known to other employees. This is information about how fairly they are being treated, and so employees are very motivated know what everyone else is getting. If you cannot defend your decision to all of your employees, you should not do it.

Trust

Trust is central to organizational behavior.[81] **Trust** is a willingness to be vulnerable to another and involves both emotion and calculation. Everyone doing organizational work must take action trusting that others later will respond in ways they expect. Managers hire employees trusting that they have been truthful about their previous experience. Employees pitch in to help others when help is needed trusting this will be appreciated. Executives trust that others in the organization have done their jobs professionally to the best of their abilities. If managers had to watch every employee and check up on what every other group has done, organizations would grind to a halt. If employees would not act unless they were assured of receiving something in return, they would do very little organizational work.

Organizations are based on trust, and trust is extremely valuable to them. Organizations work more efficiently and effectively the more employees trust their managers, their organizations, and one another.[82] Without trust, organizations must build extensive and costly surveillance and control systems, and these further undermine their flexibility to respond to changing events. The more employees trust one another, and trust their managers, the less bureaucratic and more flexible organizations can be.

Because incentive systems are an organization's formal system of rewarding performance, incentive systems can either support or undermine trust. Incentive systems that employees see as unfair or unfairly administered reduce their trust.[83] If actions speak louder than words, incentive systems are organizations' actions toward their employees. The boxed inset opinion is not only false, it is dangerous. Incentive systems based on the assumption that people cannot ever be trusted produce distrust and opportunistic behavior. Pretty words about being a team player and being all in this together will enrage employees if they are contradicted by incentive systems that make it clear that these are not really rewarded in that organization. When managers make obviously untrue statements, it is the same as saying, "Never trust anything I do or say." Some ways of building trust have been established by research.

> ***True or False?***
>
> *People will act opportunistically unless they are controlled.*

Application — Why Do Employees Trust?[84]

- Employees trust those they know longer and more frequently meet face-to-face.
- Employees trust those who treat them fairly.
- Employees trust those who have included them.
- Employees trust those who share important information with them.
- Employees trust those who trust them, and who others trust.
- Employees trust more in those organizations where trust is expected and normal.
- Employees trust those who have refrained from exploiting them when they could have done so.
- Remember: trust is easier to destroy than to create.[85]

Implications for Managing Managers

- ✓ If you want to make more money, the best way is to have skills that a labor market values highly. Don't ever expect pay for performance to get you more than a small amount more than the going rate your job commands in the labor market.

- ✓ If your organization forces you to give different pay increases to your employees, you will want to try to prevent damaging their sense of fairness and collaboration. If those establishing this policy are blind to evidence and reason, you can always do what one manager did: exchange the above-average pay increases from year to year. Those employees who get above-average increases in one year get below-average increases in the next, so that over time all are getting the same pay increases.

- ✓ If your organization doesn't reward contextual performance, take care: managers usually expect and need contextual performance from their employees, and you depend on your manager for many things. Lecturing your manager about the organization's dysfunctional incentive system is stupid. Recognize that you work with two parallel and contradictory incentive systems: one controlled by the organization's formal incentive system, and one controlled by your manager.

- ✓ What if you think you are not paid fairly? First, be absolutely sure this is the case. Remember we all have biases to view our own contributions as more deserving than others' contributions. Second, ask your manager about the reasons for the pay you receive (taking care that your tone does not imply that this is an attack). Listen without disagreeing and try to encourage your manager to be expansive and descriptive. If you still think you are not paid fairly and that you would be paid more fairly somewhere else, then you should take that other job. Remember that pay is determined by the value of your services in the labor market, not by any abstract system of pay for performance, pay for skills and responsibilities, or the cost of living. Don't dwell on unfairness, dwelling on unfairness is bad for your health.[86]

Key Words

Incentives

Join the organization

Remain with the organization

Reliably show up at work

Task performance

Contextual performance

Organizational supportiveness

Managerial supportiveness

Intrinsic and extrinsic rewards

Need theories

Pay for performance

Labor market

Internships

Pay-at-risk

Internal inequity

Employment security

Norm of reciprocity

Status

Status generalization

Recognition

Social recognition

Learning

Distributive justice

Procedural justice

Interactional justice

Trust

7

Navigating the Social Scene

Organizations bring people together to do work, and this creates social environments that affect organizational behavior in ways managers can understand but only partly control. Employees are rarely socially isolated, responding solely to their individual incentives. Instead, most work in social settings that can undermine or reinforce managerial performance measurement and incentive systems. The inset boxed opinion is not true: Many people value the good opinion and support provided by those they work with more than the incentives managers may control. When those social environments are working against the organization's incentives, those organizational incentives will not be productive.

> ***True or False?***
>
> *It's all about the incentives*

Social scientists long ago demonstrated that what we think, our ideas, our perceptions of reality, and our attitudes and feelings toward work are all created in interaction with others. Others influence what employees think the organization is, their sense of what is fair, their performance expectations, and their motivations in numerous ways. For example, employees are powerfully motivated by others' positive evaluations; they want to attain status and legitimacy in others' eyes. Also, the desire to best someone in competition can be a powerful motivator. And what is fair and unfair can only be judged in comparison to what others are getting.

The field of organizational behavior began when early 20th century researchers sought to understand why factory workers, who were paid by the piece, harassed and scorned coworkers who produced more than the group's own informal production limit.[1] Why did these employees care more about the good opinions of their coworkers than they did about making more money? Scholars have spent the last hundred years trying to understand why organizational social environments are so powerful, and how they work to support – or to undermine – employees' experiences of work and their organizations' performance.

The **organizational social environment**, or the people we interact with on a regular basis at work, is less subject to managerial control than organizational structures and policies, performance measures, and incentive systems. Because managers' control over social environments is so limited, many managers make the mistake of ignoring them. They will reorganize or change the incentives because they can take these actions quickly, rather than take the time to diagnose how the organizational social environment may be supporting or undermining organizational incentives. Yet, the power of organizational social environments for individual and organizational performance is too important to be ignored. Why can organizational social environments swamp any effects of individual performance and incentive systems? And what can managers do about it? This chapter addresses these questions.

WHY OTHERS ARE SO POWERFUL

We are highly attuned to those around us for several reasons. First, we all seek relationships with other people. A disinterest in others and an inability to read social cues are seen as serious mental disabilities.[2] Human beings have always relied on others for their survival, and attention to others' opinions and intentions is part of our biological heritage. Certainly, an interest in others also has survival value in today's organizations. Most prefer to work with and do business with those they personally know to be trustworthy.[3] This assessment of trustworthiness is so important that when we do not know others, we look to their reputations before doing business with them. If those we trust report that a stranger is trustworthy, we are more likely to trust that person ourselves.[4] So, for example, astute executives will learn as much as they can about potential business partners before their first meetings, and many lawyers, bankers, and consultants will provide reputational information about potential partners along with their technical professional services. Getting to know others personally and learning their reputations are the primary ways we learn who can or cannot be trusted at work.[5]

Second, we also seek out relationships with others for the pleasure they provide in and of themselves.[6] Conversation, shared jokes, and gossip are enjoyable and interesting. They make dull jobs fun, are a welcome break from intense concentration, and can help reduce stress and frustration. Working all day, day after day, with no social interaction can be boring. Even worse, working with others who are hostile will be intolerable for most of us. The respect and acceptance of those around us can be a powerful incentive, and it is no surprise that those who are unhappy with their organizational social environments are more likely to leave.[7]

Others are a powerful influence on us because they have been and continue to be important to our mental health, our success, and our happiness on and off the job. For this reason, whenever people regularly come together to work, they will pay attention to those around them, talk to one another about work, and create a shared social environment.

OTHERS AFFECT FEELINGS ABOUT WORK

Social environments are a powerful influence on employees' emotional experiences at work and their workplace attitudes. In previous chapters the discussion of feelings and attitudes focused on individuals. While feelings and attitudes are held by individuals, we know that the feelings and attitudes of individuals develop in response to the feelings and attitudes of others,[8] so much so, that for the practical purposes of understanding workplace feelings and attitudes, knowing the social environments underpinning them is more useful than knowing particular individuals' feelings and attitudes.

Coworkers' Moods and Attitudes Are Contagious

Feelings and attitudes are heavily affected by the feelings and attitudes displayed by coworkers. In Chapter 4 emotional contagion was introduced. This is the fact that we all tend to catch the emotions and moods of others.[9] So it is no surprise that people who work together over time tend to have a characteristic group mood.[10] Coworkers' moods mutually influence one another until they stabilize into a shared **group mood**. That is, emotions such as happiness, fear, and envy all spread among those who work together. We know from Chapter 3 that feelings affect attention to detail, creativity, employee contextual performance, absenteeism, and turnover. This means that those who work together mutually influence one another's feelings in ways that directly affect organizational behavior and performance.[11]

Attitudes also are contagious, and the attitudes of those they work with can have powerful effects on their work attitudes. This is illustrated by Seymour Lieberman's[12] classic study of attitude change at work. He had just completed a survey of unionized workers' attitudes toward management when the factory expanded. Twenty-three of the factory workers were promoted to supervisory positions, and thirty-five were elected as **union stewards** (representatives) These new supervisors' and stewards' attitudes toward management had not been any different from those of their fellow factory workers before their new responsibilities. However, a year later Seymour Lieberman found that the new supervisors were significantly more pro-management, and the union stewards were significantly less pro-management. Supervisors had spent time in management meetings with other managers hearing more positive information about management and their travails, while union stewards had spent more time in meetings with other union officials hearing stories about management perfidy at their own workplace and elsewhere. Their new positions required them to represent management or the union, and their attitudes became more consistent with others holding the same job over that year. What is particularly valuable about this study was Seymour Lieberman's opportunity to return to the factory two years later. He found that eight of the new supervisors were demoted (as part of a large layoff), and fourteen of the new stewards returned to their previous jobs as regular factory workers. In the third attitude survey these job changers' attitudes had reverted back to their original average-worker attitudes toward management. They presumably did not forget all they had learned at those management and union meetings, but they were apparently more heavily influenced by the views of those they were working alongside at the time of the surveys than they were by their former coworkers or old information. The effects of these coworker interactions are a more powerful influence on employee attitudes than direct organizational attempts to change their attitudes.[13]

This has great practical importance. To repeat: Coworkers' attitudes are a better predictor of an employee's actions at work than are that employee's own personal attitudes.[14] That is, when asked to report coworkers' perceptions of the workplace and their own perceptions, what employees believed to be their coworkers' attitudes were more powerful predictors of their actions than were their own attitudes. After all, employees know they are being observed by those they work with and want to keep the good opinion of their coworkers. Since we know from previous chapters how important employee attitudes are to their contextual job performance, absenteeism, and turnover, this means it is even more important to know what employees' perceptions of their coworkers' attitudes are in a given workplace than it is to know what any individual thinks or feels. This makes the inset boxed opinion not true: people do not make up their own minds, at least about some aspects of their workplace. They try to find out what their coworkers' thoughts are on the subject and then let that be their guide to action.

True or False?

People make up their own minds.

Application — Diagnose Employees' Moods and Attitudes

- What is the characteristic mood of your workplace? Ask, "In general, how do people feel about ___ right now?"
- When diagnosing attitudes, ask employees what they believe others' attitudes are, rather than asking them for their own attitudes. For example, "Overall, do most employees here like or dislike ___?"
- In addition to being a better predictor of workplace actions, many employees feel more comfortable describing their perception of the general mood and shared attitudes than they do describing their own mood or attitudes. This can help in producing more accurate diagnoses.

Social Support Is Critical to Many Workplaces

Organizational social processes provide vital emotional support to employees and their job performances. This is especially important in the most difficult and stressful workplaces. **Social support** is the expression of understanding, willingness to listen to another's concerns, and practical assistance provided to others. The more dangerous or stressful the job, the more important social support becomes to employees and their performance.[15] Supportive coworkers reduce anxiety, are a calming influence, and make dull or difficult workplaces more attractive.[16] Social support from managers appears to be even more beneficial. The reverse is also true: **Social undermining**, or intentional rudeness toward and harming and hindering of another, is stressful and reduces job satisfaction and organizational commitment.[17] The inset boxed opinion, fortunately, is rarely true in most organizations. Difficult and dangerous organizational work simply could not be done by employees who did not have the social support of their coworkers and managers.

True or False?

You are on your own.

Employee Burnout

Those who work at chronically stressful jobs, such as jobs that are dangerous or ones that involve helping clients who do not improve, are subject to burnout. **Burnout** is an emotional exhaustion leading to disengagement; cynicism; reduced self-efficacy, job performance, and organizational commitment; and poor employee health.[18] Employees in such jobs are much less likely to burn out if they receive social support at work.[19] The importance of social support to those doing dangerous or frustrating jobs is reflected in the many examples of organizational change failures because the changes interfered with employees' social support of one another in such jobs.[20] For example, the introduction of new mining technology that separated miners, damaging their social support of one another, led to increased accidents and employee distress. Informal systems of social support for employees doing dangerous or frustrating work are so important to these employees' ability to come to work and carry out their tasks that these organizations can collapse if this support is undermined.

How does workplace social support develop? Employees will provide one another with more social support when employees believe they have a **shared identity**: a sense that they are members of a group with common characteristics and challenges. Studies have found that those employees in dangerous circumstances, such as bomb disposal experts, who had greater shared identities provided one another with more social support, and this in turn lead them to experience less stress and provide more contextual performance.[21] Feeling as if they are not alone, and that they are surrounded by people who understand their difficulties, helps such workers to get their dangerous and frustrating jobs done. Because all jobs can be frustrating now and then, attention to fostering mutual social support can be useful in any organization.

Application -- Foster Employee Social Support[22]

- Encourage a sense of shared identity through common experiences and challenges. Bring people together to honor their collective good work.

- Social support is so important to employees that they will usually develop shared social support on their own, as long as they have opportunities to interact with those doing the same work, on or off the job.

- Foster social support by organizing regular meetings in which employees share what they have found to be effective ways to tackle difficult problems. These need to be mutual discussions, not one-way lectures.

- If there is information available about more successful approaches to work challenges, it can be shared and used as a basis for discussion.

- If employees are not providing social support for one another, this demands careful diagnosis. Do they spend too little time together with the freedom to talk about anything they want? (Build this into the work.) Are there strong informal expectations against showing vulnerability? (Find a setting where this is expected.) Do they fear freely expressing themselves in front of a hostile or unsupportive person? (Try to create settings without this person).

- Don't forget the importance of managers' own social support of employees (and especially avoid socially undermining them).

OTHERS INFLUENCE HOW WORK IS UNDERSTOOD

The influence of those around us is not confined to the effects of emotional contagion, their attitudes about work, or their willingness to listen to our problems. Others also provide information that we use to shape our understanding of the workplace. Employees do not just watch others or talk to them; they also listen to them and ask them to explain what they are doing and provide their insights on what will and will not work. For example, one study found that the social environment had a greater effect on employee absenteeism than individual employees' circumstances did.[23] In other words, employees do not interpret managerial selection, performance management, and incentive systems in vacuums; these are all discussed, analyzed, and shaped through organizational social environments.

Employees Turn to Others for Clarity about What Matters

Why do coworkers' attitudes, perceptions, and expectations matter so much to employees? We all seem to be more heavily influenced by others' views the more ambiguous the subject.[24] People standing at a bus stop in a rainstorm won't change their perceptions of the weather because someone claims it is sunny. Yet, this is faint consolation: In organizations many of the most important issues are ambiguous. What does it actually take to get a promotion in this organization? Which tasks really have the highest priority here? Can a less expensive contract supplier be trusted? For these and other important workplace matters, employees turn to others to build their own understanding of how things really work.

There is substantial evidence of the power of **social information processing** at work. This is the idea that so much at work is ambiguous that employees develop their own perceptions and beliefs from those around them, not from any objective reality.[25] Certainly ambiguity increases with more important work and greater responsibilities. When there is no clear, concrete evidence about what we should think or do to be successful, we are guided by others' ideas, hunches, and theories.

This has practical implications. For example, it means that the more ambiguous the work, the more important others become to our ability to know what should be done. For example, one study found that the more difficult good job performance was to assess, the more likely executives were to carefully construct homogeneous social environments for themselves.[26] Another study found that for jobs for which it was hard to determine good performance (staff jobs, insurance, regulated banking), employees' social class was a better predictor of who was promoted than it was in manufacturing jobs, where good job performance is clearer.[27] Without unambiguous measures of job performance, these executives promoted those like themselves, that is, those who saw the world the way they themselves did. Whether accurate or inaccurate, sometimes our social environment is the only source of information we have, and if necessary, we rely on it, consciously or not.

This means managers need to have a clear understanding of their employees' shared perceptions, and the more the work requires judgment in ambiguous circumstances, the more important it is to know how others see things. While no one person can completely control the shared understandings in an organizational social environment, research suggests that managers usually are an important source of information about the workplace to their employees,[28] a fact too few managers harness.

Application -- Be an Important Source of Information

- Don't be shy about stating how you see employees jobs: What really matters? What satisfactions and opportunities do these jobs provide?

- Be persistent. Don't make an observation just once; repetition is necessary.

- Openly disagree with those providing contradictory observations in the employees' social environment. Silence is often interpreted as agreement.

- Don't forget that managers' social cues only will be effective for ambiguous matters, that is, in the absence of objective information. Don't remark on the blazing sun while standing in a downpour.

Organizational Climates

Others' influence on employees' perceptions and expectations can extend beyond those working together face-to-face. Whenever there are repeated interactions among people, whether within one work group or across divisions or organizations, shared understandings are created. As long as there is interaction, contagion is possible. These organization-wide shared understandings are called organizational climates. An **organizational climate** is a shared perception in an organization about what is appropriate and important.[29] Climate is not always the same as individual employees' own personal beliefs. Employees can be quite sophisticated, and most would have no trouble distinguishing between their own perceptions and what they judge to be the shared climate in their organizations, if they differed. Organizations can have climates that support or hinder the free flow of communication[30] and climates about how courteously customers should be treated,[31] among many other workplace features.

Employees' perceptions of the climate in their workplace is a strong predictor of their own actions, and therefore, organizational climates are important for individual and organizational performance.[32] Benjamin Schneider and his colleagues[33] have conducted extensive studies of effective **service climates**, or the organizational or departmental climates dictating how customers or clients should be treated. They found that the better an organization's service climate, the lower employees' stress, the greater customer loyalty, the higher prices the organization could charge, and the larger its market share gain. All of these benefits came from employees' shared understandings about how to provide good customer service.

Application -- Build a Better Service Climate[34]

- Treat employees well because employees who feel well treated treat their clients and customers well.
- Assess client and customer perceptions of service quality and use the data to make improvements.
- Ensure that service employees are of high quality and that staffing levels are adequate.
- Take care that there are not confusing jobs, conflicting goals, perceived favoritism, or employees who do not know how to do their jobs.
- Reinforce formal training in service quality back on the job.
- Provide good facilities, equipment, and technology, since these are signals to employees that the organization takes service quality seriously.

OTHERS' INFLUENCE ON JOB PERFORMANCE

Others in the social environment also can powerfully affect employees' performance at work. This happens even when others are not necessarily trying to exert any influence. This can happen in several different ways: when their performance is observed by others, through the contagiousness of others' performance on their jobs, through the power of social comparisons, and through competition with one another. Each of these is discussed below.

Others Watching Affects Job Performance

Employees will work harder when working in the **mere presence** of others than they will when working alone or against a clock.[34] That is, just performing in front of others is energizing and motivating, even when no conversation or attempts to influence take place. However, this improved performance from the mere presence of others appears to work only under two conditions: for well-learned tasks and when the observer is not hostile. If employees feel evaluation apprehension, being observed by others can have the opposite effect: reduced performance on challenging tasks.[36] This is **performance anxiety**, commonly called stage fright, or becoming anxious and frightened when having to perform before an audience. If we believe those watching our performance might have a negative view of us, we will perform new or challenging tasks more poorly, but if we believe they have a positive opinion of us, performance will improve.[37] That means the inset boxed statement makes a false assumption; our job performance is always affected by others watching, sometimes for the better, sometimes for the worse.

> ***True or False?***
>
> *Don't mind me; just continue what you were doing.*

For easy tasks a benign audience is motivating. For this reason putting employees who are doing repetitive tasks, such as making nametags for an event or assembly-line work, in a room with others can lead to more effort and better productivity. And there is the bonus that the pleasure of others' company makes these workplaces more interesting and attractive.

For challenging work, such as presentations and public speaking, managing the potentially debilitating effects of stage fright is necessary. All managers must give presentations to do their work well, and the more successful they are, the more they must give speeches to large audiences and grant media interviews. Fortunately, performance anxiety can be overcome. Performance anxiety comes from perceiving performance in front of an audience as threatening. When we are threatened, adrenaline rushes, blood is diverted to our major muscles, and our heart rate increases. This is useful for outrunning a saber-toothed tiger but can interfere with giving presentations. Unfortunately, too many people fear that these anticipatory physiological reactions will worsen once they start to perform, leading them to freeze, and so they avoid public speaking, never learning that performance anxiety can be overcome.

Application -- Conquering Performance Anxiety

- The first step is to reinterpret the anticipatory physiological reactions as valuable energy for the task at hand, not as crippling anxiety. It is normal to be nervous before getting in front of an audience; think of that nervousness as the energy you need to keep your audience awake and focused.

- The second step is to focus on the task at hand, not on yourself. The audience is there to hear what you have to say, and you are there to persuade and inform them. Really, you are the only one who cares what you look like. The more you focus on what you are trying to accomplish, the more quickly you will relax. Remember, that it is about the message and achieving your goals, not about you.

- It helps to make eye contact with the audience. Try picking just one or two people (a bit toward the back of the room, not in the first row) and address those individuals. Because most people often speak to one or two people without getting anxious, this can help. If possible, you might engage the audience with a question; this will help you to keep your focus on them and their responses.

- Finally, give a lot of presentations, talks, and speeches. The more presentations you do, the more ordinary and routine they become. Volunteer to give presentations every chance you get. A worldwide voluntary association dedicated to helping people give effective speeches and presentations is Toastmasters; you can find a local group at www.toastmasters.org.

Job Performance Is Contagious

The performance of coworkers is contagious. When working alongside or with another of exceptional ability, we work harder and more persistently. This means that employees working with coworkers they believe to be superior performers – as long as they believe those coworkers do not hold a negative opinion of them – will work harder and more persistently and will perform better.[38] This performance enhancement has been documented for many jobs: Sales people sell more, scholars publish more, and golfers score better when they work with superior performers. This happens regardless of whether higher performance is rewarded; it is the sole result of the presence of high-performing coworkers. That means the inset management opinion is true. Working with the best performers improves your own performance, and con-

True or False?

Work with the best.

versely, poor coworker performance negatively influences your own.

Coworkers' performance is influential for two reasons. First, coworkers' performance is a signal. Good performers set higher standards of achievement, while poor performers send the message that no additional effort, persistence, or improvements are necessary. Second, there is evidence that employees can be labeled as poor performers merely by their association with poor performers.

Many employees are aware that their own performance is better when they have high-performing coworkers. Boris Groysberg found that star investment analysts were less likely to leave for another employer if they had more able coworkers at their current organization.[39] Having high performing coworkers was one of the most powerful ways to retain highly mobile star performers. Poor performing rotten apples really do spoil the whole performance barrel. This is another reason managers should not to turn a blind eye to poor performing employees.

The Power of Social Comparisons

The power of social comparisons, is not limited to effort and persistence on the job but affects all aspects of organizational behavior. Others are an important source of information about all aspects of the organization, as well as a source of performance calibration.[40] **Social comparison** processes, or employees' comparison of their own effort, job performance, rewards, and working conditions to that of others, are an important source of information for people at work. Which task should I do first? What is fair? Why did that person get promoted instead of me? As we saw in the previous chapters, employees' belief in the fairness of their own treatment is very important to their organizational behavior. Managers should never underestimate how enraged employees can become when they feel unfairly treated, and the primary way they decide whether they are treated fairly is by comparing themselves with others.

This means that to whom employees choose to compare themselves matters a great deal to their expectations, perceptions, attitudes, and motivation. Researchers call the individuals chosen for comparison the person's **comparison others**. If employees compare themselves to those who earn low pay, they are likely to see themselves as well paid, but if they compare themselves to someone with a big office, their own offices will seem crummy. The challenge for managers is to discover who employees are using for comparisons. From research we know:

- Employees are more likely to choose those they see as similar to themselves for comparisons.[41] The more similarities they share in job titles, ages, tasks, and so forth, the more likely they are to become comparison others.

- Employees are more likely to compare themselves to those who are in close physical proximity. Physical proximity means more interaction and thus more common understandings.

- Employees are more likely to model themselves on those they like and who are most attractive.[42] Since the best performers are more attractive in most organizations, they are more often chosen for comparison.

This means, for example, that mergers, acquisitions, and global teams all bring diverse people into proximity to one another. They tell previously unconnected employees that they are now similar ("on the same team"). Overnight, employees will begin to compare pay, benefits, vacations, furniture, and travel policies. Some employees might feel more satisfied, but unfortunately, we know that the experience of "overpayment" is temporary, and the overpaid will quickly search for comparison others who are better off.[43] Employee happiness over a favorable comparison is fleeting, but employee grievances over an unfavorable one can last decades.[44] Those who now see themselves as worse off see no need to search for other comparisons; they will feel unfairly treated and remain unhappy. Unfortunately, telling employees who to select as their comparison others, as reflected in the inset boxed opinion, is not effective. Influencing employees' choices of comparison others is not that easy.

> ***True or False?***
>
> *You shouldn't complain – look how much better off you are compared to ___.*

Finally, employees are not the only ones whose comparisons influence their perceptions, attitudes, and actions at work. Managers also are driven by comparisons of their employees when judging their job performances. For example, employees with high contextual performance received higher job performance ratings from their managers when those employees worked alongside coworkers who only rarely pitched in and helped others, but employees with the same high contextual performance were not rated as high performers when their coworkers also had high contextual performance.[45] When their coworkers were going beyond the minimum job requirements, employees did not get as much credit for their contextual performance. Managers need to take care to avoid creating unnecessary anger and resentment with unthinking implicit comparisons in their performance appraisals.

Application -- Manage Social Comparisons at Work

- Begin with a careful diagnosis of employees' comparison others: To whom do your employees compare themselves when deciding what job performance is good job performance? When deciding how hard to work? To determine if they are fairly paid? In deciding if their jobs are challenging or boring?

- Managers should do all they can to make the best performers visible and accessible to others. Providing opportunities for informal interaction with the best performers helps to reduce social distance.

- Because complainers love an audience, they often actively seek out others at work. Try to keep disgruntled employees' perspectives from dominating your organizational social environment just because the managers and high performers are too busy working to spend time with employees.

- Because organizational changes can change employees' comparison others, be aware of how changes can shift who comes into contact and who is seen as similar. Mergers, acquisitions, reorganizations, and new teams all require that any differences in circumstances be acknowledged and explained at the beginning.

Workplace Competition

Finally, one type of social comparison at work is frequently misunderstood. Employees in **competition** are working to outperform another; they are not focused on a particular performance goal but rather on beating the other on the same measure. Competition does work as a motivator. Employees will work harder and achieve higher performance when competing with others.[46] The boxed quotation from *The Economist* about the now notorious compensation of investment bankers is true for others as well.[47] Yet, competition is a double-edged sword. Competition among coworkers within the workplace can reduce the chance that they will cooperate on other tasks when cooperation is needed, or if rivalry becomes intense participants may lose sight of their own best interests.[48] No doubt, many have seen dysfunctional competition where employees sabotage and come to distrust and resent one another and intense one-to-one competitions can lead to poor decisions.

True or False?

"Money is not as important as outsiders assume: many in the industry are far more motivated by the desire to outshine their peers."

Since cooperation is so important to the flexibility and mutual support needed for organizational performance, some have argued for stamping out any coworker competition in workplaces. However, Steven Sommer finds that under certain circumstances competition does not damage future cooperation but leads to greater trust and contextual performance among competitors, and the employees thought competition was fun.[49] Competition among coworkers can have these positive outcomes if:

- The rules for determining who wins are clear.
- Everyone believes the rules are fair.
- Winning is attractive but not important.
- The competition is not a transparent manipulation to goad more effort from employees.

Many readers will recognize that these are the features of games, and we all play games with friends and family without damaging future cooperation. Competition with others can be fun and an effective motivator of job performance in those circumstances with clear, fair, unambiguous rules and small stakes.

MAJORITIES RULE

When expectations are shared by all, they have a very powerful influence on organizational behavior. But what happens when those in the organizational social environment disagree? In practice, no organization is a monolithic shared social environment with everyone in agreement about everything all the time. Disagreement is inherent when complex judgments are needed to do good work in a rapidly changing world. In real organizations employees rarely face a united chorus who sees things the same way; they face conflicting voices and views. What happens then?

When we disagree the majority is more likely to get others to agree with it than is the minority. Several voices, if they are seen to be acting independently, are more powerful than one alternative view.[50] This does not mean that majorities are all powerful. Once there are three dissenters – and three does seem to be the magic number in a wide variety of settings – the majority loses its dominance.[51] Even one dissenter reduces the chance of complete capitulation to majority opinion; this is the primary reason for use of devil's advocates.

Unfortunately, in practice, the assignment of someone as a devil's advocate does not prevent unthinking unanimity, and the inset boxed opinion is not true. A **devil's advocate** is an assigned role in which the person is supposed to question and disagree when it seems that the others are settling on a decision. This is intended to make sure that there is no rush to judgment without considering all relevant information. But apparently, formally assigned devil's advocates usually are not effective because everyone knows it is all an act.[52] It is only when dissenters are seen to genuinely believe what they are saying that others do the hard work of reconsidering their assumptions and conclusions.

> ***True or False?***
>
> *The best way to avoid a bad decision is to appoint a devil's advocate.*

Dissent is risky. Whenever dissenters speak up, they initially generate a great deal of attention, as others seek to convince them that they are incorrect.[53] As long as this discussion is focused on generating information about decisions and uncovering implicit assumptions, this active discussion can help produce better decisions. However, once those in the majority realize that all of the arguments have been made, and they have settled on a shared understanding, continuing dissent angers them. Because dissent that does not generate useful new information is frustrating and possibly threatening to the shared understandings of the issues that allow them to do their work, majorities can become very hostile to dissenters. Majorities will remove persistent dissenters if they can, or, if not, shun them. Establishing a devil's advocate is supposed to create safety for a dissenter ("It's not me, it's the role"), but that phoniness also means the dissenting information does not have to be taken seriously.

Application -- Work Effectively with Disagreement

- Disagreement and discussion of alternatives can produce better decisions and help employees to anticipate problems. However, everyone must believe they may freely raise those alternatives with out being punished as a dissenter.

- Openly discuss the need for shared understandings in order to take action. Try to separate the dissenting information from other areas where there are shared understandings. Precision helps.

- Avoid the natural inclination to blame the messenger. The use of de-personalized and very polite language helps. Say, "That idea is …", not "You are …"

- When using a devil's advocate, remember to take the dissenting information seriously. Write it down. Spend time considering each point.

- For those who enjoy the role of dissident, remember that you are contributing nothing of practical value to others after you have made your points. Repetition just makes it more likely they won't listen to anything you say, ever again.

MANAGE SOCIAL ENVIRONMENTS

Building Reputations

A **reputation** is others' shared assessment of a person, group, or organization. For individuals it can be an assessment of their skills, job performance, willingness to help others, ability, reliability, or trustworthiness; that is, anything at all relevant to working with that person. Teams, departments, organizations, and industries also can have reputations. Reputations are substitutes for first-hand experience with another and are fundamental to our willingness to work with those we have not worked with in the past. Because we all must do business with strangers in modern societies, reputations are the basis for all business; without them deals would not be made, and work would not get done. Having a good reputation makes individuals more influential and productive[54] and makes for-profit organization more profitable.[55]

Those with bad reputations can be seen as stigmatized. A **stigma** is an attribute that makes a person socially devalued or debased in that social environment. Being seen as a poor performer can be stigmatizing in many organizations,[56] and the stigma of poor performance can be transferred from poor performing organizations to their managers and employees.[57] Therefore, Groucho Marx's famous quip in the inset box is true: Those without reputations for honesty and fair dealing won't find anyone willing to work with them.

> ***True or False?***
>
> *The secret of life is honesty and fair dealing; if you can fake that you have it made.*

What contributes to a good reputation? For individuals, having high self-esteem,[58] having the ability to create an impression of effort,[59] having a good salary, getting more promotions, and performing well[60] all have been documented as contributors to good reputations. Gossip also has an important role to play in the building of reputations. **Gossip** is the informal, private sharing of evaluative information within a small select group. Gossip is how reputations are established and is the primary means by which people exert social control over members of their social environments.[61] Gossip is more common and a more powerful means of social control in smaller, isolated social environments, because there are few social alternatives in such settings. Because good reputations are so important to the trust and cooperation individuals (and organizations) need to accomplish their work, organizational gossip matters to individuals and to managers. Individuals need to ensure that they build good personal reputations, and managers need to worry that the powerful informal social controls of gossip and reputation are not working at cross purposes with their performance-measurement and incentive systems.

Application -- Build a Good Reputation[62]

- Deliver what you promised. Always remember that people will talk, and they will talk vigorously about those they believe have done them wrong.
- Associate with other people of good repute. Those with good reputations need to worry about protecting their reputations, and because we all know that, we assume that those with good reputations will not associate with bad characters.
- Work in an attractive or high-status industry or for an attractive or high-status organization. Reputations rub off.

Establishing Roles

While managers cannot control organizational social environments, they do have powerful tools to exert influence over them. One of the most powerful is their control of the roles employees are assigned. **Roles** are the parts people are expected to play: the formal and informal expectations for that position.[63] For example, the chairperson of a meeting is expected to set the agenda, manage the discussion, watch the time, and summarize the decisions and actions arising from the meeting. People at work become distressed when others do not fulfill their expected roles, as when a manager does not provide active leadership.[64] Organizational members have roles to play and jobs to do, and they come into the organization expecting some guidance about what their roles should be.

Managers are responsible for designing jobs and setting role expectations, and employees expect that guidance from their managers. As we have seen, the more ambiguity, the more likely employees are to turn for guidance to whoever will provide it. This means that managers' best chances to influence their organizational social environments is to establish clear job and performance expectations and be persistent in managing them. It is one of the role expectations of the managerial job, and when managers neglect it, they leave the power of establishing expectations to others. This means clear detailed job descriptions and time spent with new employees providing as much information and clarity as possible.

Managing Employee Socialization

Finally, the best time to influence organizational social environments is when employees are new. People in transition usually are anxious. We all like to feel competent at our jobs, and new employees will pay attention, trying to learn what they should do to be successful in a new job or organization.[65] What new employees learn at the beginning can influence their perceptions and expectations

> ***True or False?***
>
> *The best approach is to just throw new employees in the water.*

for a long time to come. Because of this, you would expect managers to try to influence what new employees learn. Unfortunately, too many follow the false popular management advice in the inset box and leave the task of shaping newcomers' perceptions, attitudes, and expectations to whoever is most interested in this work. Those who are least satisfied with their jobs often enjoy a new audience for their complaints, and the more contact employees have with dissatisfied fellow employees, the more dissatisfied they become themselves.[66] For managers, spending time with new employees is a critical investment in building clear performance expectations and a social environment that supports good performance.

The process by which newcomers learn the ropes of their new workplaces is called **socialization**. This word means literally "becoming social," i.e., knowing what others expect and value, who to consult, and who to avoid. This subtle and sophisticated knowledge is necessary for success at any job, and the more complex and ambiguous the work, the more social knowledge is needed to be competent. John Van Maanen has described how different organizational approaches to socialization can produce more or less change in the newcomer's attitudes, perceptions, and expectations.[67]

For example, the more formality, individualization, and divestiture involved in newcomers' socialization, the more likely they will be to shed their previous attitudes and views and adopt the organization's preferred attitudes and expectations. **Formal socialization** is the degree to which the newcomer is segregated from the normal workplace and given a formal newcomer's status (for example, called a recruit, trainee, or freshman). The more segregated the newcomers, the more they are stigmatized as incompetent, and so the more motivated they are to achieve veteran status and remain open to information that tells them how to do that. In addition, some newcomers are socialized individually and some collectively, as part of a class or group. Those in **collective socialization**, have more resources to potentially resist the organization's message by developing a set of contrary perceptions shared with their fellow group members. Those going through the process individually hear few alternative perspectives, and it is difficult to find social support for contrary views. Finally, **divestiture socialization** seeks to strip the newcomer of previous attitudes and identities by cutting off contact with outsiders, sometimes through harassment and long periods of demeaning dirty work. For example, in some organizations new engineers are given an impossible project in order to demonstrate to them that engineering school did not teach them everything they will need to know to be good engineers. While certain organizations have always paid careful attention to the intensive socialization of their newcomers (for example, military organizations, police departments, investment banks), all organizations can benefit from management attention to the shared understandings new employees develop about their workplaces.

Application -- Manage Socialization

- What are the attitudes, perceptions, and expectations that best support employees' success? Do not say it is "hard work," if that is not really true. If you are seen as the source of false information, you will lose credibility.

- Make sure you have a chance to explain what you think the secrets of success are to newcomers in the first week. Make the time. Take them to lunch or for a coffee. Early, accurate information influences their interpretations of subsequent information.

- Are there any coworkers who make an effort to spend time with, and so informally socialize, newcomers? If you disagree with these active socializers, in your first-week conversations with newcomers you should inoculate them by sharing what they will likely hear from these individuals and why you disagree.

- Schedule regular times to meet with newcomers in their first six months. They can ask questions, and you can make sure your views are a central part of how they come to understand what they are seeing and hearing on the job. Not only will you be seen as considerate and socially supportive, their early impressions can provide you with useful diagnostic information.

Implications for Managing Managers

- ✓ Work with the best.
- ✓ Managers will compare your performance to that of those who are in close proximity or similar to you. Work to make sure your own good performance is not buried in the clutter.
- ✓ Since you will come to share the moods, opinions, and expectations of those you work with frequently, you will need to inoculate yourself against the ones you don't like. Look for others who share your feelings and views, and try to spend as much time with them as possible.
- ✓ Be a supportive coworker. Take the time to listen.
- ✓ Remember that dissent can be threatening to others. Dissent with care.
- ✓ Never dismiss gossip; what is being said may seem trivial, but important messages about others' trustworthiness are being sent.
- ✓ Associate with people who have good reputations. Take them to lunch, and join their voluntary associations.
- ✓ Your organizational social environments will have a major influence on the way you understand and perceive your work and organizations. Select your organizational social environments carefully.

Key Words

Organizational social environment

Group mood

Union stewards

Social support

Social undermining

Burnout

Shared identity

Social information processing

Organizational climate

Service climates

Mere presence

Performance anxiety

Social comparison

Comparison others

Competition

Devil's advocate

Reputation

Stigma

Gossip

Roles

Socialization

Formal socialization

Collective socialization

Divestiture socialization

8

Understanding Cultures

Social environments usually become stable and predictable, and once stabilized they can have powerful effects on organizational performance. Stable social environments are usually called cultures, and cultures exacerbate and magnify social effects, becoming powerful supports for high performance or undermining and subverting the very performance systems managers took such pains to create. What is more, cultures are notoriously difficult to change. For example, a decade or more after a corporate merger, many employees will still see themselves as belonging to one of the two original companies, rather than to the new combination. Here the effects of cultures on organizational behavior are introduced, with special attention to how culture impedes organizational change. Different cultures, such as those that support high levels of organizational performance, are introduced. The chapter concludes by introducing the problems of colliding cultures, that is, the challenges of managing in globally dispersed and diverse workplaces.

DIAGNOSING CULTURES

A couple of decades ago management scholars turned to the study of culture to try to develop practical tools to understand and change organizational social environments that worked at cross purposes to organizational performance management systems. These are cultures that encourage dysfunctional practices such as theft, indifferent task performance, and refusal to cooperate with other divisions or departments. This practical interest in cultures began with a fascination with the power and strength of multinational Japanese corporations.[1] Here were organizations with cooperative (not hostile) labor-management relations: Managers diligently help and support their fellow managers (rather than sabotaging or withholding information from them), and employees work hard and embraced technological changes (without any of the complicated individual incentives that American managers tried to juggle). It wasn't any one thing the Japanese did. Rather, management practices, employee perceptions, expectations, and social environments all seemed to reinforce and work in concert to create Japanese corporations' successes. So began several decades of work to try to understand which cultures best contributed to organizational performance and why. Here this work is briefly introduced.

What Culture Is (and Is Not)

> ***True or False?***
>
> *I haven't got time for this culture fluff. I've got a business to run.*

Culture is a fuzzy idea. The word "culture" was adopted from the field of anthropology, and they dispute what the term means.[2] If those who spend their lives studying culture cannot agree on what it means, how can managers, who have pressing practical business, hope to make sense of it? And, more importantly, is it worth their time? Yes, there are several useful lessons from this work, and as long as everyone remembers to approach the idea of culture with caution, the opinion in the inset box is not true.

There are several different definitions of culture, but I will use Clifford Geertz's, definition because of its clarity and practical usefulness. **Culture** is a shared understanding of what actions and symbols mean.[3] For example, there is wide variation in the meaning of clothing in different organizations. In some organizations wearing shorts means the employees are youthful and innovative professionals, while in other organizations it means the employees work on the loading dock. Of course, the meaning of clothing is easy to discover in most organizations. Understanding culture is most useful in learning the meanings of subtle things that are costly to correct if you get them wrong. For example, it can be seen as politically astute in some organizations to have an informal discussion of a new proposal with others before introducing it at a meeting. By contrast, in a different organization (perhaps in the same industry, working on similar problems) this action would be interpreted as the sneaky behavior of someone trying to go behind others' backs to make secret deals. In the second organization people of integrity arc supposed to introduce their new proposals openly and honestly at meetings, where ideas are vigorously debated. In the first organization sounding out others before a meeting is seen as good professional practice, while in the second it signals the person is untrustworthy. Woc to the manager who moves from one organization to the other: Human resources management never discusses such subtleties during orientation!

Because culture develops naturally in interaction with others over long periods of time, it is often **implicit**, that is, unspoken. Unlike organizational climate, which is explicit, or spoken, culture includes all of the ways of working people know but that, to them, go without saying. Because so much of culture is implicit, it is often invisible to us until we come into contact with those from different cultures. For this reason Edward Hall said cultures were conveyed through "silent languages."[4] These silent languages of culture can have enormous effects on individuals' careers and organizational performance and are therefore worth understanding.

Norms

One way to diagnose cultures is through their **norms**, short for normative expectations. Norms are the dos and don'ts for behavior in a given social environment, the unwritten rules for what people should and should not do. Norms only govern actions, not thoughts or feelings, and they vary in intensity. Those violating **high-intensity norms** are severely punished or expelled. Violations of **low-intensity norms** are not considered very important; they receive a raised eyebrow or snide remark at worst. Finally, norms usually will develop only for those behaviors others in that social environment consider to be important.[5] For example, in North American universities neither students nor other members of those communities see the way faculty members dress as an indicator of their competence; norms about faculty clothing in these universities are low intensity. A faculty member who violates one of the few clothing norms that do exist by wearing formal attire when teaching, for example, would not face serious professional consequences. By contrast, for chief executive officers in large business firms around the world, the norms regarding proper clothing usually are high intensity, narrow, and strict. Chief executive officers could expect active attempts to force conformity because everyone in their social environment believes their clothing signals something important about their discipline, reliability, and competence.

In most organizations high-intensity norms will develop about actions that can affect resources and survival. For this reason, the relative intensity of norms in different organizations can be useful for diagnosing what is really important there. For example, in organizations in competitive industries there often are high-intensity norms about working long hours and delivering projects on time, whereas in governmental organizations the highest-intensity norms might cover employee interactions with the public and news media.

Knowing that norms grow in intensity, the more important the behavior is believed to be can be used to try to diagnose actions that otherwise might seem puzzling. For example, John Weeks wanted to know why British bankers complained so much, yet no one ever took action to fix problems. In diagnosing this puzzle he found that norms about complaints (what it is appropriate to complain about at work and how employee complaints were tailored for different listeners) were an important signal of social sophistication to these bankers.[6] Employee complaints actually built and sustained social support among coworkers; they were not calls for change. A new manager in this bank who mistakenly assumes that these complaints signal problems that should be addressed would be considered incompetent in this bank's culture.

Application -- Cultural Diagnosis for Managers

- If you are new to an organization, ask anyone and everyone what is considered good performance and what is considered bad. As often as possible ask questions such as: Who gets ahead? Why?

- Others will not always be able to tell you about all norms because so much of culture is implicit. If you violate an implicit norm, you may see anger, puzzlement, or laughter. This means that while others may not be able to explain all their norms, you can be sensitive to their reactions. If you don't understand why a reaction occurred, this is something you should try to learn. Gather more data and watch.

- Cultivate good informants. These are people who are more aware of their culture and can better articulate its meanings. Once you think you do understand something, share your interpretation with your best informants. It may not be something they could have articulated, but if it seems right or wrong, good informants should know.

- What makes sense in one social environment can seem crazy in another. Anyone changing organizations or jobs should be alert to subtle differences in the meanings of different actions.

Of course, everyone does not always conform to all of the norms in their social environments; people are not robots. Most competent people are careful to conform to others' high-intensity normative expectations for their behavior in that social environment.[7] Certainly we all conform to norms in those social environments that are important to us, since we know that dissenters can be expelled, shunned, or seen as incompetent, making it difficult for us to get our jobs done well.[8] However, some norm violations are permissible. For example, those who earn **idiosyncrasy credits** in a particular social environment have more freedom to violate more moderate- or low-intensity norms than those with fewer credits. Idiosyncrasy credits can be earned through important contributions to the organization's performance, by bringing high status from another setting to the organization so members can bask in the reflected glory, or from any other contribution others see as valuable.

This means that a careful observation of who is able to avoid conformity can provide insight into what is actually valued in a particular culture. For example, a scientist with several valuable patents may get away with screaming at colleagues, behavior that would receive chastisement from a human-resources professional if done by someone with more modest achievements. Note that it would be extremely rare to avoid conformity to high-intensity norms, no matter how many idiosyncrasy credits an employee might have. Staying with our ill-tempered scientist, a violation of (high-intensity) norms regarding careful scientific experimentation and honest reporting of results would not be tolerated no matter how distinguished the scientist may be. One useful diagnostic strategy is to observe which actions create shock and anger; those are the ones that violate high-intensity norms.

Finally, not all norm violations are done on purpose. Some norm violators are indifferent to the good opinion of their coworkers. This may be because their important social environments and social identities are outside of work. Alternatively, some people are very poor cultural diagnosticians and make unintentional mistakes. Whatever the reason, norm violation is costly: Others will seek to expel those violating their important norms at work; they will shun them, undercut them, badmouth them, and undermine their work in many different ways.

Rituals

Understanding of the role of rituals also can be useful to practical organizational work. **Rituals** are ceremonies consisting of a series of actions performed in a set order. Rituals symbolize more abstract ideas, make them physical, and reinforce the participants' own commitment to them. Many organizations have ritual practices that support employees' understandings of their organizations. As an illustration, one of the most widely misunderstood rituals in organizations is the meeting.

Meetings are events to which certain people are invited to address organizational issues or problems, receive and share information, and sometimes make decisions. Meetings are widely complained of, and the inset boxed popular opinion is one held by many. However, those studying meetings find that, when observed carefully, these gatherings are organizational rituals that explain a great deal about organizational cultures, and so that opinion need not be true.

> ***True or False?***
>
> *Meetings are a waste of time.*

Helen Schwartzman found that the formal, publicly stated purposes of meetings were rarely the only or most important purposes of meeting rituals.[9] Rather, she found that meetings were one of the few organizational settings in which power and status could be displayed. Those who could call others to a meeting demonstrated their power over those others. Those who could arrive late or leave early showed they were not subordinate to the person who called the meeting. Ritualized displays of the power and status relationships in organizations were reflected in who spoke first, who spoke the most, who was addressed, and who was ignored. Those who were never invited to meetings were invisible non-persons of no consequence. And, those who were invited to the most meetings were the most important to their organizations, suggesting that those who complain that they have too many meetings are really broadcasting their high status and power.

Meetings also reflect a great deal about their organizations. Organizations, like other social entities, have rituals they believe are necessary to make that which is most important to their members real and concrete. In practice, this means the more ambiguous the organization's tasks and the more uncertain the performance for which it is accountable, the more meetings it holds.[10] Organizations, divisions, and departments with the most ambiguity about how to achieve their goals hold more meetings. This is why governmental and non-profit organizations and organizations developing new technologies hold so many meetings. Crises in any organization create uncertainty, and so require more meetings. Rituals such as meetings are a tool for learning what the members are most in need of seeing in concrete action (status, power, information that reduces uncertainty). Thus meetings are valuable tools for astute diagnosticians of organizational behavior.

This is not to say that meetings always are fun. Those called to meetings in which they learn nothing useful or contribute nothing meaningful to decisions, all while their work piles up, are much abused. Further, because meetings are settings where power is displayed and difficult decisions are made, they can create strong negative feelings such as envy, anger, and frustration. As we saw in Chapter 4, emotions are contagious, so it is no surprise that so many leave meetings irritated, frustrated, and exhausted. One way to help make sure these common emotional experiences do not lead to in-meeting outbursts you may later regret is to try to focus your attention on learning about what is usually implicit and hidden in organizations: culture and power.

Application -- Make Good Use of Your Time in Meetings

- Meetings are comfortable places to observe displays of (and struggles for) power. Since the use of power is one of managers' most important tools, meetings are a good place to diagnose and analyze shifts in power.

- Some things to watch for: Who is addressed most frequently? Whose questions are always answered? Who is ignored? What happens when others act as if they have power that someone else does not accept? This doesn't mean you should rigidly rely solely on who speaks the most. Sometimes the most powerful people in the room rarely speak but have surrogates speak for them.

- Meetings are a good place to diagnose others' emotional intelligence: Does anyone persistently speak more often than their actual power merits? What are others' reactions?

- Opening mail (paper or electronic) while someone is speaking to you is an insult to the speaker. This means that those who do this in meetings are either very powerful or clueless (or both).

- Using meetings to read power dynamics doesn't mean that the formal, explicit purposes of meetings can be ignored. If you are running the meeting, others will be much happier if you set and stick to agendas, follow up on requests and decisions, and report on actions taken since the last meeting. [11] For more advice on the practical business of running effective meetings, see www.allbusiness.com/business_advice/articles/11341.html.

THE STABILITY OF ORGANIZATIONAL CULTURES

Why Organizational Cultures Are So Stable

Once established, social environments are very powerful forces for stability.[12] Organizational cultures are stable because many forces work to sustain that stability. First, organizational cultures are sustained and perpetuated through what has been called **attraction-selection-attrition**.[13] Different cultures attract people who believe they will best fit and prosper there; this is attraction. We have already seen in Chapter 3 that managers tend to hire those like themselves; this is selection. And people who find that they are not comfortable in a particular organization are more likely to be unhappy, possibly perform poorly, and so to leave than are those who find that their attitudes and perceptions are shared by their managers and coworkers; this is attrition. Attraction, selection, and attrition all reinforce one another, creating stable organizational cultures.

Second, socialization reinforces organizational cultural stability. Shared understandings are quickly adopted by new members and are passed down, from old hand to new recruit. Third, because cultures are so complex and implicit, it is a great deal of trouble to develop alternatives that will work. Over time attraction, selection, attrition, socialization, and the difficulty of finding better alternatives produce cultures that are passed on from person to person, leading to organizational cultures that can persist long after the original people are gone.

Finally, another force supporting organizational cultural stability arises because those creating and sustaining organizations draw on their national cultural practices in forming and sustaining their organizations.[14] For example, Ellen Westney explains that Japanese employees' strong identification with and commitment to their organizations developed because Japan shifted very rapidly from a feudal to industrialized society in the 19th century. Japanese employees took industrial jobs expecting to give feudal loyalty to their overlords and brought their village-based sense of shared fate.[15] In contrast, the United States was the first continent-sized integrated industrial economy with businesses that grew very large at a time of massive immigration. The most effective way to manage such large, diverse immigrant work forces was to import impersonal bureaucratic management systems from the military and civil service.[16] Management practice in America is dominated by concerns for procedural justice, and managers are expected to be as constrained by rules as their employees are. How organizations should operate is one part of national or ethnic cultural practices; certain practices just (implicitly) "feel right" or "feel wrong."

These powerful stability-reinforcing processes are why we can so often see the history of an organization in its current practices. For example, large military contractors have the formal policies, extensive documentation, and slow and careful decision making of their governmental customers. These practices help them to meet these customers' requirements. However, a military contractor might see the potential of its technology for commercial applications. Executives may create new divisions focused on potential new business customers to exploit these opportunities, but if the new divisions are staffed by employees from the original military contractor, they are likely to be burdened by old practices that are inappropriate to the fast-paced competitive pressures of its new commercial marketplace. This is why large former monopolies find it extremely difficult to work like nimble start-ups after moving into more competitive markets. Too many unspoken, implicit assumptions, perceptions, and practices must change.

Changing Complex Interdependent Cultural Systems

One of the most valuable management applications of cultural analysis is the anthropological insight that cultures are complex interdependent systems. Because cultures are implicit, complex, and composed of interdependent, mutually reinforcing parts, it is difficult to know how a change of one component will affect other interrelated components. For example, a chief executive might be brought into a new-product research-based organization from a successful manufacturing firm. The new executive implements the performance measurement and incentive system that worked so well in the previous organization. However, it is not as easy to fairly measure scientists' output, and attaching rewards and punishments to nonsensical measured outcomes can lead to a heavy turnover among the company's best scientists, decimating the new-product pipeline.

The challenge of complex interdependencies is most apparent in attempts at organizational change. Organizational change is so very difficult, in part, because it attempts to change employees' shared implicit understandings of important interdependent features of their work and organizations. Until action is taken and the effects observed, it is virtually impossible to know what the effects of a major change will be. This is why the success rate of organizational changes is so poor.[17] Managers can rarely know all of the meanings in organizations of any size, they cannot know how those interdependent systems will react to any major change, and certainly they cannot control all of the meanings different participants will construct. With such inherent complexity, the popular management opinion in the inset box is not just false, it is absurd.

> ***True or False?***
>
> *Employees have to be sold on change.*

There is a long history of research demonstrating that shared attitudes in a social environment are much more resistant to change than are attitudes individuals hold privately.[18] This is why most organizational-change programs involve discussions with others. Organizational-change consultants are aware of the World War II-era research on attempts to get American housewives to try recipes using culturally shunned visceral meats. They found that if the women could discuss preparing meals with visceral meats in regular meetings with their peers, change was more likely.[19] Such discussions must occur among those who feel they are free to voice their concerns, and the meetings must continue over time. In such settings employees can hear how others have coped with similar problems and can get informal advice and encouragement. In these discussions they can develop new shared understandings and provide one another with social support for cultural change.

Alas, this documented process for successful cultural change has too often been mismanaged in actual organizational-change programs. For example, employees might be gathered together to listen to sales pitches for change, not to freely discuss their concerns and difficulties. Because everyone is busy, employees are convened once, before the change has started. This means there is no possibility for new shared understandings and social support for change to develop. Further, those who control real rewards and punishments often are present at these discussions, making many employees unwilling to honestly voice their fears and difficulties. The boxed inset opinion is false: Cultural change comes from open discussion, collaboratively solving problems as they arise, and sincere social sup-

> ***True or False?***
>
> *The leader's purpose has to belong to everyone in the organization.*

port for new ways of working, not from a hard sell. Sales pitches for change are worse than useless. They are public displays of failed attempts at manipulation, inviting cynicism rather than the new shared understandings the change agents had in mind.

Application -- Change Organizational Cultures

- Begin with a diagnosis of how the proposed changes may involve unspoken norms and cultural meanings. Most change involves new techniques and technologies, which are concrete and explicit. However, even technical changes can fail if they involve implicit norms, expectations, and cultures in ways not anticipated.

- Have your change consultants or champions conduct careful diagnoses of how the proposed changes will affect implicit under standings and norms in your particular organization. Do the consultants and champions know the critical performance-supporting aspects of your current culture and how the change may impact them? Insist that they do.

- Hold frequent meetings, giving all involved sufficient time to explain how the change is affecting their work, and give them opportunities to share ideas about making it less costly and more effective. Build this continuous work into the change program.

- Take employees' problems seriously and adjust the program in response to the new information being generated by the change. Make this a regular part of the change. Organizations are too implicit, complex, and interdependent for anyone to get it all right the first time. Successful change programs adjust as new information is generated.

- Politically astute managers attach their own preferred policies and organizational structures to the change program. Organizational changes foster active politicking, and so is a time of both peril and opportunity.

- Determine if executives really are committed to the change. If those championing organizational change are not putting in the time and attention that real organizational change requires, assume they are more interested in grand gestures to support their next career moves. It is probably better to assume they are not stupid, but know exactly what they are doing so you can simply wait them out.

THE RISKS OF STRONG CULTURES

One of the fads that came out of the fascination with Japanese corporate cultures was a belief in the power of strong cultures. In **strong cultures** everyone in the organization tends to agree on what is important and what different actions mean. These are organizations in which all of the employees share the same understanding of the organization's purpose.[20] In strong cultures there are shared stories and rituals and a sense that everyone in the organization has a shared identity and values. Strong cultures should support outstanding organizational performance because everyone has a shared understanding of what they should be doing, and employees should have more contextual performance because they are committed to the organization. Certainly it makes sense that if everyone shares a common goal and assumptions, they will be less likely to be working at cross purposes. However, research suggests that the inset boxed management opinion is not true. Strong cultures have both advantages and disadvantages for organizational performance.

> ***True or False?***
>
> *The most effective organizations have strong corporate cultures.*

First, strong cultures have employees who see things the same way. Yet, if their shared understanding is not performance focused, strong cultures will not produce high levels of organizational performance. Strong cultures need not be performance focused. They can support negligence, hostility to clients, and anything else you can imagine. In strong cultures, everyone agrees on what should be done; this shared understanding doesn't necessarily support high levels of organizational performance.

Second, even when strong cultures are performance focused, they have disadvantages. In a study of several Silicon Valley high-technology companies, the advantages of their strong performance-focused cultures included employee hard work, persistence, and focus on improving organizational performance.[21] However, the study's researchers documented several problems among employees, such as resistance to needed changes, neglect of families and other non-work activities, stress, and burnout. Strong cultures can be so powerful that they can foster behavior among employees that is dysfunctional for their own health and safety. Similarly, others also have found that organizational success has bred failures in strong cultures.[22] This was because success fostered a strong cultural belief that what everyone was doing was right, but these assumptions harnessed the power of the social environment to resist change when the marketplace changed. Even when strong organizational cultures are performance focused and foster high levels of employee effort, they come at a cost of reduced organizational flexibility.

Your Organization Has a Strong Culture If ...

- Employees usually refer to the organization using "we," rather than "they" or "it."
- New employees are confused for months on end and struggle to understand the organization's particular norms.
- The organization avoids hiring managers from the outside.
- Employees socialize with one another after work.
- Employees protect one another from attack, whether the attack is right or wrong.
- Employees are reluctant to leave the organization for better opportunities elsewhere.

HIGH-PERFORMANCE ORGANIZATIONAL CULTURES

A number of studies have documented that a certain kind of strong organizational culture produces better organizational performance in many different industries. These successful cultures have been called **high-performance organizational cultures**. High-performance organizational cultures vary somewhat, but all have mutually reinforcing interdependent management practices and cultural processes that foster high levels of employee performance and commitment.

High-performance Organizational Cultures Have ...[23]

- Promotions from within the organization as much as possible.
- Employees hired because they share the organization's values and have high skill levels.
- Higher pay than comparable jobs in other organizations.
- Team-, division-, and organization-based incentives.
- Performance-focused appraisals that include plans for long-term employee development.
- Extensive employee and managerial training.
- Use of teams and other forms of direct collaboration among employees.
- Employee discretion and freedom to make decisions about how to do their work.
- As much employment security as possible.

In high-performance organizational cultures employees' shared understandings and expectations all reinforce and support management hiring and performance management systems rather than working at cross purposes. For example, if employees are delegated more decision-making responsibility, it is important that they have the necessary information and skills. If organizations want to hire those with high-level skills, they will have to pay above-market salaries to attract and retain them. If the organization wants employees to collaborate with others and adapt to changing demands, they need to assure employees that they will not be working themselves out of a job by providing employment security to them. If only one (or a few) of these practices are in place, management practices and culture will work at cross purposes and undermine one another. The lesson from cultural research is that it is not just one or two individual systems that contribute to organizational performance, but that hiring systems, performance measurement, incentives, and organizational social processes. They can undermine one another, or they can support and reinforce one another. Those claiming that managers need to focus on just one practice – listen to their employees, instill a shared vision, or change the incentive system – do not understand how complex and interdependent organizations are. A number of studies demonstrate that the boxed inset opinion is not true.[24]

> ***True or False?***
>
> *You only need to do [insert this year's fad] to be a successful manager.*

There is substantial research evidence that high-performance organizational cultures produce higher-performing organizations. Studies in many countries have documented higher sales, higher sales from new products, and higher profits in organizations with high-performance organizational cultures.[25] Research has found that high-performance organizational cultures had lower employee quit rates and greater sales growth.[26] And those organizations with high-performance cultures did not lose productivity after layoffs, as did other organizations, as long as they persisted with their high-performance investments in employees.[27] These positive effects occurred because these cultures and management systems together fostered higher levels of trust, cooperation, and shared understanding among employees.[28]

Finally, high-performance organizational cultures include practices like employment security, so that many confuse high-performance cultures with **protected organizational cultures**. Examples of protected cultures are inexpensive state colleges with unionized tenured faculty members or monopoly service providers with extensive employee-protection policies. While both high-performance and protected organizational cultures emphasize employment security, there are important differences:

Application -- Distinguish Protected Cultures from High-performance Cultures

- Employment security in high-performance cultures is dependent on superior employee performance; employment security is not performance-dependent in protected cultures.

- High-performance cultures provide extensive training focused on performance improvement; protected cultures provide training as a benefit.

- In high-performance cultures employees take broad responsibility for the organization's performance; in protected cultures employees focus on defending their own occupational prerogatives.

- Extensive business information is provided to all employees in high-performance cultures; information is hoarded to build power in protected cultures.

- In high-performance cultures human-resources professionals seek to support and assist managers; in protected cultures human-resources professionals seek to control managers.

WHEN CULTURES COLLIDE

Because so much of culture is implicit, cultures often become visible only when people from different ones come into contact with one another. Whether through a merger, an acquisition, a new outsourcing relationship, or a joint venture, increasingly employees find that their jobs require them to work with those who have developed their own separate and different cultural systems of meaning. Sometimes differing cultural practices will become apparent at first contact, and other times cultural clashes will surprise everyone months later.

Colliding cultures matter because people tend to like and trust those who are similar to themselves (**homophily**). This means more cooperation and less employee turnover when employees work with those they see as similar to themselves.[29] As described earlier, the ability of employees to work together collaboratively is important to organizational performance. However, today we work in an organizational world that does not allow trust and shared meanings to develop at a leisurely pace among people who have had a lifetime of shared experiences. We all must work with employees, contractors, vendors, and customers from differing cultures, and we must do so under unrelenting pressures for speed and responsiveness. All of the social influences described in Chapter 7 and the implicit norms and pressures for cultural stability work against these rapid collaborations, and managers need to know how to be effective when cultures collide. Here three aspects of managing in different cultures are introduced: managing geographically dispersed virtual workplaces, managing across national cultures, and managing diverse workplaces.

WHEN WORK IS DONE VIRTUALLY

Information technology has made the problem of colliding cultures worse. It used to be that working with people from different organizations was a slow and cumbersome process involving travel and time. That slow process gave people time to talk, to interact, and to work out common meanings and shared understandings. And because these processes were so slow and costly, many executives avoided the challenges of creating rapid collaborations across great distances by slowly growing their organizations.[30] Now, with the pervasive use of electronic communication media, more and more organizations find that they can reduce costs by developing virtual workplaces for even the most complex products and services. In **virtual workplaces** people work together to produce a common product or service, but they do not meet face to face while doing their shared work.

Virtual work is often stressful and frustrating for everyone.[31] Virtual workplaces are especially challenging places to build the shared understandings necessary to take action when there is ambiguity. And it is worse when virtual teams span differing national cultures. Without informal face-to-face contact it is difficult to establish trust and shared understandings. Electronic communication eliminates subtle facial movements, gestures, voice pauses, and modulations, making the development of shared meanings slow and difficult. Electronic communication also makes anger-fueled, escalating miscommunication more likely.[32] This a major reason why virtual teams do not perform as well as ones that physically meet together for complex work requiring information sharing, managing the unexpected, and innovation. The boxed inset opinion is only partly true: Information technology has made it easier to communicate simple straightforward technical information. But it has made it more difficult to communicate the subtle, implicit information necessary for complex organizational work. Nevertheless, Cristina Gibson and Jennifer Gibbs have found that virtual workplaces can overcome these barriers and perform well if they are carefully managed.[33]

> ***True or False?***
>
> *Information technology has made it easier to communicate.*

Application -- Manage More Effective Virtual Workplaces

- Select members who already know each other, if possible, and post background information about all team members on an online site for the team so they can get to know one another before beginning work.

- Try to keep membership and procedures stable. The difficult process of developing shared expectations in virtual workplaces is made worse by changing structures and personnel.

- Hold mandatory, regularly scheduled **e-meetings** (meetings via video or online tools) for all members. When some members miss different meetings, this adds to miscommunication and frustration.

- Teams should meet face to face at the beginning of projects and at regular intervals during their work.

- The more members use the words "empathy," "openness," and "understanding" to describe other members of the virtual work place, the more effective they are.

- The most effective virtual workplaces did all of the above. They had stable memberships, had full attendance at e-meetings, they trusted one another, and they met face to face at least occasionally.

MANAGING ACROSS DIFFERENT NATIONAL CULTURES

All of the challenges of working across different organizational cultures are magnified when working across different national cultures. Because working, buying, and selling across national borders affects nearly everyone working in organizations today, working across national cultures is an important management challenge. Those who work across national boundaries not only face the formidable challenges of working with different legal systems, governmental practices, regulatory environments, and educational systems, they also face the challenges of working through different implicit, unspoken cultural meanings. National cultures are much richer, more complex, and much more likely to be implicit than single-nation organizational cultures. This is because national cultures have been built over generations and learned over lifetimes, rather than in a few months or years. While biologists and philosophers may agree with the inset boxed opinion, organizational

> ***True or False?***
>
> *Down deep we are all the same.*

behavior does not go that deep, and national cultural differences affect all aspects of organizational behavior and management in ways that make the opinion false for our practical management purposes.

Because managers from North America and Europe could not become country experts in all of the dozens of countries in which they found themselves having business relationships, they became interested in theories that explained the cultural differences of many nations in ways that would be useful in their work. Because of that demand, over the past two decades researchers have developed many different ways of dividing the world's cultures along dimensions.[34] Three dimensions with the most extensive research detailing their management implications follow.

Universalism-particularism

Cultures can be distinguished by the extent to which people believe that universal rules should be applied whenever possible (**universalism**). This is in contrast to those cultures in which people tend to believe that every person should be treated as a unique individual (**particularism**).[35] In universalistic cultures what is fair is to apply the same rules to everyone. So, for example, under universalism good managers should judge all of their employees based on their individual job performances, whether they like or dislike the employees personally. Similarly, benefits such as sick pay and vacation should be administered according to a set of rules that applies equally to all. By contrast, under particularism, good managers treat their employees differently depending on their employees' differing needs, skills, or relationships with others. In particularistic cultures managers may pay an employee whose husband has a well-paying job less than one doing the same work who must support her family. Particularistic managers would give more paid days off to someone with a sick relative who needed care than to one who did not have those obligations. More universalistic cultures tend to be found in Northern and Western Europe and the former British colonies, while particularism dominates in many of the least-developed countries.

Because universalism and particularism govern fundamental judgments about what is fair, this cultural dimension has a significant impact on how people manage and how employees feel about their managers.[36] Those from universalistic cultures tend to extensively document the rules and expect everyone to apply rules without regard to their personal relationships. Those from particularistic cultures rely on personal relationships for the predictability and trust they need at work, making them uncomfortable doing business with anyone they do not personally know. For someone from a universalistic culture, a business dinner can be just a pleasant evening; for someone from a particularistic culture, it is a critical first step in seeing whether a personal relationship (and so a business relationship) can be built.[37] No one from a particularistic culture would expect someone with whom they do not have a personal relationship to tell them the truth. This means that for employees in particularistic cultures, it is important to establish close personal relationships with others. A manager or coworker from a universalistic culture who keeps arms-length professional relationships would be seen as someone who does not want to establish trust and good working relationships and thus could not be trusted.

Collectivism-individualism

In those cultures high in **individualism** people see the "self" as restricted to one's own self only, while under **collectivism** the emphasis is on the self as part of a larger social group.[38] Those in individualist cultures emphasize personal achievement at work, while collectivists focus on group or organizational achievement. For example, individualists are more likely to avoid working hard on a team task if they can get away with loafing, while collectivists would not let the team down whether they could get away with it or not. However, managers should not assume that collectivists are all selfless altruists. Because collectivists define the self as part of a collective, they are highly attuned to who is in their own collective and who is an outsider. This makes it difficult for collectivists to trust anyone not in their own collective, and so they avoid business relationships with outsiders,[39] making large-scale multi-organizational collaborations difficult. The most individualistic cultures are The Netherlands, Great Britain, and the former British colonies, with the United States and Australia (with their long histories of lightly populated frontiers) scoring highest. The most collectivist cultures are in Central America and the Asian Muslim countries.[40]

Individualists prefer that their pay be determined by their individual performance, while collectivists prefer that pay be based on collective effort. As we learned in Chapter 6, perceptions that money and other incentives are allocated fairly are very important to employees, and so we find that performance measurement and pay systems are almost always adapted to local national cultures. Research has found that those managers who did adapt their pay and performance management practices to local cultures had higher returns on sales and assets.[41]

Power Distance

As a final example, national cultures can vary in the extent to which they are low or high in power distance. In **low power distance** cultures, differences in power between people are expected to be masked in social interaction. In low power distance cultures, those with more power expect those with less power to address them by first names, and when they ask for something, they do so by avoiding using language that emphasizes power distance (for example, "Would you please …"). By contrast, in **high power distance** cultures, those with unequal power expect to behave quite differently toward one another. People with low power in such cultures are deferential in interactions with those with higher power; those with high power are expected to be imperious and to carry themselves with the respect their positions merit.[42] Note that this says nothing about the actual power of anyone; it only illustrates how those who have different power are expected to interact with one another. The Nordic countries have the lowest power distance, and Malaysia, Indonesia, and the Latin American countries around the Caribbean have the highest power-distance cultures.

Because most organizations have power differences, culturally based expectations about how those with different gradations of power should behave toward one another have implications for how managers and employees interact. For example, mangers from low power distance cultures communicate with employees more frequently, expect their employees to approach them with problems, and delegate more decision making to their subordinates.[43] Employees in high power distance cultures avoid bringing information and problems to their managers and expect their managers to take full responsibility for their own work.[44] That is, there is more **upward delegation**, or the shifting of work problems to bosses, in high power-distance national cultures. Managers in high power distance cultures often complain of being overworked, and they rarely manage through the delegation of accountability and empowerment.

Application -- Management in Different National Cultures[45]

- Begin with a careful diagnosis. While organizations that adapt their management practices to local cultures are more successful, this needs to be balanced against the fact that some national cultures do not have a history of effective large-scale organization. Ask yourself: What is critical to organizational success? Alternatively, what is a cultural preference and can be adapted to local conditions?

- Research the country in which you will be doing business. Be aware that the more its culture varies from your own, the less likelihood of success.[46]

- Become aware of your own cultural perspectives and assumptions.

- Work to diagnosis the meaning of the foreign managerial practices you encounter. What problems do they solve (or might once have solved)?

- Develop your **cultural intelligence**, or your ability to recognize cultural differences and adapt your actions to differing local cultural contexts.[47] For example, Americans, who are taught to be confident talkers, should practice using silence when that is locally valued.

Grouping countries by cultural dimensions can help illuminate similarities and differences. This is an important matter when we observe that cross-border joint ventures are more likely to fail the farther apart the partners are on cultural dimensions such as the ones described here.[48] Such cultural dimensions can help alert managers to possible adjustments they may need to consider in the management practices they have developed in their own cultures, ones they implicitly assume will be seen as fair and professional to everyone. However, caution is in order. Grouping national cultures by just a few highly abstracted dimensions provides only limited information when working with those from an unfamiliar national culture. Fortunately, the internet has many easily accessible resources, making country-specific cultural research only a few clicks away.

Application -- Learn About National Cultures

- For country cultures and political economies:

  http://globaledge.msu.edu/ReferenceDesk
  http://lcweb2.loc.gov/frd/cs/cshome.html
  www.state.gov/www/background_notes/index.html
  www.bspage.com/1netiq/Netiq.html
  www.WTO.org
  www.un.org/en/

- For travel warnings:

  http://travel.state.gov

- For news and country-specific current events:

  http://newslink.org/
  www.economist.com

WORKING WITH DIVERSITY

Different cultures can collide within organizations as well as across them. Globalization, information technology, cost pressures, and the need for rapid responses to competitive pressures have meant the pulling together of teams of engineers, marketing professionals, and designers from around the world to develop innovative products and services. Further, movements in the late 20th century, such as reductions in racial and gender barriers to jobs and more immigration, have increased the diversity of employees working together throughout the world. These changes usually are discussed as diversity management. **Diversity** refers to variety in the backgrounds and experiences of those who work together – diversity in age, race, gender, or national or ethnic culture or diversity in occupational specialization or industrial experience.

Before discussing the effects of diversity on organizational behavior, we need to address prejudice. **Prejudice** is a negative evaluation or feeling about another because of his or her membership in a group. Racial, ethnic, and gender prejudice have received the most attention, but it also is common in organizations to find prejudice against individuals based on their occupational training and experience. Recent research on racial prejudice in the workplace can be summarized: Although overt statements of prejudice have nearly disappeared in most American organizations, unarticulated feelings of prejudice are still widespread.[49] And research continues to demonstrate than non-whites are less likely to be hired or promoted and more likely to receive biased treatment and performance appraisal ratings than are whites.[50] And in a shocking twist, one study found that the better the actual job performance of Asian-American employees, the less likely they were to receive good performance ratings![51]

Similar effects are found in relation to gender. In this case, it is a matter of differing role expectations that men and women hold for each other. For example, women at work are punished for expressing negative feelings and for not acting altruistically (but men are not).[52] Women must demonstrate superior job performance to avoid being considered poor performers.[53] In one study women business students made greater contributions to study-team performance but received less credit and social support than men did.[54] And finally, it seems that women and racial minorities need to engage in more ingratiation, more agreeing with the boss, more flattery and favor rendering to get promoted to corporate boards than do white men.[55] So the boxed inset opinion is true: Most women and men do communicate differently, because they are punished if they don't.

> ***True or False?***
>
> *Men and women communicate differently.*

While most of us will work to remove prejudice (in feelings as well as deeds), some will not want to wait for society to change and will need to take action to protect themselves today.

Application -- Succeed in a White Man's World

- Because prejudice can be shared by those who are disadvantaged and advantaged, check your own implicit assumptions: Am I dis counting some employees' actions, but not others? Do I provide more support and encouragement to some based on their demography and background rather than their performance?
- Look for opportunities to demonstrate your skills early. In most organizations that care about performance, good performance will trump prejudice, so act quickly and well.
- You increase your chances of success by working in a job with unambiguous individual measures of performance. If the metrics don't exist, develop some, and then be sure to report your performance against them.
- Flattery, agreeing with the boss, and doing favors does help, but take care to do this with nuance and sophistication; heavy-handed ingratiation is an insult to the recipient and can backfire.
- Don't expect diversity training to do much good.[56] The only reliable way to overcome prejudice is to do excellent work that is unambiguously yours.
- In today's global economy all of us can expect to find ourselves in the minority at some point in our careers. This puts those who have never had to practice the above skills at a disadvantage.

True or False?

Diverse workplaces have higher performance.

Finally, as will surprise no one who has read this far, the inset boxed opinion is not true: Diverse teams, departments, and organizations do not have higher performance than more homogeneous ones.[57] Although it makes intuitive sense that diverse workplaces, which can draw on a wider range of talents and experiences, should be more productive, studies show that diverse workplaces have more problems with cooperation, coordination, and the development of shared identities.[58] However, all of these problems can be overcome with open discussion and time together;[60] but time is required. Of course, some tasks need those with different experiences and skills to work together to produce a product, service, or decision that would be the poorer for not using all of that relevant knowledge. Those who put such teams and workplaces together need to realize that the more diverse they are, the more time employees and managers will need to develop the shared understandings and trust that allow them to work effectively. The most reliable way for all organizations to be successful is to provide more effective shared experiences for people who will be working together; this cannot be rushed.

Implications for Managing Managers

✓ Cultivate multiple informants who can explain what things mean and how things work. Recognize that the first person you get to know may not be the best source for reliable information.

✓ Learn the norms and rituals in your organizations. If a practice is puzzling, there is a good chance it has an implicit purpose, and a careful diagnosis will be more useful than loud complaints about it.

✓ Be wary of organizational change programs. Many younger employees are less invested in the older ways of doing things and see change programs as an opportunity to shine. Older and wiser employees have learned to wait and see if the bandwagon is really going anywhere before jumping aboard.

✓ Do not underestimate the difficulties of working in a foreign country. Because it is such a challenge, it can be easier to take those opportunities while you are young, flexible, and strong.

Key Words

Culture

Implicit

Norms

High-intensity norms

Low-intensity norms

Idiosyncrasy credits

Rituals

Meetings

Attraction-selection-attrition

Strong cultures

High-performance organizational Cultures

Protected organizational cultures

Homophily

Virtual workplaces

E-meetings

Universalism-particularism

Individualism-collectivism

Power distance

Upward delegation

Cultural intelligence

Diversity

Prejudice

9

Mastering Power

Power is an essential tool of management. No organization is a command-and-control machine that gives every manager the authority to get others to do all of the things necessary to meet their responsibilities. Organizations and people are too complex, change too often, and are too concerned with their own goals for that to ever happen. Managers need to enlist the cooperation of bosses, peers, subordinates, and those outside the organization because they cannot do it all alone. They are responsible for getting work done, and that means they need to obtain resources, permissions, and authority from others to do that work. Power is how you get organizational work done.

For these reasons it isn't surprising that those managers who have mastered power have been more successful in their careers.[1] In fact, one of the most common misconceptions is the one in the inset box: All you need to do is present your clever idea to the world, and the world will rush to implement it. It never happens this way. Others are focused on their own wants and clever ideas, and they will not drop everything they care about to work on someone else's project without a good reason. Their support and effort must be enlisted and directed, and that is done through the understanding and effective use of power. This is why employees report that the most effective leaders are the ones who can protect them and get them the resources they need, not the nicest and most considerate bosses.[2] No manager can be successful without enlisting others' support.

> ***True or False?***
>
> *Good ideas sell themselves.*

Traditionally, managers have been taught about power under the label *leadership* with a focus on how to exert effective influence over their subordinate employees. Leadership is addressed in the following chapter. However, managers also need to enlist the support of peers, bosses, vendors, contractors, and suppliers, as well as that of their employees. Managers depend on the cooperation of more than the few employees who report to them, and they need to know how to enlist that support to do their jobs well.

This chapter introduces what research can tell us about power. Because power is complex, ambiguous, and so often mismanaged, this chapter begins by laying a foundation for the diagnosis of organizational power. The foundation begins by clarifying what power is and distinguishing it from similar things such as authority and manipulation. Next we'll look at a description of some of the most important bases of power in organizations and common reasons for organizational politicking. This section ends by discussing what research can tell us about why people submit or resist others' attempts to wield power over them. With this foundation in place, managers can become more adept at diagnosing and understanding the power and politics in their workplaces. The chapter then continues by introducing some of the most common and successful political tactics available to managers.

Warnings you have found throughout this book about the importance of careful diagnosis are particularly important for mastering power: Normative expectations about the use of power vary dramatically from organization to organization, and what might be seen as competent management influence in one organization could be seen as back-stabbing betrayal in another. The effective use of power is critically dependent on careful and nuanced diagnoses of situations. The need for careful diagnoses in the exercise of power is especially important to keep in mind when reading popular management advice books on exercising power. The inset boxed advice, taken from one of those books,[3] may be true if you are waging a shooting war or seeking to poison an early Han emperor, but in the kinds of organizations in which most of you find yourselves, if you follow such popular advice to lie, mislead, and sabotage, you will get into serious trouble. There are organizations in which the worst is required of anyone seeking to survive, but those places are rare. While popular power advice books can be fun to read, research suggests that there is a real danger that risky power plays can make things worse. Here less risky and more reliable practical approaches to mastering power in organizations are described.

> ***True or False?***
>
> *Keep people off-balance and in the dark by never revealing the purposes behind your actions.*

UNDERSTANDING POWER

What Power Is (and Is Not)

Power, like culture, is widely misunderstood, and many managerial careers have been destroyed by superficial assumptions and rash acts taken by those who did not understand how power worked in their organizations. This means some time must be spent understanding the nuances of organizational power, authority, politicking, manipulation, and the personal effects of wielding power and of powerlessness.

While we usually can distinguish who does and does not have power in our own organizations,[4] once we try to get precise, opinions about power differ. For example, there is great debate in the scholarly community about definitions of power,[5] a debate that draws attention to the reality that any two people may use the word "power" to mean very different things. We need to be able to clearly state what power is and what it is not in order to understand and use it in organizational work.

Here **power** is defined as the ability of an individual, group, or organization to get other people, groups, or organizations to do what they would otherwise not have done. Power is the ability to get others to take action, not the actions themselves; this means that power is rarely visible in any objective way. For example, those confident in their power usually do not shout, scream, or strut, and sometimes they don't speak publicly but let others do that for them. What is more, power is not prediction: Just because you declare, "Arise, sun!" at dawn does not mean you have power over the sun. Power involves overcoming opposition or inertia;[6] it is the ability to make something you want to happen actually happen when it would not have happened on its own. Power is easy to misunderstand and diagnose because it is potential, not something you can actually see or touch.

Finally, power is not possessed by a person, group, or organization in isolation, but it is always part of the situation and the particular people in that situation. While personal political skills can help, they are rarely as important in an organization as what people control, the legitimacy of their exercise of power, and the assumptions and expectations of those they want to influence.[7] There are no powerful people in the abstract. For example, senior executives may have the power to hire and fire those working in their business units but be unable to obtain the parent corporation's backing for all of their investment proposals. This means too many managers who could get things done in one organization find themselves frustrated and impotent in a new one. The tactics that worked so well with the people in one situation can be useless in another. Building effective organizational power requires constant diagnoses.

Formal Authority

Power is not authority, although authority is one possible source of organizational power. **Formal authority** is an organization's or official's allocation of specific powers to someone over certain people and resources.[8] For example, in some organizations managers are given the authority to hire and fire, but in others someone else (for example, higher-level managers, those interpreting union contracts) has the authority to hire and fire employees.

This distinction between power and authority is an important one, because too many new managers assume their organizational authority is enough and mis-

> ***True or False?***
>
> *I'm their boss, so my subordinates will do what I say.*

takenly hold the false management opinion in the inset box. Authority is certainly important to managers, but it is rarely sufficient to get their work done. It does not cover contextual performance, and no supervisor can be everywhere watching everyone at once. Successful managers need to learn how to build and effectively exercise power above and beyond their organizational authority.

Application -- Build Power to Support Organizational Authority[9]

- Build on successes. Others need to be confident that you are someone who takes action to solve problems before they will follow your direction. Find small, easy problems to solve as soon as possible.

- Begin by solving individuals' problems. Help employees with tools, training, or other assistance.

- Be flexible when it is reasonable. All employees face uncertainty in their lives and so want to know that their managers will understand if they have an emergency. Managers who won't yell at an employee who is late because of a car accident on the way to work or who will understand when a family tragedy disrupts a valued employee's performance are necessary to employees' sense of personal security. Managers who are reasonable and understanding create reasonable and understanding employees who will reciprocate when those manager have to ask for assistance.

- Do not tolerate insubordination. Insubordination is disastrous to a manager's power; avoid it at all costs. Public insubordination can be avoided by taking care to conduct a careful diagnosis of your power: Will you face resistance? Where? If you think public insubordination is possible, avoid giving the order, if at all possible. If you do face public insubordination, you must respond immediately and forcefully. Public insubordination creates confusion: Watching someone smoke under the "No Smoking" sign means employees do not know which requirements are real and which are just suggestions.

Politicking

Power is not the same as politicking. **Politicking** involves actions to influence others or to build one's power. Examples of politicking are providing information in order to persuade another, doing someone a favor in exchange for a favor in return, or working through a trusted colleague to get others to do what they otherwise would not have done. **Politics** is a way of summarizing such acts. Politicking and politics are overt actions intended to influence, while power is the potential ability to get others to do something they otherwise would not have done.

Some people conducting organizational behavior research reserve the terms "politics" and "politicking" only for those actions that are illegitimate or self-serving, actions such as lying, withholding needed information from a colleague, and administering organizational resources in exchange for personal favors.[10] Certainly such actions are dysfunctional for organizations (to say nothing of the harm they do to their targets). However, here the terms "politicking" and "politics" are used the way political scientists use them to refer to any action undertaken to influence another or to build power.[11] As will be detailed below, there are many political acts that do not depend on secrecy or dirty tricks and even may be welcomed by their targets. Managers must politick to do their jobs, and their actions to influence and build power are not all bad. Here politicking and politics mean both acceptable and unacceptable actions to build and exercise power, making the boxed inset management opinion false.

> ***True or False?***
>
> *Politics are dirty.*

Manipulation

Many confuse politicking with manipulation. **Manipulation** is influencing others by deceiving them. The effective exercise of power does not depend on manipulation or lying. Everyone can know exactly what you are doing and why, and they will still do what they otherwise would not have done. For example, most would accept that their managers have the formal authority to make a new project the priority. A change in priorities is not manipulation.

Seeking to exercise power through manipulation is not a good idea. One reason is because deception and lying are unethical. So, manipulation should not be done for that reason alone. However, even for those willing to behave badly, manipulation is a very risky tactic. This is because it depends on complete secrecy for its effects, and complete secrecy is very hard to maintain in organizations.[12] This is the reason why popular power advice so often fails: Eventually employees see the pattern and resent being manipulated. Certainly, people can become very angry if they feel that have been manipulated or tricked. As we saw in Chapter 6, those who feel they have been treated unfairly will retaliate when they can, leave if possible, and sullenly withhold cooperation if that is their only option.[13]

Power through deception and manipulation is often called being **Machiavellian**. However, those who have read Niccolò Machiavelli's entire book would find this warning: *"If you are going to attack a prince you better be sure to kill him, because a wounded prince is dangerous."*[14] In today's bureaucratic organizations many people are princes, that is, they have the ability to retaliate. Those who are attacked will act to protect themselves, and when possible, take revenge on their attackers. Even the least intelligent employees, with sufficient time and motivation, can find ways to punish their attackers. They have the time, can wait, and are very motivated. Do you want to build an army of motivated enemies lying in wait for you to stumble? Those who hold the inset boxed management opinion are risk takers indeed.

> ***True or False?***
>
> *To get what you want from others, you need to be Machiavellian.*

Unfortunately, those adopting Machiavellian methods often do so because they distrust others, and so they never try any other approach.[15] This is called the **sinister attribution error**, or mistakenly assuming that others are out to get you. Of course, those who assume others cannot be trusted, and that they must attack before they are attacked, lead others to distrust and attack in self defense. Morgan McCall and David Lombardo found that those managers who advanced early in their careers through Machiavellian deception were most likely to derail before reaching executive positions.[16] Why? Because eventually others learned how to effectively respond to their deceptions, and the higher they rose, the more likely they were to find themselves working with people who understood power and politics. Of course, situations differ, and some may find themselves working in organizations that can somehow function in the midst of such a war of all against all. But such organizations are rare.

As unwise as Machiavellian manipulations can be, you might find that you need to defend yourself from such attacks. Below are some of the most common defenses against them. Clearly, such defenses, while sometimes necessary for personal protection, undermine organizational performance.

Application -- Defend Yourself from Manipulation[17]

- Develop detailed documentation of your decisions and actions.
- Strictly adhere to defined responsibilities, guidelines, and precedents.
- Associate yourself with high-status people and events, and disassociate yourself from problems.
- Play it safe by avoiding dangerous situations or decisions.

Effects of Politicking and Power

Active politicking and wielding power have consequences for the participants, although the widely held management opinion in the inset box is false. There is no evidence that active politicking hurts organizational performance.[18] However, active politicking can be distressing to those who practice it and those who observe it.[19] Politicking is emotionally engaging to most, often involves frustration, and can seem unfair and corrupt. While a few enjoy the sport of politicking, many more do not. One study found that employees reporting substantial politicking in their workplaces had lower contextual and task performance, were absent more often, and reported more dissatisfaction.[20] Later in the chapter ways to minimize some of the negative effects of active politicking are described in detail.

> ***True or False?***
>
> *Politicking hurts organizational performance.*

Holding more or less power also affects the people involved. Research has documented the harm of powerlessness. Powerlessness makes people unhappy and hurts them,[21] and a lack of autonomy and freedom impedes creativity and innovation.[22] When employees feel they are the victims of managers who misuse their power,[23] they do not like feeling powerless, it is not good for their health, and watching others engage in dirty tricks politicking leads to poorer employee performance.

Power also has consequences for those wielding relatively more power. Some of the positive effects of having relatively more power include more promotions and better job performance, especially for managers.[24] Those with more power are happier and more likely to take actions that lead to building more power.[25] However, there also are negative consequences for those wielding power. The old Russian saying in the inset box appears to be true: Those with more power are less inhibited, are poorer at self monitoring, overestimate their personal effectiveness, and are more self indulgent. Acting on passing feelings and whims surely does not help a manager's effectiveness. High-powered individuals are more likely to be impolite, bossier, to speak out of turn, and to act aggressively toward others.[26] The more powerful you are, the less likely you are to conform to social and moral conventions, and the more likely you are to ignore your effects on others. All of these flaws damage managers' observational and diagnostic skills and thus can hurt their job performance. So having power can be good for your career and health but also can damage your social intelligence and diagnostic skills. Power is a dangerously double-edged tool.

> ***True or False?***
>
> *Power makes you stupid.*

Power Can Be Used for Good or Bad

Finally, to understand power managers need to recognize that power is neither good nor bad in itself but rather just a tool. Just as a kitchen knife can chop vegetables for dinner or kill someone, power can be used for good or bad. Without power very little good work would get done: Relief supplies could not be delivered halfway around the world to those dispossessed by war, life-saving medicines would not make it to the local pharmacy, and grain could not be planted, fertilized, harvested, converted into ethanol, and put into fuel tanks. Even writers and artists, those stereotypical loners, depend on publishers, gallery owners, newspaper reviewers, and bloggers, among many, many others, to get their work to their admirers. We all depend on the organized efforts of others, and organization depends on the ability to get others to do things they otherwise would not have done. Those who disdain power will not spend the diagnostic time needed to understand it. While Lord Acton's epigram in the inset box may well be true, Rosabeth Kanter has persuasively argued that powerlessness, which leads to frustration and the inability to get important work done, also corrupts.[27]

> ***True or False?***
>
> *Power tends to corrupt and absolute power corrupts absolutely.*

Of course, power can be and too frequently is used for bad purposes. In organizations people who have been allocated authority to enable them to pursue the organization's objectives have been known to misuse that power for their own personal gain, to entertain themselves, or to satisfy nasty desires. One example is **sexual harassment**, the creation of an abusive work environment by giving targets persistent sexual attention, repeatedly asking them for dates, repeatedly making sexual comments, or bringing sexually explicit materials into the workplace. Sexual harassment is not about sexual desire or gratification but rather the use of something about which many have strong feelings (sex) to demoralize and denigrate another. Sexual harassers always feel they have power over their targets, and they use that power to try to intimidate them into further submission.[28]

Because power is vague, drawing clear lines between good and bad power can be difficult in practice. It is not simply a matter of intention (helping the organization or clients is good, but helping one's self is bad). Many appalling acts have been justified as serving some higher goal. Nevertheless, we can draw on the work of those seeking to rid organizations of sexual harassment for guidance:

Application -- Eradicate Bad Uses of Power Without Destroying Its Good Uses

- It helps to formally identify legitimate and illegitimate uses of power. Explaining the organization's policies with examples educates employees and managers about what are and are not acceptable uses of power.

- The most effective way to prevent the misuse of power is to provide its potential victims with protected ways to report misuse. The most well known of these are whistleblower protections, but they can include any well-publicized complaint process.

- Providing informal counseling can help employees understand whether a misuse of power has occurred before they decide to formally file a complaint. Counselors can include ombudspersons, as well as problem-specific specialists such as sexual harassment counselors.

- Since holding power can so often cloud judgment, one way to help guard against misuse of your own power is to apply **The Mom Test**: If you explained your actions to your mother, would she approve? Mom is not a fool, and if she would disapprove of your actions, that should be a warning that others also would not approve.

SOURCES OF ORGANIZATIONAL POWER AND POLITICS

Those seeking to exercise power need to diagnose the potential sources of power that might be available to them. Inexperienced managers too often assume some sources provide more power than they really do, while neglecting others with valuable potential. Similarly, some organizational circumstances foster active managerial politicking while others tend to suppress it. Too often managers do not recognize the organizational conditions that produce more active politicking, and they instead jump to the conclusion that personalities are to blame. In this section some of the most widely used sources of organizational power and the situations that lead to active organizational politicking are described.

Power Comes from Dependence

Much power arises out of dependence.[29] That is, people, teams, and organizations have power over others to the degree that those others depend on them for something they want. That dependence may be obvious, such as employees' dependence on employers for rent and food money. Dependence can also be less obvious, as when factory managers depend on highly skilled mechanics to keep machines running. In workplaces, everyone depends on others. For example, employees depend on their managers to obtain resources and protection from unreasonable demands needed to do their jobs, managers depend on their employees' willingness to pitch in and help when a new challenge arises, and all are dependent on the organization's prosperity for their paychecks. Mutual dependence on others is inherent in organizations, even though some may have relatively more power than others. Absolute organizational power is very rare in our societies; even the less dependent party has some potential power in most relationships. This means the diagnosis of dependencies is central to effectively building and exercising power.

A practical implication is that people, teams, and organizations can seek to increase their power by reducing their dependence on others.[30] The less dependent people are on others, the more power they have to do what they want the way they want to do it. For example, a sales associate may want to spend more time calling on clients rather than writing reports used by the marketing department. Increasing others' dependence on you and reducing your own dependence are central to many effective political tactics, as detailed below.

Scarcity Leads to Politicking

All those doing organizational work depend on resources such as skilled employees, tools, and support staff. When resources are abundant and everyone can get most of what they want, there is little need to exercise power. However, the scarcer the resources, the more people will politick to ensure themselves a share of those limited resources. For example, in a study of budget allocations to university departments, those departments most pinched for resources engaged in the most politicking.[31] Daniel Katz and Robert Kahn argued that resource scarcity is one of the primary reasons organizations seek to grow: Larger organizations mean more managerial positions for the ambitious, larger organizational budgets, and so less aggressive politicking among managers for resources.[32] When executives have sufficient resources to get their work done, there is less need to argue, plot, and seek to persuade. By the same token, declining sales, budget cuts, and other resource reductions will produce more active politicking.

Conflict Leads to Politicking

Division of labor is inherent in large, complex organizations, and dividing labor breeds conflicts. Division of labor is rarely simple and clear cut: Different divisions and departments can be created by product, processes, geography, or anything else.[33] This means most managers can make a case for a different division of labor. Managers will seek to incorporate staff resources in their own group to ensure more reliable and speedy service, and others will seek to rid themselves of difficult and unpromising tasks while trying to acquire promising new ones. These conflicts over tasks and goals are popularly called **turf battles**. Turf battles are inherent anytime an organization's undertaking is divided in ways that allow the specialization and accountability necessary to get large-scale, complex work done. The more organizations change, the more often work needs to be re-divided, and so the more turf battles.

In addition, divided labor creates departments and teams with different perspectives and goals, and so efforts among managers to have their own perspectives and goals take precedent.[34] There is evidence that even simple job specialization leads people to see management problems in different ways, skewing their arguments toward their own training and experience.[35] For example, strategic challenges tend to be seen as operations problems by manufacturing managers and as financial problems by finance managers. Goal setting for accountability means that different people can have conflicting goals. To illustrate, the marketers at a publishing house may want to continue publishing books that rely on their established marketing channels, but the editors may want to take advantage of a new opportunities where they believe there is more growth potential. The marketers will bear the costs of learning about these new markets and building new marketing channels in unfamiliar areas. Both are doing the jobs they were assigned, jobs that have led them to pursue goals that now conflict with one another, conflicts that need to be resolved through political processes.

These political processes are not some dysfunction that needs to be fixed. In fact, suppressing these political processes can lead to poorer organizational performance. Paul Lawrence and Jay Lorsch found that organizations that tried to reduce politicking by reducing division of labor had poorer performance than those that kept their professionals highly specialized and focused yet developed effective political processes to integrate information and settle differences.[36] Political processes also help bring useful information to decision makers. If power is too lopsided (one department is too powerful), it means that valuable expertise and knowledge from other departments were not fully considered, leading to poor strategic decisions. Kathleen Eisenhardt found that executive teams in start-up high-technology firms that more effectively managed their executives' politicking prospered, while those who could not effectively manage their inherent conflicts failed.[37] The successful firms used the following processes.

Application -- Manage Conflicting Views

- Focus on facts and measure as much as possible. As one chief executive said, "Everyone is entitled to a personal opinion, but not to personal facts." In this way the executives could focus on what the facts might mean, rather than quibble about one another's unsubstantiated guesses about the facts.

- Deliberately develop multiple alternatives. The successful start-ups considered four or five options at once, focusing executive attention on creating combinations rather than clinging to their support of, or opposition to, one proposal.

- Keep attention in executive committee meetings focused on the common organizational goal rather than on individual personal or unit goals that might be in competition with one another.

- Make the chief executive powerful, but not all powerful. When others had significant participation in decisions with relatively more influence in their own areas of expertise, and when the chief executive did not shrink from taking ultimate responsibility, the conflicts produced productive exchanges of information and less rigidity.

- Make decisions with **consensus with qualification**. First, attempt to reach consensus (all agree on a decision), but if consensus cannot be achieved rather quickly, the responsible executive makes the decision. In this way different perspectives are fully discussed and understood, but the organization is not paralyzed trying to achieve a complete agreement that may never come.

Ambiguity and Uncertainty Lead to Politicking

As we saw in Chapter 7, ambiguity can be extremely distressing.[38] Those working in organizations must take some kind of action in the face of uncertainty, and so others with explanations that reduce ambiguity become more influential. This means that many will submit to others' influence for reassurance that reduces uncertainty.[39] If others appear to be very confident, and we are uncertain, we are more likely to be persuaded.[40] Uncertainty and ambiguity foster politicking, and the greater the ambiguity, the more people report that others politick for self-serving reasons[41] and that others threaten and intimidate them more.[42]

Ambiguity and uncertainty in organizations can come from many sources. Sometimes departments can have overlapping responsibilities,[43] or the work itself may be uncertain, as when unproven technologies need to be developed, or new materials need to be used.[44] Ambiguity also arises when organizations face rapid changes.[45] Since the more strategic the work, the more uncertainty there is about exactly what should be done, it isn't surprising that we find that the higher a manager's rank, the more managers see politics and politicking as a normal part of their jobs.[46] Whatever the cause, the more ambiguity and uncertainty, the more managerial time spent politicking.

Centralized Power Reduces Politicking

When there is highly **centralized power**, one person or group has dominating power over others, and more decisions are made at higher organizational levels. Centralized power has the benefit of reducing active politicking among managers and employees.[47] There is no need to work to influence those who do not control anything you want. Taken to the extreme, highly centralized power leads to a form of organizational politics called **palace politics**, in which politicking consists of everyone struggling to get the ear and favor of one all-powerful boss.[48]

While centralized power reduces managerial and employee politicking, it often leads to poor organizational performance in all but the smallest and simplest organizations.[49] The one dominating leader cannot know all relevant information for complex work nor monitor the work of numerous differing specialists, which means that the larger the organization, and the more complex the work, the more likely the person with dominating power is to lack relevant information. What is more, when power is highly centralized, the only security for employees is to retain the favor of the dominating leader, turning employees into ingratiating courtiers rather than managers with the confidence to report relevant information. In most modern performance-focused organizations power is dispersed to foster better organizational performance.

When executives at higher levels delegate power over certain decisions to a department or business unit, this is called **decentralization**. Then individual managers delegate power over certain decisions or provide more autonomy to their subordinate employees. This is called **empowerment**.[50] Decentralization and empowerment lead to higher team and organizational performance by moving decisions down to where the information is, rather than waiting while questions and recommendations slowly move up and down the hierarchy.[51] Empowerment also is motivating. This makes the boxed inset opinion is false: Power is not fixed but can expand or contract based on how well it is managed.[52] Power that is delegated and subordinates who have been empowered do not reduce the power of executives and managers. They can always step in and reverse the poor decisions of subordinates or rescind their power if it was used ineffectively.

> ***True or False?***
>
> *Power is fixed; what I give away I can never get back.*

Decentralization and empowerment are necessary for effective organizational performance, but they do require a more active management of political processes to share information and make decisions. Those now empowered to make decisions must have the necessary information about the organization's goals and how their decisions might affect others. Empowerment needs to be managed through establishing systems of communication, accountability, and political processes for decision making.

Application -- Successful Empowerment[53]

- Decentralization and empowerment require investments in moving information to where it is needed. This means more downward communication of the organization's strategic goals and marketplace challenges, as well as more committees and meetings among peers in which information can be exchanged. Meetings are the price of decentralization and empowerment.

- Decentralization and empowerment must be supported by systems to ensure accountability: job descriptions, goal setting, feedback, and active problem solving.

- Executives need to recognize that with more dispersed information, political systems for making decisions need to be established. If all disputes are simply brought back to the boss, this is a reversion to palace politics and runs the risk of incomplete information and poor performance. Better to establish committees, other open forums for presenting information, and clear decision rules, such as consensus with qualification, to manage the politicking.

Some Enjoy Politicking More Than Others Do

Finally, some seek power and politick simply because they enjoy it; they see every situation as an opportunity to roll logs, trade horses, and bargain hard. Others avoid politicking. We have already learned that those with a higher Need for Power are more successful as managers.[54] In addition, those occupying more powerful positions tend to be those who prefer autonomy, are more gregarious and enthusiastic, and enjoy fostering enthusiasm in others. They are less likely to be conscientious and easygoing or to let well enough alone.[55] Yet, again, situations do matter: Extraverts were more influential in team-based organizations, while the more conscientious attained greater influence when organizational work was based on technical tasks.[56] While these personality differences are not nearly as important as situations are in determining why people seek to exercise power,[57] they do serve as a reminder that those who are uncomfortable exercising power might not be effective as managers, roles in which politicking is a job requirement.

Just as individuals differ in their preferences to exercise power, so can they differ in their preferred ways of exercising power. While there is a great deal of research on the different types of tactics individuals habitually use, usually called their influence styles, such work is of limited practical use. This is so for several reasons. First, there have been problems identifying individuals' influence styles; people really do vary their tactics by the situation and so report different styles for different situations. Second, we are not reliable reporters of our own influence styles, consistently reporting that we use more socially acceptable tactics than what others who observe us report.[58] We already saw that people can misperceive how others see them, and when it comes to something as sensitive and vague as political tactics, self-enhancement bias can be strong. Third, influence-style political tactics should and usually do vary by circumstances: Different relationships, settings, and issues all mean that different tactics would best fit the influence challenge at hand. For example, researchers disagree about whether women are more likely to successfully use influence styles that better match expectations for their gender roles.[59] A few studies show that women have the same success with the same tactics as men do, while other research finds that women need to confine themselves to gender-expected indirect methods.
This makes the inset boxed opinion true sometimes and false other times. While some people do tend to rely exclusively on certain tactics, more effective managers will be more flexible, adapting their styles and tactics to their situations.

> ***True or False?***
>
> *People have different influence styles.*

Application -- Diagnose Politicking in Your Organization

To repeat: Not all politicking is problematic, so any attempt to understand politicking must start with a careful diagnosis: Why is there politicking in your organization?

- If politicking arises from scarcity, first check to see that scarcity is not imagined or the result of misunderstandings. If scarcity is real, it is best to openly acknowledge it and develop clear procedures about how allocation decisions will be made. In this way, scarcity is handled in a legitimate, taken-for-granted way, rather than through escalating paranoia and defensive politicking.

- If politicking arises from conflicts, work to reduce departmental identification with teams or departments and increase organization-wide identification through cross-unit socializing, transfers, and rewards tied to organizational goal achievement.

- If politicking arises from ambiguity, first check to see if the ambiguity can be removed with clearer job descriptions or procedures. If not, develop explicit procedures for how decisions get made under uncertainty.

- If politicking arises from dispersed power, develop and explain the formal policies and practices for reconciling differences and the rationales for them.

- If politicking arises from personal desire to politick, a judgment is in order: If the person creates purely self-serving or self-indulgent conflicts that serve no useful organizational purpose, one way to eliminate the behavior is to alert everyone else to the actions. Once everyone understands that someone's actions are self indulgent, self serving, and manipulative, these actions rarely will be effective. Finally, since politicking can engage emotions, create frustrations, and make many people uncomfortable, be sure that your own personal discomfort with politicking is not blinding you to the possibly valuable roles these activities are playing in your organization.

WHY DO ANOTHER'S BIDDING

The final diagnostic foundation for the effective use of power is an understanding of why people willingly do what they otherwise would not have done. If you want to get people to do something they would not otherwise have done, you need to know why they would do it. There is no question that in doing organizational work, most willingly submit without a fuss to others' power. Why should that be? After all, psychologists are convinced that we all seek to gain the freedom of action that power can bring.[60] There is a substantial literature documenting why people let themselves be influenced by others. First, there is no personality or individual difference that makes some people more susceptible to influence than others,[61] making the inset opinion false.

> ***True or False?***
>
> *Some people are easy to influence.*

To Get the Organization's Work Done

We submit to others' power because it leads to better organizational performance, or improved services to clients. Everyone understands what happens when the left organizational hand does not know what the right hand is doing. When it makes sense, submitting to legitimate power is necessary to coordination and organizational performance. **Legitimate power** is power that everyone involved accepts as right and appropriate. When power is legitimate, others will voluntarily defer to it, even when it is not in their self interest.[62] Authority, when allocated according to known rules and for reasons everyone believes are necessary, is an example of power that is accepted without thought; it is legitimate. Organizations have hierarchies because they are quicker and more efficient political systems than politicking over every little decision.

In practice, this means that managers are expected to exercise their formal authority, that is, to make decisions about how to adapt to the unexpected and to reallocate resources when necessary. When those with formal authority do not take action, they create a **power vacuum**, leading to employee distress and poorer unit performance.[63] As needed political work does not get done, others step in to try to exercise power, but since they lack legitimacy, their decisions are not accepted by all. Some may resist or may contend for power themselves, leading to time consumed in politicking rather than in getting the work done. Anyone who has lived through power vacuums knows how unpleasant and frustrating they can be.

To Be Liked

Most of us want to be liked, and one way to make ourselves more likeable is to submit to that person's influence.[64] In our closest relationships we are more likely to be mutually influential. We want to be liked by those we like, and we tend to assume that those we like are more knowledgeable.[65] Making yourself likeable is a common political tactic for those with few resources; being seen as likeable, warm, and charming is a way to gain relative power that anyone can use.

> ***True or False?***
>
> *People care more about being accurate than they do about being liked.*

In a similar way, we submit to another's influence in order to reduce interpersonal conflict.[66] The more our opinions and beliefs are in conflict with those around us, the more distress we experience. Holding the same attitudes, opinions, beliefs, and theories about our workplaces as those of our coworkers is reassuring and calming. For many people, more often than they care to admit, the boxed inset opinion is false.

One way to make ourselves likeable is through **impression management**, or trying to present a positive image of ourselves to others. Virtually all social interaction involves presenting public versions of ourselves and trying to persuade others that they should accept our presentation.[67] Impression management dominates much social interaction, and the only time we are not concerned with strategic self presentation is when we are overcome by emotion, are highly involved in the task at hand, or doing highly ritualized tasks such as ordering a drink on an airplane. We all usually choose our words so as not to offend, and we know that impression management is considered a normal and expected part of social interaction.[68] People seek to manage others' impressions of them because it works. For example, those who more actively managed their impressions were more likely to attain promotions and seats on boards of directors.[69]

Impression management tactics and strategies have been widely studied. Examples include the use of ingratiation, excuses and justifications to repair bad impressions, apologies, and self handicapping to manage others' performance expectations, civility, and much more.[70] These techniques can get quite sophisticated, such as deliberately making mistakes to avoid additional work, broadcasting your limitations to others so you won't have to take the time to help them, and threatening lawsuits to get what you want. Another example of sophisticated impression management is strategic conversation for political advantage, as described below:

Application -- Manage Impressions in Conversation

- Those who speak first can often set the agenda and lead the conversation.
- Persistence matters: The number of times a point of view is expressed influences others' adoption of that view, even when only one person keeps repeating it.[71]
- Most nonverbal behaviors reflect quick emotional reactions and so are seen as more sincere; be aware of how others are reading your nonverbal reactions.
- When reporting an action that could be seen as bizarre, you can undercut the impression that you are crazy by introducing it with a rational disclaimer that undercuts the craziness impression. For example, "You might think I am crazy, but I think we should stop advertising on television."
- As we saw in Chapter 7, majorities tend to produce conformity, so asking for others' open support before a meeting can help produce majority conformity pressures.

Why Defiance?

Of course, submission to others' power can never be taken for granted. Defiance and resistance are as common as deference,[72] and those seeking to wield power need to be sensitive to signs of resistance. Who is likely to be defiant, and when might we expect others to defy attempts to influence them? Defiance and resistance can include overt acts (such as sabotage) and indirect defiance (such as neglecting to take action or report a problem). Resistance in organizations can be targeted directly at those holding the unwelcome power, but because this can be risky, resistance also takes the indirect form of wearing inappropriate clothes, strictly following the rules to slow work down, or taking extra time in the bathroom.[73] Interestingly, Blake Ashforth found that because managers identified more strongly with their organizations than other employees did, they were more likely to engage in indirect resistance, while production workers were more likely to take the direct route of complaining, criticizing, and arguing.[74] This means that those working with professionals and managers need to be particularly sensitive to indirect signs of resistance.

What leads to defiance or resistance? When power is legitimately acquired, wielded fairly, and kept within legitimate bounds, there is less chance of defiance.[75] The holding of power illegitimately is a primary cause of organizational defiance or resistance. Finally, those seeking to wield power will not welcome resistance and defiance, but these acts are central to the adaptation of organizations to changes in their environments. If those with more power are wrong, resistance prevents organizational failure. Acts of resistance can precipitate organizations' adaptations to environmental changes.[76] And, of course, everyone working in organizations will want to resist others' influence attempts sometimes in their organizational careers.

Application -- Successful Resistance[77]

- Careful diagnosis is required: What means and resources can you use to resist? What are others' perceptions and expectations? Who will support you and who may not?
- It is more effective to identify a particular issue and keep focused on it. No one can get practical work done by opposing something as vague as "the system."
- Is it possible to resist within the rules? Are there formal grievance procedures or other legitimate resources available?
- Successful resistance requires that you debunk the reasons others have for not joining you. Rationalizations for inaction can be powerful.
- Unceasing pressure is necessary; don't give up. However, individual tactics that drag on too long are not effective.
- Tactics need to be adapted as the situation changes.
- Have specific solutions or counterproposals; if your target is persuaded, you need to be ready with a constructive, realistic alternative.
- Organized resistance requires clear communication: Everyone must understand the objectives and strategies.
- Others must have confidence in your eventual success. If people do not think resistance will be effective, they simply will not think about it.
- Compromise is one of your most valuable tools: It is a concrete victory and can buy time so you can regroup and plan.

POLITICAL STRATEGIES AND TACTICS

Because the effective exercise of power is so critical to a managers' job performance and is so often mismanaged, here practical approaches to exercising power are introduced. Scholars have developed an endless list of political strategies and tactics.[78] Some of the most management-relevant ones are discussed below.

Solve Others' Most Important Problems

> ***True or False?***
>
> *Nice guys finish last.*

This is an approach that always works. It does not rely on deception or intimidation and works as well when everyone knows what you are doing as when they do not. It allows its practitioners to prove the inset management opinion false. **Strategic Contingencies Theory** proposes that the extent to which a person, function, or department solves the organization's most important problems (what those scholars called their strategic contingencies), the greater the power the person or department will have in that organization.[79] For example, some organizations, such as personal-care consumer products, operate in very competitive markets with little real difference between products (think: toothpaste). In these organizations marketing helps solve their most important problem by discovering trends, developing marketing campaigns, and getting consumers to pick their products off the store shelf rather than their competitors' product. In personal-care consumer product companies, marketing will have more power than other divisions. This is reflected in marketing's relatively larger budgets and the presence of fellow marketers in top executive positions.[80] In contrast, a large state research university does not have much difficulty attracting undergraduates to enroll because it is comparatively inexpensive for state residents. Most such universities can predict undergraduate enrollment a decade in advance based on the birth rates in their states and other historical patterns. Attracting undergraduates is not an important problem for these universities, and those responsible for attracting and enrolling undergraduates rarely obtain executive positions or high pay for their work. The important problem for large state research universities is money. In practice, most of their money comes from the research grants that faculty scientists bring to their campuses. These scientists get a disproportionate amount of their respective university's resources, and university presidents who began as scientists are common, but those who began in admissions or marketing are rare.[81]

The logic of Strategic Contingencies' Theory is straightforward: If someone is solving your most important problems, if someone is the one that you depend on for your survival or success, then that is a person, or group of people, to keep happy at all costs. If they quit and go work for your competitor, you are sunk. If they demand a lot, well, you don't really have much choice but to give them what they demand. And research supports giving them what they want: If the department or person who solves those most important problems has the most power in

> ***True or False?***
>
> *Them that has, gets.*

that organization, the organization's performance is better.[82] It is no surprise that there is ample research evidence supporting Strategic Contingencies' Theory, stated in its crudest form in the boxed inset management opinion.[83] Those who solve others' most important problems gain organizational power.

Solving others' most important problems directs attention to several practical actions:

- You need to solve others' most important problems, not the problems you are best at solving. Too many complain that their work is not appreciated. If what you do isn't appreciated, maybe it really isn't that important to others. Focus your diagnosis on what the organization (or people you wish to influence) believe to be their most important problems, the ones critical to their survival.

- Others are dependent on you to the extent that they **need** what you can do (they need their most important problems solved) and they lack **alternatives** to you. Dependence is based on both: The organization may need what you can do, but if it has many alternative problem solvers, you will not have a great deal of power. For example, organizations need to have their accounts kept according to accepted accounting standards, but licensed accountants are plentiful, and so they rarely have great power outside professional accounting organizations. Similarly, we all need food, but it is easily found in widely accessible grocery stores and restaurants, so any one grocery or restaurant has little power.

- If you want to wield power over others, the most effective and least risky way is to find ways to solve their most important problems.

Most recognize this method of solving others' most important problems, because they have seen its effects in practice in their own organizations. But this knowledge has not led to most people occupying positions of great power in their organizations. If it is so obvious, why isn't everyone using it? Certainly many choose to do the work they love, regardless of whether it makes them indispensable to others. However, because power is an essential tool of management, managers need to find ways to solve others' important problems if they are to do their jobs well. You may not be able to solve the organization's most important problems, but you can solve the problems of peers, subordinates, bosses, and that one very important department. The key is a careful diagnosis and creativity in solving others' important problems.

An example of the kind of diagnoses and creativity involved in effectively using this method is the story of United States President Lyndon Johnson and the Little Congress.[84] Lyndon Johnson arrived in Congress in 1931, one of 435 representatives in an organization that rewarded seniority with committee chairmanships and other access to power and resources. Lyndon Johnson didn't want to wait 30 years to reach a powerful position and so looked for opportunities. He noticed that with the Great Depression, government became more active than it had been before. There was a flurry of proposed new legislation, legislation that could have far-ranging effects on many people. This meant that the newspapers wanted to get the latest information about important pending legislation. He also noticed that there was an organization for the staff members of the elected representatives called the Little Congress. It provided staff training but was seen primarily as a place for staff members to socialize. However, Lyndon Johnson saw Little Congress's potential. Since few cared about this organization, he easily got himself elected its speaker and added speeches and discussions about pending legislation (which staff members develop). Then, he invited newspaper reporters. The reporters were happy to get the latest inside information about the pending legislation of interest to their readers. Once reporters began writing stories about what they heard in Little Congress meetings, powerful senior representatives and senators, who always want to see their names in newspapers, clamored to get on the agenda. Who controlled the agenda of speakers for Little Congress meetings? Lyndon Johnson. He traded these speaking opportunities for favors and influence, and Little Congress was the beginning of his extensive Washington, D. C., power base. His success was based on a careful diagnosis of who depended on whom for their most important problems and creatively putting together solutions for those that he controlled. Some of the questions you can ask yourself as you seek to build power through building others' dependence on you.

Application -- Diagnose Others' Important Problems

- What do you want to accomplish?
- On whom are you dependent for achieving this?
- Why?
- What are their points of view likely to be?
- Which ones are the most influential?
- On whom and what are they dependent?
- Why?
- How can you help solve their important problems?

Have Valued Resources

One of most frequent ways that managers can solve others' most important problems is through providing them with the resources they need to get their work done. The possession of resources has long been recognized as an important source of organizational power.[85] Resources can be used to do better work, and they can be traded with others for their support, as when a manager loans professionals to peers to help them get through a heavy work load.

Interestingly, you don't need a lot of resources to gain power. Relatively small amounts of **discretionary resources**, that is, uncommitted resources that can be used freely, can be a source of power in organizations.[86] This happens because most of an organization's budget is already committed, projects have been promised multi-year funding, necessary employees must be paid, and so forth. Yet, as everyone can always use a little extra, say, those loaned employees, they can quickly come to expect them as a standard. Managers' own larger budgets may be relatively stable, but because those loaned employees can be taken away at any time, the manager providing them can assume greater power than the higher-level executive providing the department's large budget.

Information technology is an example of a once discretionary resource that has quickly become a necessity. Of course, information itself is a valuable resource in organizations,[87] putting information systems at the center of power in most organizations. Because information is critical, and much of is stored and delivered electronically, the design of information systems is a common cause of turf battles in organizations. For example, the movement of information about customer buying patterns to corporate headquarters via electronic data collection reduces the power of store managers over ordering merchandise for their stores. Similarly, because keeping information systems up and running is so important to departmental and organizational performance, the location of information technology support becomes a critical resource for managers. Managers ask themselves, "Do I have sufficient information technology support personnel in my department?" or, "Must I beg for service from an overwhelmed central support office?" No managers are fooled by soothing language about the benefits of improved services from consolidating such a critical service in corporate headquarters. Such consolidations of services are almost always intended to save money by reduced services. Managers seeking to deliver good performance will try to control all of the resources necessary to deliver that performance, and information systems are often critical to that performance. This is why so many information technology professionals, who may have no interest in power or politics, find themselves in the middle of difficult organizational politicking.

Application -- Information Systems and Politicking

- Managers' first political acts usually are to seek authority over the information processing resource (the service reports to them) or have sufficient budget and permission to directly purchase the service from outside vendors. This provides the most reliable supply of the resource.

- Failing that, managers will seek to assert influence over those who provide the critical resources through tactics such as ingratiation, seeking to solve the service providers' most important problems, managing impressions about the criticality of their need (that is, screaming the loudest), and so forth. Being the target of this onslaught from powerful managers can be very stressful to central information service providers, and so executives will seek to buffer their centralized providers by making communication difficult, for example, by requiring that requests must be made only by e-mail.

- Astute managers recognize that reorganizations involving critical information services pose a direct threat to their ability to control the resources needed to do their jobs well, and they will politick to ensure they have reliable service provision in any reorganization.

Be an Expert

In addition to resources, knowledge useful to the solutions of others' most important problems is an important resource that can be deployed to gain power. Organizations depend on specialized knowledge of all sorts to get work done. There is substantial evidence that those departments (and individuals) providing the most important irreplaceable knowledge (high need with no alternatives) are most powerful in their organizations.[88] Such powerful employees can be difficult to manage.[89] Prima donnas can get more of what they want, whether that is longer breaks, more pay, or more administrative support. All of the authority and resources managers control can be more than counterbalanced by the prima-donna employee's ability to solve important problems.

Sometimes managers find they need expertise that is not available in their organizations, so they hire outside experts for advice or temporary assistance. However, if such expertise is critical to solving important organizational problems, outside experts will be pulled into politicking. Jeffrey Pfeffer argued that outside experts, or consultants, are often used by managers as a political tactic.[90] Even the most technical of outside consultants have jobs that force them to manage the politicking of those who will be affected by their recommendations. This is why consulting is often highly politicized work. In practice, outside consultants find themselves making political misjudgments because they lack knowledge of the local relationships and situations in their client organizations. For example, consultants working in more centralized manufacturing industries develop a business model based on discovering what chief executives want and making sure that goal is central to their recommendations. However, this model does not work in organizations such as hospitals or law firms, where the most prominent professionals can hold more power than the chief executives. These powerful professionals are as likely to publicly mock a consultant's report repeating the chief executive's pet ideas as they are to defer to the consultant's expertise.

Application -- Use Outside Consultants Effectively

- Consultants will be used more for new threats to the survival of the organization. Here outside expertise genuinely is needed, and knowledgeable consultants can recommend a set of actions to take in the face of paralyzing uncertainty.

- Consultants will be used for advice on policy matters when power is dispersed in the organization. In organizations with highly centralized power the dominant person has no need to rely on outside expert power to get things done.

- When power is dispersed and balanced in the organization, and the major parties are in disagreement, consultants can be called in to break the deadlock.

- If expertise already exists in the organization, and there is no deadlock, consultants should not be used. Outside consultants retained under these circumstances reflect serious organizational dysfunction.

- Because consultants can make recommendations that fundamentally change the jobs and careers of executives, the hiring of consultants usually is something controlled by the most powerful.

Create Social Capital

Social relationships are an important source of power. Social relationships become **social capital** when they are mobilized for a purpose. For example, friends become social capital when they make a recommendation for a job at their organizations, and colleagues become social capital when they share information about how to use the new enterprise management software. Social capital is valuable: Organizations that employ executives who have good social relationships with their clients are more profitable than those that do not; social capital is especially important for entrepreneurial companies.[91] Those who have good relationships with their bankers do not lose as much on their investments as other clients do,[92] and managers who have more social relationships with a variety of colleagues have better job performance than those who do not.[93] People are more likely to help their friends, as the Beatles' lyric in the inset box says.[94] Of course, friendship is not one-way exploitation: Francis Flynn found that those engineers who both gave and accepted help were the most productive (and the most respected).[95]

> ***True or False?***
>
> *I get by with a little help from my friends.*

However, helping friends is not the only value of social capital. Social capital also provides access to the rich informal information that will not appear in written reports. Most people will not provide sensitive information unless they trust the recipient, and a personal relationship is a reliable way to build trust. Managers are especially dependent on this flow of nuanced information, making building social capital important to their job performance. Further, for those with little opportunity to solve others' important problems on their own, gathering the support of others and forming alliances is a reliable way to gain power.

Application -- Build Alliances[96]

- Allies outside the organization are less likely to be competing for the same organizational resources, but outside alliances must be used with great finesse in most organizations, since few welcome being lobbied by outsiders on internal organizational matters.

- The advantage of internal organizational allies are that they are more likely to have influence and are more legitimate than outside allies, but they may be less willing to help you if they see you as a threat or competitor. Earning others' trust is critical to building alliances.

- Organizational alliances can be built on common interests; when these are not available, those with minority interests can bundle their divergent interests together into one proposal that contains all individual proposals.

- One of the most useful political skills is the ability to see the organization from another's perspective (that is, to have empathy) and so be able to frame your desired outcome as serving another's interests. For example, in many organizations executives fear litigation, and so legal departments can shut down many organizational practices by evoking this fear.

- Organizational alliances are usually much bigger than the minimum necessary to gain support. Implementation requires widespread support in organizations, and no one wants to feel cut out of important decisions. When building organizational alliances, don't overlook anyone.[97]

As useful as allies are, restricting yourself to working only with your friends has a cost: fewer new ideas and opportunities and poorer performance.[98] Those who only work with those they already know learn less, and the social capital they can call on for assistance is more limited. It is better to have bridging social relationships with many others. There is strong evidence that those who have **bridging social capital** have higher job performance.[99] Those who have bridging social capital serve as a link (or bridge) between those with no other connection to others. Those with bridging social capital provide that rich informal information that people otherwise would not get. If the information is useful, that means the bridging person is the only one providing something valuable, that is, solving others' important problems. Bridging social capital is built by going places to meet new people, joining task forces and committees, attending company social events, and joining associations of all kinds.

Hold Formal Positions of Authority

There is no question that holding formal positions with the right to dictate others' actions matters.[100] This legitimate power is not a result of dependence on a supervisor (although that may be added, just to be safe) but is the result of an acceptance that such power is right and correct. It is unthinking power. The legitimate power of authority means there is less need for active politicking; formal authority is the quickest and least stressful form of power. Saying, "because the boss said so" settles a lot of issues. Because authority is such a common source of power, it goes without notice much of the time, except when opportunities arise to amass authority.

Because new chief executives often make changes in an organization's strategy and act to replace other senior executives with those loyal to their own vision, executive succession is one of the most politicized of organizational decisions. Research has documented some of the tactics found in succession politicking.[101]

Application -- The Politics of Executive Succession

- Those who can make the most credible claims that they can solve the organizations' most important problems tend to be made chief executive; this means that the choice of chief executive usually reflects what the governance board believes to be the organization's most important problems.

- Chief executives are key to organizational adaptations to major environmental shifts, so outsiders are most often appointed chief executives when the board believes the organization is failing.

- Chief executives will often replace existing senior executives with those they believe are loyal to their own policies (or themselves); replacements are more widespread if the chief executive was brought in from the outside. This means that appointing new chief executives leads managers to be preoccupied with their survival (or finding their next jobs) for a year or more.

- New chief executives from the outside are more likely to initiate significant organizational changes and more likely to have difficulty implementing those changes because they and their new loyalists lack knowledge of relationships and power bases in the organization.

Authority rarely is as straightforward is many might hope. As noted above, managers' formal authority usually is insufficient to the work they need to accomplish. Interestingly, the reverse is also true: Those in positions of authority can have influence far beyond the formal authority assigned to the position.[102] Laboratory subjects have given deadly electric shocks to others if told to do so by a person in authority and students randomly assigned as prison guards bullied, while those students assigned to be prisoners cowered and grew fearful. Authority like all power is rarely unambiguous.

Because authority can be ambiguous, people search for cues about who has authority: Who has the best office or the best furniture? The person running the meeting conventionally sits at the head of the table, and so sitting at the head of the table suggests authority. Because territory can reflect power, politicking over workplace territory can be fierce.[103] Much of the politicking about offices, parking spaces, windows and the like, what is called **petty office politics**, is really politicking over symbols of authority. Given its ambiguity, these signals can be important. Since the meanings of symbols of authority and power are culture specific, interpreting symbols of power in different cultures is one of the challenges of globalization.

Application -- Interpret Symbols of Power

- In high power distance cultures those with more power are expected to act the part: haughty, disdainful of inferiors, giving commands. This can be very offensive to people from low power distance cultures who feel that their essential dignity as human beings is being disrespected.
- In low power distance cultures those with more power are expected to act as equals to those with less power, with similar demeanor, styles of dress, and use of first names. This can be very confusing to people from high power distance cultures, since they can mistakenly interpret egalitarian managers as weak and powerless.
- The meanings of symbols of relative power such as offices, clothing, and demeanor do not mean the same things in other cultures, requiring great care in diagnosis when working in a foreign culture.

Write (and Avoid) the Rules

A powerful political tactic in organizations involves controlling the rules, budgets, and job descriptions that constrain actions in organizations. **Rules** are decisions made in advance, written instructions about what to do in a particular situation. Written rules are necessary to decentralization and empowerment because they are vital to making sure actions in large complex organizations are coordinated. Most comply with rules unthinkingly; people search for direction when they are uncertain about what to do, and rules are formal attempts to provide that guidance. Like centralized power, rules reduce politicking. Rules say what should be done by whom and are often accepted unthinkingly. After all, the primary alternative to written rules is constant surveillance and politicking. This means the inset boxed management opinion is false: Without rules large organizations would grind to a halt. Of course, some rules might be outdated. However, astute managers know that superficially nonsensical rules may be serving some organizational purpose that executives have not done a good job of explaining or may not want to explain.

> ***True or False?***
>
> *The rules prevent us from getting any work done.*

The authority to write rules, structure and restructure organizations, and write job descriptions are important sources of legitimate power.[104] The power to write the rules is usually carefully guarded, available only to those who are solving important problems, as asserted in the inset boxed opinion. However, everyone is free to learn the rules. For those working in large bureaucracies, understanding the many rules and how they are created and changed can be an important source of power. For example, a skilled manager learns the rules for job reclassifications in order to redesign high-performing employees' jobs so that the job can be reclassified into a higher pay grade, thus earning the gratitude of valuable employees.

> ***True or False?***
>
> *Those who have the gold make the rules.*

If politically astute managers cannot write the rules, they will seek to leave them unwritten. Those who are unconstrained by rules have more scope for personal discretion. Rules, strictly enforced, are a primary means of constraining the powerful.[105] One way to avoid such constraints on your actions is through purposeful ambiguity in their communication. Such **strategic ambiguity** means that the message has been purposefully left unclear, allowing it to be interpreted many different ways.[106] Eric Eisenberg argues that strategic ambiguity provides deniability (if something goes wrong), and makes it easier to change direction without seeming to be inconsistent. Avoiding the constraint of rules and clear public commitments is a common tactic of those seeking absolute power, as is reflected in the quotation in the inset box is from Nikita Khrushchev of the Soviet Union.[107]

> ***True or False?***
>
> *Who's the boss: the law or we? We are masters over the law, not the law over us.*

Control the Agenda

In organizations one of the most effective political tactics is to seek to control the agenda, that is, help shape what gets considered and when. Managers can influence expectations about what is feasible, what can be accomplished in the current difficult budget environment, and in many other ways influence which issues are noticed and discussed. For example, much organizational works gets done in meetings and committees. This means that those who set the agendas for those groups also control what gets debated and decided. One tactic is to put issues you don't want to resolve or address at the bottom of a lengthy meeting agenda. In most meetings the participants speak at length on the first few agenda items, using up valuable time. Those chairing meetings could cut off lengthy speeches and remind everyone that there are important issues to come, but they don't have to do this. Other participants don't have the legitimacy to cut off others' conversation and so sit in frustration as time is wasted on less important issues.

Committees often serve political as well as purely information and decision purposes. When power is dispersed, and broad support is needed, a tactic to build support is to staff committees with those whose support is critical to the potential success of the project. Members of the committee have more influence over the shape of the proposal, but in turn they will have publicly committed themselves to any decision coming out of their committee. In this way they are **co-opted**, or won over by their involvement in the decision process.

Application -- Use Committees Effectively[108]

- In many organizations much real work gets done between meetings where committee members sound out others' support and set up the flow of discussion at meetings. However, make sure this is legitimate in your organization, or you could be disparaged as Machiavellian.

- The smaller the committee, the easier it is for it to work effectively; very large committees (15 or more members) tend to become hierarchical and formal, with most talking done by the high-status members. Committee members who do not feel they have had any real input will not feel committed to its decisions. The larger and more diverse the committee, the more time members must spend together to be able to work effectively.

- Ideally committees are composed only of those who have information directly relevant to the task at hand or whose political support is necessary.

- Committees become frustrating when members' interests are very diverse, when the participants have strong independent power bases, or when some members would prefer that no decision or action be taken and so act to slow down decisions and block action.

- If you find yourself chairing committees that might become contentious, you should learn **Robert's Rules of Order**. These are formal rules of procedure that can be used to prevent individuals from blocking actions the majority wishes to take and can keep business moving in the face of highly emotional politicking. The complete formal procedures need not be followed rigidly in most meetings, but when meetings get ugly, these rules can prevent a meeting from being derailed. The rules can be found at www.robertsrules.org.

- If you find yourself on a committee that exists to publicly demonstrate concern rather than take real action, it will be very frustrating You will work very hard to produce a report that will be buried and forgotten the day it arrives. It will become an opportunity to learn and practice your anger-management and political-diagnostic skills.

Develop Your Political Skills

Political skills do matter. Managers with better **political skills** have better job performance, and their business units have better performance.[109] What are political skills? Gerald Ferris and his colleagues have found that political skills involve:[110]

- Social astuteness, or the ability to understand and read differing social environments. This is used to develop a deep knowledge of particular people, their relationships, and the environments in which they work.
- Knowledge of which tactics to use in a particular situation: what is likely to work, when, and where; when to persuade; when to present facts; and when to seek allies and supporters.
- The ability to build strong friendships, alliance and coalitions.
- Having the trust of others who believe you are sincere and honest.

Political skills are built on the ability to **self monitor**. This is the ability to keep track of how others react to you and to control your own emotions and actions.[111] How did the target of your influence attempt react? Do others see you as sincere or sneaky? Accuracy in reading the social situation and restraining any of your own reactions that could be insulting or threatening to others are important to effective political skills. This knowledge of how others see you and your actions means you can avoid the danger of inaccurately seeing yourself as more politically skilled than you really are. For too many, the inset boxed management opinion is just not true. They misjudge the situation and the relationships or use tactics that backfire. Fortunately, political skills can be learned.

True or False?

I understand how things work around here

Application -- Build Political Skills[112]

- Begin by working to improve your self awareness. Questionnaires asking you to rate your preferences and skills can help, if used with good counselors who can help you reflect and interpret the information. Alone they are much less useful than carefully examining your reactions to events, asking why certain things seem to irritate you, and working to better understand your own and others' reactions.
- Practice (with feedback and reflection) makes perfect. If you have trouble understanding why something occurred (and as a check on the self-flattering biases we all have), try to find someone who can help you interpret and understand what happened.
- Take training in drama. It can help you become more aware of others' reactions to what you do. It teaches you to become aware of yourself as an object and to be more aware of how others read and interpret your actions.

Be Attractive

People will do things for those they find attractive, not because of any calculation of need and alternatives, but because associating with attractive people makes us more attractive.[113] There is substantial evidence that most of us are motivated to be seen as attractive by others. For example, individuals and organizations often seek to mimic those who have an attractive identity they wish to share.[114]

People can be attractive, and so gain power, in any number of ways. One way is through having higher status. Those with high status have more influence.[115] Since those with higher status are assumed to be competent, act with more confidence, and more likely to speak more often and more forcefully, having high status provides a general resource that can be used to get more of what you want.[116] All of the effort to attain higher status is not just mere vanity; higher status results in real ability to get others to do what you want. And status striving is everywhere; for example, studies have documented how status is claimed and asserted, even in e-mail messages. E-mail senders claim status by signature inserts (high-status people have their own phone number and office), shorter messages (high-status people are very busy), and the use of informal salutations and language (only permissible among equals or when higher-status people address lower-status ones).[117]

Another common way to make yourself attractive to someone is through ingratiation. Through **ingratiation** people try to make themselves more attractive to others by trying to please them. Those executives with practice in ingratiation were more likely to be asked to join the boards of other firms; and receive better reviews from security analysis.[118] However, like all political tactics, ingratiation must be done with finesse.

Application -- Judiciously Ingratiate[119]

- Find things in common: People tend to like others who are similar to themselves.
- Agree with their opinions, flatter them, do favors for them, and directly and indirectly promote yourself. Chose actions based on the situation: For example, high-status people are more likely to ingratiate themselves to a lower-status person through flattery than through agreement, and people interviewing for jobs are more likely to use direct self promotion.
- Be sincere; blatant ingratiation will backfire if ulterior motives are suspected. Fortunately, the targets of ingratiation are less likely to see the motives to please in blatant ingratiation than are bystanders.

Persuade

The rational presentation of supportive facts is the most socially acceptable way to politick in most organizations. Everyone wants to believe they will be persuaded by the evidence, and research suggests that the tactic of marshalling facts to support an argument is a more successful approach than arguing without presenting supportive facts or by threatening others.[120] By all means, if you can find facts to support what you want to get done and organize them in a thoughtful way, you should do so.

However, the real challenge is reflected in the all too true inset boxed opinion attributed to Peter Drucker. We all tend to be more attuned to facts that are more favorable to ourselves. We tend to remember arguments that support our own ideas and pay attention to the facts that support our own preferred courses of action.[121] As a practical matter, when there is disagreement, attempts to rationally present supporting facts becomes a war of facts, placing decision makers in the role of a judge trying to sort out the claims and counterclaims. Unfortunately, marshalling the facts rarely is a guaranteed way to get what you want all the time.

True or False?

Most of us can find the facts to support our own positions.

Persuasion is changing another's belief using emotion and argument and can be effective. Chief executives who worked to persuade their institutional investors were able to increase their personal power over their own pay and the company's strategy.[122] Robert Cialdini has summarized a great deal of research on how to harness the science of persuasion.[123]

Application -- Persuasion Is More Effective if ...

- They like you: People are more likely to accept the influence of people they like.
- They see you as similar to themselves: People are more likely to accept influence from those who are more like them.
- You can demonstrate that what you want is consistent with their previous public and voluntary commitments.
- You are seen as an expert: People are more likely to be influenced by those who know more about the subject.
- You can phrase the issue as one in which they can avoid losses: People are more likely to be moved by fear of losses than by the promise of gains.
- They were able to influence you: People tend to reciprocate.

Managers and other professionals often find themselves making presentations. Presentations should always be seen as attempts to persuade others, if not to take a particular action, then to persuade your audience that you are articulate and competent. Too many inexperienced employees and managers miss these persuasion opportunities, loading up their slides with volumes of small-font data, written points that do not track with the oral presentation, and in other ways confuse and irritate audience members rather than persuade them.

Application -- Make Persuasive Presentations[124]

- Grab the audience's attention: What will you be doing? Work on making this short and snappy.
- Be clear about the steps you will follow to get there. Remember that an audience, unlike a reader, does not know whether you are in the middle, almost there, or at the end, so let them know where you are throughout the presentation.
- Select only the data necessary to support your points. Remember that people will focus on the numbers, so do not overwhelm them. If the presentation is a technical one that you are giving to other experts, put tables and charts into handouts that you pass out at the beginning; this will give your audience members time to formulate their disagreements and quibbles, increasing their delight.
- No PowerPoint font smaller than 20 point, ever. Less and larger text is more.
- All major points should appear on a slide. No background or explanation in slides. Use quotations sparingly, and never use a long quotation.
- All graphs, charts, and tables need explanations; plan the time for them.
- Use no more than three colors consistently throughout.
- Avoid cutesy; it is irritating.
- Keep it simple; the presentation should only summarize or highlight major points.

Threaten Harm

The final tactic is threatening to harm others if they will not do what you want them to do. There is no question that a lot of power in organizations is based on explicit and implicit threats of harm, such as loss of jobs, promotions, pay increases, attractive job assignments, and the like. Theoretically, these are all rewards that are bestowed for favored performance, but many employees will view the threat of withholding a reward as a harmful punishment. Even though it is common in organizations, threatening harm is a risky political tactic. Managers who threaten punishments, had employees who produced fewer innovations, were more distressed, and withdrew or quit the first chance they got.[125] Employees who were threatened felt they were humiliated, were less likely to help others, and saw their workplaces as less just.[126] Threats of harm undermine employee trust, contextual performance, and organizational performance.[127] Remember Machiavelli's warning that those you threaten have the time and motivation to retaliate. Explicit threats can only be used if you do not expect any future relationship and do not depend on that person for anything, a rare situation in most organizational work.

THE CHALLENGE OF POWER AND POLITICS

This chapter has laid out some of the things that research can tell managers about building and exercising organizational power. However, Henry Mintzberg warns that power is as much a matter of will as skill.[128] Many of us are uncomfortable analyzing dependencies, practicing ingratiation, and thinking about their work places as political arenas. While this is certainly understandable and even admirable, it is not something that managers can afford to do if they want to be good at their jobs.[129] Power is an essential tool of managers, and no manager can hope for success without understanding and successfully wielding it.

Because few things are more complex than the effective building and effective use of power, effective managers read widely about those who have successfully built and wielded it. Some of the best instruction in the use of power comes from biographical descriptions of how particular people amassed and deployed power in their own organizations. The description of Lyndon Johnson and the Little Congress is one of many excellent analysis of individuals' rise to power.[130]

Implications for Managing Managers

- ✓ How effective is your manager at getting what you need to be able to do your job? Powerless managers are a misery for their employees and are unlikely to change.
- ✓ If you want more of something, you need to treat it as a problem of building power: What important problems can you solve for your manager (or anyone else who controls what you want)?
- ✓ Do not confuse formal authority with power: Those without authority can still solve others' important problems, be experts, and ingratiate.
- ✓ Everything discussed throughout this chapter is as relevant for employees who want to succeed as it is for managers. Even the dullest job can be enriched by diagnosing and practicing influence, and remember the ability to build and use power leads to health and wealth.

Key Words

Power	Power vacuum
Formal authority	Impression management
Politicking	Strategic Contingencies' Theory
Politics	Need plus alternatives
Manipulation	Discretionary resources
Machiavellian	Social capital
Sinister attribution error	Bridging social capital
Sexual harassment	Petty office politics
The Mom Test	Rules
Turf battles	Strategic ambiguity
Consensus with qualification	Co-opted
Centralized power	Political skills
Palace politics	Self monitor
Decentralization	Ingratiation
Empowerment	Robert's Rules of Order
Legitimate power	Persuasion

10

Leading Others

Leadership has always been important to those concerned with organized action. Organization requires coordinating everyone's actions to achieve shared goals, as well as changing those goals when necessary -- the usual tasks of leaders. In practice, without some form of leadership, organizational work cannot get done.[1] The importance of leadership is reflected in civilizations' earliest writings, which include descriptions of the qualities that leaders should have, and advice to leaders about how to be successful.[2] The fascination with leadership continues today and is reflected in the devotion of large sections of bookstores to books on leadership. It is hard to find a college that does not claim to develop leaders, and it would be a rare profession, industry, or nation that does not have its own writings and practical advice about effective leadership. The existence of this vast collection of material on leadership presents two challenges.

True or False?

True leaders embrace failure; they do not fear failure.

The first challenge is how to cope with the quantity of material: much of it can be considered ambiguous preaching, like that shown in the inset box. Leaders who fear failure probably have good reason to believe they will be punished for failure, which makes statements like this boxed management opinion silly. Unfortunately, too much practical leadership advice (and early leadership research) can be boiled down to precisely this type of advice: be good, kind, true to yourself, brave, do not tell a lie, and so forth. While being good is a fine idea, you already know that; and if being good was enough, successful leaders would be common – something we know isn't true. Because all managers, entrepreneurs, and management students seek the golden key of leadership success, all too many writers have offered to provide such advice for modest (and immodest) fees.

In this chapter, the challenge of too much opinion-based leadership advice is addressed by keeping a focus on what real research can usefully say to real managers, and by avoiding the advice of the many self-appointed leadership gurus. It is not that valuable insights cannot be gleaned from others' leadership advice; it is that this book reports and applies systematic research on what makes some leaders successful. This research is grouped into the following sections: what differentiates successful from unsuccessful leaders and what makes no difference at all; challenges to effective leadership decision making; charismatic leadership; different situations that call for different kinds of leadership; and what research can tell us about how to develop leadership skills.

There is a second challenge that is particular to leadership. We all suffer from the romance of leadership. The **romance of leadership** is the tendency we have to attribute success and to blame the leaders personally for anything that happens in team or organized work. Of course, leaders do not control everything and cannot always predict the future. Sports teams need strong players to win but it is easier (and cheaper) to fire the manager rather than replace the whole team. Too often, people avoid the hard work of diagnosing the causes of bad (and good) performance, the difficult job of hiring and retaining the best people, and the challenges of setting up strong performance management practices and high-performance cultures, and instead hope that a change of leaders is all that is needed. All of us feel more in control if we can attribute credit or blame to individual people, and changing a leader helps us to feel that productive action is underway.[3] Too many of us welcome this simplistic dodging of the hard work of diagnosis and management, and attribute both good and bad performance to leaders that they could not possibly have caused alone.[4]

Application -- Manage the Romance of Your Leadership

- Because many will assume that you have more influence than you do, they will over interpret what you do, where you go, and what you say – act cautiously.
- Accept that you will be blamed even if it was not your fault.
- Don't fall into the trap of assuming you are more important than you really are; be humble.

Does the romance of leadership mean that leaders don't matter? To answer this question, we need to be clear that leaders can have two distinct effects: on their employees or followers, and on the performance of their organization or team.[5] The substantial research that exists on leaders' impacts on their followers can be summarized as follows: leaders matter a great deal to those they lead. Numerous studies routinely find that the vast majority of employees report that interaction with their supervisors is the worst or most stressful aspect of work, making leaders one of employees' chief complaints.[6] Leaders do matter to their followers' attitudes, commitment, and turnover.

Since leadership matters so much to employees, does this mean it also matters to organizational or team performance? In short, leadership does *not* matter as much to organizational performance as does the favorability of the organization's market, its business cycle, or industry.[7] Anyone can look like a great leader in a booming market. In addition, the more successful the company, the more likely the leader will be seen as charismatic.[8]

Where leader quality does matter most for team or organizational performance is in those situations that are the most fluid and unconstrained. For example, research has shown that mayors had more influence over the libraries and parks in their cities than they did in areas where they faced powerful interest groups, such as firefighting and policing.[9] Leaders are more important to performance at organizational foundings, because policies and cultures are not yet established.[10] Leaders have more influence on the performance of autonomous professionals than they do on those doing more routine work, because the latter are more constrained by metrics and machines.[11] Leaders also matter more when organizations needed to adapt and change.[12] The boxed inset management opinion is true, up to a point. Leadership does matter to leaders' followers, and matters most to performance when the situation is uncertain or fluid. However, in large stable organizations that are not facing radical changes in their environments, leaders do not matter as much as might be assumed by many, such as executive compensation committees.[13]

> ***True or False?***
>
> *Do leaders matter?*

WHAT IS LEADERSHIP?

Because leadership has always been fascinating, many different definitions of leadership have been proposed, some of them quite complex,[14] and most of them emphasizing something the writer wants other people to do.[15] In this chapter, we keep it simple and stick close to the dictionary definition: **leadership** is the guiding of others toward an objective. Leadership may or may not be exercised from a position of formal authority, although we expect those in positions of formal authority to act as the leaders. Leadership always involves influencing others, and that aspect of leadership has already been discussed in detail in the previous Chapter 9, *Mastering Power*.

This definition of leadership directs our attention to three fundamental tasks of leaders: they have visions, they enlist others to work toward these visions, and they take action.

Establish a Vision

Establishing a vision or direction for the team or organization is central to the idea of leadership; leaders must have some idea of the future before anyone would follow them. A **vision** is an idea of a future for the organization or team. It is more abstract than a goal: for example, Ikea's vision is to achieve "affordable solutions for better living."[16] Another company might have a goal like, "to become a global company with US$200 million in revenue by 2015." A successful vision is an attractive future that can be meaningful to everyone, not a specific goal or economic metric that may be of interest only to a small group like a sales team or executives.[17]

An Effective Vision Is...[18]

- Brief
- Clear
- Abstract
- Challenging
- Oriented Toward the Future
- Stable
- Able to Inspire Followers

Joel Baum and his colleagues found that leaders with effective visions had more successful organizations and more committed employees. Entrepreneurial organizations (for profit and not-for-profit) with visions grew faster than those that only had goals.[19] Those executives and middle managers who developed and actively communicated visions produced better-performing and more innovative businesses.[20] Compelling visions of the future were especially useful in successful organizational change.[21] Managers who identified attractive visions had employees who believed that their managers shared their own values, were more stimulated by their work, had greater self-efficacy, were more committed and identified with the organization, had greater trust in their managers, saw their managers as more charismatic,[22] and identified with and were more involved with their organizations.[23] Effective visions were particularly helpful in providing a framework that helped employees respond to crises.[24]

Visions work in several ways. First, they clarify the meaning of employees' work. For example, most employees would find it more meaningful to work to help others live better lives than to provide yet more money for investors who are already a lot richer than the employees are.[25] Second, visions provide a guide to action that can help employees respond to changing circumstances, such as those that might have made a metric-based goal obsolete.[26] So, for example, a new online magazine may have a vision of providing youth with the best source of entertainment news, and may initially set high-traffic goals to demonstrate to potential investors that they have a large audience. Later in their growth, the goal can shift to revenue growth targets while maintaining the same vision. Third, visions reflect employees' values and expectations and are grounded in the particular situation. Examples might include focusing on a vision of achievement in a competitive sports equipment organization, but on meeting client needs in a non-profit social-services organization.[27]

Despite the importance of visions, researchers have found that the leadership role of "vision setter" is the one least often pursued by executives.[28] We don't know if this is because too many managers don't appreciate the power of visions, or if they do not have the skills to develop and communicate their visions.[29] The following are several ideas for developing an effective vision.

Application – Develop an Effective Vision

- Visions are more meaningful if they focus on the team or organization's positive effects on others.
- Vision statements are more effective when leaders have thought through the causes and implementation.[30]
- Visions appeal to shared ideals such as beauty, order, honesty, dignity, and a meaningful life, but they also need to be based in reality: don't say anything in a vision statement that employees see contradicted in practice.
- Successful visions are based on deep understandings of their environments, opportunities, and constraints.
- Employees must have confidence that the vision can be achieved.
- Visions build a sense of community and common fate.
- Review examples of others' vision statements: a wide variety of business and non-profit organizational vision statements can be found at www.samples-help.org.uk/mission-statements/corporate-vision-statements.htm

Enlist Followers

Why people choose to follow someone else has long fascinated social scientists. Because engaging and retaining followers is central to effective leadership, this is by far the largest area of leadership research. This section begins with what research can tell us about how leaders enlist others in support of their vision and why initiating action is necessary to leadership. Later sections then cover other approaches for successfully enlisting followers.

Employees cannot become committed to a particular vision if they have never heard of it, so they must know what the vision is. Communicating a vision requires that leaders interpret and reinterpret what the organization has done and is doing in ways that appeal to higher and more universal purposes.[31] So, for example, Herb Kelleher, a founder of Southwestern Airlines, (and now his successors) framed the challenges the airline faced as a war. At its founding, Southwestern's large competitors succeeded in securing legislation that barred Texas-based Southwestern Airlines from the primary Dallas-Fort Worth Airport, making it virtually impossible for its passengers to make connections to other airlines.[32] Herb Kelleher framed these moves as a mortal attack, what is called creating a **superordinate goal**. This is an overarching, compelling goal that requires everyone's cooperation. This type of goal is particularly effective at bringing together group members.[33] What began as a response to an early attempt to kill the airline continues to be used to enlist employees in a compelling common cause, contributing to this airline's continued success. Employees are more likely to follow visions if vision statements are repeated frequently, in a variety of ways, using eye-to-eye contact, with animated facial expressions.[34] Leaders who do something dramatic and visible are more likely to grab employees' attention and convince them that their vision is more than empty talk.[35] It helps to be able to tell stories that capture who you are, and who you would like to be. We remember stories better than we remember lists of facts or achievements; stories stay with us. So, for example, at Southwestern Airlines, stories of pilots helping to load bags onto the planes help support statements about everyone working together as a team.

All too often, lofty vision statements fail to enlist others because they have not been linked to the work that needs to be done, to goals, and most importantly, to the leaders' own actions.[36] If the leader's vision calls for saving lives, but employees are given goals for seeing at least six patients per hour, the vision will be empty talk, and everyone will know it. An obviously phony vision statement is worse than no vision statement at all, because it means that managers do not do what they say, and so cannot be trusted.

Application – Enlist Others to the Vision

- Communicate the vision often (a web page posting does not count). Come back, again and again, to what the team or organization does that is meaningful.
- Communicate the vision in person to as many employees as possible.
- Find and repeat good stories that illustrate the vision.
- Tie the vision to goals and incentives.
- Demonstrate the vision yourself: If you want the employees to put customers or clients first, they need to see you put customers or clients first.

Initiate Action

Finally, leaders need to be willing to act if they want to enlist followers. Leaders initiate team and organizational actions. People are willing to follow someone because they believe that person will help the team or organization to get its work done and overcome its challenges. The earliest leadership researchers called these actions initiating structure.

Initiating structure is the extent to which a leader initiates activity, organizes the work to be done, and maintains standards and deadlines. When leaders initiate action, whether that action is giving directions, consulting with employees, or negotiating, the result is that employees show higher performance and feel greater satisfaction with their work.[37] Managers who employees rated high in initiating structure by their employees had higher performing teams,[38] and increased sales.[39] Those with leaders with better initiating structure had research teams with higher quality work, who met deadlines and had better performance.[40] Effective leaders take action to structure the work, follow up when something isn't completed, and in other ways ensure that things get done.[41] Taking action is particularly important when a leader is faced with the most difficult issues. No one wants to follow a coward. The application below can assist a leader to take action on one of the most challenging issues faced by managers today: managing the personal privacy, favoritism, and anger that can arise due to workplace romances.

Application – Initiate Action on Difficult Problems: Workplace Romance[42]

- Romances between managers and their direct-report employees should be prohibited, because these can lead to favoritism and exploitation.
- Romances among those of equal rank or indirect reporting relationships should not be prohibited unless they create a conflict of interest or cause work disruption: if there is no impact on job performance, a workplace romance is a personal privacy matter.
- Prohibit workplace romances for senior-level executives because their visibility means that these can lead to major conflicts of interest and negative publicity.
- Managers should not intervene in non-prohibited workplace romances unless they can tie the relationship directly to the work performance of the participants or team.

Leaders who take action contrast with those with formal authority who adopt **laissez-faire leadership**, that is, who leave their employees free to do whatever they want to do. In these teams, employees have reported more feelings of uncomfortable ambiguity and incidences of bullying among coworkers.[43]

Taking action to organize work and initiate action should not be confused with being autocratic. Many once thought that leaders who initiated action would show less consideration. **Consideration**, or the extent to which leaders are friendly and considerate of employees' feelings and desires, was long thought to be a necessary component of employee happiness.[44] However, considerate managers only had high performing employees when the leaders also took actions like setting goals and defining responsibilities and priorities.[45] While employees prefer nice, considerate leaders, employees also recognize that leaders' actions necessary for the success of the team or organization are more important. The fundamental tasks of a leader are to have a vision, and to take the actions necessary to keep everyone focused on what needs to be done to achieve that vision. Initiating structure and consideration are not mutually exclusive and the most effective leaders will do both.

Application – Combine Initiating Structure and Consideration[46]

- Encourage employees to set high goals for themselves.
- Show confidence in employees' ability to meet performance expectations.
- Provide developmental experiences for employees.
- Provide coaching to improve employee job performance.
- Encourage employees to look at old problems in new ways.
- Give positive feedback when employees perform well.

SUCCESSFUL LEADERSHIP

All successful leaders must carry out the fundamental leadership tasks of establishing a vision, enlisting followers, and initiating action, and yet beyond these basic tasks, few can agree on what makes a successful or unsuccessful leader. In the popular press, one writer will declare an elected official a great leader while others dispute that claim; executives are proclaimed great visionary leaders one year, but in the next, those same strengths are exposed as fatal flaws.[47] Those who study leadership are no better: they disagree on ever-shifting lists of personality characteristics and actions for differentiating good from bad leaders.[48] Numerous, sometimes lengthy, lists of traits and competencies are produced with no research that clearly establishes that any one list is better than another.[49] Readers can avoid wasting time on each new trendy leadership must-do by recognizing that such lists arise from two biases we all have.

The first is bias is the romance of leadership described above: people attribute both too much success and too much failure to leaders. When a company or politician is doing well, we assume it must be because the person is extraordinary, and so we study that person's characteristics or actions so that we can be successful too. Because we all suffer from the romance of leadership, journalists know that any personality profile of the leader of a currently successful organization will gain readers, thereby encouraging our romantic, but inaccurate, belief that it is all about the person.

The second bias is **hindsight bias**, or a distorted remembering and evaluation of people and events after we already know the results.[50] Hindsight bias leads us to search for, and pay attention to, positive reasons if we know a team or organization has been successful, as well as the possible negative ones if it has been unsuccessful. Hindsight bias allows us to construct explanations for ourselves that make sense of the world, but it can lead to inaccurate diagnoses.

When hindsight bias is combined with the romance of leadership, we assume that successful teams and organizations must have successful (e.g., decisive) leaders. In contrast, when that same organization stumbles a year later, the same formerly decisive leader is now assumed to be at fault for arrogance. With the romance of leadership, hindsight bias, and the desire of all writers to say something new, we will always have new lists of leadership skills, competencies, and advice, packaged as necessary for the unique leadership challenges of our times. Readers can enjoy these lists as inspirational tracts and, if well written, as entertainment, while recognizing that inspiration and entertainment are their real purposes.

What Successful Leaders Do

Are there certain personal characteristics that make some leaders more successful than others? Only two characteristics have strong and consistent research evidence to support them: First, cognitive ability, or intelligence, reliably predicts more successful leadership performance.[51] Leaders must be able to diagnose the environments their teams or organizations face now, and far into the future, and they must evaluate the resources they can bring to bear for success. Successful leaders must analyze ambiguous and complex information and then articulate a clear and meaningful vision. They must also be able to adapt their own actions and those of the organization or team when what they are doing at present is not working. Cognitive ability helps with all of these demanding abstract tasks.

Second, leaders who are more confident in their abilities, or have higher leadership self-efficacy, also are more effective.[52] Self-efficacy, as described in Chapter 5, *Managing Performance*, when combined with clear goals and an attractive vision that was clearly communicated, led to greater new venture growth.[53] Self-confident leaders are more willing to try new directions and are more likely to use effective influence tactics like rational persuasion, rather than coercion.[54] The combination of leaders' self-confidence, optimism, hope, and resiliency has been called leaders' **psychological capital**. Recent research suggests leaders with greater levels of psychological capital have higher performing organizations, and employees with better job performance job satisfaction, commitment, and lower turnover.[55]

In addition to the well-established personal qualities of cognitive ability and leadership self-efficacy, studies have found that successful leaders often are more likely to do certain things and not others. The following are a few of the features of successful leadership that have been best established by research.

Divergent thinking has been associated with more successful leadership.[56] **Divergent thinking** is the generation and tying together of many different ideas, commonly called "thinking outside the box." Robert Sternberg proposes that successful leaders engage in more divergent thinking because this type of thinking helps them to redefine the team or organization for new circumstances, to redirect it if such redirection is required, and to integrate different ideas in productive ways.[57] Successful leaders are more creative and can see problems from different angles when compared to less successful leaders. Of course, divergent thinking is not just throwing out ideas, which can create chaos for others; rather, it is focused on challenges and effective ways to address them. Erratically throwing out one idea after another does not build others' confidence.

True or False?

Leaders must communicate, communicate, communicate.

The common assumption in the inset box is true. Successful leaders communicate more often. They communicate with their followers more frequently and are more available to answer their questions.[58] Leaders who held regular meetings had more productive teams than those who did not.[59] Active communication improves team and organizational performance in two ways. First, managers often have access to unique information and expertise, and regular communication with employees helps others to access that information. Second, leaders who actively communicate make sure their own vision and goals are continuously brought to the attention of others; this helps to keep everyone aware of the direction and purpose of the work. While no one can control all conversations, increased frequency of communication does increase the odds that the leaders' message will be heard and not forgotten.

An important part of communication is what Deborah Anacona calls sensemaking. **Sensemaking** is making sense of the team or organization's world. It is what leaders do when they combine divergent thinking and communication. Successful leaders are constantly trying to understand the world in which they work and how it might be changing, and then they explain these insights to others. Sensemaking is the result of diagnosis and then providing direction when the familiar ways are not working. Unfortunately, she has found that sensemaking is the leadership skill least understood by managers.[60]

Application – The Leadership Skill of Sensemaking

- Seek out many different sources of data.
- Try to understand the nuance of every situation – don't oversimplify.
- Be very sensitive to those closest to the front line: those employees who work with customers, clients, and new technologies.
- Avoid interpreting new situations using your old understandings; avoid rigidity.
- Test your own understanding by discussing it with others. Conduct experiments.
- Use images, metaphors, and stories to try to capture elements of the situation.

Integrity is the consistency between a person's words and actions. People are said to have more integrity when they do what they say they will do. The importance of integrity to successful leadership is one of the most popular claims of those providing leadership advice based on their own experience as leaders. This is reflected in the boxed inset management opinion. However, research conclusions are mixed regarding this common management opinion. Employees had higher performance when they saw their leaders as authentic and sincere.[61] When followers believe that their leader lacks integrity there are problems. For example, employees receiving direction from those they see as lacking integrity are more likely to sabotage and engage in other organization-harming actions.[62] On the other hand, other researchers report that no reliable research evidence exists to confirm and effect of leader integrity on team or organizational performance.[63] These mixed research results might be explained in two ways: employees may report that their leaders have no integrity when they are angry at the leader for any number of other reasons, or alternatively people may disagree on what integrity actually is in practice, making systematic research difficult.

True or False?

Leaders are judged by their actions.

Successful leaders tend to be those who are viewed by their followers as engaging in **self-sacrifice**, or forgoing personal interests for the good of the team or organization. Leaders seen as self-sacrificial had employees who were themselves more likely to help others,[64] and had higher performing teams.[65] Clearly, if leaders are exploitive or greedy, they can hardly expect any different behavior from others, which supports the boxed inset management opinion.

True or False?

Leaders should model the behavior they want from others.

All of these actions – articulating a clear and compelling vision that makes work meaningful, making sense of the organization's environment, taking action, frequent communication, acting consistently with your words, and sacrificing for the organization's interests – increase the chances of successful leadership. These actions work because they build employee trust in their leaders. When employees trust their leaders they are more likely to help others at work and engage in other types of contextual performance, are less likely to quit, have more positive attitudes toward the job and the organization, have higher job performance, and are more likely to accept their leaders' decisions.[66] Nevertheless, even though we know that these leadership actions build trust, Kurt Dirks and Daniel Skarlicki have argued that many managers are not trusted as much as they want to be, because leaders face trust dilemmas.[67] **Trust dilemmas** arise because managers often must mediate between many people. To meet the expectations of one person (say, their own boss's demand that they cut costs), managers may have to violate the expectations of others (say, their employees' expectations of merit pay increases for working so hard to meet all of their goals). Sometimes managers are forced to choose whose trust they must damage. This is another reason why managers' jobs are so challenging. Research does suggest how to limit the damage from trust dilemmas.

Application – Manage Trust Dilemmas[68]

- It is extremely difficult to repair trust when the trust violator is seen to have done it for selfish, personal reasons.
- If you suspect trust may be damaged by your actions, explain how you were forced by circumstances beyond your control.
- If that is not plausible, explain how the act was done for someone else's benefit, not your own.
- If you anticipate that others will see your actions as a betrayal, then if at all possible, explain the reasons before they are shocked by the betrayal.
- Apologies work if they are timely, sincere, assume responsibility, and seek to maintain others' goodwill.

What Unsuccessful Leaders Do

There is growing interest in understanding what leaders do that can damage their effectiveness. If we focused only on employees' complaints about their leaders, we would find a long list of faults, such as avoiding conflicts, having poor emotional control, over-controlling, poor planning, disorganization, rumor-mongering, and so forth and so on.[69] However, apparently, these long lists of follower complaints seem to be unrelated to how others view a leader's performance: one survey found that 45% of the follower-identified bad leaders were promoted or rewarded.[70] Of course, we cannot know why employees characterized their leaders as bad. It could be because employees blame their leaders for things beyond the leader's control (romance of leadership), or it is possible that other matters were seen as more important by those rewarding these leaders. These types of employee surveys are good at identifying unhappy employees, but are not always useful in identifying what is causing them to be unhappy. Rather, surveys are best used as spurs for diagnosis.

Systematic research has identified two particularly unsuccessful leadership approaches: autocratic and abusive leadership. We have long known that autocratic leaders produce disengaged followers, and less creative and poorer team and organizational performance.[71] **Autocratic leaders** are coercive and punitive, making all the decisions themselves, and care more about getting the job done than about their followers' needs. Kurt Lewin and his colleagues conducted the earliest studies on the effects of autocratic leadership. Followers with autocratic leaders were more submissive, more afraid to approach the leader, more likely to wait for orders rather than initiating action on their own, and were more hostile to one another. Those working for autocratic leaders got into fights with one another and sabotaged the workplace as their frustration grew. Autocratic leaders clearly undermine employee collaboration and contextual performance.[72] While productivity can often be higher in the short-run, over the long run teams with autocratic leaders did not perform well.[73]

Recently, interest has been growing in the effects of abusive supervision or leadership. **Abusive leaders** are callous and arbitrary in their use of power, they mistreat employees by using derogatory names, yelling, intimidating, withholding needed information, humiliating, and ridiculing their followers.[74] Note the difference between autocratic and abusive leaders: autocratic leaders insist on complete control and emphasize punishment, while abusive leaders do not necessarily want to control all decisions, but are more capricious and maliciously harmful. Those who see their leaders as abusive report they have more stress, lower contextual performance, reduced organizational commitment, and more absenteeism.[75] Employees with abusive leaders were more likely to try to harm the organization, or if that was too risky, they engaged in passive acts of resistance.[76] Abusive leaders degrade and offend their employees, providing them with strong motivation to retaliate in any ways they possibly can. Not surprisingly, organizations with abusive leaders have lower organizational performance.[77]

Lest readers assume that leaders' own personalities make them abusive, recent evidence indicates that abusive leadership is a trickle-down process, as managers who are themselves abused, or who work in a hostile, chaotic, and disorganized workplace, are more likely to abuse those who report to them.[78] Apparently, when abusive actions and hostility are seen as the organizational norm, or when the workplace is so confused that managers feel that they must shout and intimidate employees in order to motivate them, managers are more likely to be abusive. In contrast, managers who were supported by their own managers were in turn more supportive of their employees.[79]

Application – Manage an Abusive Leader[80]

- Don't be aggressive, hostile, very obliging, or avoid your manager; these all tend to foster an abusive reaction.
- Avoid being seen by your manager as cynical; this encourages hostility.
- Engage in contextual performance (as described in Chapter 6, *Managing Incentives*); this has been shown to reduce abuse.
- Maintain self-confidence; those in doubt get picked on more.
- Diagnose the situation: if the organizational climate is abusive, do not blame this on your manager personally, but view it as a feature of the organization that you will need to learn to live with.
- Abusive leadership in organizations can be minimized by having clear policies on accountability and performance management, and by establishing grievance channels.

What Has Nothing to Do with Successful Leadership

This section concludes by noting that much of the popular advice about what can make you a successful leader has been studied and found to have no effect on successful leadership. This means that many of the criteria by which leaders are selected and large parts of many leadership development programs have been found to have no relationship to successful leadership. Having knowledge about popular practices that do not work is useful so that time and money are not wasted on them.

For example, many leaders are selected based on their experience, but experience in a job, or as a leader, has no relationship to later leadership success.[81] The inset boxed management opinion is not true. Why do so many persist in selecting leaders based on experience when it simply is not a good predictor of leadership success? Fred Fiedler speculates that this is done because, without a diagnosis of what skills a particular leadership position demands, people tend to fall back on what is most easily measured: time in a similar job.[82]

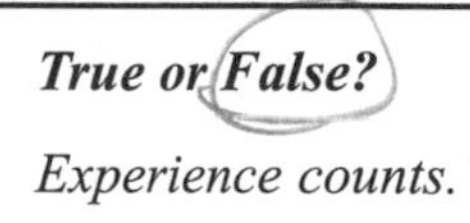

In addition, many leadership development programs are dominated by assessments and discussions of participants' temperaments, leadership capabilities, personalities, and the like. There is simply no evidence that any self-assessed temperament or capability produces a more successful leader.[83] A few moments' reflection makes it clear why this is so. First, people possibly lack self-insight and therefore inaccurately report their true temperaments. After all, a widely-used temperament instrument has only a two-thirds chance of reporting the same temperament if taken again.[84] What is more, the circumstances and challenges different leaders face are simply too varied for any one personality type to be more successful in all circumstances. Of course, it is fun to find out about yourself, discuss yourself with others, and become more tolerant of those who approach problems from a different angle. Nevertheless, none of this has anything to do with becoming a more successful leader.

EFFECTIVE DECISION MAKING

Leaders make decisions – important decisions – and the wrong decision can be devastating. Historians write books analyzing the decisions of political and military leaders, investment analysts pore over chief executives' strategic decisions, and everyone second-guesses their own manager's decisions.

A **decision** is necessary when a choice must be made between two or more alternatives. If one alternative is obviously the right one, no decision is required; only if uncertainty really exists regarding which alternative is best does someone face a decision. Since leaders make decisions for their teams and organizations, decision-making is one of their most important responsibilities.

Because we can only know if a decision was actually a good one after the fact, most research tries to identify the decision-making processes that result in successful (or unsuccessful) decisions. The following describes a few of the common errors that interfere with good decision-making processes, and then notes some of the advantages and disadvantages of involving followers in decisions. However, remember that excellent decision-making processes can result in bad decisions and poor decision-making processes can result in good decisions: there is never a guarantee.

Common Errors

Decisions are only as good as the information on which they are based, and so anything that causes us to ignore or dismiss relevant information can lead to poor decisions. Psychologists have identified a large number of errors that we all tend to make when gathering and evaluating information. A few of the ones most relevant to leaders' decision-making follow.

A **framing bias** results from weighting certain information more or less heavily based on how the decision is framed.[85] For example, if the decision is framed as a risk of loss (say, the expense of integrating an acquisition), leaders will be more conservative to minimize losses, but if the gains are featured (say, new market share in a rapidly growing industry) leaders will tend to act more positively. Similarly, in negotiations, we tend to move to the middle of the two starting offers, which is why negotiators will start with extreme offers and try not to be the first to make a concession. Diagnoses will be more accurate when leaders become aware of how the decisions they face have been framed.

Escalation of commitment refers to our tendency to stick with a prior decision even when evidence is mounting that it was wrong.[86] We simply do not like to admit that we made a mistake so we tend to discount information suggesting our previous decisions were wrong. For example, leaders might stay longer with a dysfunctional inventory management system if they had been the one who decided to purchase it. Even small commitments tend to bind us to a particular course of action and so care must be taken to continuously attend to new information.

An **overconfidence bias** is our tendency to be too optimistic about how successful we will be.[87] The very self-confidence that is so necessary to successful leadership can distort our decisions. Leaders are prey to confidence that they will get lucky, be the winner, or beat the odds, and they tend to underweight the chances that things will not work out for the best. Leaders need to plan for the bad as well as the good.

All of these biases result from our natural desire to save time and trouble (framing bias) and we all like to think of ourselves as competent and capable (escalation of commitment and overconfidence bias). For low-stakes decisions that do not matter much, these biases do not cause enough harm to overshadow their benefits in efficiency and supporting self-efficacy. However, leaders often make complex, important decisions where these biases can be devastating. In order to counteract these decision-making biases, researchers have identified a process for making important complex decisions that should produce better decisions by counteracting most biases and insuring that all available information is carefully considered.[88] Many variants of what is usually called the **rational decision-making model** can be found. As more of the following steps were used in making decisions, policy decision makers had increasing success in international crises.[89]

Application – Make Rational Decisions

1. Identify what you want to achieve.
2. Generate a comprehensive list of clear alternatives.
3. Search widely for information about all of the alternatives.
4. Carefully evaluate all of the information for all of the alternatives.
5. Before making the final decision, review all of the advantages and disadvantages of each alternative.
6. Select the best alternative, and take action to reduce the possible negative consequences of that alternative.

Involve Followers in Decisions

Many of the steps in the rational decision-making model involve gathering and evaluating information, and among leaders' most important information sources are their followers. However, several different ways can be employed to involve employees in decisions and confusion among these methods can create misunderstanding and distrust.

In **participation**, the leader and followers jointly make the decision.[90] In this way, more information is presented and evaluated from multiple perspectives. Since participation means that a team is responsible for the decision, one of the challenges of participative decision-making is deciding how to integrate the different participants' views into a final decision. These **decision rules** can vary a great deal. Some common ones include consensus (all agree on the final decision), consensus with qualification (if all cannot agree, the person designated in advance makes the final decision), majority voting, or charging a subgroup in advance with making the final decision. Needless to say, decision rules developed after disagreement has surfaced will rarely be accepted, since everyone will propose (or suspect others of proposing) decision rules that favor themselves. Simultaneous fighting by team members over both the decision and the decision rules is very dysfunctional.

Although there are many advantages of participation, it also has costs. Those whose views are rejected by the team may feel alienated. Participative decision-making also can be a slow process, which impairs decisions that need to be made rapidly, and some issues simply aren't important enough to take large numbers of people away from other work for lengthy discussions.[91] However, participation does reduce perceptual biases and promotes the acceptance of decisions. Followers usually prefer it, and it fosters trust and motivation.[92] If participation is active and honest, open discussion can improve commitment to a decision, and even foster acceptance of decisions that favor others,[93] resulting in improved performance. Participation does this by providing more information on the trade-offs and all of the alternatives, and by generating social support for the decision. The discussion makes the rationale clearer, and allows people to talk through different strategies for achieving challenging goals.

Participation does lead to a better understanding of the issues and commitment to the final decision, but it does not necessarily produce better decisions. The quality of team decisions is usually better than what the average member of the team would have decided, but often it is worse than the decision that the best member of the team would have made.[94] Those participants with the most expertise can be swamped during participation, diluting their contributions and the quality of the decision. If some members of the team clearly know more about the problem, participation does not result in better team performance, which makes the boxed inset management opinion false.

> ***True or False?***
>
> *Encouraging participation will result in better decisions.*

Too often managers confuse consultation with participation. **Consultation** involves seeking information from others so that the leader can make an informed final decision alone. Unfortunately, some managers ask for participation, but what they really want is to collect information to consider while making the final decision (consultation). Even worse, they sometimes try to sell their idea through persuasion and argument, thinking that this selling will lead to the decision commitment that comes from the open discussion of participation. Naturally, those called to participate in a decision meeting will assume that they are being asked to make a decision. When they find that this isn't the case, employees can feel manipulated and become cynical and distrusting of the leader. It is not that they would have been opposed to being consulted; it is that they can feel manipulated into believing they were going to be full decision makers when they were not. This problem is made even worse when some employees take their cues from their positions as citizens in a democracy and assume that any group discussion must entail a democratic group decision. Participation does not motivate simply by letting people speak in public, and those leading these types of discussions need to be absolutely clear about who will be making any decisions and how.

Application – Be Clear about What You Want from Participation

- The word participation should be avoided – it simply means too many different things to different people. Your own use of it prevents clear thinking about exactly what you expect from a discussion.
- The purpose of each discussion should be written clearly on the agenda or invitation. For example, "Hear status reports on the implementation of the new accounting software, and discuss obstacles;" or "Present preliminary proposals for the new marketing campaign and solicit constructive criticism and ideas for improvement."
- Decision rules for reaching agreement always should be known in advance of any discussion.

HARNESS EMOTIONS: CHARISMATIC LEADERSHIP

One of the things that can differentiate leadership from other forms of influence is the potential engagement of followers' emotions. We have already learned that employees pick up on their managers' emotions in Chapter 4, *Making Sense of Feelings at Work*. In the following, we discuss one of the most widely studied ways in which leaders engage their followers' emotions: charismatic leadership.

The word charisma has been adapted by social scientists from theology (where it means the manifestation of a divine spirit) to characterize leaders who use particularly powerful forms of emotional appeals in leading. **Charismatic leaders** harness emotion to motivate and engage followers. Charismatic leaders develop and communicate an emotionally captivating vision that engages followers to become committed to common aspirations.[95] Charismatic leaders are highly esteemed by followers who are devoted and unquestioning, becoming imbued with moral inspiration and purpose. Charismatic leaders act as if they have no doubts, are highly expressive, active, and eloquent. Charismatic power is not based on others' calculations or analyses of what will lead to the highest payoff, but is a result of contagious emotions, of belief and commitment. Charismatic leadership gains its power by arousing and directing followers' emotions,[96] and by articulating and engaging their values.[97]

Charismatic leaders are undoubtedly powerful. They foster more creative[98] and entrepreneurial employees.[99] They are seen as more effective in many different cultures, and contribute to more profitable organizations.[100] It is no surprise that Rakesh Khurana found that boards of directors of American Fortune 500 companies now seek chief executive officers who can be charismatic leaders as well as competent managers; and that even mediocre executives who are seen as charismatic receive high salaries.[101] Therefore, the boxed inset management opinion is true: the more inspirational you can be, the more effective you can be.

> ***True or False?***
>
> *Be inspirational.*

Note, however, that a fundamental contradiction exists between enlisting followers' emotions as a charismatic leader and operating in a modern organization where employees are supposed to be chosen on merit (not loyalty) and formal authority is to be respected regardless of the person holding the position.[102] Charismatic leadership is very personal, and fosters unthinking loyalty rather than thoughtful analyses. This is why many consider charismatic managers to be dangerous for organizations. This is because employees become more committed to the leader personally than to the organization, placing the organization at risk for rivalries and splits.[103]

Because of the power of charismatic leaders, researchers have long tried to understand the kind of person who becomes a charismatic leader, and the situations and organizations where charismatic leaders are most often found. Based on that work, we know that charismatic leaders tend to be older, to have greater cognitive ability, to score higher with respect to extraversion, agreeableness, and openness to experience and lower on neuroticism. Charismatic leaders express more positive emotions, and are better able to read and understand others' emotions.[104] However, situations matter at least as much as leaders' personal qualities. Charismatic leaders are rarely found at the top of large organizations if they are not founders, and are more commonly encountered as executives in smaller, decentralized, and more flexible organizations.[105] Charismatic leaders more often appear during crises, or at other times of high stress and uncertainty.[106]

Application – Learn Charisma[107]

- Pay attention to your own and others' emotions. Develop an understanding of how emotions affect actions.
- Encourage identification with the organization and leader; use we.
- Make sure that employees work in cohesive teams.
- Have employees make public statements of commitment.
- Communicate both your high-performance expectations of employees and their ability to meet them.
- Project a powerful, confident, and dynamic presence.
- Articulate a clear, inspirational vision.

DIFFERENT SITUATIONS NEED DIFFERENT LEADERS

If leaders make organized action possible, then what leaders must do depends on the team or organization's purpose, its environment, the people available, and the pace of change – all of which will differ in different situations. Leaders must diagnose and clearly understand the situations in which they find themselves. Thousands of studies have sought to document what kinds of leaders and actions are more successful in different situations. A few of these are described in the following paragraphs.

Instability

Onc of the best-established situations that require different leadership actions is the stability of the team or organization's environment. A more stable environment, such as that established by repeat customers, slowly changing technologies, or the same competitors, allows more rules to be written and less involvement of active leaders in sensemaking and communicating about changes in other parts of the environment or organization.[108] This means that managers can supervise more employees, because they can rely on **substitutes for leadership** such as stable rules, goals, and policies. On the other hand, a more turbulent and rapidly changing environment requires leaders be active in sensemaking and in constant communication with their employees, and that they spend more time in consultative and participative decision-making.

Sector Differences

Different demands are placed on leaders in profit-making, non-profit, and governmental sectors. For example, those who manage volunteers must rely more heavily on persuasion and charismatic leadership because they have less power over their followers than do those managing employees.[109] University leaders are more successful with less obtrusive approaches, and because implementation can be blocked by so many, they must convene frequent large meetings to allow opposing views to be discussed before any significant decisions can be made.[110] Leaders in governmental organizations must adhere more closely to national cultural values than do those managing businesses. For example Khalid Al-Aiban and the author found that Saudi Arabian governmental managers needed to demonstrate that family loyalty was paramount (for example, by practicing nepotism), whereas Saudi businesses had less pressure to do so; in contrast, governmental leaders in the United States needed to demonstrate more commitment to meritocracy in their hiring (by using objective tests) than did businesses in that country.[111] What many think of as differences in governmental vs. business practices really are a reflection of greater pressure on governmental leaders to implement their societies' values in their organizations, whether or not those values contribute to organizational efficiency.

Executive Leadership

Those leading at different organizational levels often face different demands. Attention is now increasingly paid to the different requirements of middle managers and chief executives. No particular personality characteristics distinguish successful executives from other managers.[112] However, in any but the smallest organizations, executives must delegate more than middle managers, and need to rely on other managers' recommendations because they simply do not have the detailed information about many different, often globally dispersed, functions.[113] Executives must be careful not to overrule lower-level managers, since that can paralyze decision making in their organizations. Chief executives must invest significant time in managing their governing boards and outside officials and community leaders. Because executives personify the organization to insiders and outsiders alike, they also need to act in ways that reflect the values that people expect from their organizations. In addition, everything they say and do is carefully examined, which limits their personal freedom. Based on their extensive work with corporate chief executives, Michael Porter and Nitin Nohira make the following recommendations for new executives.

Application – Lead as a Chief Executive[114]

- A clear strategy is critical to leading large organizations.
- Use indirect influence by shaping the context for others' decisions, for example, through goal setting and budgeting.
- Establish an organizational structure that directs attention to priorities; for example, a global divisional structure empowers the global regions' needs, whereas a centralized structure directs attention to costs and product or service standardization.
- Financial, operating, and human resources reviews are important arenas for gathering information and setting directions.
- Chief executives are the only ones who can connect all aspects of the organization and its environments, and so they need to be analyzing this diverse information continuously and share it with others.
- Executives need to visibly enact the leadership role expected for their organizations.

Women and Men as Leaders

True or False?

Women have a different (and more effective) leadership style.

Despite the popularity of this boxed inset management opinion, systematic research finds almost no differences between the ways women and men lead: this inset management opinion is simply not supported by research. While women leaders are slightly more likely to be charismatic and use more participation in decision making,[115] they also are more likely to suffer from conflict in the role stereotypes of leaders (dominant) and women (nurturing).[116] Employees prefer men as leaders when they see aggressive competition as critical to performance, but prefer women as leaders when building supportive relationships in the team is seen as the most important task.[117] Stereotyping is a problem for ethnic minorities, with Asian-Americans judged as less competent when leading sales departments than when leading engineering groups.[118] Although women and ethnic minorities with unambiguously strong qualifications are often evaluated fairly in the United States, the more ambiguous the kind of leadership that is needed, the more strongly gender and ethnic stereotypes influence evaluations of their leadership effectiveness.

Followers

Leaders' followers will vary in their experience, expertise, and professional normative expectations. Because what is expected and valued by some followers may be offensive to others, those who find themselves leading new teams or organizations will need to invest in diagnosing followers' skills, needs, and experience. For example, many employees now take what are called bridge jobs between their career positions and full-time retirement. This means that many managers will find that they are leading teams of workers older than they are. Peter Cappelli and Bill Novelli have found that many managers do an especially poor job of leading older employees.[119] They offer the following advice.

Application – Lead Older Employees

- Lead by example rather than by command.
- Do not assume you have expertise that older employees do not (they certainly will not assume it).
- If older employees have more industry experience, consult with them. After an incident, seek them out for a debriefing to learn how they understood what happened.
- While all employees want respect, older employees are particularly sensitive to overt disrespect.
- Of course, older employees themselves have to adapt, for example, by not letting their distaste for organizational politics make them look like grumpy cynics.

These are just a few of the situations requiring leaders to adjust. As always, a careful diagnosis of your own situation is the most important leadership skill.

Lead in Different Cultures

True or False?

When in Rome, do as the Romans do.

Surprisingly, as powerful as cultural differences are, only slight differences are seen regarding what makes leaders successful in different cultures, which makes the inset aphorism false.[120] Although national and organizational cultures differ, what successful leaders do depends much more on their particular situations than it does on matching cultural leadership practices to stereotyped images of another's culture. For example, recent research finds that Indian employees, despite working in a high power-distance culture (see Chapter 8, *Understanding Cultures*), are more collaborative with teammates and clients, and have higher commitment and job satisfaction when their leaders share more information, and are more consultative than autocratic.[121] This does not mean you should rigidly stay with your own familiar culture, but it means you need to conduct a more detailed diagnosis of exactly what may be interfering with the ability to lead a culturally diverse group, or one with a culture new to you. Addressing specific problems of misunderstanding is the best approach.

Application – Develop Third Culture Bonding[122]

- In Third Culture Bonding, leaders seek to develop a deeper understanding of the actual differences that lead to difficulties among those from different cultures who work together, and then develop agreed-upon practices (the third culture) to bridge those differences.

- Individuals from the different cultures begin by meeting face-to-face to build mutual trust and commitment to developing alternative ways of working.

- Next, members of each culture identify cross-cultural conflicts that have made work difficult for them. These must describe behaviors (not intentions or personal characteristics) and be illustrated with specific examples.

- These examples are shared and discussed, and then everyone works to develop new third-culture operating procedures and tools to replace the two conflicting approaches.

- The leader's role is to coordinate the discussion and make sure that any solutions can be implemented in that organization.

LEADERS ARE BORN AND MADE

Because leaders are so critical to organizational success, research on leadership training has a long history. The effectiveness of various types of leadership training and coaching is introduced below. As will be clear, the boxed inset management opinion is false: leaders are born *and* made.

True or False?

Leaders are born, not made.

Leadership Training

Extensive evidence shows that leadership development training can make a significant difference in leaders' effectiveness.[123] Of course, many different kinds of leadership training exist and many of them are not effective.

One reason for failure is that much leadership training is focused on self-awareness, in the belief a better understanding of yourself and your reactions will lead to more effectiveness as a leader.[124] However, much self-awareness training consists of completing various questionnaires where people are asked how they perceive or react to situations. This kind of leadership training can have positive effects on participants' self-awareness, their tolerance, and flexibility, and if everyone in a team participates together, it can build team cohesion. However, several studies indicate that self-awareness training has a negative effect on team performance.[125] Researchers speculate that this happens because the trainees now focus more on themselves and their team members rather than on critical outsiders such as customers or clients. The boxed inset management opinion is not true.

> ***True or False?***
>
> *Self-awareness training will make you a more successful leader.*

In contrast, training that is focused on specific skills has been shown to improve charismatic leadership,[126] coordination between teams,[127] and leaders' fostering of a feeling of interactional justice among employees.[128] Training that is focused on specific leadership skills or challenges tends to be more effective. However, how training is delivered does not seem to matter. While certain training techniques can be particularly effective, even the much-despised lecture-plus-discussion can be effective if the content is targeted to useful skills relevant to leaders' particular challenges.[129] This means that the boxed inset management opinion is not true.

> ***True or False?***
>
> *Leadership training is a waste of time.*

Finally, the most effective preparation for successful leadership appears to be a combination of challenging experiences and extensive feedback.[130] Leadership is too complex and situation-specific for abstract principles to be useful. It is better to take action on real problems, and then have an opportunity to get feedback from someone who has worked with those challenges before.

The **after-event review** has been particularly successful. In this type of review, the successes and failures are appraised with a focus on what happened, what went well, and what could be done differently next time.[131] The emphasis is on diagnosis rather than self-congratulation. For example, your quality problems may not be as bad as your competitors' are, but it is better to analyze in detail what caused any failures and to develop plans to eliminate those causes. Many organizations practice half-after-event reviews by analyzing mistakes and failures but ignoring successes. Valuable information can be gleaned from successes as well as failures, and developing a richer understanding of what is working and what is not working allows leaders to develop a more sophisticated working model of leadership effectiveness.

Application – Conduct After-Event Reviews

1. Identify the specific event or events to be reviewed.
2. Conduct reviews during or immediately after the event.
3. Analyze how the outcome came about, step-by-step. The focus is on exactly what happened.
4. Use open-ended questions and involve all participants in the discussion.
5. Identify which procedures produced successful outcomes and which were not successful.
6. Analyze unsuccessful outcomes to see what might be the cause. Develop an alternative and see if that was effective or not.
7. These procedures can become part of standard operating procedures, training programs, and checklists.
8. Continue to conduct reviews to revise and update procedures.

Coaching

Coaching has become an increasingly popular form of leadership development. Coaching provides individualized feedback on another's actions, with a focus on future improvement. Informal coaching of employees has always been a manager's responsibility. Yet, in recent years, coaching has become professionalized and organizations increasingly send their executives to independent coaches, either to work on a specific problem, or for general leadership development. Coaches are not psychotherapists, but experts on organizations and management. However, the relationship with a coach is much like that with a psychotherapist, based on personal confidence and trust.

Coaches work with their clients to identify actions clients can take, then the client experiments with a new action before the next session. Both will then analyze what worked and what did not work. The coach and client collect ongoing diagnostic information, and test their ideas about what might work. Having a coach is like having your own expert organizational-behavior diagnostician working on your challenges. Managers can use professional coaching techniques in their own informal employee coaching.

Application – What Good Coaches Do[132]

1. The managers present the problems they wish to address to their coach.

2. The managers state their own theories about what is causing problems.

3. Next, the managers describe the actions they have been taking to address the problems and what the outcomes of those actions were.

4. The coach has a discussion with the managers to help them reframe the problems, drawing on the coach's expertise.

5. New actions are developed, and the managers take those actions before the next session.

6. The managers return to describe the actions and what happened and this new information is analyzed, possibly resulting in new or additional actions.

Finally, you can expect to find yourself in new leadership positions throughout your career. The following are some tips for those new to leadership positions, whether assigned or self-created.

Application – Get Off to a Good Start[133]

- Do not wait to begin learning the ropes on your first day: as soon as you know you might be taking a leadership position begin to learn the people and issues so you can start your first day with a preliminary plan of action.

- Who is powerful there? If you report to a board or directors or trustees, who are the individuals who really run the show? Do not forget your peers and employees. Learn the social networks and others' resources and social capital.

- Have a preliminary chart of who is solving the organization's most important problems before the first day.

- Beware of employees who have their own personal connections to other powerful people. You should learn about these within the first few months.

- Remember that formal authority does not automatically confer power, but producing quick successes does. A priority in those first days is exploring what these opportunities for demonstrating success might be.

Implications for Managing Managers

- ✓ Take a leadership job in an organization with a booming demand for what it produces; unfortunately, this is no secret and so the competition for these leadership jobs is fierce.
- ✓ If your manager is a laissez-faire leader, do not take your frustrations out on your coworkers: get together to decide which actions to take.
- ✓ Be alert to your manager's trust dilemmas: do not assume it is all about you.
- ✓ It is exciting, invigorating, and fun to work for charismatic leaders, but beware: they often march their followers off to their deaths.
- ✓ Be alert to the common perceptual errors in making your decisions.
- ✓ Never assume you have been called to a meeting to make a decision, unless this has been made absolutely clear.
- ✓ Conduct honest, regular after-event reviews of your own performance.

Key Words

Romance of leadership
Leadership
Vision
Superordinate goal
Initiating structure
Laissez-faire leadership
Consideration
Hindsight bias
Psychological capital
Divergent thinking
Sensemaking
Integrity
Self-sacrifice
Trust dilemmas
Autocratic leaders
Abusive leaders
Decision
Framing Bias
Escalation of commitment
Overconfidence bias
Rational decision-making model
Participation
Decision rules
Consultation
Charismatic leaders
Substitutes for leadership
After-event review
Coaching

11

d Retain

annot escape the fact that sooner or
night be for economic reasons: budg-
n that there simply isn't enough
cannot do the work required. Telling
a doubt the most difficult thing a
the wrong job hurts everyone. It harms the departing employees' financial security and careers. Their co-workers become unhappy about having to do the extra work the departing employees had done. And if a terminated employee brings a wrongful termination lawsuit, everyone gets to devote many distressing hours to depositions and lawyers.

In contrast, managers also must fight "the war for talent." The must retain their high-performers, sometimes in the face of continuous contacts by competitors and recruiters. Losing employees to competitors is especially harmful to organizational performance.[1] This chapter covers the guidance organizational behavior research can provide to managers who are facing the prospect of letting an employee go, and in retaining employees they don't want to lose. Both are real challenges, but we begin with the challenge that most engages emotion: firing.

We need to begin by distinguishing between **layoffs**, in which employees are let go because the organization does not have the money or work to support them, and **terminations**, in which employees are let go because their work was judged inadequate. Clearly no blame can be attributed to employees who have been laid off, since they do not personally control the economic conditions of their organizations, and so being laid off holds less of a stigma or disgrace. However, in practice the distinction between being laid off and terminated is not so clear cut. Many chosen for layoffs are the poorer performers; managers may collude with terminated employees by supporting their claim that they were laid off to be more humane and to help them get another job, to maintain the cooperation of the departing employees, and to keep the support of their friends remaining at work. And for many jobs, layoffs and terminations are often managed in the same way. So, although the legal distinctions are important, here the distinction is made only when directly relevant to the discussion of how to best manage employee terminations.

We'll address the challenge of letting employees go by discussing first what must be done in preparation, second how to do it in a way that is least damaging to organizational effectiveness, third the most effective ways to learn from the experience, and finally, the giving and getting of honest and defensible references about former employees. Because letting employees go is governed by legal considerations, managers will need to be sure they are professionally advised so that their actions are defensible. No legal advice is offered here. However, because so many managers dread being sued by former employees, and this dread so often leads to dysfunctional management practices, research that can provide insights into more effective management actions will be shared. This information is offered only to counter panicky popular management opinions; it is not legal advice and is no substitute for getting such advice. Finally, the chapter concludes with a discussion of **retention**, that is the challenge of keeping your best performers.

PREPARING TO LET EMPLOYEES GO

Before getting into the details of preparing to let employees go, we need to discuss the unfortunately all-too-common situation of managers who do not let go those employees who should be fired. When this particular form of management neglect occurs, it is usually justified by this boxed opinion, really an excuse to avoid a difficult task. It may be difficult but it is almost never impossible. Tenured professors can (and should) be terminated for poor performance, and civil servants working for governments can (and should) be terminated for poor performance. Certainly some organizations and local labor laws require more paperwork than others. Many governments or organizations require that poor performance be documented, written feedback provided, and a time period for the employee to improve be provided before terminating many classes of employees. And terminated employees might file a **grievance**, a formal organizational or labor union complaint of unfair treatment. Sure, it can be costly to terminate employees in many organizations. So what?

> ***True or False?***
>
> *It is impossible to fire employees in this organization.*

The very organizations that have cumbersome formal requirements for documentation and feedback before an employee can be terminated are also the ones that have well-staffed professional human resources departments that can guide managers through these processes and then manage any employee grievances. It is much worse for small entrepreneurs who thought they could terminate someone for poor performance but then have to face a perhaps unjustified legal action that could bankrupt them. However managers who do not take action against poor performers incur the hostility of the coworkers who resent carrying extra work, contributing to widespread employee dissatisfaction. These managers are making their own lives easier at the expense of their other employees, and the employees know it. A manager's job is full of difficulties, but effective managers actively seek the information and support they need to carry out even their most difficult tasks.

There are two aspects of the preparation for letting employees go that pose problems for managers. The first is actually deciding to let someone go, and the second is how much information to share with the employees at risk for termination — and all employees in the case of possible layoffs. Both reflect on managerial trustworthiness in important ways. We already saw how important employee trust is to organizational performance. Because letting employees go is one of the most traumatic events that can occur in a workplace, the way it is managed will be discussed, analyzed, and parsed for a long time to come. Emotionally charged, negative events are attended to and remembered longest.[2] The reasons for the termination decision, and the way it was carried out, will form the basis for employees' trust in the organization and its managers for a long time.

Basis for the Decision To Let Employees Go

Why was one employee let go and another spared? Employees want to know the answer to this question, and if managers do not make the reasons clear, employees will develop their own theories about it. If they judge that the decision was arbitrary, based on favoritism or whim, employee trust in their managers and the organization is undermined.[3] Layoffs seen as unfair lead to anger, retaliation, and sometimes, to violence[4].Layoffs seen as unjust amplify anxiety, fear, guilt and shame among remaining employees.[5] **Workplace aggression**, or purposeful acts to harm another or the organization, are rightly feared. There is evidence that those who feel victimized, and unfairly treated are more likely to act against others.[6]

Here is a case in which detailed labor union contracts that specify explicit rules, such as seniority, to govern layoffs help support effective management. Such rules reassure employees that the decision was not based on a whim or personal bias. Formal policies such as grievance procedures, anti-harassment and evaluation policies also increase the likeliehood that judges will view the organization as fair and defer to it in a suit brought by an employee.[7] Although the poorest performers may not have been let go when formal rules are applied, at least employee trust in management has not been damaged.[8] Layoffs seen as unjust amplify anxiety, fear, guilt and shame among remaining employees.

Was the decision to terminate based on the employee's poor performance? Although this may be so and is clear in the manager's mind, too often the performance criteria for this important decision are not at all clear to the remaining employees. So it is not enough that the decision actually be a fair one; it is necessary that both departing and remaining employees believe it is a fair one. It is important for departing employees to believe it was fair because they are much more likely to sue a former employer if they feel the decision was an unfair one.[9] It is important for the remaining employees to believe it was fair so their commitment and trust are not undermined.[10] The best way to make sure that others see the decision as fair is to explain the reasons for the decision.

Sharing Information

Managers usually know that employees will be let go for financial reasons or for poor performance long before they actually let them go: How much should they let them know in advance? There are good reasons for providing as much information as possible as soon as possible.

First, many organizations have found that this popular opinion is not true. Because sharing information and not exploiting employees when possible creates trust,[11] information about something as important as layoffs is an opportunity to either reinforce employee trust or destroy it. When managers notify employees that layoffs are pending, they make themselves vulnerable, realizing that many employees might find other jobs before the date of the layoff. Yet because managers are open and forthright with them, employees are more likely to believe their future promises. Those executives implementing mergers and layoffs who explained how it would affect the business and groups of employees quickly rebounded while those who did not provide detailed information found their employees distrusted them and performed poorly months after the transition.[12] Effective managers share as much information as possible because they recognize that organizational performance will suffer much more from employee distrust and perfunctory effort than it will from the possibility that some employees will spend some time at work looking for another job, and others might leave a week or two early.

> ***True or False?***
>
> *If I tell employees a layoff is coming, they'll stop doing their work.*

Second, in the case of terminating for poor performance, managers and their organizations also benefit from advance information. There are reasons why highly bureaucratic organizations require written notice of performance and then a time period for the employee to improve: many performance problems are correctable. To reiterate a message from Chapter 5 on managing performance: managers are prone to the fundamental attribution bias of seeing employee performance as coming from some inherent fault of the employee, but many performance problems result from mistaken expectations, lack of information or a break down in the performance support systems. Letting employees know when they have a performance problem is seen as fair and reduces the chance that employees will think the manager or organization is unfair and untrustworthy.[13]

Finally, employees often sense when a layoff or termination is coming. Even if the organization does not provide explicit organizational or personal performance data with an explanation of what this means for the future, employees in sales, marketing and accounting will all know if organizational or unit revenue is dropping. Engineers and scientists will know whether or not customers are interested in their innovations. These employees all have friends in the organization who are very interested in any signals about their future security, and this is a recipe for rumors. **Rumors** are theories about what is really going on without any solid data to back them up. Rumors can be wildly unrealistic, completely nonsensical, or startlingly accurate.[14] They can become inaccurate because rumors are spread through talk, and we all partially hear or misunderstand what we hear. Clearly, when employees believe wildly inaccurate ideas about what is really going to happen at work, their actions will be based on those beliefs, potentially causing havoc.

Managers complain of employee rumors, but they can easily eliminate them. How? Rumors only develop about something important to employees that they lack accurate information about. Managers might wish that employees wouldn't talk about important workplace matters, but that will never happen. The absolutely reliable way to eliminate rumors is to provide accurate information about the things that are important to employees. If they can get the truth from a reliable source who has not had a history of misleading them, they don't need to speculate and invent explanations.

Application — Rumor Control

- Provide information about revenue prospects (or budgetary debates, if a governmental organization) and their implications for the organization. If the information is too confidential to put in a newsletter, it can be shared in large meetings held on a regular basis.

- Be honest about how possible financial or performance shortfalls will be addressed. For example, the organization may try to avoid layoffs by not filling vacancies and redeploying employees when possible. It may need to avoid cuts in strategically critical jobs; identify those jobs and explain why they're critical.

- Set up a formal rumor control system. In such systems, employees can anonymously ask questions or repeat rumors that are then honestly addressed. These can be the collection of written rumors discussed at those regular meetings, or the rumors and responses can be posted.

LETTING AN EMPLOYEE GO

Too often, the pain of employee layoffs and terminations is made worse by insensitive management of the process. All employees judge their managers and organizations by how they handle these important events. This boxed statement is not so much a popular management opinion, but a popular legal opinion as implemented by fearful managers. Attorneys are paid to prevent low-probability-but-costly individual actions and are not trained to focus on the larger management and organizational costs of their actions and advice. But attorneys are not in charge; managers are, and managers need to weigh both the costs and benefits of blindly following the advice of people who have limited organizational expertise. Although managers must take care that confidential information is not carried out the door, they need to consider the organizational consequences of the ways departing employees are treated. Treating departing employees disrespectfully or like criminals damages employee trust for several reasons. First, if managers have prepared properly, most of those who are being let go have good reasons to suspect this may be coming, and so already have had plenty of time to remove any information. That is, a bum's rush out the door enrages the terminated employee and their friends at work without really protecting the organization. Second, most departing employees are painfully aware that they should not destroy any relationships they will want for references and leads for future jobs. So, as a practical matter in most organizations, the odds are very low that a terminated employee will steal or damage confidential company information. Rather, the greater risk is that insensitive treatment of departing employees will lead to retaliation such as lawsuits, and result in the distrust of the remaining employees.[15]

> ***True or False?***
>
> *Employees should be escorted to their desks, watched carefully, and then escorted off the premises after their employment has been terminated*

Costs of the Insensitive Management of Departures

Terminations and layoffs are one of the most brutal assaults that an employee can experience. It is not just a financial calculation of lost wages, although this is certainly important. It is much more than this to many employees. First, for many, the organization is an important source of **social identity**. Our social identity is how we define ourselves in terms of group memberships. For example, someone might define himself as a Pakistani-American chemical engineer, husband and father of two, who works in the Optics Division of the world's most innovative medical device company. Any one of us may belong to a very large number of groups (e.g., people born in Edmonton, Canada now living in Dublin, Ireland), but we will vary in how important any of these groups may be to our own social identity. For example, people who work in more prestigious professions are more likely to identify themselves with their jobs, and people are more likely to identify themselves with a sports team when it is winning.[16] Organizations can be an important source of identity to many people, and the status of "unemployed" lacks prestige in most countries. For many, losing a job for any reason is a public, personal failure, and so is humiliating. Losing their job can, for some, be a powerful assault on how they see themselves and will require them to try to redefine themselves in a way that restores their sense of self-respect. How they are treated by their organizations and managers at this difficult time matters to them and can have a powerful effect on their future actions.

A serious cost of an insensitive termination is that wrongful termination lawsuits are much more likely to be filed if employees feel that they have been unfairly treated.[17] Employees who have been escorted to their desks and then out the door, in full view of their colleagues, will rarely feel that they have been treated with the respect and fairness they deserved. Rather, they will remember all of the overtime they put in, the weekends they sacrificed for the organization, and become angrier and angrier that they were betrayed and humiliated. In short order, they may decide that they have not been let go for legitimate business reasons, but have been stabbed in the back. Transgressions such as insulting treatment at departure unnecessarily create a feeling of unfair treatment and betrayal that could have been avoided.

The emotional costs of an insensitive layoff or termination are not borne by the departing employees alone. Even if coworkers did not directly witness any public humiliation, at least some of them will be on friendly terms with a departing employee and more than willing to provide a sympathetic ear. What these informants learn will be of compelling interest to all of their co-workers, and so the departed employee's story (embellished and enriched in ways that cannot be controlled) will be widespread throughout the organization in short order. Again, remaining employees' judgments about how their co-workers were treated will affect their attitudes toward the organization, their manager, and their actions at work. Research shows that those co-workers surviving layoffs were more disengaged and less committed to their organizations when they thought their former co-workers were treated unfairly.[18]

Finally, the managers making these decisions may be wracked with guilt and fear. Terminations and layoffs create powerful and painful emotions. One indicator of how emotionally difficult this can be for managers is that virtually all can remember in vivid detail the first time they had to fire an employee. While this distress is natural, too often it leads managers to try to get rid of these painful feelings as quickly as possible by hustling the shamed and stigmatized departing employees out the door immediately. These are important organizational events that need to be carefully managed.

Effective Management of Departures

One of the most effective ways of managing terminations and layoffs is through explanation. Robert Bies and his colleagues have established that explanations that reframe the actions so the offender is no longer seen as morally culpable reduces outrage.[19] Explanations matter. Both departing and remaining employees should understand the rationale for the decisions and feel that they were fairly administered. Why was this decision a business necessity? What criteria were used to decide who should go? By their nature, managers must dispense the good and bad things under their control differentially. An important managerial task is to be sure that employees believe that these unequal distributions are fair distributions.

Similarly, as we saw in Chapter 6, even unfavorable outcomes can be seen as fair ones if the decision and its implementation are seen as fair. Remember, employees' perceptions that their manager and organization are procedurally and interactionally just leads to greater job satisfaction and organizational commitment, less propensity to sue their employers, less turnover, and higher customer satisfaction ratings.[20] Below are some of the characteristics of organizational layoff or termination decision processes and implementation that lead employees to judge them as fair.

- *Clear rules and policies applied consistently and without bias.*[21] Do employees know in advance the criteria for selecting those who will be let go? Did the person fired for poor performance know what needed to be corrected? Are these rules and policies unambiguously based on job performance, or some other legitimate distribution rule, such as seniority? If the rules and policies are not written down, how do you know that employees really understand them?

- *Voice.* When employees have had a chance to provide information and tell their side of the story, they will be more likely to judge the procedures as fair.[22]

- *Opportunity to correct errors.* Having a system for appeals and a way to make corrections leads employees to judge their organizations as fair.[23]

Particularly with something as emotionally wrenching as layoffs and terminations, active efforts to ensure that all employees perceive the actions to be fair are critical to preventing wrongful termination lawsuits and better commitment and contextual performance of the remaining employees. All are watching how the departing employees are treated and asking, Is this a fair organization? They will wonder: If I invest a lot of my time and make a commitment to this organization, will I be betrayed or exploited? Managers need to be concerned that an insensitive layoff or termination does not motivate critical employees to begin searching for another job. All of these considerations need to be weighed against any possibility that departing employees will remove information in the few hours after they return to their desks. Is that information more valuable to the organization than the possible legal costs, reduced commitment, increased turnover and poorer performance produced by treating departing employees with disrespect? If the answer is, "Yes," and company information must be protected, feelings of betrayal and unfairness can be prevented by explaining these reasons to everyone.

Application — Separation with Respect and Sensitivity

- Do the small things that you can do to help employees avoid humiliation when let go. For example, you can allow them to draft and send the announcement themselves (after reviewing it); publicly thank them for their contributions (mentioning specific projects or accomplishments); provide a job search office for a month; and so forth.
- Be as generous as you can possibly be with severance pay. Explain what you are giving and why this is the maximum possible. Whatever the amount, it is a lot less than the cost of a wrongful termination lawsuit.
- Be aware of your own emotions and make sure that you are not just pushing through a painful task as quickly as possible. Rushing a departing employee can inadvertently lead others to think you are treating the departing employee unfairly and with disrespect. When managers stopped by just to chat this was helpful in large study of layoffs in private and public sector organizations.[24]

LEARNING FROM AN EMPLOYEE'S DEPARTURE

Whether a poorly performing employee had to be let go or a good performer is leaving, effective managers will recognize that this is an opportunity to learn more about what is or is not working as well as it should. Departures are excellent opportunites for after-event reviews.

Exit Interviews

One approach to learning from an employees' departure is to conduct exit interviews with them. Many organizations conduct **exit interviews** hoping to learn more about what may be unattractive to employees. In exit interviews, departing employees are interviewed by someone outside their work group, usually a human resources management professional. The assumption is that departing employees have nothing to lose from telling the truth and so are accurate sources of information about compensation, benefits, and the cli-

True or False?

Exit interviews are a good way to discover why an employee quit.

mate of their workplace. Unfortunately, these assumptions and the boxed opinion are wrong. In practice, departing employees usually are non-committal in their exit interviews.[25] In fact, recent studies have discovered that these interviews provide distorted data — encouraging employees to blame their work environment for their departure when they really are leaving for better pay, benefits, or opportunities.[26]

Neither of these results should be surprising. With expected job mobility so high, many employees recognize that they may need to ask for future references from former managers or co-workers. Departing employees will gain only a momentary emotional satisfaction from pouring their complaints and dissatisfactions into the ear of a stranger, at the potentially high cost of damaging professional relationships they may need in the future.

The practice of exit interviews really stems from a mistaken assumption about information in organizations. As organizations grow in size, executives lose the ability to know everyone, and so they substitute formal systems like written job descriptions, performance goals and audits, along with the delegation that large organizational size compels in order to maintain organizational coherence. Although formal systems such as these are necessary to the management of large organizations, there is a limit to what they can do. Most of us are reluctant to confide negative or nuanced information in writing or to strangers. We are not confident it will not be distorted or turn up somewhere later in a way that can hurt us. Large organizational size requires more sophisticated formal management systems than do small organizations, but such formal systems are no substitute for the kind of information gained through the grapevine or informal organization.

Understanding the Informal Organization

Informal organization is the name for the networks of advice, friendship and influence among people who know one another in an organization and across organizations. Of course, people get to know those they work with daily, but they may also know people in other departments or in outside organizations through previous work experience, outside-work contacts, or from temporary task forces or committees. We all are more willing to share honest and risky information like gossip and complaints with those we know personally because we trust them not to use that information against us. Managers and employees draw on their informal contacts to get help with problems, to learn useful information, and otherwise to get the assistance and knowledge that would come slowly, if at all, from formal organizational systems.

The informal organization is essential to managerial success; its existence is not an error or a reflection of organizational incompetence, but rather a necessity for coping with the unexpected and the need to gather the complex and sensitive information necessary to effective management. Effective managers build their own extensive networks of informal contacts, and they know who else has networks covering areas outside their own networks. If a manager really does not know why someone is quitting and does not have a sufficiently trusting relationship with someone who does, this is a strong signal of an incomplete informal network. Exit interviews cannot substitute for the strong informal organizational contacts all effective managers need.

Application — Build an Effective Informal Network

- Look for **good informants**. That is what anthropologists call the people who always seem to know what is going on and can describe it clearly. Some people at work always want to be in the know, others pay no attention until absolutely necessary, and others are somewhere in between. It should not be hard to find the good informants in different work groups and divisions: just ask, everyone will know who they are.

- Cultivate informants in all key areas. Take advantage of those times when you are thrown together with people from different departments and organizations to get to know them. Ask them to lunch later. Lunches are opportunities to learn, and effective managers do not just go to lunch with the same group, day after day. They build friendly, comfortable relationships with as many people in as many areas as possible that could be relevant to their work.

- If you hold a high-level position, create opportunities for informal conversations with employees through informal lunches and discussions on targeted topics. If you visit a distant workplace, ask that the human resources professional at that site take you on a tour and describe the programs.

- If you have a high-level position, do not try to seem like "one of the little people" by focusing your attention on front-line employees alone. This is disrespectful to supervisors and middle managers; they should receive executive attention at least proportional to their rank. Supervisors and middle managers are central to more information flows than are employees stuck at their work stations, and so can make excellent informants.

GETTING AND GIVING USEFUL EMPLOYEE REFERENCES

Most departing employees will seek references from their former managers, and yet many managers do not provide honest references because they hold the overly cau-

> ***True or False?***
>
> *When called for a reference about a former employee, I cannot give an honest assessment because I will get sued.*

tious inset boxed opinion. This fear arises because too many managers do not know how to give legal and honest evaluations. There is no doubt that a managerial fear of lawsuits has many things to recommend it, one being that it keeps those who have become drunk with power within the law. This is unquestionably a good thing, as those who have worked in countries without a strong rule of law will be the first to tell you;[27] these managers have learned that there are worse things than lawyers. Nevertheless, in a country as litigious as the United States, a salutary desire to avoid illegal acts can sometimes metastasize into a fear of providing an accurate description of a former employee's performance. This is because many managers fear that employees who didn't like what they said might sue. This fear is particularly widespread among middle and lower-level managers in large organizations and among Americans with small businesses. High-level executives in large organizations frequently work with lawyers and have grown used to their folkways. They see lawyers as just one more piece of their offensive and defensive weaponry. Lower-level managers do not have lawyers on their own staffs (and are likely to be blamed and threatened by those attorneys they do encounter), and lawyers are a very expensive luxury for small businesses. Although I am not an attorney, and nothing written here should ever be seen as legal advice, I feel duty bound to address what is one of practicing managers' most distressing challenges: fear of employee lawsuits.

First, managers need to distinguish between getting sued and losing a lawsuit. In the United States, anyone can file a lawsuit for any ridiculous reason at all. Most of the horror stories we read regarding companies being sued for some silly reason are dismissed by a judge. Newspapers love these stories: lawsuit filings are public documents that reporters can easily access from electronic databases, and these stories are interesting precisely because they are outrageous. Newspapers do not bother to waste ink on the uninteresting subsequent judicial dismissal some months later. So anyone can sue anyone in the United States, but if managers have not broken the law, they should not run their organizations into the ground worrying that someone somewhere might some day sue. This is not intended to downplay the distress and costs of frivolous lawsuits, only to remind managers that there is little they can do to avoid the truly ridiculous ones, and that actions taken in an irrational fear of lawsuits can be costly to organizational performance.

How can you avoid doing something that might inadvertently lead to legal trouble for getting and giving employee references? Recently Ann Ryan and Marja Lasek[28] studied court cases regarding successful and unsuccessful lawsuits about providing and obtaining references for potential employees; they suggest.

- If the job has a "special duty of care" (employees have access to private residences or lodgings, or have special access to property), managers are obligated to make an effort to screen out those employees who could foreseeably use such access to harm others. For such jobs, a check of the applicant's criminal history is appropriate and necessary.

- Credentials (e.g., driving licenses) necessary to job performance must be confirmed.

- Managers may not defame anyone in writing (libel) or orally (slander). **Defamations** are statements about former employees for which the truth cannot be demonstrated and that harm their reputations.

- **The truth is an absolute defense.**[29] It is easier to demonstrate the truth of concrete employee actions and performance outcomes (number of days absent, project deadlines missed, investment decisions that resulted in losses) than the truth of personality characterizations. The truth of characterizations (e.g., stupid, lazy, not a team player) are very difficult to establish and so should be avoided. A good rule of thumb is to ask for, and to provide, only accurate descriptions of job-relevant past behaviors and performance, avoiding all character descriptions.

- Managers can lose their qualified or conditional privileges to provide information on former employees if managers' malicious intent can be demonstrated. This means managers should never try to get revenge through references; they should just be happy that the troublesome employee is gone.

Application — Give Legal and Honest Evaluations of Former Employees

- If your organization has a formal policy about providing references, follow it. Even if it is a dumb policy, violating it is not worth losing your job.
- Describe concrete behaviors; do not summarize or characterize.
- If a reference-seeker asks for a general characterization ("Was Miguel a good employee?") do not provide it; stick to descriptions of behaviors and performance.
- Make sure any employees who might be asked for references understand the difference between describing job-relevant behaviors or performance and personal characterizations. Make them practice so you know they understand.
- If the person who calls for a reference is a robotic professional reference checker who obviously is not interested in really learning about the prospective employee, do not bother doing anything other than confirming employment. If that other manager cares so little about getting accurate information about the past performance of prospective employees, why should you care?

RETAIN YOUR BEST EMPLOYEES

Retaining your best employees also challenges managers. Any organization that expects to get its work done needs to retain those employees who best do its work and the recruitment and retention of the best employees consistently tops the concerns of executives in international surveys and managers' efforts to retain employees often backfire.[30] Too many managers find themselves trapped in a vicious circle of making counter-offers to retain employees, but then find that those employees' coworkers become unhappy because they believe they should be paid as much. Managers with unhappy employees can find themselves in a trap of desperately seeking to retain employees with outside offers by countering with higher salaries, which can lead other employees to feel the only way to be fairly paid is to bring in an outside offer, and so on in a costly spiral. This can be stopped.

As we saw in throughout this book employees are more likely to stay if they are happy with their jobs, coworkers, managers and organizations, if their coworkers are strong performers and happy and provide them with social support, and if they have a shared identity with coworkers and the organization. Employees who trust their managers and organizations see no need to protect themselves by moving. Unhappy employees begin a self-reinforcing cycle: they are more likely to start looking around and asking around about other jobs, thinking about taking another job leads to less emotional engagement and lowered commitment, which leads to a more active search. The best employees will find it easiest to obtain a job offer, increasing the chances that they will leave. Better to avoid this spiral by doing the things that tend to foster trust and make employees happy: offering better pay, autonomy, congenial colleagues, and fair treatment. Trust does matter – the future is uncertain and employees are more likely to stay with managers and organizations they trust.

Retention is especially difficult in organizations undergoing **downsizing**, or systematically laying off large numbers of employees. Naturally, broad lay offs lead employees to have doubts about the future of the organization and their own future there. Such job insecurity leads employees to become less satisfied, to distrust, to reduce their contextual performance,[31] and to begin searching for jobs elsewhere.[32] However, a survey of Canadian organizations found that there was no increase in turnover or reduction in employee productivity when the layoffs were conducted with extensive information and were seen as fair.[33] Those organizations with high-performance organizational cultures that maintained those practices during downsizing continued to prosper. Unfortunately, too many managers resist providing information because they believe the false boxed inset opinion. From public accountants to equity research analysts, the better performers are less likely to quit than are average or poor performers when they are happy in their work and trust their managers and organizations.[34] It seems that the respectful and sensitive management of terminations is also key to retaining the best employees.

True or False?

I can't provide any information about possible downsizing because the best employees will leave.

Implications for Managing Managers — Coping with Job Loss

- ✓ Try not to permanently damage any relationship at any job you have. You will never be able to perfectly control who will get called for a reference. This especially applies if you are getting fired; behaving nobly increases the chance that former co-workers and managers will reciprocate your good behavior by saying as many good things about you as they can.

- ✓ Never threaten to sue someone; only jerks do that. And in the important practical matter of managing your own emotional stability, be wary of actually suing an employer, no matter how wrong they were. You will spend many painful years reliving past hurts, and possibly incurring new, worse ones. For you it will be very personal and frightening, but the organization's lawyers will just handle it as a routine cost of doing business. And you will never get a good reference from someone you forced into a legal deposition. If you are considering suing, talk to someone else who has done so before making your decision.

Key Words

Layoffs	Exit interviews
Terminations	Informal organization
Retention	Good informants
Grievance	Defamation
Rumors	The truth is an absolute defense.
Social identity	Downsizing

Endnotes

Chapter 1 Why Organizational Behavior

1. Hatchuel, A. (2005) Towards an epistemology of collective action. *European Management Review*, 2, 36–47.
2. *New York Times Sunday Magazine*, November 7, 2004, p. 19.
3. McCall, M. W., Lombardo, M. W. & Morrison, A. M. (1988) *Lessons of experience*. New York: Simon Schuster.
4. Oatley, K. (2004) *Emotions*. Malden, MA: Blackwell.
5. From page 2: Massey, D. S. (2002) A brief history of human society. *American Sociological Review*, 67, 1–29.
6. See, for example, Blanchard, K. & Johnson, S. *The one minute manager*, The Blanchard Family Partnership and Candle Communications. It was first published in 1981 and has sold more than 3.5 million copies.
7. Ashford, S. J. & Tsui, A. S. (1991) Self-regulation for managerial effectiveness. *Academy of Management Journal*, 34, 251–280.
8. Church, A. H. (1997) Managerial self-awareness in high performing individuals in organizations. *Journal of Applied Psychology*, 82, 281–292.
9. Galinsky, A. D. & Kray, L. J. (2004) From thinking about what might have been to sharing what we know. *Journal of Experimental Social Psychology*, 40, 606–618.
10. The best laid plans. *The Wall Street Journal*. July 6, 1993. A1, 6.
11. Business fads: What's in and what's out. *Business Week*, July 12, 1986. 52–56.
12. Abrahamson, E. (1991) Managerial fads and fashions. *Academy of Management Review*, 16, 586–612.
13. Pfeffer, J. (1996) *Competitive advantage through people*. Boston, MA: Harvard Business School Press.
14. Welbourne, T. M. & Andrews, A. O. (1996) Predicting the performance of initial public offerings. *Academy of Management Journal*, 39, 891–919; see also, Cascio, W.F. The economic impact of employee behaviors on organizational performance. In E.E. Lawler III & J. O'Toole (Eds.) *America at work*, 241-256. New York: Palgrave MacMillan.
15. Sinclair, R. R., Tucker, J. S., Wright, C. & Cullen, J. C. (2005) Performance differences among four organizational commitment profiles. *Journal of Applied Psychology*, 90, 1280–1287.
16. Greenberg, J. (2001) Promote procedural justice to enhance acceptance of work outcomes. In E. A. Locke (Ed.) *A handbook of principles of organizational behavior Malden*. MA: Blackwell, pp. 181–195.
17. The Corporate Research Foundation UK (2000) *Britain's best employers*. New York: McGraw-Hill.
18. Thornhill, S. & Raphael, A. (2003) Learning about failure. *Organization Science*, 14, 497–509.
19. McKenzie, C. (2003) Rational models as theories not standards of behavior. *Trends in Cognitive Sciences*, 7, 403–406.
20. Sandler, J. (with Anna Freud) (1985) *The analysis of defense*. New York: International Universities Press.
21. Ibid.
22. Snyder, C. R. & Lopez, S. J. (Eds.) (2003) *Handbook of positive psychology*. New York: Oxford University Press.

Chapter 2 Why Managers

1. Quick, J. C., Quick, J. D., Nelson, D. L. & Hurrell, J. J. Jr. (1997) *Preventive stress management in organizations*. Washington, D. C.: American Psychological Association.
2. Sullivan, S. E. & Bhagat, R. S. (1992) Organizational stress, job satisfaction, and job performance. *Journal of Management*, 18, 353–374; and Motowidlo, S. J. Packard, J. S. & Manning, M. R. (1986) Occupational stress: Its causes and consequences for job performance. *Journal of Applied Psychology*, 71, 618–629.
3. The first to write of the benefits of division of labor was Adam Smith in 1776; see Smith, A. (1993) *An inquiry into the nature and causes of the wealth of nations*. New York: Oxford University Press.
4. Mintzberg, H. (1973) *The nature of managerial work*. New York: Harper & Row.
5. Ibid.
6. Guest, R. H. (1955-1956) Of time and the foreman. *Personnel*, 32, 478–486.
7. Stewart, R. (1967) *Managers and their jobs*. London: Macmillan.
8. Martin, N. H. (1956) Differential decisions in the management of an industrial plant. *Journal of Business*, 29, 249–260.
9. Mintzberg, H. (1973) Op. Cit.
10. Mintzberg, H. (1973) Op. Cit.
11. See Hill, L.A. (2003) *Becoming a manager*. 2nd ed. Boston: Harvard Business School Press.
12. McClelland, D. C. & Boyatzis, R. E. (1982) Leadership motive pattern and long-term sucess in management. *Journal of Applied Psychology*, 67, 737-743.
13. Ibid.
14. Ibid.
15. Ibid.
16. Braybrooke, D. (1964) The mystery of executive success re-examined. *Administrative Science Quarterly*, 8, 533–560.
17. Peters, T. J. & Waterman, R. H. (1982) *In search of excellence*. New York: Warner.
18. Luthans, F., Hodgetts, R., & Rosenkrantz, (1988) *Real managers*. New York: Harper Row.
19. Ibid. Adapted from Table 2-2, pp. 14–19.
20. Schneider, B., Ehrhart, M. G., Mayer, D. M., Saltz, J. L. (2005) Understanding organization-customer links in service settings. *Academy of Management Journal,* 48, 1017–1032.
21. Luthans, F et al. (1988) Op. Cit.
22. Pfeffer, J. (1992) *Managing with power.* Boston: Harvard Business School Press.
23. De Lorean, J. Z. (1979) *On a clear day you can see General Motors.* Grosse Pointe, MI: Wright Enterprises.
24. Burrough, B. & Helyar, J. (1990) *Barbarians at the gate.* New York: Harper Collins.
25. Hoag, A, J, & Hoag, J. H. (2002) *Introductory economics.* River Edge, NJ: World Scientific.
26. For example, the Hungarian word for leader, *vezeto,* does not carry the prestige of *menedjer* (say it out loud), and the German word for leader *(Furher)* is out of favor for obvious reasons.
27. Mintzberg, H. (1973) Op. Cit.
28. Martin, N. H. (1956) Op. Cit.
29. Mintzberg, H. (1973) Op. Cit.
30. Donaldson, L. (2001) *The contingency theory of organizations.* Thousand Oaks, CA: Sage.
31. Mitroff, I. (2000) *Managing crises before they happen.* New York: American Management Association.
32. The first three are adapted from *How to keep a crisis from happening.* Harvard Management Update, December 2000. Boston: Harvard Business School.
33. Pelz, D. C. (1952) Influence. *Personnel*, 29, 209–217.

34. Winter, D. G. (1991) A motivational model of leadership. *Leadership Quarterly*, 2, 67–80.
35. McClelland, D. C. & Boyatzis, R. E. (1982) Leadership motive pattern and long-term success in management. *Journal of Applied Psychology*, 67, 737–743.
36. Levine, J. M. & Moreland, R. L. (1990) Progress in small group research. *Annual Review of Psychology*, 41, 585–634.
37. Katz, D. & Kahn, R. L. (1978) *The social psychology of organizations.* New York: Wiley.
38. McNutt, D. B. & Judge, T. A. (2004) Boundary conditions of Galatea. *Academy of Management Journal*, 47, 550–565.
39. Hackman, J. R. & Oldham, G. R. (1980) *Work redesign.* Englewood Cliffs, NJ: Prentice-Hall.
40. Marmot, M. (2004) *The status syndrome.* New York: Times Books.
41. Ibid.
42. McClelland, D. C. & Boyatzis, R. E. (1982) Op. Cit.

Chapter 3 How to Hire

1. Herbert A. Simon (1945) *Administrative behavior*. New York: MacMillan.
2. Poundstone, W. (2003) *How the world's smartest companies select the most creative thinkers*. New York: Little, Brown.
3. Greengard, S. Gimme attitude. *Workforce Management*, July 1, 2003, p. 57.
4. Arthur, W. Jr., Bell, S. T., Villado, A. J. & Doverspike, D. (2006) The use of personal organization fit in employment decision making. *Journal of Applied Psychology*, 91, 786-801.
5. Lauver, K., & Kristof-Brown, A. (2001) Distinguishing between employees' perceptions of person-job and person-organization fit. *Journal of Vocational Behavior*, 59, 454–470.
6. Pulakos, E. D. Wexley, K. N. (1983) The relationship among perceptual similarity, sex, and performance ratings in management-subordinate dyads. *Academy of Management Journal*, 26, 129–139.
7. Costa, P. T. & McCrae, R. R. (1992) *The NEO-PI Personality Inventory.* Odessa, FL: Psychological Assessment Resources.
8. Hurtz, G. M. & Donovan, J. J. (2000) Personality and job performance. *Journal of Applied Psychology*, 85, 869–879.
9. Ibid.
10. Costa & McCrae, Op. Cit.
11. Thorensen, C. J., Bradley, J. C., Bliese, P. D. & Thorensen, J. D. (2004) The big five personality traits and individual job performance growth trajectories in maintenance and transitional jobs. *Journal of Applied Psychology*, 89, 835–853.
12. Collins, C. J., Hanges, P. J. & Locke, E. A. (2004) The relationship of achievement motivation to entrepreneurial behavior. *Human Performance*, 17, 95-117.
13. Brett, J. F., Brief, A, P, Burke, M. J. & George, J. M. (1990) Negative affectivity and the reporting of stressful life events. *Health Psychology*, 9, 57–68.
14. Van Yperen, N. W. (2003) On the link between different combinations of Negative Affectivity (NA) and Positive Affectivity (PA) on job performance. *Personality and Individual Differences*, 35, 1873–1881.
15. Staw, B. M. & Barsade, S. G. (1993) Affect and managerial performance: A test of the sadder-but-wiser vs. happier-and-smarter hypothesis. *Administrative Science Quarterly*, 38, 304–331.
16. Aquino, K. & Bradfield, M. (2000) *Perceived victimization in the workplace. Organization Science*, 11, 525–537.
17. Watson, D., Clark, L. A. & Tellegen, A. (1988) Development and validation of brief measures of positive and negative affect, *Journal of Personality and Social Psychology*, 54, 1063–1070.
18. Schmitt, F. L. & Hunter, J. E. (2000) Select on intelligence. In E. A .Locke (Ed) *Handbook of principles of organizational behavior*, Oxford, UK: Blackwell, 3–14.

19. Murphy, K. R., Cronin, B. E., Tam, A. P. (2003) Controversy and consensus regarding the use of cognitive ability testing in organizations. *Journal of Applied Psychology*, 88, 660–671.
20. Schmitt, F. L. & Hunter, J. E. (1998) The validity and utility of selection methods in personnel psychology. *Psychological Bulletin*, 124, 262–274.
21. The Wonderlic is available from www.wonderlic.com and the Hexaco from www.hexaco.org. For a review, see Murphy, K. (1984) The Wonderlic Personnel Test. In J. Hogan & R. Hogan (Eds.), *Business and industry testing.* Austin: Pro-Ed, 191–197.
22. Rynes, S., Brown, K. G. & Colbert, A. E. (2002) Seven common misconceptions about human resources practices. *Academy of Management Executive*, 16, 92–102.
23. Hofstadter, R. (1996) *Anti-intellectualism in American life.* New York: Alfred A. Knopf.
24. Schmitt & Hunter (1998), Op. Cit.
25. United States Equal Employment Opportunity Commission (1978) Uniform Guidelines on Employee Selection Procedures. *Federal Registry*, 43, 38290–38315.
26. Feingold, A. (1994) Gender differences in personality. *Psychological Bulletin*, 116, 429–456.
27. Viser, M. Suit charges Newton Fire Dept. on quotas. *The Boston Globe*, December 16, 2004, Metro/Region, p. A1.
28. The following text does not constitute legal advice but summarizes the research findings of Campion, J. E. & Arvey, R.D. (1989) Unfair discrimination in employment interview. In R. W. Eder & G. R. Ferris (Eds.) *The employment interview.* Newbury Park, CA: Sage, 61–73.
29. Levington, J. A., Field, S. H., Veres, G. J. & Lewis, M. P. (1996) Effects of race on interview ratings in a situational panel interview. *Journal of Applied Psychology*, 81, 178–186.
30. Berscheid, E. & Walster, E. (1974) Physical attractiveness. In L. Berkowitz (Ed.) *Advances in experimental social psychology.* Vol. 7. New York: Academic Press.
31. Bruner, J. S, & Tagiuri, R. (1954) Person perception. In G. Lindsey (Ed.) *Handbook of social psychology*, Vol 2. Reading MA: Addison-Wesley.
32. Kelley, H. H. (1972) Attribution in social interaction. In E. E. Jones, D. E. Kanous, H. H. Kelley, R. E. Nisbett, S. Valins, & B. Weiner (Eds.) *Attribution.* Morristown, NJ: General Learning Press, 1–26.
33. Jones, E. E. & Nisbett, R. E. (1972) The actor and observer. In E. E. Jones, D. E. Kanous, H. H. Kelley, R. E. Nisbett, S. Valins, & B. Weiner (Eds.) *Attribution.* Morristown, NJ: General Learning Press, pp. 79–94.
34. Pulakos, E. D. Wexley, K. N. (1983) Op. Cit.
35. Asch, S. (1946) Forming impressions of personality. *Journal of Abnormal Psychology*, 41, 258–290.
36. Dipboye, R. L. (1989) Threats to the incremental validity of interviewer judgments. In R. W. Eder & G. R. Ferris (Eds.) *The employment interview*. Newbury Park: Sage, 45–60.
37. Barrick, M. R., Swider, B. W. & Stewart, G. L. (2010) Initial evaluations in interviews. *Journal of Applied Psychology*, 95, 1163–1172.
38. Cascio, W. F. (1982) *Applied psychology in personnel management.* Reston, VA: Prentice-Hall.
39. Jonas, E., Schaulz-Hardts, S., Frey, D & Thelan, N. (2001) Confirmation bias in sequential information search after preliminary decisions. *Journal of Personality and Social Psychology*, 80, 557–571.
40. That lying causes stress for many people is the basis for lie detection technology; for a review of the effectiveness of this technology see Knight, J. (2004) The truth about lying, *Nature*, 428, 692–694.
41. Granovetter, M. (1995) *Getting a job*. Chicago: University of Chicago Press.
42. Pearce, J. L. (2000) Employability as trustworthiness. In C. R. Leana & D. M. Rousseau (Eds.) *Relational wealth*. New York: Oxford University Press, 79–90.
43. Dougherty, T. W., Turban, D. B. Callender, J. C. (1994) Confirming first impressions in the employment interview. *Journal of Applied Psychology*, 79, 659–665.
44. Eder, R. W. & Ferris, G. R. (Eds.) (1989) Op. Cit.

45. Borman, W. C. & Motowidlo, S. J. (1997) Task performance and contextual performance. *Human Performance*, 10, 99–109.
46. Ibid.
47. McDaniel, M. A., Whetzel, D. L., Schmidt, F. & Maurer, S. D. (1994) The validity of employment interviews, *Journal of Applied Psychology*, 79, 599–616.
48. Dougherty, T. W., Ebert, R. J. & Callender, J. C. (1986) Policy capturing in the employment interview, *Journal of Applied Psychology*, 71, 9–15.
49. Pulakos, E. D., Schmitt, N., Whitney, D. & Smith, M. (1996) Individual differences in interviewer ratings, *Personnel Psychology*, 49, 85–102.
50. Adapted from Campion, M. A., Palmer, D. K. & Campion, J. E. (1997) A review of structure in the selection interview, *Personnel Psychology*, 50, 655–702; and Virj, A. et al. (2011) Outsmarting the liars. *Current Directions in Psychological Science*, 20, 28-32
51. Meriac, J. P., Hoffman, B. J., Woehr, D. J. & Fleisher, M. S. (2008) Further evidence for the validity of assessment center dimensions. *Journal of Applied Psychology*, 93, 1042–1052.
52. Lawler, E. E., III (1973) Motivation in work organizations. Monterey, CA: Brooks/Cole.
53. Gilliland, S. W. (1994) Effects of procedural and distributive justice on reactions to a selection system, *Journal of Applied Psychology*, 79, 691–701.
54. Phillips, J. M. (1998) Effects of realistic job previews on multiple organizational outcomes. *Academy of Management Journal, 41, 673–690.*
55. *Ibid.*
56. Adapted for managers from Wanous, J. P. (1989) Installing a realistic job preview. *Personnel Psychology*, 42, 117–133.
57. Mueller-Hanson, R., Heggestad, E. D. & Thornton, G. C., III (2003) Faking and selection, *Journal of Applied Psychology*, 88, 348–355.

Chapter 4 Making Sense of Feelings at Work

1. Weber, M. (1946) *From Max Weber*. New York: Oxford University Press, 215–216.
2. Ashcraft, K. L. (2001) Organized dissonance. *Academy of Management Journal, 44, 1301–1322.*
3. Friedman, H. S., Prince, L. M. Riggio, R. E. & DiMatteo, M. R. (1980) Understanding and assessing nonverbal expressiveness. *Journal of Personality and Social Psychology,* 39, 331–351.
4. Ekman, P., Friesen, W. V. & O'Sullivan, M. (1988) Smiles when lying. *Journal of Personality and Social Psychology*, 54, 414–420.
5. Rafaeli, A. & Sutton, R. I. (1989) The expression of emotion in organizational life. In L. L. Cummings & B. M. Staw (Eds.) *Research in Organizational Behavior, Vol. 11.* Greenwich, CT: JAI Press, 1–42.
6. The term was introduced by Hochschild, A. R. (1983) *The managed heart.* Berkeley: University of California Press; for a more recent review see Elfenbein, H. A. (2007) Emotion in organizations. *The Academy of Management Annals*, 1, 315-386.
7. Ibid.
8. An excellent brief introduction to the differences between emotions, moods and temperament can be found in Gray, E. & Watson, D. (2001) Emotions, mood, and temperament. In Payne, R. L. & Cooper, C. L. (Eds.) *Emotions at work.* New York: Wiley.
9. Ibid.
10. George, J. M. (1995) Leader positive mood and group performance. *Journal of Applied Social Psychology,* 25, 778–794.
11. Hsee, C. K., Hatfield, E., Carlson, J. G. & Chemtob, C. (1990) The effect of power on susceptibility to emotional contagion, *Cognition & Emotion,* 4, 327–340.

12. Kelly, J. J. & Barsade, S. G. (2001) Mood and emotions in small groups and teams. *Organizational Behavior and Human Decision Processes,* 86, 99–130.
13. Ashcraft, K. L. (2001) Op. Cit.
14. Finkenauer, C. & Rime, B. (1998) Keeping emotional memories secret. *Journal of Health Psychology,* 3, 47–58; and Rime, B., Finkenauer, C., Luminet, O., Zech, E. & Philippot, P. (1998) Social sharing of emotion. *European Review of Social Psychology,* 9, 145–189.
15. The interested reader can read about a mandated requirement to share feelings at a major metropolitan newspaper's editorial department in Argyris, C. (1974) *Behind the Front Page.* San Francisco: Jossey-Bass.
16. Lazarus, R. S. & Cohen-Charash, Y. (2001) Discrete emotions in organizational life. In Payne, R. L. & Cooper, C. L., (2001) Op. Cit.
17. Salovey, P. & Mayer, J. (1990) Emotional intelligence. *Imagination, Cognition and Personality,* 9, 185–211.
18. Seligman, M. E. P. (2002) *Authentic Happiness.* New York: Free Press.
19. Ibid.
20. Oatley, K. (2004) *Emotions.* Malden, MA: Blackwell.
21. Cheniss, C. (2010) Emotional intelligence. *Industrial and Organizational Psychology,* 3, 110-126.
22. Costanza, M. & Archer, D. (1989) Interpreting the expressive behavior of others. *Journal of Nonverbal Behavior,* 13, 225–245.
23. Funder, D. C. & Harris, M. J. (1986) On the several facets of personality assessment. *Journal of Personality,* 54, 528–550.
24. DiMatteo, M. R., Friedman, H. S. & Taranta, A. (1979). Sensitivity to bodily nonverbal communication as a factor in practitioner-patient rapport. *Journal of Nonverbal Behavior,* 4, 18–26; and Rosenthal, R., Hall, J. A., DiMatteo, M. R., Rogers, P. L. & Archer, D. (1979) Sensitivity to nonverbal communication. Baltimore: Johns Hopkins University Press.
25. Seo, M. & Barrett, L. F. (2007) Being emotional during decision making – good or bad? *Academy of Management Journal*, 50, 923-940.
26. Byron, K. (2007) Male and female managers' ability to "read" emotions. *Journal of Occupational and Organizational Psychology,* 80, 713-733; see also Won, C. & Law, K.S. (2002) The effects of leader and follower emotional intelligence on performance and attitude. *The Leadership Quarterly*, 13, 243-274; and Zeidner, M., Matthews, G. & Roberts, R.D. (2004) Emotional Intelligence in the workplace. *Applied Psychology: An International Review*, 53, 371-399.
27. Hall, J. A. (1984) *Nonverbal Sex Differences.* Baltimore: Johns Hopkins University Press; and Shao, P. T. & Schaubroeck, J. (2008) *Testing a role congruence model of emotional display*. Annual Meeting of the Academy of Management, Anaheim, CA.
28. Yukl, G. A. (1989) *Leadership in organizations* (2nd ed.) Englewood Cliffs, NJ: Prentice Hall; and Ashkenasay, N. M. & Tse, B. (2000) Transformational leadership as management of emotion. In Ashkenasay, N. M., Hartel, C. E. J, & Zerbe, W. (Eds.) *Emotions in the workplace.* Westport, CT: Quorum Books.
29. Kostera, M. Proppé, M. & Szatkowski, M. (1995) Staging the new romantic hero in the old cynical theatre. *Journal of Organizational Behavior,* 16, 631–642.
30. Adapted from Ledford, G. E. (1999) Comment. *Journal of Organizational Behavior,* 20, 25–30.
31. Iaffaldano, M. T. & Muchinsky, P. M. (1985) Job satisfaction and job performance. *Psychological Bulletin,* 97, 251–273.
32. Borman, W. C. & Motowidlo, S. J. (1993) Expanding the criterion domain to include elements of contextual performance. In N. Schmitt & W. C. Borman (Eds.) *Personnel Selection in Organizations:* pp. 71–98. San Francisco, CA: Jossey-Bass.
33. Judge, T. A., Thoresen, C. J., Bono, J. E. & Patton, G. K. (2001) The job satisfaction–job performance relationship. *Psychological Bulletin*, 127, 376-407.

34. Baldwell, W. A., Ensign, W. Y. & Mills, P. J. (2005) Negative mood endurance after completion of high altitude military training. *Annals of Behavioral Medicine,* 29, 64–69.
35. Bless, H., Clore, G. L., Schwartz, N., Golisano, V., Rabe, C., Wilk, M. (1996) Mood and use of scripts. *Journal of Personality and Social Psychology,* 71, 665–679; and Foo, M.-D. Uy, M. A. & Baron, R. A. (2009) How do feelings influence effort? *Journal of Applied Psychology,* 94, 1086-1094.
36. Kaufmann, G. & Vosburg, S. K. (2002) The effects of mood on early and late idea production. *Creativity Research Journal,* 14, 317–330.
37. Wright, T. A. & Staw, B. M. (1999) Affect and favorable outcomes. *Journal of Organizational Behavior,* 20, 1–23; and Staw, B. M. & Barsade, S. G. (1993) Affect and managerial performance. *Administrative Science Quarterly,* 38, 304–331.
38. Cropanzano, R., James, K. & Konovsky, M. A. (1993) Dispositional affectivity as a predictor of work attitudes and job performance. *Journal of Organizational Behavior,* 14, 595–606.
39. Gray, E. & Watson, D. (2001) Op. Cit.
40. Locke, E. A. (1976) The nature and causes of job satisfaction. In Dunnette, *M. D. Handbook of Industrial and Organizational Psychology.* Chicago: Rand McNally, pp. 1297–1349.
41. Brief, A. P. (1998) Op. Cit.
42. Ibid.
43. Barker, R. G. & Gump, P. V. (1964) *Big school, Small School. Stanford,* CA: Stanford University Press.
44. Smith, F. J. Work attitudes as predictors of attendance on a specific day. *Journal of Applied Psychology,* 62, 16-19.
45. Tsai, W., Chen, C. & Liu, H. (2007) Test of a model linking employee positive moods and task performance. *Journal of Applied Psychology*, 92, 1520-1583.
46. Estimates of the costs of turnover are provided in Cascio, W. F. (2006) The economic impact of employee behaviors on organizational performance. In E. E. Lawler, III & J. O'Toole (Eds.) *America at Work*, 241-256, New York: Palgrave MacMillan. and of absenteeism in Armour, S. Workplace absenteeism soars 25%, costs millions. *USA Today,* November 6, 1998, p. 1A.
47. Ibid.
48. Mowday, R. T., Porter, L. W. & Steers, R. M. (1982) *Employee-organization Linkages.* New York: Academic Press.
49. Meyer, J. P., Stanley, D. J., Herscovitch, L. & Topolnytsky, L. (2002) Affective, continuance, and normative commitment to the organization. *Journal of Vocational Behavior,* 61, 20–52.
50. For a meta-analysis of studies largely conducted in the United States, Riketta, M. (2002) Attitudinal organizational commitment and job performance. *Journal of Organizational Behavior,* 23, 257–266; for China see Chen, Z. X. & Francesco, A. M. (2003) The relationship between the three components of commitment and employee performance in China. *Journal of Vocational Behavior,* 62, 490–510; and for Israel see Carmeli, A. (2005) Perceived external prestige, affective commitment, and citizenship behaviors. *Organization Studies,* 26, 443–464.
51. Murphy, W. H. (2004) The pursuit of short-term goals. *Journal of Business Research,* 57, 1265–1275.
52. Van Breugel, G., Van Olffen, W. & Olie, R. (2005) Temporary liaisons. *Journal of Management Studies,* 42, 539–566.
53. O'Reilly, C. A. III, Caldwell, D. F. & Barnett, W. P. (1989) Work group demography, social integration, and turnover. *Administrative Science Quarterly,* 34, 21–37.
54. Ostroff, C. (1992) The relationship between satisfaction, attitudes, and performance. *Journal of Applied Psychology,* 77, 963–974.
55. Staw, B. Bell, N. & Clausen, J. 1986. The dispositional approach to job attitudes. *Administrative Science Quarterly,* 31, 56–77; and Judge, T. A. & Ilies, R. (2004) Affect and

job satisfaction. *Journal of Applied Psychology,* 89, 661–673.
56. Assouline, M. & Meir, E. I. (1987) Meta-analysis of the relationship between congruence and well-being measures. *Journal of Vocational Behavior,* 31, 319–332.
57. Greenberg, J. (1990) Organizational justice. *Journal of Management,* 16, 399–432.
58. Fried, Y. & Ferris, G. R. (1987) The validity of the job characteristics model. *Personnel Psychology,* 40, 287–322.
59. Doran, L. I., Stone, V. K., Brief, A. P. & George, J. M. (1991) Behavioral intentions as predictors of job attitudes. *Journal of Applied Psychology,* 76, 40–45.
60. Documentation of women's lower pay when performing the same tasks as men can be found in England, P. & McLaughlin, S. D. (1979) Sex segregation of jobs and income differentials. In Alvarez, R., Lutterman, K. G. & Associates (Eds.) *Discrimination in organizations.* San Francisco: Jossey-Bass; and one of the many studies finding no relationship between gender and job satisfaction is Witt, L. A. & Nye, L. G. (1992) Gender and the relationship between perceived fairness of pay or promotion and job satisfaction. *Journal of Applied* Psychology, 77, 910–917.
61. Krackhardt, D. & Porter, L. W. (1985) When friends leave. *Administrative Science Quarterly,* 30, 242–261.
62. Summarized from Brief, A. P. (1998) Op. Cit.
63. Wright, T. A. & Cropanzano, R. (2004) The role of psychological well-being in job performance. *Organizational Dynamics,* 33, 338–351.
64. For civil servants, see Marmot, M. G., Bosma, H., Hemingway, H., Brunner, E, (1997) Contribution of job control and other risk factors to social variations in coronary heart disease incidence, *The Lancet,* 350 (073) 235–239; for Swedish workers see, Theorell, T., Tsu, T., Hallquist, J. & Reuterwallet, C. Decision latitude job strain, and myocardial infarction. *American Journal of Public Health,* 88, 382–388; for nurses, see Fox, M. L., Dwyer, D. J., Ganster, D. C. (1993) Effects of stressful job demands and control on physiological and attitudinal outcomes in a hospital setting. *Academy of Management Journal,* 36, 289–318; and for factory workers see, Timio, M. & Gentili, S. (1976) Adrenosympathetic overactivity under conditions of work stress. *British Journal of Preventive and Social Medicine,* 30, p. 262–265.
65. Ibid.
66. Weick, K. E. (1993) The collapse of sensemaking in organizations. *Administrative Science Quarterly,* 38, 628–652.
67. Staw, B. M., Sandelands, L. E. & Dutton, J. E. (1981) The threat rigidity effects in organizational behavior, *Administrative Science Quarterly,* 26, 501–524.
68. Fiedler, F. E. (1995) Research in leadership selection and hiring, *Administrative Science Quarterly,* 40, 241–250.
69. Adapted from Quick, J. C., Quick, J. D., Nelson, D. L. & Hurrell, J. J. Jr. (1997) *Preventative stress management in organizations.* Washington, D. C.: American Psychological Association; and Sutherland, V. J. & Cooper, C. L. (1990) *Understanding stress.* London: Chapman & Hall.
70. Hackman, J. J. & Oldham, G. R. (1980) *Job redesign.* Reading, MA: Addison-Wesley.

Chapter 5 Managing Performance

1. For example, the (combined) performance of service employees was a good predictor of which stores had the most satisfied and loyal customers; see Liao, H. & Chuang, A. (2004) A multilevel investigation of factors influencing employee service performance and customer outcomes. *Academy of Management Journal,* 47, 41–58.
2. Mitchell, T. R. (1997) Matching motivational strategies with organizational contexts. In L. L. Cummings & B. M. Staw (Eds.) *Research in organizational behavior,* vol. 19: 60–62.

Greenwich, CT: JAI Press.

3. Vroom, V. (1964) *Work and motivation.* New York: Wiley.
4. Ibid.
5. Erez, A. & Isen, A. M. (2002) The influence of positive affect on the components of expectancy motivation. *Journal of Applied Psychology*, 87, 1005–1067.
6. Kerr, S. (1995) On the folly of rewarding A, while hoping for B. *Academy of Management Executive*, 9, 7–14.
7. Bandura, A. (1997) *Self-efficacy*. New York: Freeman.
8. Speirer, C. & Frese, M. (1997) Generalized self-efficacy as a mediator and moderator between control and complexity at work and personal initiative. *Human Performance*, 10, 171–192.
9. Krueger, N. F. Jr. & Dickson, P. R. (1993) Self-efficacy and perceptions of opportunities and threats. *Psychological Reports*, 72, 1235–1240.
10. Jex, S. M. & Bliese, P. D. (1999) Efficacy beliefs as a moderator of the impact of work-related stressors. *Journal of Applied Psychology*, 84, 349–361.
11. Whyte, G., Saks, A. & Hook, S. (1997) When success breeds failure. *Journal of Organizational Behavior*, 18, 415–432; and Vancouver, J. B., Thompson, C. M., Tischner, E. C. & Putka, D. J. (2002) Two studies examining the negative effect of self-efficacy on performance. *Journal of Applied Psychology*, 87, 506–516.
12. Chen, C. C., Greene, P. G. & Crick, A. (1998) Does entrepreneurial self-efficacy distinguish entrepreneurs from managers? *Journal of Business Venturing*, 13, 295–316; and Cox, L. & Sommer, S. M. (1998). "Attributional styles of entrepreneurs." *Ventures*, proceedings of the 1998 Babson Conference.
13. See, Ahearne, M., Mathieu, J. & Rapp, A. (2005) To empower or not to empower your sales force? *Journal of Applied Psychology*, 90, 945–955; and McNatt, D. B. & Judge, T. A. (2004) Boundary conditions of the Galatea Effect. *Academy of Management Journal,* 47, 550–565.
14. Adapted from Bandura, A. (2004) Cultivate self-efficacy for personal and organizational effectiveness. In E. A. Locke (Ed.) *Handbook of principles of organizational behavior:* 120–136. Malden, MA: Blackwell.
15. Kerr, S. (2004) Editor's introduction: Establishing organizational goals and rewards. *Academy of Management Executive,* 18, 122–123.
16. For reviews see, Locke, E. A. & Latham, G. P, (1990) *A theory of goal setting and task performance*, Englewood Cliffs, NJ: Prentice-Hall; and Locke, E. A. & Latham, G. P. (2002) Building a practically useful theory of goal setting and task motivation. *American Psychologist*, 57, 705–717.
17. Locke, E. A. & Latham, G. P, (1990) *A theory of goal setting and task performance*, Englewood Cliffs, NJ: Prentice-Hall.
18. Latham, G. P., Erez, M. & Locke, E. A. (1988) Resolving scientific disputes by the joint design of crucial experiments. *Journal of Applied Psychology*, 73, 753–772.
19. Locke & Latham (1990) Op. Cit.
20. Locke & Latham (2002) Op. Cit.
21. Harackiewicz, J. M. & Elliott, N. J. (1998) The joint effect of target and purpose goals on intrinsic motivation. *Personality and Social Psychology Bulletin*, 24, 675–689.
22. Locke, E. A. (2000) Motivation, cognition, and action. *Applied Psychology: An International Review*, 49, 408–429.
23. Seijts, G. H. & Latham, G. P. (2001) The effects of learning, outcome, and proximal goals on a moderately complex task. *Journal of Organizational Behavior*, 22, 291–302.
24. Pearce, J. L. (1993) *Volunteers*. New York: Routledge.
25. Dossett, D. L., Latham, G. P. & Mitchell, T. R. (1979) Effects of assigned vs. participatively set goals, knowledge of results, and individual differences on employee behavior when goal

difficulty is held constant. *Journal of Applied Psychology*, 64, 291–298.
26. For the classic description of employee collaboration to limit performance in response to goal ratcheting see, Roethlisberger, F. J. & Dickson, W. J. (1939) *Management and the worker*. Cambridge, MA: Harvard University Press.
27. Jex & Bliese (1999) Op. Cit.
28. Locke, E. A., Smith, K., Erez, M., Chah, D. & Schaffer, A. (1994) The effects of intra-individual goal conflict on performance. *Journal of Management*, 20, 67–91.
29. Schweitzer, M. E., Ordonez, L. & Douma, B. (2004) Goal setting as a motivator of unethical behavior. *Academy of Management Journal,* 47, 422–432.
30. Earley, P. C., Connolly, T. & Ekegren, G. (1989) Goals, strategy development and task performance. *Journal of Applied Psychology,* 74, 24–33.
31. Luthans, F. & Stajkovic, D. (1999) Reinforce for performance. *The Academy of Management Executive,* 13, 49–57.
32. Ibid.
33. Meyer, H. H. (1980) Self-appraisal of job performance. *Personnel Psychology,* 33, 291–295; and Brown, J. D. (1986) Evaluations of self and others. *Social Cognition*, 4, 353-376.
34. Sully de Luque, M. & Sommer, S. M. (2000) The impact of culture on feedback seeking behavior: An integrated model and propositions. *Academy of Management Review,* 25, 829–849.
35. Rogers, R. (1978) *Metaphor*. Berkeley: University of California Press.
36. Arnett, J. (1969) *Feedback and human behavior.* Hammondsworth, UK: Penguin.
37. Kopelman, R. E. (1986) Objective feedback. In E. A. Locke (Ed.) *Generalizing from laboratory to field settings:* 119–145. Boston: DC Heath; and Vigoda-Gadot, E. & Angert, L. and (2007) Goal setting theory, job feedback and OCB. *Basic and Applied Social Psychology*, 29, 119-128.
38. Ibid.
39. Ashcroft, S. J. & Tsui, A. S. (1991) Self-regulation for managerial effectiveness. *Academy of Management Journal,* 34, 251–280.
40. Weiner, B. (1985) An Attribution Theory of achievement motivation and emotion. *Psychological Review,* 92, 548–573.
41. Aguayo, R. (1990) *Dr. Deming.* New York: Simon & Schuster.
42. Cleveland, J. N., Lim A. S. & Muray, K. R. (2007) Feedback phobia? In J. Langan-Fox, C. Cooper, & R. J. Klimoski (Eds.) *Research companion to the dysfunctional workplace*; 168-186. Northhampton, MA: Edward Elgar; and Dugan, K. W. (1989) Ability and effort attributions. *Academy of Management Journal,* 32, 87–114.
43. Jawahar, I. M. & Williams, C. R. (1997) Where all the children are above average. *Personnel Psychology*, 50, 905-926.
44. Ilgen, D. R. & Knowlton, W. A., Jr. (1980) Performance attributional effects on feedback from superiors. *Organizational Behavior and Human Performance,* 25, 441–456.
45. Adapted from Kluger, A. N. & Densi, A. S. (1996) the effects of feedback intervention on performance. *Psychological Bulletin*, 119, 254-284; and Porter, L. W., Lawler, E. E., III & Hackman, J. R. (1975) *Behavior in organizations.* New York: McGraw-Hill.
46. Gino, F. & Schneitzer, M. E. (2008) Blinded by anger or feeling the love. *Journal of Applied Psychology*, 93, 1165-1173.
47. Blau, P. M. & Scott, W. R. (1962) Formal organizations. San Francisco, CA: Chandler.
48. Meyer, M. W. (1994) Measuring performance in economic organizations. In N. J. Smelser & R. Swedberg (Eds.) *Handbook of economic sociology:* 556–580. Princeton, NJ: Princeton University Press.
49. Adapted from Ghorpade, J. & Chen, M. M. (1995) Creating quality-driven performance appraisal systems. *Academy of Management Executive,* 9, 32–41.
50. Thomke, S. & Nimgade, A. (2002) *Bank of America (A) and (B)*. Harvard Business School cases 603-022 and 603-023. Boston, MA: Harvard Business School Press.

51. Lee, F., Edmondson, A. C., Thomke, S. & Worline, M. (2004) The mixed effects of inconsistency on experimentation in organizations. *Organization Science,* 15, 310–326.
52. Meyer, M. W. (1992) Op. Cit.
53. Maier, N. R. F. (1958) Three types of appraisal interviews. *Personnel,* March–April.
54. Pulakos, E. D. Wexley, K. N. (1983) The relationship among perceptual similarity, sex, and performance ratings in management-subordinate dyads. *Academy of Management Journal,* 26, 129–139.
55. See, Mitchell, T. R. & Kalb, L. S. (1982) Effects of job experience on supervisor attributions for a subordinate's poor performance. *Journal of Applied Psychology,* 67, 181–188; and Helsin, P. A., Latham, G. P. & VandeWall, D. (2005) The effect of implicit personality theory on performance appraisals. *Journal of Applied Psychology,* 90, 842–856.
56. Bernardin, H. J., Cardy, R. L. Carlyle, J. J. (1982) Cognitive complexity and appraisal effectiveness. *Journal of Applied Psychology,* 67, 151–160.
57. Jacobs, R., Kafry, D. & Zedeck, S. (1980) Expectations of behaviorally anchored rating scales. *Personnel Psychology,* 33, 595–640.
58. Bernardin, H. J. & Buckley, M. R. (1981) Strategies in rater training. *Academy of Management Review,* 6, 205–212; and London, M., Mone, E. M. & Scott, J. C. (2004) Performance management and assessment. *Human Resource Management*, 43, 319-336.
59. Thompson, P. H. & Dalton, G. W. (1970) Performance appraisal. *Harvard Business Review,* January–February, 149–157; and Schleicher, D. J., Bull, R. A. & Green, S. G. (2009) Rater reactions to forced distribution ratings. *Journal of Management*, 35, 899-927.
60. Atwater, L. E. (1998) The advantages and pitfalls of self-assessment in organizations. In J. W. Smither (Ed.) *Performance appraisal:* 331–342. San Francisco: Jossey-Bass.
61. Thornton, G. C. III (1980) Psychometric properties of self-appraisals of job performance. *Personnel Psychology,* 33, 263–271.
62. Motowidlo, S. J. (1982) Relationship between self-rated performance and pay satisfaction among sales representatives. *Journal of Applied Psychology,* 67, 209–213.
63. DeNisi, A. S., Randolph, W. A. & Blencoe, A. G. (1983) Potential problems with peer ratings. *Academy of Management Journal,* 26, 457–464.
64. Dipboye, R. L. & de Pontbriand, R. (1981) Correlates of employee reactions to performance appraisals and appraisal systems. *Journal of Applied Psychology,* 66, 248–251.
65. Hackman, J. R. & Oldham, G. R. (1980) *Work redesign.* Reading, MA: Addison-Wesley.
66. Smith, D. C. & Bratton, W. J. (2001) Performance management in New York City. In D. W. Forsythe (Ed.) *Quicker, better, cheaper?:* 453–482. Albany, NY: Rockefeller Institute.
67. Hackman, J. R. & Oldham, G. R. (1980) Op. Cit.
68. Morgeson, F. P., Delaney-Klinger, K. & Hemingway, M. A. (2005) The importance of job autonomy, cognitive ability, and job-related skill for predicting role breadth and job performance. *Journal of Applied Psychology,* 90, 399–406.

Chapter 6 Managing Incentives

1. Kerr, S. (1995) On the folly of rewarding A, while hoping for B. *Academy of Management Executive*, 9, 7–14.
2. Updated from the original found in Katz, D. & Kahn, R. L. (1966) *The social psychology of organizations*. New York: John Wiley.
3. Not surprisingly, employees tend to choose and stay in jobs that are better paid. See Feldman, D. C. & Arnold, H. J. (1978) Position choice. *Journal of Applied Psychology*, 63, 706–710; and Mobley, W. H., Hand, H. H., Meglino, B. M. & Griffith, R. W. (1979) Review and conceptual analysis of the employee turnover process. *Psychological Bulletin*, 86, 493–522.
4. Estimates of the costs of turnover are provided in Macy, B. A. & Mirvis, P. H. (1976) A

methodology for assessment of quality of work life and organizational effectiveness in behavior-economic terms. *Administrative Science Quarterly*, 21, 217–226.

5. Absenteeism costs are described in Armour, S. Workplace absenteeism soars 25%, costs millions. *USA Today,* November 6, 1998, p. 1A.
6. Gibson, R. O. (1966) Toward a conceptualization of absence behavior. *Administrative Sciences Quarterly,* 11, 107–133.
7. Dalton, D. R. & Perry, J. L. (1981) Absenteeism and the collective bargaining agreement. *Academy of Management Journal,* 24, 425–431.
8. Rosse, J. G. & Hulin, C. L. (1985) Adaptation to work. *Organizational Behavior and Human Decision Processes,* 36, 324–347.
9. Lawler, E. E., III & Hackman, J. R. (1969) The impact of employee participation in the development of a pay incentive plan. *Journal of Applied Psychology,* 53, 467–471.
10. Ibid.
11. For conscientiousness see, Hurtz, G. M. & Donovan, J. J. (2000) Personality and job performance. *Journal of Applied Psychology,* 85, 869–879; for affect see, Staw, B. M. & Barsade, S. G. (1993) Affect and managerial performance: A test of the sadder-but-wiser vs. happier-and-smarter hypothesis. *Administrative Science Quarterly,* 38, 304–331.
12. Francis Flynn found that the most generous employees were also the most productive. See Flynn, F. J. (2004) How much should I give and how often? *Academy of Management Journal* 46, 539-553.
13. Roethlisberger, F. J. & Dickson, W. J. (1939) *Management and the worker.* Cambridge, MA: Harvard University Press.
14. Rabbie, J. M. (1963) Differential preferences for compensation under threat. *Journal of Abnormal and Social Psychology,* 67, 643–648.
15. Terborg, J. R. & Ungson, G. R. (1985) Group-administered bonus pay and retail store performance. *Journal of Retailing,* 61, 63–77.
16. Roethlisberger, F. J. & Dickson, W. J. (1939) Op. Cit.
17. Judiesch, M. K. & Lyness, K. S. (1999) Left behind? *Academy of Management Journal,* 42, 641–651.
18. MacKenzie, S. B., Podsakoff, P. M. & Ahearne, M. (1998) Some possible antecedents and consequences of in-role and extra role salesperson performance. *Journal of Marketing,* 62, 87–98.
19. Adapted from the research of Farh, J-L., Earley, P. C. & Lin, S-C. (1997) Impetus for action. *Administrative Science Quarterly,* 42, 421–444; Moorman, R. H., Blakely, G. R. & Niehoff, B. P. (1996) Does perceived organizational support mediate the relationship between procedural justice and organizational citizenship behavior? *Academy of Management Journal,* 41, 351–357; Netermeyer, R. G., Boles, J. S., McKee, D. O. & McMurrian (1997) An investigation into the antecedents of organizational citizenship behaviors in a personal selling context. *Journal of Marketing,* 61, 85–98; and Grant, A. M. & Mayer, D. M. (2009) Good soldiers and good actors. *Journal of Applied Psychology*, 94, 900-912.
20. Andersson, L. M. & Bateman, T. S. (1997) Cynicism in the workplace. *Journal of Organizational Behavior,* 18, 449–469.
21. Pearce, J. L. (1983) Job attitude and motivation differences between volunteers and employees from comparable organizations. *Journal of Applied Psychology,* 68, 646–652.
22. Hackman, J. L. & Oldham, G. R. (1980) *Job redesign.* Reading, MA: Addison-Wesley.
23. Hackman, J. L. & Oldham, G. R. (1980) Op. Cit.
24. Adapted from Hackman, J. L. & Oldham, G. R. (1980) Op. Cit.
25. Murray, H. A. and collaborators. (1938) *Explorations in personality.* New York: Oxford University Press.
26. Hall, C. S. & Lindzey, G. (1970) *Theories of personality.* 2nd ed. New York: John Wiley.
27. Herzberg, F., Mausner, B. & Snyderman, B. B. (1959) *The motivation to work.* New York:

Wiley; and Alderfer, C. P. (1972) *Existence, relatedness, and growth.* New York: Free Press.
28. See King, N. (1970) Clarification and evaluation of the two-factor theory of job satisfaction. *Psychological Bulletin,* 74, 18–31; and Wahba, M. A. & Bridwell, L. G. (1976) Maslow reconsidered: A review of research on the need hierarchy theory. *Organizational Behavior and Human Performance,* 15, 212–240.
29. Aguayo, R. (1990) *Dr. Deming.* New York: Simon & Schuster.
30. For executives, see, Tosi, H., Werner, S., Katz, J. & Gomez-Meija, L. (2000) How much does performance matter? *Journal of Management,* 26, 301–339; for employees, see Lawler, E. E., III (1971) *Pay and organizational effectiveness.* New York: McGraw-Hill.
31. Cadsby, C. B., Song, F. & Tapon, F. (2007) Sorting and incentive effects of pay for performance. *Academy of Management Journal*, 50, 387-405.
32. Jurgensen, C. E. (1978) Job preferences (what makes a job good or bad?) *Journal of Applied Psychology,* 63, 267–276; and Shaw, J. D. et al. (2009) Employee–organization exchange relationships, human resources practices and quit rates of good and poor performers. *Academy of Management Journal*, 52, 1016-1033.
33. Locke, E. A., Feren, D. B., McCaleb, V. M., Shaw, K. N. & Denny, A. T. (1980) The relative effectiveness of four methods of motivating employee performance. In K. D. Duncan, M. M. Gruneberg & D. Wallis (Eds.) *Changes in work life:* 363–388. London: Wiley.
34. Andrews, I. R. & Henry, M. M. (1963) Management attitudes toward pay. *Industrial* Relations, 3, 29–49.
35. Ibid.
36. Harris, J. & Bromiley, P. (2005) *Incentives to cheat.* Paper presented at the Annual Academy of Management Meeting, Honolulu, HI.
37. Mahoney, T. A. (1983) Approaches to the definition of comparable worth. *Academy of Management Review,* 8, 14–22.
38. Brown, K. A. & Huber, V. L. (1992) Lowering floors and raising ceilings. *Personnel Psychology,* 45, 279–311.
39. Pearce, J. L. (1987) Why merit pay doesn't work. In D. B. Balkin & L. R. Gomez-Meija (Eds.) *New perspectives on compensation:* 169–178. Englewood Cliffs, N. J.: Prentice-Hall.
40. Pearce, J. L., Stevenson, W. B. & Perry, J. L. (1985) Managerial compensation based on organizational performance. *Academy of Management Journal,* 28, 261–279.
41. Lawler, E. E., III (1971) Op. Cit
42. Messersmith, J. G., et al. (2011) Executive turnover. *Journal of Applied Psychology,* 96, 457-469.
43. Siegel, P. A. & Hambrick, D. C. (2005) Pay disparities within top management groups. *Organization Science,* 16, 259–274.
44. Miceli, M. P., Jung, I., Near, J. P. & Greenberger, D. B. (1991) Predictors and outcomes of reactions to pay-for-performance plans. *Journal of Applied Psychology,* 76, 508–521.
45. DeVoe, S. E. & Pfeffer, J. (2007) Hourly payment and volunteering. *Academy of Management Journal*, 50, 783-798. Groysberg, B., Nanda, A. & Nohira, N. (2004) The risky business of hiring stars. *Harvard Business Review,* May, 1–10.
46. Lawler, E. E., III (1971) Op. Cit.
47. Chilton, K. W. (1994) Lincoln Electric's incentive system. *Compensation & Benefits Review,* 26, 29–34.
48. Miller, C. & Schuster, M. H. (1995) The anatomy of a failure. *Public Administration Quarterly,* 19, 217–224.
49. For example, Morgenson, G. Big bonuses still flow, even if bosses miss goals. *The New York Times,* June 1, 2006. p. A1.
50. Pearce, J. L. (1998) Job insecurity is important, but not for the reasons you might think. In C. L. Cooper & D. M. Rousseau (Eds.) *Trends in organizational behavior,* Vol. 5: 31–46.

New York: John Wiley.

51. Cappelli, P. (1995) Rethinking employment. *British Journal of Industrial Relations,* 35, 563–602.
52. Chandler, A. D. (1977) *The visible hand. Cambridge,* MA: Harvard University Press.
53. Tsui, A. S., Pearce, J. L., Porter, L. W. & Tripoli, A. M. (1997) Alternative approaches to the employee-organization relationship. *Academy of Management Journal,* 40, 1089–1121.
54. Pfeffer, J. (1995) Producing sustainable competitive advantage through the effective management of people. *Academy of Management Executive,* 9, 55–69.
55. Tsui, A. S., et al. (1997) Op. Cit.
56. Pearce, J. L. and Randel, A. (2004) Expectations of organizational mobility, workplace social inclusion and employee job performance. *Journal of Organizational Behavior*, 25, 81–98.
57. Pearce, J. L. (1998) Op. Cit.
58. Gouldner, A. W. (1960) The norm of reciprocity. *American Sociological Review*, 25, 161–178.
59. Pfeffer, J. (1995) Op. Cit.
60. Marmot, M. (2004) *The status syndrome*. New York: Times Books.
61. Stuart, T. E., Hoang, H. & Hybels, R. C. (1999) Interorganizational endorsements and the performance of entrepreneurial ventures. *Administrative Science Quarterly*, 44, 315–349.
62. Levine, J. M. & Moreland, R. L. (1990) Progress in small group research. *Annual Review of Psychology*, 41, 585–634.
63. Webster, M. & Hysom, S. J. (1998) Creating status characteristics. *American Sociological Review*, 63, 351–378.
64. Pearce, J. L., Ramirez, R. R. & Branyiczki, I. (2001) Leadership and the pursuit of status. In W. H. Mobley & M. W. McCall, Jr. (Eds.) *Advances in global leadership. Vol. 2*: 153–178. New York: JAI Press.
65. For example, Pfeffer, J. (1995) Op. Cit.
66. Petersen, D. E. (1991) *A better idea*. Boston: Houghton Mifflin.
67. Pearce, J. L. et al. (2001) Op. Cit.
68. Stajkovic, A. D. & Luthans, F. (1997) A meta-analysis of the effects of organizational behavior modification on task performance, 1975–95. *Academy of Management Journal,* 40, 1122–1149.
69. Harter, J. K. & Creglow, A. (1999) A meta-analysis and utility analysis of the relationship between core employee opinions and business outcomes. In M. Buckingham & C. Coffman (Eds.) *First, break all the rules:* 255–267. New York: Simon & Schuster.
70. Luthans, F. & Stajkovic, A. D. (2004) Provide recognition for performance improvement. In E. A. Locke (Ed.) *Handbook of principles of organizational behavior:* 166–180. Malden, MA: Blackwell.
71. Adapted from Nelson, B. (1994) *1001 ways to reward employees.* New York: Workman.
72. See Greenberg, J. (1988) Equity and workplace status. *Journal of Applied Psychology*, 73, 606–613; and Greenberg, J. (1990) Employee theft as a reaction to underpayment inequity. *Journal of Applied Psychology*, 75, 561–568.
73. Simons, T. & Roberson, Q. (2003) Why managers should care about fairness. *Journal of Applied Psychology,* 88, 432–443; and Luo, Y. (2007) The interdependent and interactive roles of procedural, disruptive and interactional justice in strategic alliances. *Academy of Management Journal*, 50, 644-654.
74. Pearce, J. L. & Henderson, G. R. (2000) Understanding acts of betrayal: Implications for industrial and organizational psychology. In C. L. Cooper and I. T. Robertson (Eds.) *International Review of Industrial and Organizational Psychology 2000:* 165–187 London: John Wiley.

75. Erdogan, B. & Bauer, T. N. (2010) Differentiated leader-member exchanges. *Journal of Applied Psychology*, 95, 1104-1120; and Dornstein, M. (1985) Perceptions regarding standards for evaluating pay equity and their determinants. *Journal of Occupational Psychology,* 58, 321–330.
76. Cropanzano, R. & Greenberg, J. 1997. Progress in organizational justice: Tunneling through the maze. *International Review of Industrial and Organizational Psychology,* 12, 317–372.
77. Greenberg, J. (1990) Op. Cit.
78. Adapted from Folger, R. & Cropanzano, R. (1998) *Organizational justice and human resource management.* Thousand Oaks, CA: Sage.
79. Konovsky, M. A. & Cropanzano, R. (1993) Justice considerations in employee drug testing. In R. Cropanzano (Ed.) *Justice in the workplace*. Hillsdale, NJ: Erlbaum, 171–192.
80. Ibid.
81. Bigley, G. A. & Pearce, J. L. (1998) Straining for shared meaning in organization science. *Academy of Management Review,* 23, 405–421.
82. Kramer, R. M. (1999) Trust and distrust in organizations. *American Review of Psychology*, 50, 569-598: and Salaman, S. D. & Robinson, S. L. (2008) Trust that binds. *Journal of Applied Psychology*, 93, 593-601.
83. Folger, R. & Konovsky, M. A. (1989) Effects of procedural justice, distributive justice, and reactions to pay raise decisions. *Academy of Management Journal,* 32, 115–130.
84. Adapted from Pearce, J. L., Bigley, G. A. & Grubb, A. R. (2006) *What really causes trust?* The Paul Merage School of Business University of California, Irvine Working Paper; and Lau, D. C. & Liden, R. C. (2008) Antecedents of coworker trust. *Journal of Applied Psychology*, 93, 1130-1138; and Slovic, P. (1993) Perceived risk, trust and democracy. *Risk Analysis*, 13, 765-682. Greenburg, J. (2010) Organizational injustice as an occupational health risk. *Academy of Management Analysis*, 4, 205-243.

Chapter 7 Navigating the Social Scene

1. Roethlisberger, F. J. & Dickson, W. J. (1939) *Management and the worker*. Cambridge, MA: Harvard University Press.
2. American Psychiatric Association (1987) *Diagnostic and statistical manual of mental disorders* (3rd ed.) DSM-III-R, Washington, D. C.: American Psychiatric Association.
3. Granovetter, M. S. (1985) Economic action, social structure, and embeddedness. *American Journal of Sociology*, 91, 481-510.
4. For the apparel industry, see Uzzi, B. (1999) Embeddedness in the making of financial capital. *American Sociological Review*, 64, 481-505; for law, see Uzzi, B. & Lancaster, R. (2004) Embeddedness and the price of legal services in the large law firm market. American Sociological Review, 69, 319-344; and for banking, see Jensen, M. (2003) The role of network resources in market entry. *Administrative Science Quarterly*, 48, 466-497.
5. Alderfer, C. P. (1972) *Existence, relatedness and growth*. New York: The Free Press.
6. Ibid.
7. Brief, A. P. (1998) *Attitudes in and around organizations*. Thousand Oaks, CA: Sage; and Heaphy, E. D. & Dutton, J. E. (2008) Positive social interactions and the human body at work. Academy of Management Review, 33, 137-162..
8. The Europeans have led research on the social context of emotions and attitudes. An excellent example is Tajfel, H. (1984) *The social dimension. Vol. 2*. Cambridge, UK: Cambridge University Press.
9. George, J. M. (1995) Leader positive mood and group performance. *Journal of Applied Social Psychology*, 25, 778-794; Hsee, C. K., Hatfield, E., Carlson, J. G. & Chemtob, C. (1990) The effect of power on susceptibility to emotional contagion. *Cognition & Emotion*,

4, 327-340; and Hatfield, E., Cacioppo, J. T. & Rapson, R. L. (1994) *Emotional contagion*. Cambridge, UK: Cambridge University Press.

10. Bartel, C. A. & Saavedra, R. (2000) The collective construction of work group moods. *Administrative Science Quarterly*, 45, 197-231; and Totterdell, P. et al. (2004) Affect networks. *Journal of Applied Psychology*, 89, 854-867.
11. Bakker, A. B. & Xanthopoulou, D. (2009) The crossover of daily work engagement. *Journal of Applied Psychology*, 94, 1562-1571; and Felps W., et al. (2009) Turnover contagion. *Academy of Management Journal*, 52, 545-561.
12. Leiberman, S. (1956) The effects of changes in roles on the attitudes of role occupants. *Human Relations*, 9, 385-402.
13. Brehm, J. W. & Mann, M. (1975) Effects of importance of freedom and attraction to group members on influence produced by group pressure. *Journal of Personality and Social Psychology*, 31, 816-824.
14. Blau, P. M. & Scott, W. R. (1962) *Formal organizations*. San Francisco: Chandler; and Chiaburu, D.S. & Harrison, D.A. (2008) Do peers make the place? *Journal of Applied Psychology*, 93, 1082-1103.
15. Trist, E. L., Susman, G. I. & Brown, G. R. (1977) An experiment in autonomous working in an American underground coal mine. *Human Relations*, 30, 201-236.
16. For a recent meta-analysis, see Duffy, M. (2008) *Consequences of social undermining and support*. Society for Industrial and Organizational Psychology Annual Meeting, San Francisco.
17. Ibid.; and Porath, C. L. & Erez, A. (2007) Does rudeness really matter? *Academy of Management Journal*, 50, 1181-1197.
18. Halbesleben, J. R. B. & Buckley, M. R. (2004) Burnout in organizational life. *Journal of Management*, 30, 859-879.
19. Halbesleben, J. R. B. (2006) Sources of social support and burnout. *Journal of Applied Psychology*, 91, 1134-1145.
20. Trist, E. L., et al. (1977) Op. Cit.
21. Haslam, S. A. & Reicher, S. (2006) Stressing the group. *Journal of Applied Psychology*, 91, 1037-1052; and Blader, S. L. & Tyler, T. R. (2009) Testing and extending the group engagement model. *Journal of Applied Psychology*, 94, 445-464.
22. Some of the ideas are adapted from the Take Care! Program described in Le Blanc, P. M., Hox, J. J., Schaufeli, W. B., Taris, T. W. & Peeters, M. C. W. (2007) Take Care! *Journal of Applied Psychology*, 92, 213-227.
23. Sanders, K. (2004) Playing truant within organizations. *Journal of Managerial Psychology*, 19, 136-155.
24. Asch, S. E. (1955) Opinions and social pressure. *Scientific American*, 193, 31-35; and Weiner, M. Certainty of judgment a variable in conformity behavior. *Journal of Social Psychology*, 48, 257-263.
25. Salancik, G. R. & Pfeffer, J. (1978) A social information processing approach to job attitudes and task design. *Administrative Science Quarterly*, 23, 224-253; and Gino, F., Ayal, S. & Ariley, D. (2009) Contagion and differentiation in unethical behavior. *Psychological Science*, 26, 393-398.
26. Westphal, J. D. & Stern, I. (2006) The other pathway to the boardroom. *Administrative Science Quarterly*, 51, 169-204.
27. Pfeffer, J. (1977) Toward an examination of stratification in organizations. *Administrative Science Quarterly*, 22, 553-567.
28. Griffin, R. W. (1983) Objective and social sources of information in task redesign. *Administrative Science Quarterly*, 28, 184-200; and Newman, S., Griffin, M. A. & Mason, C. (2008) Safety in work vehicles. *Journal of Applied Psychology*, 93, 632-644.
29. Glick, W. H. (1985) Conceptualizing and measuring organizational and psychological cli-

mate. *Academy of Management Review*, 10, 601-616.

30. Drexler, J. A., Jr. (1977) Organizational climate. *Journal of Applied Psychology*, 62, 38-42.
31. Schneider, B., Parkington, J. J. & Buxton, V. M. (1980) Employee and customer perceptions of service in banks. *Administrative Science Quarterly*, 25, 252-267.
32. Ibid.
33. For a summary of their work, see Schneider, B. & Bowen, D. E. (1995) *Winning the service game*. Boston: Harvard Business School Press.
34. Ibid
35. Zajonc, R. B. (1965) Social facilitation. *Science*, 149, 269-274.
36. Szymanski, K., Garczynski, J. & Harkins, S. (2000) The contribution of potential for evaluation to coaction effects. *Group Processes & Intergroup Relations*, 3, 269-283.
37. Cottrell, N. B., Wack, D. L., Sekerak, G. J. & Rittle, R. H. (1968) Social facilitation of dominant responses by the presence of an audience and the mere presence of others. *Journal of Personality and Social Psychology*, 9, 245-250.
38. Messe, L. A., Hertel, G., Kerr, N. L., Lount, R. B., Jr., & Park, E. S. (2001) Knowledge of partner's ability as a moderator of group motivation gains. *Journal of Personality and Social Psychology*, 82, 935-946.
39. Groysberg, B. (in press) *The portability of stardom*. Princeton, NJ: Princeton University Press.
40. Festinger, L. (1954) A theory of social comparison processes. *Human Relations*, 7, 117-140.
41. Goldstein, N. & Cialdini, R. (2007) The spyglass self. *Journal of Personality and Social Psychology*, 92, 402-417.
42. Shah, P. P. (1998) Who are employees' social referents? *Academy of Management Journal*, 41, 249-268; and Feldman, N. S. & Ruble, D. N. (1981) Social comparison strategies. *Personality and Social Psychology*, 7, 11-16.
43. Colquitt, J. A., Greenberg, J. & Zapata-Phelan, C. P. (2005) What is organizational justice? In J. Greenberg & J. A. Colquitt (Eds.) *Handbook of organizational justice*: 3-55. Mahwah, NJ: Lawrence Erlbaum Associates.
44. Hansson, R. O., Jones, W. H. & Fletcher, W. L. (1990) Troubled relationships in later life. *Journal of Social & Personal Relationships*, 7, 451-463.
45. Bommer, W. H., Dierdorff, E. C. & Rubin, R. S. (2007) Does prevalence mitigate relevance? *Academy of Management Journal*, 50, 1481-1494.
46. Sommer, S. M. (1995) Social competition. *International Journal of Conflict Management*, 6, 239-256.
47. *The Economist*, May 17th, 2008, page 16.
48. Poortvliet, P. M. & Darnon, C. (2010) Toward a more social understanding of achievement goals. *Current Directions in Psychological Science*, 19, 324-328; and Ku, G., Malhotra, D. & Murninghan, J. K. (2005) Toward a competitive arousal model of decision-making. *Organizational Behavior and Human Decision Processes*, 96, 89-103.
49. Sommer, S. M. & Farner, S. (1996) *The impact of cooperation and competition on performance and affect*. Western Academy of Management Annual Meeting, Banff, Alberta.
50. Festinger, L. (1953) An analysis of compliant behavior: 232-256. In M. Sherif & M. O. Wilson (Eds.) *Group relations at the crossroads*. New York: Harper.
51. Allen, V. & Levine, J. (1971) Social support and conformity. *Journal of Experimental Social Psychology*, 7, 48-58.
52. Nemeth, C. (2001) Devil's advocate versus authentic dissent. *European Journal of Social Psychology*, 31, 707-720.
53. For a review, see Hackman, J. R. (1976) Op. Cit.
54. Ferris, G. R., Blass, F. R., Douglas, C., Kolodinsky, R. W. & Treadway, D. C. (2003) Personal reputation in organizations. In J. Greenberg (Ed.) *Organizational behavior* (2nd

ed.): 211-246. Mahwah, NJ: Lawrence Erlbaum & Associates.
55. Huang, Z. (2006) *From chaos to order*. Annual Meeting of the Academy of Management Meeting. Atlanta, GA.
56. Weisenfeld, B. M., Wurthmann, K. A. & Hambrick, D. C. (2008) The stigmatization and devaluation of elites associated with corporate failures. *Academy of Management Review*, 33, 231-251.
57. Kulik, C. T., Bainbridge, H. T. J. & Cregan, C. (2008) Known by the company we keep. *Academy of Management Review*, 33, 216-230.
58. Baumeister, R. (1982) Self-esteem, self-presentation, and future interaction. *Journal of Personality*, 50, 29-45.
59. Greenberg, J. (1990) Looking fair vs. being fair. In B. M. Staw & l. L. Cummings (Eds.) *Research in organizational behavior*. Vol. 12: 111-157. Greenwich, CT: JAI.
60. Ferris, G., Treadway, D., Kolodinsky, R., Hochwarter, W., Kacmar, C., Douglas, C. & Frink, D. (2005) Development and validation of the political skill inventory. *Journal of Management*, 31, 126-152.
61. Merry, S. E. (1984) Rethinking gossip and scandal: 271-302. D. Black (Ed.) *Toward a general theory of social control*. New York: Academic Press.
62. Adapted from Ferris, G. R. et al. (2003) Ibid.
63. Biddle, B. J. (1979) *Role theory*. New York: Academic Press.
64. Hackman, J. R. (1976) Group influences on individuals. In M. D. Dunnette (Ed.) *Handbook of industrial and organizational psychology*: 1455-1525. Chicago: Rand McNally.
65. Bandura proposes that in order to learn something, the information must attract the learner's attention, and it is more likely to attract the learner's attention if it seems useful or might have future benefits. See Bandura, A. (1986) *Social foundations of thought and action*. Englewood Cliffs, NJ: Prentice-Hall.
66. Krackhardt, D. & Porter, L. W. (1985) When friends leave. *Administrative Science Quarterly*, 30, 242-261.
67. Van Maanen, J. (1976) Breaking in. In R. Dubin (Ed.) *Handbook of work, organization, and society*: 67-130. Chicago: Rand McNally.

Chapter 8 Understanding Cultures

1. Ouchi, W. G. (1981) *Theory* Z. Reading, MA: Addison-Wesley.
2. Geertz, C. (2000) *The interpretation of cultures*. New York: Basic Books.
3. Ibid.
4. Hall, E. T. (1990) *The silent language*. New York: Doubleday.
5. Thibaut, J. W. & Kelley, H. H. (1959) *The social psychology of groups*. New York: Wiley.
6. Weeks, J. (2003) *Unpopular culture*. Chicago: University of Chicago Press.
7. Davis, K. (1950) *Human society*. New York: Macmillan.
8. Kiesler, C. A. & Kiesler, S. B. (1969) *Conformity*. Reading, MA: Addison-Wesley.
9. Schwartzman, H. B. (1987) The significance of meetings in an American mental health center. *American Ethnologist*, 14, 271-294.
10. Ibid.
11. Rogelberg, S. G., Allen, J. A., Shanock, L., Scott, C. W. & Shuffler, M. (2008) *Meetings at work*. Society for Industrial and Organizational Psychology Annual Meeting, San Francisco.
12. Hannan, M. T. & Freeman, J. (1977) The population ecology of organizations. *American Journal of Sociology*, 82, 929-964.
13. Schneider, B. (1987) The people make the place. *Personnel Psychology*, 40, 437-543.
14. Hofstede, G. (1980) Motivation, leadership, and organization: Do American theories apply abroad? *Organization Dynamics*, Summer, 42-63; and Miller, D. & Friesen, P. H. (1980)

Momentum and revolution in organizational adaptation. *Academy of Management Journal*, 23, 591-614.

15. Westney, D. E. (1987) *Imitation and innovation*. Cambridge, MA: Harvard University Press.
16. Zucker, L. (1986) Production of trust. *Research in Organizational Behavior*, 8, 53-112.
17. Caincross, F. (2002) *The company of the future*. Boston, MA: Harvard Business School Press.
18. Kelley, H. H. & Volkart, E. H. (1962) The resistance to change of group anchored attitudes. *American Sociological Review*, 17, 453-465.
19. Lewin, K. (1958) Group decision and social change. In E. Macoby, T. Newcombe & E. Hartley (Eds.) *Readings in social psychology* (3rd ed.) : 197-211. New York: Holt, Rinehart and Winston.
20. Deal, T. & Kennedy, A. (1982) Corporate cultures. Reading, MA: Addison-Wesley.
21. Jelenik, M. & Schoonhoven, C. B. (1993) *The innovation marathon*. San Francisco: Jossey-Bass.
22. Miller, D. (1994) What happens after success. *Journal of Management Studies*, 31, 325-358.
23. Adapted from Batt, R. (2002) Managing customer services. *Academy of Management Journal*, 45, 587-597; and Collins, C. J. & Smith, K. G. (2006) Knowledge exchange and combination. *Academy of Management Journal*, 49, 544-560.
24. Ichniowski, C., Shaw, K. & Prennushi, G. (1997) The effects of human resource management practices on productivity. *American Economic Review*, 87, 291-313.
25. Datta, D. K., Guthrie, J. P. & Wright, P. M. (2005) Human resource management and labor productivity. *Academy of Management Journal*, 48, 135-145; Collins, C. J. & Smith, K. G. (2006) Collins, C. J. & Smith, K. G. (2006) Knowledge exchange and combination. *Academy of Management Journal*, 49, 544-560; Iverson, R. D., Zatzick, C. D. & McCrae, M. M. (2008) High performance work systems. In J. Barling & C. L. Cooper (Eds.) *The Sage handbook of organizational behavior*: 393-409. Thousand Oaks, CA: Sage; and Flood, P. C. et al. (2010) *Partnership Climate High Performance Work Systems and Organizational Effectiveness*. Annual Meeting of the Academy of Management, Chicago, IL.
26. Batt, R. (2002) Managing customer services. Academy of Management Journal, 45, 587-597.
27. Zatzick, C. D. & Iverson, R. D. (2006) High involvement management and workforce reduction. *Academy of Management Journal*, 49, 999-1015.
28. Collins, C. J. & Smith, K. G. (2006) Op. Cit.
29. McPherson, M., Smith-Lovin, L. & Cook, J. (2001) Birds of a feather. *Annual Review of Sociology*, 27, 415-444; and Edwards, J. R. & Cable, D. M. (2009) The value of congruence. *Journal of Applied Psychology*, 94, 654-677.
30. Chandler, A. D. (1977) *The visible hand*. Cambridge, MA: Harvard University Press.
31. Gibson, C. B. & Gibbs, J. L. (2006) Unpacking the concept of virtuality. *Administrative Science Quarterly*, 51, 451-495; and Kelliher, C. & Anderson, D. (2010) Doing more with less? *Human Relations*, 63, 83-106.
32. Byron, K. (2008) Carrying too heavy a load. *Academy of Management Review*, 33, 309-327.
33. Adapted from Gibson, C. B. & Gibbs, J. L. (2006), Op. Cit.; and Govindarajan, V. & Gupta, A. K. (2001) Building an effective global business team. *MIT Sloan Management Review*, 42(4), 63-71.
34. For manager-friendly reviews, see Steers, R. M. & Nardon, L. (2006) *Managing in a global economy*. Armonk, NY: M. E. Sharpe; and Adler, N. J. (1997) *International dimensions of organizational behavior*. (3rd ed.) Cincinnati, OH: South-Western.
35. Parsons, T. & Shils, E. A. (1951) *Toward a general theory of action*. Cambridge, MA: Harvard University Press.
36. Smith, P. B., Dugan, S. & Trompenaars, F. (1996) National culture and the values of organizational employees. *Journal of Cross-Cultural Psychology*, 27, 231-264.

37. Xin, K. and Pearce, J. L. (1996) Guanxi: Connections as substitutes for formal institutional support. *Academy of Management Journal*, 39, 1641-1658; and Henrich, J. (2000) Does culture matter in economic behavior? *American Economic Review*, 90, 973-979..
38. Hofstede, G. (2001) *Culture's consequences* (2nd ed.) Thousand Oaks, CA: Sage.
39. Ibid.
40. Earley, P. C. (1989) Social loafing and collectivism. *Administrative Science Quarterly*, 34, 565-581.
41. Hofstede, G. (2001) Op. Cit.
42. Newman, K. L. & Nollen, S. D. (1996) Culture and congruence. *Journal of International Business Studies*, 27, 753-779.
43. Offerman, L. R. & Hellmann, P. S. (1997) Culture's consequences for leadership behavior. *Journal of Cross-Cultural Psychology*, 28, 342-351.
44. Pearce, J. L. (2001) *Organization and management in the embrace of government*. Mahwah, NJ: Lawrence Erlbaum Associates.
45. Shipper, F., Hoffman, R. C. & Rotondo, D. M. (2007) Does the 360 degree feedback process create actionable knowledge equally across cultures? *Academy of Management Learning & Education,* 6, 33-50.
46. Erez, M. (2004) Make management practice fit organizational culture. In E. A. Locke (Ed.) *Handbook of principles of organizational behavior*: 418-434. Malden, MA: Blackwell.
47. Tihany, L., Griffith, D. A. & Russell, C. J. (2005) The effect of cultural distance on entry mode, choice, international diversification and MNE performance. *Journal of International Business Studies*, 35, 270-283.
48. Ng, K. & Earley, P. C. (2006) Culture + intelligence. *Group and Organization Management*, 31, 4-19.
49. Barkema, H. G., Shenkar, O., Vermeulen, F. & Bell, J. (1997) Working abroad, working with others. *Academy of Management Journal*, 40, 426-442.
50. Brief. A. (2008) *Diversity at work*. Cambridge: Cambridge University Press.
51. Bendick, M., Jr., Jackson, C. W. & Reinoso, V. A. (1994) Measuring employment discrimination through controlled experiments. *Review of Black Political Economy*, 23, 25-48; James, E. H. (2000) Race-related differences in promotions and support. *Organizational Science*, 11, 493-508; Dietch, E. A., et al. (2003) Subtle yet significant. *Human Relations*, 56, 1299-1324; and Stauffer, J. M. & Buckley, M. R. (2005) The existence and nature of racial bias in supervisory ratings. *Journal of Applied Psychology*, 90, 586-591.
52. Chartier, G. & Fritzche, B. A. (2007) *Discrimination against Asian Americans*. Annual Meeting of the Society for Organizational and Industrial Psychology, New York, New York.
53. Simpson, P. A. & Stroh, L. K. (2004) Gender differences. *Journal of Applied Psychology*, 89, 715-721; and Heilman, M. E. & Chen, J. J. (2005) Same behavior, different consequences. *Journal of Applied Psychology*, 90, 431-441.
54. Foschi, M. (1996) Double standards in the evaluation of men and women. *Social Psychology Quarterly*, 59, 237-254; and Heilman, M. E. & Haynes, M. C. (2005) No credit where credit is due. *Journal of Applied Psychology*, 90, 905-916.
55. Graves, L. M. & Elsass, P. M. (2005) Sex and sex dissimilarity effects in ongoing teams. *Human Relations*, 58, 191-221.
56. Westphal, J. D. & Stern, I. (2006) The other pathway to the boardroom. *Administrative Science Quarterly*, 51, 169-204.
57. Bezrukova, K., Joshi, A. & Jehn, K. A. (2008) *Diversity training research in organizational settings*. Annual Meeting of the Society for Industrial and Organizational Psychology, San Francisco, CA; and Kalev, A., Dobbin, F. & Kelly, E. (2006) Best practices or best guesses? *American Sociological Review*, 71, 589-617.
58. van Knippenberg, D. & Schippers, M. C. (2007) Work group diversity. *Annual Review of Psychology*, 58, 515-541.

59. Milliken, F. J. & Martins, L. L. (1996) Searching for common threads. *Academy of Management Review*, 21, 402-433.
60. Flynn, F., Chatman, J. A. & Spataro, S. E. (2001) Getting to know you. *Administrative Science Quarterly*, 46, 414-442.

Chapter 9 Mastering Power

1. See Gentry, W. (2008) *Political skills as an indicator of managerial success*. Annual Meeting of the Society of Industrial and Organizational Psychology, San Francisco, CA; and Luthans, F., Hodgetts, R., & Rosenkrantz, (1988) *Real managers*. New York: Harper Row.
2. Pelz, D. C. (1952) Influence. *Personnel*, 29, 209-217
3. The inset boxed opinion was taken from Greene, R. (1998) *The 48 laws of power*. New York: Penguin. The classics in this genre include Machiavelli, N. (1999). *The prince*. New York: Penguin; and Sun Tzu, (2004) *The art of war*. New York: Barnes and Noble Classics series.
4. Pfeffer, J. (1981) *Power in organizations*. Marshfield, MA: Pitman.
5. See Lux, S. (2008) A *multi-level conceptualization of organizational politics*. Annual Meeting of the Society of Industrial and Organizational Psychology, San Francisco, CA.
6. Emerson, R. M. (1962) Power-dependence relations. *American Sociological Review*, 27, 31-41; and Bierstedt, R. (1950) An analysis of social power. *American Sociological Review*, 15, 730-738.
7. Pfeffer, J. & Salancik, G. R. (1977) Administrator effectiveness. *Human Relations*, 30, 641-656; and Bedi, A. & Schat, A. C. H. (2008) *Perceptions of organizational politics*. Annual Meeting of the Society of Industrial and Organizational Psychology, San Francisco, CA.
8. Weber, M. (1947) *The theory of social and economic organization*. New York: Free Press.
9. Sayles, L. (1979) *Leadership*. New York: McGraw-Hill.
10. Kacmar, K. M. & Carlson, D. S. (1997) Further validation of the perceptions of organizational politics scale (POPS). *Journal of Management*, 23, 627-658; and Ferris, G. R., Adams, G., Kolodinsky, R. W., Hochwarter, W. A. & Ammeter, A. P. (2002) Perceptions of organizational politics. In F. J. Yammarino & F. Dansereau (Eds.) *The many faces of multi-level issues*: 179-254. New York: Elsevier Science.
11. Lasswell, H. D. (1936) *Politics*. New York: McGraw-Hill; and in organizational behavior, Pfeffer, J. (1981) Op. Cit.
12. For a good discussion of the costs of secrecy, see Lawler, E. E., III (1971) *Pay and organizational effectiveness*. New York: McGraw-Hill.
13. Simons, T. & Roberson, Q. (2003) Why managers should care about fairness. *Journal of Applied Psychology*, 88, 432–443.
14. Machiavelli, N. (1999). Op. Cit.
15. Gilovich, T. (1991) *How what we know isn't so*. New York: Free Press.
16. McCall, M. W., Lombardo, M. W. & Morrison, A. M. (1988) *Lessons of experience*. New York: Simon Schuster.
17. Adapted from Ashforth, B. E. & Lee, R. (1990) Defensive behavior in organizations. *Human Relations*, 43, 621-648
18. Pfeffer, J. (1981) Op. Cit.
19. Allen, R. W., et al. (1979) Organizational politics. *California Management Review*, 22, 77-83.

21. Ibid.

20. Bedi, A. & Schat, A. C. H. (2008) Op. Cit.

22. Nemeth, C. J. (1997) Managing innovation. *California Management Review*, 40, 173-189; and Kosmala, K. & Herrbach, O. (2006) The ambivalence of professional identity. *Human Relations*, 59, 1393-1428.

23. Magee, J. C., Galinsky, A. & Gruenfeld, D. (2007) Op. Cit.
24. Drory, E. & Singh, V. (2008) *The challenge of organizational politics*. Annual Meeting of the Academy of Management, Anaheim, CA.
25. Magee, J. C., Galinsky, A. & Gruenfeld, D. (2007) Power, propensity to negotiate, and moving first in competitive interactions. *Personality and Social Psychology Bulletin*, 33, 200-212.
26. Keltner, D., Gruenfeld, D. H. & Anderson, C. (2003) Power, approach, and inhibition. *Psychological Review*, 110, 265-284; and see, K. E., Rothman, N. B. & Soll, J. B. (2010) *Powerful and Unpersuaded*. Annual Meeting of the Academy of Management, Montreal, Quebec.
27. Kanter, R. M. (1979) Power failure in management circuits. *Harvard Business Review*, July-August, 65-75.
28. Berdahl, J. (2007) Harassment based on sex. *Academy of Management Review*, 32, 641-658.
29. Jones, E. E. (1964) *Ingratiation*. New York: Appleton-Century-Crofts.
30. Brehm, J. W. (1966) *A theory of psychological reactance*. New York: Academic Press.
31. Salancik, G. R. & Pfeffer, J. (1974) The bases and use of power in organizational decision making. *Administrative Science Quarterly*, 19, 453-473.
32. Katz, D. & Kahn, R. L. (1966) *The social psychology of organizations*. New York: Wiley.
33. Galbraith, J. R. (1995). *Designing organizations*, San Francisco: Jossey-Bass.
34. Goldner, F. H. (1970) The division of labor. In M. N. Zald (Ed.) *Power in organizations*: 97-143. Nashville, TN: Vanderbilt University Press..
35. Dearborn, D. C. & Simon, H. A. (1958) Selective perception. *Sociometry*, 21, 140-143.
36. Lawrence, P. R. & Lorsch, J. W. (1967) *Organization and environment*. Boston, MA: Harvard Business School Press.
37. Eisenhardt, K. M., Kahwajy, J. L. & Bourgeois III, L. J. (1997) How management teams can have a good fight. *Harvard Business Review*, 75:4, 77-85.
38. Goffman, E. (1959) *The presentation of self in everyday life*. New York: Overlook Press.
39. Tannenbaum, P. H. (1967) The congruity principle revisited. In L. Berkowitz (Ed.) *Advances in experimental social psychology*, Vol. 3: 271-320. New York: Academic Press.
40. Pearce, J. L., Ramirez, R. R. & Branyiczki, I. (2001) Leadership and the pursuit of status: Effects of globalization and economic transformation. In W. S. Mobley & M. McCall (Eds.) *Advances in Global Leadership*, 2, 153-178.
41. Goldner, F. H. (1970) Op. Cit.
42. Gray, B. & Ariss, S. S. (1985) Politics and strategic change across life cycles. *Academy of Management Review*, 10, 707-723.
43. Gandz, J. & Murray, V. V. (1980) The experience of workplace politics. *Academy of Management Journal*, 23, 237-251.
44. Rosen, C. C., Levy, P. E. & Hall, R. J. (2006) Placing perceptions of politics in the context of the feedback environment, employee attitudes, and job performance. *Journal of Applied Psychology,* 91, 211-230.
45. Hodson, R., Roscigno, V. J., & Lopez, S. H.. (2006) Chaos and the abuse of power. *Work and Occupations*, 33, 382-416.
46. Galbraith, J. R. (1995) Op. Cit.
47. For a description of how Japanese companies extend and expand power within their organizations, see Ouchi, W. G. (1982) *Theory Z*. New York: HarperCollins.
48. Pearce, J. L., Stevenson, W. B., & Porter, L. W. (1986) Coalitions in the organizational context. In R. J. Lewicki, M. H. Bazerman, & B. Sheppard (Eds.), *Research on negotiation in organizations*, Vol. 1: 97-115. Greenwich, CT: JAI Press.
49. For a discussion of the organizational behavior under the highly centralized power of communism, see Pearce, J. L. (2001) *Organization and management in the embrace of government*. Mahwah, NJ: Lawrence Erlbaum.

50. Thomas, K. W. & Velthouse, B. A. (1990) Cognitive elements of empowerment. *Academy of Management Review*, 15, 666-681
51. Galbraith, J. R. (1995) Op. Cit.
52. See discussion in Drory, E. & Singh, V. (2008) Op. Cit.
53. Srivastava, A., Bartol, K. M. & Locke, E. A. (2006) Empowering leadership in management teams. *Academy of Management Journal*, 49, 1239-1251.
54. McClelland, D. C., & Boyatzis, R. E. (1982) Leadership motive pattern and long-term success in management. *Journal of Applied Psychology*, 67, 737-743; & Treadway, D. C., Hochwater, W. A., Kacmar, C. J., & Ferris, G. R. (2005) Political will, political skill and political behavior. *Journal of Organizational Behavior*, 26, 229-245.
55. Burt, R. S. (1998) Personality correlates of structural holes: 221-250. In R. M. Kramer & M. A. Neale (Eds.) *Power and influence in organizations*. Thousand Oaks, CA: Sage.
56. Anderson, C., Spataro, S. E. & Flynn, F. J. (2008) Personality and organizational culture as determinants of influence. *Journal of Applied Psychology*, 93, 702-710.
57. Bedi, A. & Schat, A. C. H. (2008) *Perceptions of organizational politics*. Annual Meeting of the Society of Industrial and Organizational Psychology, San Francisco, CA; and in those studies finding individual effects, for those trained in statistics: The amount of variance explained by individual differences variables is always less than 20%, sometimes substantially less.
58. Podsakoff, P. M. & Schriesheim, C. A. (1985) Field studies of French and Raven's Bases of Power. *Psychological Bulletin*, 97, 387-411.
59. A study finding gender differences: Carli, L. L., LaFleur, S. J., & Loeber, C. C. (1995) Nonverbal behavior, gender, and influence. *Journal of Personality & Social Psychology*, 68, 1030-1041; a study finding no gender differences: Aguinis, H. & Adams, S. K. (1998) Social-role versus structural models of gender and influence use in organizations. *Group & Organization Management*, 23, 414-446.
60. Jones, E. E. & Pittman, T. S. (1982) Toward a general theory of strategic self-presentations. In J. Suls (Ed.) *Psychological perspectives on the self*, Vol. 1: 231-262. Mahwah, NJ: Lawrence Erlbaum.
61. McGuire, W. J. (1968) Personality and susceptibility to social influence. In E. F. Borgatta & W. W. Lambert (Eds.) *Handbook of Personality Theory and Research*: 1130-1187, Chicago: Rand McNally.
62. Tyler, T. (1998) The psychology of authority relations. In R. M. Kramer & M. A. Neale (Eds.) *Power and influence in organizations*: 251-260. Thousand Oaks, CA: Sage.
63. Skogstad, A., Einarsen, S., Torsheim, T., Aasland, M. S., & Hetland, H. (2007) The destructiveness of laissez-faire leadership behavior. *Journal of Occupational Health Psychology*, 12, 80-92.
64. For example, see Bovard, E. W., Jr. (1953) Conformity to social norms in stable and temporary groups. *Science*, 117, 361-363.
65. For a review, see Moscovici, S. (1985) Social influence and conformity. In G. Lindzey & Aronson, E. (Eds.) *Handbook of Social Psychology* (3rd ed.): 347-412. New York: Random House; & Jones, E. E. (1964) Op. Cit.
66. Ibid.
67. Jones, E. E. & Pittman, T. S. (1982) Op. Cit.
68. Liden, R. C. & Mitchell, T. R. (1988) Ingratiatory behaviors in organizational settings. *Academy of Management Review*, 13, 572-587.
69. For example, see Westphal, J. D. & Stern, I. (2007) Flattery will get you everywhere (especially if you are a male Caucasian). *Academy of Management Journal*, 50, 267-288.
70. An excellent practical discussion of sophisticated impression management acts can be found in Rosenfeld, P., Giacalone, R. A., & Riordan, C. A. (2002) *Impression management*. London: Thompson Learning.

71. Cacioppo, J. T. & Petty, R. E. (1979) Effects of message repetition and position on cognitive response, recall, and persuasion. *Journal of Personality and Social Psychology*, 37, 97-109.
72. For example, see Sidanius, J., Pratto, F., van Laar, C., & Levin, S. (2004) Social Dominance Theory. *Political Psychology*, 25, 845-879.
73. Gottfried, H. (1994) Learning the score. In J. M. Jermier, D. Knights, & W. R. Nord (Eds.) *Resistance and power in organizations*: 102-127. London: Routledge.
74. Ashforth, B. E. (1989) The experience of powerlessness in organizations. *Organizational Behavior and Human Decision Processes*, 43, 207-242.
75. Morgan, D. H. J. (1975) Autonomy and negotiation in an industrial setting. *Sociology of Work and Occupations*, 2, 203-226.
76. Lammers, J., Galinsky, A. D., Gordijn, E. H., & Otten, S. (2008). Legitimacy moderates the effects of power on approach. *Psychological Science*, 19, 558-564.
77. Alinsky, S. (1971) *Rules for radicals*. New York: Vintage.
78. Pfeffer, J. (1981) Op. Cit.
79. Hickson, D. J., Hinings, C. R., Lee, C. A., Schneck, R. E., & Pennings, J. M. (1971) A Strategic Contingencies' Theory of intraorganizational power. *Administrative Science Quarterly*, 16, 216-229.
80. Salancik, G. R. & Pfeffer, J. (1977) Who gets power – and how they hold on to it. *Organizational Dynamics*, 5, 3-21.
81. Salancik, G. R. & Pfeffer, J. (1974) Op. Cit.
82. Ibid; and Carpenter, M. A. & Wade, J. B. (2002) Microlevel opportunity structures as determinants of non-CEO executive pay. *Academy of Management Journal*, 45, 1085-1103.; & Casciaro, T. & Pisjorski, M. J. (2005) Power imbalance, mutual dependence, and constraint absorption. *Administrative Science Quarterly*, 50, 167-199.
83. Summarized in Donaldson, L. (2001) *The contingency theory of organizations*. Thousand Oaks, CA: Sage, who also discusses some of the critiques.
84. Caro, R. A. (1982) *The path to power*. New York: Knopf.
85. French, J. R. P. & Raven, B. (1959) Op. Cit.
86. Pfeffer, J. (1981) Op. Cit.
87. Pettigrew, A. M. (1972) Information control as a power resource. *Sociology*, 6, 187-204.
88. For example, see Won, S., Ho, V. T., & Lee, C. H. (2008) A power perspective to interunit knowledge transfer. *Journal of Management*, 34, 127-150; & Foddy, M. & Smithson, M. (1996) Relative ability, paths of relevance, and influence in task-oriented groups. *Social Psychology Quarterly*, 59, 140-153.
89. For a classic example, see Crozier, M. (1964) *The bureaucratic phenomenon*. Chicago: The University of Chicago Press.
90. Pfeffer, J. (1981) Op. Cit; and more recently, Levina, N. & Orlikowski, W. J. (forthcoming) Understanding shifting power relations within and across organizations. *Academy of Management Journal*.
91. Hitt, M. A., Bierman, L., Uhlenbruck, K., & Shimizu, K. (2006) The importance of resources in the internationalization of professional service firms. *Academy of Management Journal*, 49, 1137-1157; & Hochberg, Y. V, Ljundqvist, A., & Lu, Y. (2007) Whom you know matters. *Journal of Finance*, 112, 251-301..
92. Discussed in Burt, R. S. (2005) *Brokerage and closure*. Oxford, UK: Oxford University Press.
93. Ibid.
94. Bowler, W. M. & Brass, D. J. (2006) Relational correlates of interpersonal citizenship behavior. *Journal of Applied Psychology*, 91, 70-82.
95. Flynn, F. J. (2003) How much should I give and how often? *Academy of Management Journal*, 46, 539-553.
96. Adapted from Pfeffer, J. (1981) Op. Cit.

97. Pearce, J. L., Stevenson, W. B., & Porter, L. W. (1986) Op. Cit.
98. For examples see, Pearce, J. L. (2001) Op. Cit; & Sorenson, O. & Waguespack, D. M. (2006) Social structure and exchange. *Administrative Science Quarterly*, 51, 560-589.
99. Brass, D. J. (1984) Being in the right place. *Administrative Science Quarterly*, 29, 518-539; & Brass, D. J. & Burkhardt, M. A. (1993) Potential power and power use. *Academy of Management Journal*, 36, 44-470.
100. French, J. R. P. & Raven, B. (1959) The bases of social power. In D. Cartwright (Ed.) *Studies in social power*: 150-167. Ann Arbor: University of Michigan Press; and for a discussion of the dark side of authority, see Kelman, H. C. & Hamilton, V. L. (1989) *Crimes of obedience*. New Haven, CT: Yale University Press.
101. Adapted from Pfeffer, J. (1981) Op. Cit.
102. Milgram, S. (1974) *Obedience to authority*. New York: Harper & Row.
103. Brown, G., Lawrence, T. B., & Robinson, S. L. (2005) Territoriality in organizations. *Academy of Management Review*, 30, 577-594.
104. For example, see Schneper, W. D. & Guillén, M. F. (2004) Stakeholder rights and corporate governance. *Administrative Science Quarterly*, 49, 263-295.
105. Pearce, J. L. (2001) *Organization and management in the embrace of government*. Mahwah, NJ: Lawrence Erlbaum.
106. Eisenberg, E. (1984) Ambiguity as a strategy in organizational communication. *Communication Monographs*, 51, 227-242.
107. Simis, K. M. (1982) *USSR*. New York: Simon Schuster.
108. Hackman, J. R. (1987) The design of work teams. In J. W. Lorsch (Ed.) *Handbook of organizational behavior*: 315-342. Upper Saddle River, NJ: Prentice Hall.
109. Priven, F. F. (2008) Can power from below change the world? *American Sociological Review*, 73, 1-14.
110. Ferris, G. R., Treadway, D. C., Kolodinsky, R. W., & Hochwarter, W. A. (2005) Development and validation of the Political Skill Inventory. *Journal of Management*, 31, 126-152; and Ferris, G. R. et al. (2012) Political skill in the organizational sciences. In, G. R. Ferris & D. C. Treadway (Eds.) *Politics in Organizations*: 487-528. New York: Routledge.
111. Kramer, R. M. & Hanna, B. A. (1998) Under the influence? In R. M. Kramer, R. M. & M. A. Neale (Eds.) *Power and influence in organizations*: 145-179. Thousand Oaks, CA: Sage.
112. Adapted from Ferris, G. R., Perrewé, P. L., Anthony, W. P., & Gilmore, D. C. (2000) Political skill at work. *Organizational Dynamics*, 28, 25-37.
113. Higgins, C. A., Judge, T. A. & Ferris, G. R. (2003) Influence tactics and work outcomes. *Journal of Organizational Behavior*, 24, 89-106.
114. Jones, E. E. & Pittman, T. S. (1982) Op. Cit; Simon, B. & Oakes, P. (2006) Beyond dependence. *Human Relations*, 59, 105-139; & Meyer, J. W. & Rowan, B. (1991) Institutionalized organizations. In W. W. Powell & P. J. DiMaggio (Eds.) *The new institutionalism in organizational analysis*. Chicago: University of Chicago Press.
115. Berger, J., Cohen, B. P. & Zelditch, M. (1966) Status characteristics and expectations states. In J. Berger, M. Zelditch & B. Anderson (Eds.) *Sociological theories in progress* Vol. 1: 29-46. Boston: Houghton-Mifflin.
116. Asch, S. (1946) Forming impressions of personality. *Journal of Abnormal Psychology*, 41, 258-290.
117. Owens, D. A., Neale, M. A. & Sutton, R. I. (2000) Technologies of status management, *Research on Managing Groups and Teams*, 3, 205-230.
118. Stern, I. & Westphal, J. D. (2010) Stealthy footsteps to the boardroom. *Administrative Science Quarterly*, 55, 278-319; and Westphal, J. D. & Clement, M. B. (2008) Sociopolitical dynamics in relations between top managers and security analysts. *Academy of Management Journal*, 51, 873-897.

119. Adapted from Norton, M. I. & Frost, J. H. (2007) Less is more. *Journal of Personality and Social Psychology*, 92, 97-105; Jones, E. E., Stires, L. K., Shaver, K. G., & Harris, V. A. (1968) Evaluation of an ingratiatory by target persons and bystanders. *Journal of Personality*, 36, 349-385; Ellis, A. P. J., West, B. J., Ryan, A. M., & DeShon, R. P. (2002) The use of impression management tactics in structured interviews. *Journal of Applied Psychology*, 87, 1200-1208; & Treadway, D. C. et al. (2007) The moderating role of subordinate political skill on supervisors' impressions of subordinate ingratiation and ratings of subordinate interpersonal facilitation. *Journal of Applied Psychology*, 92, 848-855.
120. Wayne, S. J., Liden, R. C., Graf, I. K., & Ferris, G. R. (1997) The role of upward influence tactics in human resource decisions. Personnel Psychology, 50, 979-1006; & Keys, J. B., et al. (1987) Lateral influence tactics. *International Journal of Management*, 4, 425-431.
121. Zalkind, S. S. & Costello, T. W. (1962) Perception. *Administrative Science Quarterly*, 7, 218-235.
122. Westphal, J. D. & Bednar, M. K. (2008) The pacification of institutional investors. *Administrative Science Quarterly*, 53, 29-72.
123. Cialdini, R. B. 1988. *Influence*. Glenview, IL: Scott, Foresman.
124. Adapted from Baldwin, T. T., Bommer, W. H. & Rubin, R. S. 2008, *Developing management skills*, New York: McGraw-Hill-Irwin.
125. Krause, D. (2008) *Effects of power-based leadership on innovative behaviors at work.* Annual Meeting of the Society of Industrial and Organizational Psychology, San Francisco, CA.
126. Sparrowe, R. T., Soetjipto, B. W., & Kraimer, M. L. (2006) Do leaders' influence tactics relate to members' helping behavior? *Academy of Management Journal*, 49, 1194-1208.
127. Detert, J. R., Treviño, L. K., Burris, E. R., & Andiappan, M. (2007) Managerial modes of influence and counterproductivity in organizations. *Journal of Applied Psychology*, 92, 993-1005.
128. Mintzberg, H. (1983) *Power in and around organizations*. Englewood Cliffs, NJ: Prentice-Hall.
129. Thompson, J. A. Proactive personality and job performance. *Journal of Applied Psychology,* 90, 1011-1017.
130. Unfortunately good detailed descriptions of the exercise of power in business and non-profits are rare (those who know don't say), but they are plentiful in government. Two excellent examples are Goodwin, D. K. (2006) Team of rivals: *The political genius of Abraham Lincoln*. New York: Simon and Schuster; and Caro, R. A. (1975) *The power broker*: *Robert Moses and the fall of New York*. New York: Random House

Chapter 10 Leading Others

1. Van Vugt, M., Hogan, R. & Kaiser, R. B. (2008) Leadership, followership and evolution. *American Psychologist*, 63, 182-196.
2. Bass, B. M. (1990) *Bass & Stogdill's Handbook of Leadership* (3rd ed.) New York: Free Press.
3. Pfeffer, J. (1977) The ambiguity of leadership. *Academy of Management Review*, 2, 104-112.
4. Meindl, J. R. Ehrlich, S. B. (1987) the romance of leadership and the evaluation of organizational performance. *Academy of Management Journal*, 30, 90-109; and Meindl, J. R. Ehrlich, S. B. & Dukerich, J. M. (1985) The romance of leadership. *Administrative Science Quarterly*, 30, 78-102.
5. Kaiser, R. B., Hogan, R. & Craig, S. B. (2008) Leadership and the fate of organizations. *American Psychologist*, 63, 96-110.

6. Hogan, R., Curphy, G. J. & Hogan, J. (1994) What we know about leadership effectiveness and personality. *American Psychologist*, 49, 493-450.
7. Lieberson, S. & O'Connor, J. F. (1972) Leadership and organizational performance. *American Sociological Review*, 37, 117-130.
8. Agle, B. R., Nagarajan, N. J. & Sonnenfeld, J. A. (2006) Does CEO charisma matter? *Academy of Management Journal*, 49, 161-174.
9. Tucker, R. C. (1981) *Politics as leadership*. Columbia: University of Missouri Press.
10. Ling, Y., Simsek, Z., Lubatkin, M. H. & Veiga, J. F. (2008) The impact of transformational CEOs on the performance of small- to medium-sized firms. *Journal of Applied Psychology*, 93, 923-934.
11. Smith, J. E., Carson, K. P. & Alexander, R. A. (1984) Leadership: It can make a difference. *Academy of Management Journal*, 27, 765-776.
12. Mintzberg, H. & Waters, J. A. (1982) Tracking strategy in an entrepreneurial firm. *Academy of Management Journal*, 25, 465-499.
13. Podsakoff, P. M., MacKenzie, S. B. & Bommer, W. H. (1996) Meta-analysis of the relationship between Kerr and Jerimer's substitutes for leadership and employee job attitudes, role perceptions, and performance. *Journal of Applied Psychology*, 81, 380-399; and Khurana, R. (2002) *Searching for a corporate savior*. Princeton, NJ: Princeton University Press.
14. See Bass, B. M. (1990) Op. Cit., for a review.
15. Just a few of the more recent examples include authentic leadership (acting consistently with your own values), servant leadership (leaders should see their role as serving their followers not the other way around), ethical leadership (acting based on a set of ethical precepts), martyred leadership (you cannot expect followers to sacrifice for the organization if leaders do not demonstrably do so first), and so on.
16. www.samples-help.org.uk/mission-statements/vision-statements.htm.
17. De Luque, M. S., Washburn, N. T., Waldman, D. A. & House, R. J. (2008) Unrequited profit. *Administrative Science Quarterly*, 53, 626-654.
18. Baum, J., Locke, E. & Kirkpatrick, S. (1998) A longitudinal study of the elation of vision and vision communication to venture growth in entrepreneurial firms. *Journal of Applied Psychology*, 83, 43-54.
19. Ibid; and Rubio, A., Rosenblatt, Z. & Hertz-Lararowitz, R. (2010) Entrepreneurial leadership vision in nonprofit vs. for-profit organizations. *Leadership Quarterly*, 21, 144-158.
20. Hart, S. L. & Quinn, R. E. (1993) Roles executives play. *Human Relations*, 46, 543-574; Howell, J. M. & Higgins, C. A. (1990) Champions of change. *Organizational Dynamics*, 19, 40-55.
21. Larwood, L., Falbe, C. M., Kriger, M. P. & Miesing, P. (1995) Structure and meaning of organizational vision. *Academy of Management Journal*, 38, 740-769; and Griffin, M. A., Parker, S. K., & Mason, C. M. (2010) Leader vision and the development of adaptive and proactive performance. *Journal of Applied Psychology*, 95, 174-182.
22. Awamleh, R. & Garner, W. (1999) Perceptions of leader charisma and effectiveness. *Leadership Quarterly*, 10, 345-373; Kirkpatrick, S. & Locke, E. (1996) Direct and indirect effects of three core charismatic leadership components on performance and attitudes. *Journal of Applied Psychology*, 81, 36-51; Locke, E. (1991) *The essence of leadership*. New York: Maxwell Macmillan International; and Shamir, B., et al. (1993) Op. Cit.
23. Dutton, J. E., Dukerich, J. M., & Harquail, C. V. (1994) Organizational images and members' identification. *Administrative Science Quarterly*, 39, 239-263.
24. Hunt, J. G., Boal, K. B. & Dodge, G. E. (1999) The effects of visionary and crisis-responsive charisma on followers. *Leadership Quarterly*, 10, 433-448.
25. Cameron, K. (2008) *Positive leadership*. San Francisco: Berrett-Koehler.
26. Ligon, G. S., Hunter, S. T. & Mumford, M. D. (2008) Development of outstanding leadership. *Leadership Quarterly*, 19, 367-374.
27. Shamir, B., et al. (1993) Op. Cit.

28. Hart, S. L. & Quinn, R. E. (1993) Roles executives play. *Human Relations*, 46, 543-574.
29. Shipman, A. S., Byrne, C. L. & Mumford, M. D. (2010) Leader vision formation and forecasting. *Leadership Quarterly*, 21, 439-456.
30. Ibid; and Strange, J. M. & Mumford, M. D. (2005) The origins of vision. *Leadership Quarterly*, 16, 121-148.
31. Shamir, B., Arthur, M. B., & House, R. J. (1994) The rhetoric of charismatic leadership. *Leadership Quarterly*, 5, 25-42.
32. *Southwestern Airlines*. Graduate School of Business Stanford University Case HR-1A.
33. Sherif, M. & Hovland, C. I. (1961) *Social Judgment*. New Haven, CT: Yale University Press.
34. Howell, J. M. & Frost, P. J. (1989) A laboratory study of charismatic leadership. *Organizational Behavior and Human Decision Processes*, 43, 243-269.
35. Emrich, C. G., Brower, H. H., Feldman, J. M. & Garland, H. (2001) Images in words. *Administrative Science Quarterly*, 46, 527-557.
36. Conger, J. A. & Kanungo, R. N. (1998) *Charismatic leadership in organizations*. Thousand Oaks, CA: Sage.
37. Colbert, A. E. & Witt, L. A. (2009) The role of goal-focused leadership in enabling the expression of consideration. *Journal of Applied Psychology*, 94, 790-796.
38. Evans, M. G. (1970) The effects of supervisory behavior on the path-goal relationship. *Organizational Behavior and Human Performance*, 5, 277-298.
39. Graham, W. K. (1973) Leader behavior, esteem for least preferred coworker, and group performance. *Journal of Social Psychology*, 90, 59-66.
40. Keller, R. T. (2006) Transformational leadership, initiating structure, and substitutes for leadership. *Journal of Applied Psychology*, 91, 202-210.
41. Stogdill, R. M. (1974) *Handbook of leadership*, New York: Free Press.
42. Pierce, C. A. & Aquinis, H. (2009) Moving beyond a legal-centric approach to managing workplace romances. *Human Resources Management*, 48, 447-464.
43. Skogstad, A., Einarsen, S., Torsheim, T. Aasland, M. S. & Hetland, H. (2007) The destructiveness of laissez-faire leadership behavior. *Journal of Occupational Health Psychology*, 12, 80-92.
44. Bass, B. M. (1990) Op. Cit.
45. Ibid.
46. Adapted from the MLQ Form 5X-Short in Avolio, B. J. & Bass, B. M. (2004) *Multifactor Leadership Questionnaire* (3rd ed.) Redwood City, CA: Mind Garden.
47. For an example, see "Incompetent? No just not a leader." *New York Times*, October 3, 2009, p. B1.
48. Hollenbeck, G. P., McCall, M. W. & Silzer, R. F. (2006) Leadership competency models. *Leadership Quarterly*, 17, 398-413; and Burnkrant, S. R. (2005) *Funny math, serious misinterpretation*. Society for Industrial and Organizational Conference Annual Conference. Los Angeles, CA.
49. Jongbloed, L. & Frost, P. J. (1985) Pfeffer's model of management. *Journal of Management*, 11, 97-110.
50. Hölzl, E., Kirchler, E. & Rodler, C. (2002) Hindsight bias in economic expectations. *Journal of Applied Psychology*, 87, 437-443.
51. Bass, B. M. (1990) Op. Cit.
52. Ng, K. Y., Ang, S. & Chan, K. Y. (2008) Personality and leader effectiveness. *Journal of Applied Psychology*, 93, 733-743.
53. Baum, J. R. & Locke, E. A. (2004) The relationship of entrepreneurial traits, skill, and motivation to subsequent venture growth. *Journal of Applied Psychology*, 89, 587-598.
54. House, R. J.& Howell, J. M. (1992) Personality and charismatic leadership. *Leadership Quarterly*, 3, 81-108.
55. Peterson, S. J., Walumbwa, F. O., Byron, K. & Myrowitz, J. (2009) CEO psychological traits

transformational leadership, and firm performance in high-technology start-up and established firms. *Journal of Management*, 35, 348-368; and Luthans, F., Avolio, B. J., Avey, J. & Norman, S. (2007) Positive psychological capital. *Personnel Psychology*, 60, 541-572.

56. Mumford, M. D. & Connelly, M. S. (1991) Leaders as creators. *Leadership Quarterly*, 2, 289-316.
57. Sternberg, R. J. (2007) A systems model of leadership. *American Psychologist*, 62, 34-42.
58. Farrow, D. L., Valenzi, E. R. & Bass, B. M. (1980) *A Comparison of Leadership and Situational Characteristics with Profit and Non-Profit Organizations*. Academy of Management Annual Conference, Detroit, MI.
59. Roby, T. B. & Forgays, D. G. (1953) *A problem solving model of communication in B-29 crews*. Technical Report 53-32. San Antonio, TX: Lackland Airforce Base, Human Resources Research Center; Dyer, J. L. & Lambert, W. E. (1953) *Coordination of flying activities in bomb wings*. Chapel Hill, NC: University of North Carolina, Institute for Research in Social Science; and O'Reilly, C.A. (1977) Supervisors and peers as information sources, group supportiveness, and individual decision-making performance. *Journal of Applied Psychology*, 62, 632-635
60. Anacona, D. (forthcoming) Sensemaking. In *Harvard Handbook of Leadership*. Boston, MA: Harvard Business School Press.
61. Eberly, M. B. (2010) *To fake or not to fake*. Doctoral Dissertation, University of Washington.
62. Dineen, B. R., Lewicki, R. J. & Tomlinson, E. C. (2006) Supervisory guidance and behavioral integrity. *Journal of Applied Psychology*, 91, 622-635.
63. Palanski, M. E. & Yammarino, F. J. (2009) Integrity and leadership. *Leadership Quarterly*, 20, 405-420.
64. De Cremer, D., Mayer, D. M., van Dijke, M., Schouton, B. C. & Bardes, M. (2009) When does self-sacrificial leadership motivate prosocial behavior? *Journal of Applied Psychology*, 94, 887-899.
65. van Knippenberg, B. & van Knippenberg, D. (2005) Leadership self-sacrifice and leadership effectiveness. *Journal of Applied Psychology*, 90, 25-37.
66. Dirks, K. T. & Ferrin, D. L. (2002) Trust in leadership. *Journal of Applied Psychology*, 87, 611-628.
67. Dirks, K. T. & Skarlicki, D. P. (2004) Trust in leaders: 21-40. In R. M. Kramer & K. S. Cook (Eds.) *Trust and distrust in organizations*. New York: Russell Sage.
68. Adapted from Kramer, R. M. & Lewicki, R. J. (2010) Repairing and enhancing trust. *Academy of Management Annals*, 4, 245-277.
69. Shen, W., Davies, S. E., Rasch, R., & Bono, J. E. (2008) *The Development of a Taxonomy of Ineffective Leadership Behaviors*. Society of Industrial and Organizational Psychology 2008, San Francisco, CA.
70. Shaw, James B., Erickson, A. & Harvey, M. (2011) A method for measuring destructive leadership and identifying types of destructive leaders in organizations, *Leadership Quarterly*, 22, 575-590.
71. Lewin, K., Lippitt, R. & White, R. K. (1939) Patterns of aggressive behavior in experimentally created social climates. *Journal of Social Psychology*, 10, 271-301.
72. Ashforth, B. (1997) Petty tyranny in organizations. *Canadian Journal of Administrative Sciences*, 14, 126–140.
73. Bass, B. M. (1990) Op. Cit.
74. Tepper, B. J. (2007) Abusive supervision in work organizations. *Journal of Management*, 33, 261-289; and Zhang, X. & Bartol, K. M. (2010) Linking empowering leadership and employee creativity. *Academy of Management Journal*, 53, 107-128.
75. Tepper, B. J. (2000) Consequences of abusive supervision. *Academy of Management Journal*, 43, 178-190.
76. Brehm, J. W. (1966) *A theory of psychological reactance*. New York: Academic Press.

77. Hmieleski, K. & Ensley, M. (2007) The effects of entrepreneur abusive supervision. *Academy of Management Proceedings*, 1-6.
78. Bardes, M., Mayer, D. M., Hoobler, J. M., Wayne, S. J., & Marinova, S. J. (forthcoming) A trickle-down model of abusive supervision. *Personnel Psychology*.
79. Shanock, L. R. & Eisenberger, R. (2006) When supervisors feel supported. *Journal of Applied Psychology*, 91, 689-695.
80. Adapted from Roscigno, V. J., Lopez, S. H. & Hodson, R. (2009) Supervisory bullying, status inequalities and organizational context. *Social Forces*, 87, 1561-1589.
81. Fiedler, F. E. (1992) Time-based measures of leadership experience and organizational effectiveness. *Leadership Quarterly*, 3, 5-23.
82. Ibid.
83. Bjork, R. A. & Druckman, D. (1991) *In the Mind's Eye*. Washington, D.C.: National Academy Press.
84. McCalley, M. H. (1981) Jung's theory of psychological types and the Myers-Briggs Type Indicator: 294-352. In P. McReynolds (Ed.) *Advances in Personality Assessment*, Vol. 5. San Francisco: Jossey-Bass.
85. Kahneman, D., Slovic, P. & Tversky, A. (Eds.) (1982) *Judgment Under Uncertainty*. New York: Cambridge University Press.
86. Staw, B. M. (1981) The escalation of commitment to a course of action. *Academy of Management Review*, 6, 577-587.
87. Kruger, J. & Dunning, D. (1999) Unskilled and unaware of it. *Journal of Personality and Social Psychology*, 7, 1121-1134.
88. Janis, I. L. (1989) *Crucial decisions*. New York: Free Press.
89. Herek, G., Janis, I. L. & Huth, P. (1987) Decisionmaking during international crises. *Journal of Conflict Resolution*, 31, 203-226.
90. Vroom, V. H. & Yetton, P. H. (1973) *Leadership and decision-making*. Pittsburgh, PA: University of Pittsburgh Press.
91. Miner, J. B. (1973) *The management process*. New York: Macmillan.
92. Deci, E. L., Cornell, J. P. & Ryan, R. M. (1989) Self-determination in a work organization. *Journal of Applied Psychology*, 74, 580-590; and Bass, B. M. (1990) Op. Cit.
93. Locke, E. A., Alavi, M. & Wagner, J. (1997) Participation in decision making.: 293-331. In G. Ferris (Ed.) *Research in Personnel and Human Resource Management Vol. 15*. Greenwich, CT: JAI Press; and Hideg, I., Michela, J. L. & Ferris, D. L. (2011) Overcoming negative reactions of nonbeneficiaries to employment equity. *Journal of Applied Psychology*, 96, 363-376.
94. Morse, N. C. & Reimer, E. (1956) The experimental change of a major organizational variable. *Journal of Abnormal Psychology*, 52, 120-129; and Locke, E. A. & Schweiger, D. M. (1979) Participation in decision making: 265-339. In B. Staw & L. L. Cummings, (Eds.) *Research in Organizational Behavior Vol. 1*. Greenwich, CT: JAI Press.
95. Shamir, B. et al. (1993) Op. Cit.
96. Weber, M. (1947) *The Theory of Social and Economic Organization* (trans and ed. A. M. Henderson & T. Parsons) New York: Free Press.
97. Bass, B. M. (1990) Op. Cit.
98. Gong, Y., Huang, J.-C. & Farh, J.-L. (2009) Employee learning orientation, transformational leadership, and employee creativity. *Academy of Management Journal*, 52, 765-778.
99. Ling, Y., Simsek, Z., Lubatkin, M. H. & Veiga, J. F. (2008) Transformational leadership's role in promoting corporate entrepreneurship. *Academy of Management Journal*, 51, 557-576.
100. Rowland, J. & Laukamp, L. (2008) Charismatic leadership and objective performance indicators. *International Journal of Applied Psychology*, 58, 602–621.
101. Khurana, R. (2002) Searching for a corporate savior. Princeton, NJ: Princeton University Press; Tosi, H. L. (2004) CEO charisma, compensation, and firm performance. *Leadership Quarterly*, 15, 405-420.

102. Erez, A., Misangyi, V. F., Johnson, D. E., LePine, M. A. & Halverson, K. C. (2008) Stirring the hearts of followers. *Journal of Applied Psychology*, 93, 602-615.
103. Walter, F. & Bruch, H. (2009) An affective events model of charismatic leadership behavior. *Journal of Management*, 35, 1428-1452.
104. Brown, M. E. & Treviño, L. K. (2009) Leader-follower values congruence. *Journal of Applied Psychology*, 94, 478-490.
105. Walter, F. & Bruch, H. (2009) Op. Cit.
106. Ibid; House, R. J. & Aditya, R. N. (1997) The social scientific study of leadership. *Journal of Management*, 23, 441-473; and Pastor, J. C., Mayo, M. & Shamir, B. (2007) Adding fuel to the fire. *Journal of Applied Psychology*, 92, 1584-1596.
107. Adapted from Conger, J. A. and Kanungo, R. N. (Eds.) *Charismatic Leadership in Organizations*. Thousand Oaks, CA: Sage.
108. Burns, T. & Stalker, G. M. (1961) *The management of innovation*. Chicago: Quadrangle.
109. Pearce, J. L. (1983) Comparing volunteers and employees in a test of Etzioni's compliance typology. *Journal of Voluntary Action Research*, 12, 22-30.
110. Cohen, D. & March, J. G. (1974) *Leadership and Ambiguity*. New York: McGraw-Hill.
111. Al-Aiban, K. M. & Pearce, J. L. (1993) The influence of values on management practices. *International Studies of Management and Organization*, 23, 35-52.
112. Nahavandi, A. & Malekzadeh, A. R. (1993) Leader style in strategy and organizational performance. *Journal of Management Studies*, 30, 405-425.
113. Porter, M. E. & Nohria, N. (2010) What is leadership?: 433-473. In Nohira, N. & Khurana, R. (Eds.) *Handbook of Leadership Theory and Practice*. Boston: Harvard Business Press.
114. Adapted from Ibid.
115. Eagly, A. H., & Johnson, B. T. (1990) Gender and leadership style. *Psychological Bulletin*, 108, 233-256.
116. Eagly, A. H. & Karau, S. J. (2002) Role congruity theory of prejudice toward female leaders. *Psychological Review*, 109, 573-598.
117. van Vught, M. & Spisak, B. R. (2008) Sex differences in the emergence of leadership during competitions within and between groups. *Psychological Science*, 19, 854-858.
118. Sy, T., et al. (2010) Leadership perceptions as a function of race-occupation fit. *Journal of Applied Psychology*, 95, 902-919.
119. Cappelli, P. & Novelli, B. (2010) *Managing the older worker*. Boston: Harvard Business Press.
120. Gelfand, M. J., Erez, M. & Aycan, Z. (2007) Cross-cultural organizational behavior. *Annual Review of Psychology*, 58, 479-514.
121. Rao, A. N. & Pearce, J. L. (2011) *Should management practice adapt to cultural values?* Annual Meeting of the Academy of Management, San Antonio, TX.
122. Adapted from Graen, G. B., Hui, C. & Gu, Q. L. (2004) A new approach to intercultural cooperation: 225-246. In G. B. Graen (Ed.) *New Frontiers of Leadership, LMX Leadership, Vol. 2.* Greenwich, CT: Information Age.
123. Latham, G. (1988) Human resource training and development. *Annual Review of Psychology*, 39, 545-582.
124. Argyris, C. (1982) The executive mind and double-loop learning. *Organizational Dynamics*, 11, 5-22.
125. Bass, B. M. (1990) Op. Cit.
126. Howell, J. M., Frost, P. J. (1989) A laboratory study of charismatic leadership. *Organizational Behavior and Human Decision Making Performance*, 43, 243-269; Dvir, T., Eden, D., Aolio, B. J. & Shamir, B. (2002) Impact of transformational leadership on follower development and performance. *Academy of Management Journal*, 45, 735-744; and Frese, M., Beimel, S. & Schoenborn, S. (2003) Action training for charismatic leadership. *Personnel Psychology*, 56, 671-697.

127. DeChurch, L. A. & Marks, M. A. (2006) Leadership in multiteam systems. *Journal of Applied Psychology*, 91, 311-329.
128. Greenberg, J. (2006) Losing sleep over organizational injustice. *Journal of Applied Psychology*, 91, 58-69.
129. Bass, B. M. (1990) Op. Cit.
130. DeRue, D. S. & Wellman, N. (2009) Developing leaders via experience. *Journal of Applied Psychology*, 94, 859-875; Dragoni, L., Tesluk, P. E., Russell, J. E. A. & Oh, I.-S. Understanding managerial development. *Academy of Management Journal*, 52, 731-743; and Ellis, S., Mendel, R. & Nir, M. (2006) Learning from successful and failed experience. *Journal of Applied Psychology*, 91, 669-680; Readers might find the U. S. Army's guide to conducting after-action reviews helpful: www.au.af.mil/awc/awcgate/army/tc_25-20/tc25-20.pdf .
131. Tripoli, A. Personal communication. August 22, 2007.
132. Adapted from "That tricky first 100 days," *The Economist*, July 15, 2006, p. 65.

Chapter 11 How to Fire and Retain

1. Somaya, D., Williamson, I. O. & Lorinkova, N. (2008) Gone but not lost. *Academy of Management Journal*, 51-936-953.
2. Burke, A., Heuer, F. & Reisberg, D. (1992) Remembering emotional events. *Memory and Cognition*, 20, 277–290; and Le Doux, J. (1996) *The emotional brain*. New York: Simon and Schuster.
3. Brockner, J., Konovsky, M., Cooper-Schneider, R., Folger, R., Martin, C. & Bies, R. J. (1992) Interactive effects of procedural justice and outcome negativity on victims and survivors of job loss, *Academy of Management Journal*, 37, 397–409.
4. Dietz, J., et al. (2003) The impact of community violence and an organization's procedural justice climate on workplace aggression. *Academy of Managment Journal*, 46, 317-326; and Barclay, L. J., Skarlicki, D. P. & Pugh, S. D. (2005) Exploring the role of emotions in injustice perceptions and retaliation. *Journal of Applied Psychology*, 90, 629-643.
5. Colquitt, J. A. (2008) Two decades of organizational justice. In J. Barling & C. L. Cooper (Eds.) *The Sage Handbook of Organizational Behavior*: 73-88. Thousand Oaks, CA: Sage.
6. Robinson, S. L. (2008) Dysfunctional workplace behavior. In J. Barling & C. J. Cooper (Eds.) Op. Cit.
7. Edelman, L. B. (2008) *When organizations rule*. Center for Organizational Research Seminar, University of California, Irvine.
8. Freeman, R. B. & Medoff, J. L. (1984) *What do unions do?* New York: Basic Books
9. Lind, E. A., Greenberg, J., Scott, K. S., & Welchans, T. D. (1998) *The winding road from employee to complainants*. Academy of Management Annual Meeting, San Diego, CA.
10. Brockner, J. et al. (1992) Op. Cit.
11. Pearce, J. L., Bigley, G. A. & Grubb, A. R. (2006) *What really causes trust?* The Paul Merage School of Business University of California, Irvine Working Paper.
12. Schweiger, D. M. & DeNisi, A. S. (1991) Communication with employees following a merger. *Academy of Management Journal*, 34, 110-135; and Maertz, Jr. C. P. et al. (2010) Downsizing effects on survivors. *Industrial Relations*, 49, 275-285.
13. Brockner, J., et al. (1992) Op. Cit.
14. Rosnow, R. L. & Fine, G. A. (1976) *Rumor and gossip*. New York: Elsevier.
15. Lind, E. A., et al. (1998) Op. Cit.
16. Cialdini, R. B., Borden, R. J., Thorne, A., Walker, M. R., Freeman, S. & Sloan, L. R. (1999) Basking in reflected glory. In R. F. Baumeister (Ed.) *The self in social psychology*: 436–445. Philadelphia: Taylor & Frances.

17. Brockner, J. et al. (1992) Op. Cit.
18. La Tendresse, (2000) Social identity and intergroup relations within the hospital. *Journal of Social Distress and the Homeless*, 9, 51–69.
19. Bies, R. J. (1987) The predicament of injustice. *Research in Organizational Behavior*, 9, 289–319.
20. Simons, T. & Roberson, Q. (2003) Why managers should care about fairness. *Journal of Applied Psychology*, 88, 432–443.
21. Greenberg, J. (1997) *The quest for justice on the job*. Thousand Oaks, CA: Sage.
22. Ibid.
23. Konovsky, M. A. & Cropanzano, R. (1993) Justice considerations in employee drug testing. In R. Cropanzano (Ed.) *Justice in the workplace*. Hillsdale, NJ: Erlbaum, 171–192.
24. Amundson, N. E., Borgen, W. A., Jordan, S. & Erlebach, A. C. (2004) Survivors of downsizing. *Career Development Quarterly*, 52, 256-271.
25. Lefkowitz, J. & Katz, M. L. (1969) Validity of exit interviews. *Personnel Psychology*, 22, 445–455; and Hennen, M. E. (2005) *Exploring Relations Between Employee Opinion and Exit Interview Questionnaire Data*. Society for Industrial and Organizational Psychology Annual Convention, Los Angeles, CA.
26. Ibid.
27. Pearce, J. L. (2001) *Organization and management in the embrace of government*. Mahwah, NJ: Erlbaum.
28. Ryan, A. M. & Lasek, M. (1991) Negligent hiring and defamation. *Personnel Psychology*, 44, 293–319.
29. Ibid. p. 308.
30. For example, CEO Briefing (2006) *The Economist Intelligence Unit*. London.
31. Reisch, W. D., Chia, S. L., Malobes, C. M. & Slocum, J. W. III (2007) *Job insecurity, job satisfaction and oganizational performance*. Paper Presented at the Annual Meeting of the Academy of Managment, Philadelphia, PA.
32. Pearce, J. L. & Randel, A. (2004) Expectations of organizational mobility, workplace social inclusion and employee job performance. *Journal of Organizational Behavior*, 25, 81-98.
33. Zatzick, C. D. & Iverson, R. D. (2006) High-involvement management and workforce reduction. *Academy of Management Journal*, 49, 999-1015.
34. Peters, L. H. & Sheridan, J. E. (1988) Turnover research methodology. In G. F. Ferris, & K. M. Rowland (Eds.) *Research in Personnel and Human Resource Management*: 231-262. Greenwich, CT: JAI Press; and Groysberg, B. & Nanda, A. (2005) *Does stardom affect job mobility?* Harvard Business School Working Paper.

What the Research Says: True or False?

Readers are sent to the pages because memorized answers will not help them take effective action.

Popular Management Opinion	True?	False?	See Page
Isn't management just common sense?	❑	❑	2
Don't get trapped in analysis paralysis.	❑	❑	8
Today's successful companies have the secrets to your success.	❑	❑	10
Competitive success is attained through people.	❑	❑	11
People are irrational.	❑	❑	12
If I can just figure out these people I will be successful.	❑	❑	14
Everything I need to know I learned in kindergarten.	❑	❑	17
I don't do any real work, I'm a manager.	❑	❑	19
Effective managers plan, organize, coordinate, and control.	❑	❑	23
To be a successful manager it is more important to kiss up to your bosses than to produce good results.	❑	❑	27
Leaders have a long-range perspective.	❑	❑	31
Managers' most important job is to be sensitive to their employees' needs.	❑	❑	32
Employees will slack off if they are not watched.	❑	❑	34
Managerial stress leads to heart attacks.	❑	❑	35
Hire the best.	❑	❑	39

I'll know it when I see it.	❑	❑	46
Call references only when you are ready to make a job offer.	❑	❑	50
Selection interviews are the best way to pick the best employee.	❑	❑	53
When hiring employees, you need to sell them on the job.	❑	❑	56
Check your emotions at the door.	❑	❑	61
Employees should express their feelings at work.	❑	❑	62
Successful managers have high emotional intelligence.	❑	❑	66
Happy workers are more productive workers.	❑	❑	69
Committed employees are better employees.	❑	❑	73
Stress kills.	❑	❑	75
Employees need to have a fire lit under them or they won't perform.	❑	❑	76
Employees will not do something if there isn't anything in it for them.	❑	❑	82
All they need is a kick in the pants.	❑	❑	85
Just hire the right people and get out of their way.	❑	❑	86
Employees usually know when they are performing poorly.	❑	❑	91
We just need to design a better performance measurement system.	❑	❑	94
Performance appraisals should be abolished.	❑	❑	98
Having employees engage in self-evaluation makes performance appraisal more democratic.	❑	❑	100

You will get the behavior you reward.	❑	❑	113
Extrinsic rewards reduce the intrinsic rewards employees get from their work.	❑	❑	115
Once employees are paid enough, they are no longer motivated by money.	❑	❑	117
Employees should be paid for performance.	❑	❑	117
Money doesn't motivate.	❑	❑	118
Make the workplace as egalitarian as possible.	❑	❑	126
Your praise is in your paycheck.	❑	❑	127
Reward employees fairly.	❑	❑	129
People will act opportunistically unless they are controlled.	❑	❑	131
It's all about the incentives.	❑	❑	137
People make up their own minds	❑	❑	140
You are on your own.	❑	❑	141
Don't mind me, just continue what you were doing.	❑	❑	146
Work with the best.	❑	❑	148
You shouldn't complain – look how much better off you are compared to ___.	❑	❑	150
"Money is not as important as outsiders assume: many in the industry are far more motivated by the desire to outshine their peers."	❑	❑	151
The best way to avoid a bad decision is to appoint a devil's advocate.	❑	❑	153
The secret to life is honesty and fair dealing; if you can fake that you have it made.	❑	❑	154
The best approach is to just throw new employees in the water.	❑	❑	156

I haven't got time for this culture fluff. I've got a business to run.	❑	❑	162
Meetings are a waste of time.	❑	❑	165
Employees have to be sold on change.	❑	❑	169
The leader's purpose has to belong to everyone in the organization.	❑	❑	169
The most effective organizations have strong corporate cultures.	❑	❑	171
You only need to do [insert this year's fad] to be a successful manager.	❑	❑	174
Information technology has made it easier to communicate.	❑	❑	176
Down deep we are all the same.	❑	❑	178
Men and women communicate differently.	❑	❑	182
Diverse workplaces have higher performance.	❑	❑	183
Good ideas sell themselves.	❑	❑	187
Keep people off-balance and in the dark by never revealing the purposes behind your actions.	❑	❑	188
I'm their boss so my subordinates will do what I say.	❑	❑	190
Politics is dirty.	❑	❑	191
To get what you want from others you need to be Machiavellian.	❑	❑	192
Politicking hurts organizational performance.	❑	❑	193
Power makes you stupid.	❑	❑	193
Power tends to corrupt and absolute power corrupts absolutely.	❑	❑	194
Power is fixed; what I give away I can never get back.	❑	❑	199

People have different influence styles.	❑	❑	201
Some people are easy to influence.	❑	❑	203
People care more about being accurate than they do about being liked.	❑	❑	204
Nice guys finish last.	❑	❑	207
Them that has, gets.	❑	❑	208
I get by with a little help from my friends.	❑	❑	213
The rules prevent us from getting work done.	❑	❑	217
Those who have the gold make the rules.	❑	❑	217
Who is the boss: the law or we? We are the masters over the law, not the law over us.	❑	❑	217
I understand how things work around here.	❑	❑	220
Most of us can find the facts to support our own positions.	❑	❑	222
I can't provide any information about possible downsizing because the best employees will leave.	❑	❑	275
True leaders embrace failure; they do not fear failure.	❑	❑	229
Do leaders matter?	❑	❑	231
Leaders must communicate, communicate, communicate.	❑	❑	239
Leaders are judged by their actions.	❑	❑	240
Leaders should model the behavior they want from others.	❑	❑	240
Experience counts.	❑	❑	243
Encouraging participation will result in better decisions.	❑	❑	246
Be inspirational.	❑	❑	248
Women have a different (and more effective) leadership style.	❑	❑	251

When in Rome, do as the Romans do.	❑	❑	252
Leaders are born, not made.	❑	❑	253
Self-awareness training will make you a more successful leader.	❑	❑	254
Leadership training is a waste of time.	❑	❑	254
It is impossible to fire employees in this organization.	❑	❑	262
It I tell employees a layoff is coming, they'll stop doing their work.	❑	❑	264
Employees should be escorted to their desks, watched carefully, and then escorted off the premises immediately after their employment has been terminated.	❑	❑	266
Exit interviews are a good way to discover why an employee quit.	❑	❑	269
When called for a reference about a former employee, I cannot give an honest assessment because I will get sued.	❑	❑	272

Index

About the Author

Jone L. Pearce is Dean's Leadership Professor and Director of The Center for Global Leadership at The Paul Merage School of Business, University of California, Irvine. She has published over 90 scholarly articles in her field of organizational behavior, has edited several volumes, and the books: *Volunteers: The Organizational Behavior of Unpaid Workers* (Routledge, 1993), *Organization and Management in the Embrace of Government* (Erlbaum, 2001), and *Status in Management and Ogranization* (Cambridge University Press, 2011) She is a Fellow and past president of the Academy of Management, a Fellow of the American Psychological Association, and The Association for Psychological Science and International Association of Applied Psychology. She has received numerous honors, including several teaching excellence awards, has provided expert testimony on management reform legislation pending before the U. S. House of Representatives, and serves as an advisor to universities and reserach institutes throughout the world.

"We have been using this book for our graduate level Organizational Behavior class for a couple of years now, in conjunction with supplementary readings. The feedback from the students in consistently and overwhelmingly positive. The book is well-written, and eminently practical, yet solidly grounded in research. I have not found any other book that so successfully bridges the academic-practitioner divide, and translates research so effectively for the student. The new chapter on leadership in the third edition is equally well done, and a very welcome addition. I cannot recommend this book highly enough."

– Lucy R. Ford, Saint Joseph's University

"I've found that the more management experience my students have, the more they like *Organizational Behavior Real Research for Real Managers*. This is a book that cuts through the fuzz to get to what matters to working, practicing managers. It's the book I wish I'd had when I started my career in the army and in industry."

– John N. Davis, Hardin-Simmons University

"Professor Pearce's book was extremely well written. It is a super reference for managers. I have used it in my job and will refer back to it in the future. When the new expanded version comes out, I will be the first to buy a copy."

– Executive

"The book has applications for practicing managers. I think this real-world focus makes this book unique compared to other undergraduate textbooks, and it is helpful and appropriate for an undergraduate class."

– Undergraduate Student

"I actually enjoy reading this textbook very much -- it is interesting, applicable even to undergraduate students, and it is fairly easy to read. I like the fact that it gives a lot of examples."

– Undergraduate Student

"I think the textbook it very useful and easy to understand. I was surprised at how much I enjoyed reading it. Breaking it down into smaller sections was helpful and I really enjoyed reading the applications. Not only did I learn concepts, I learned how to apply them in my daily life."

– Undergraduate Student

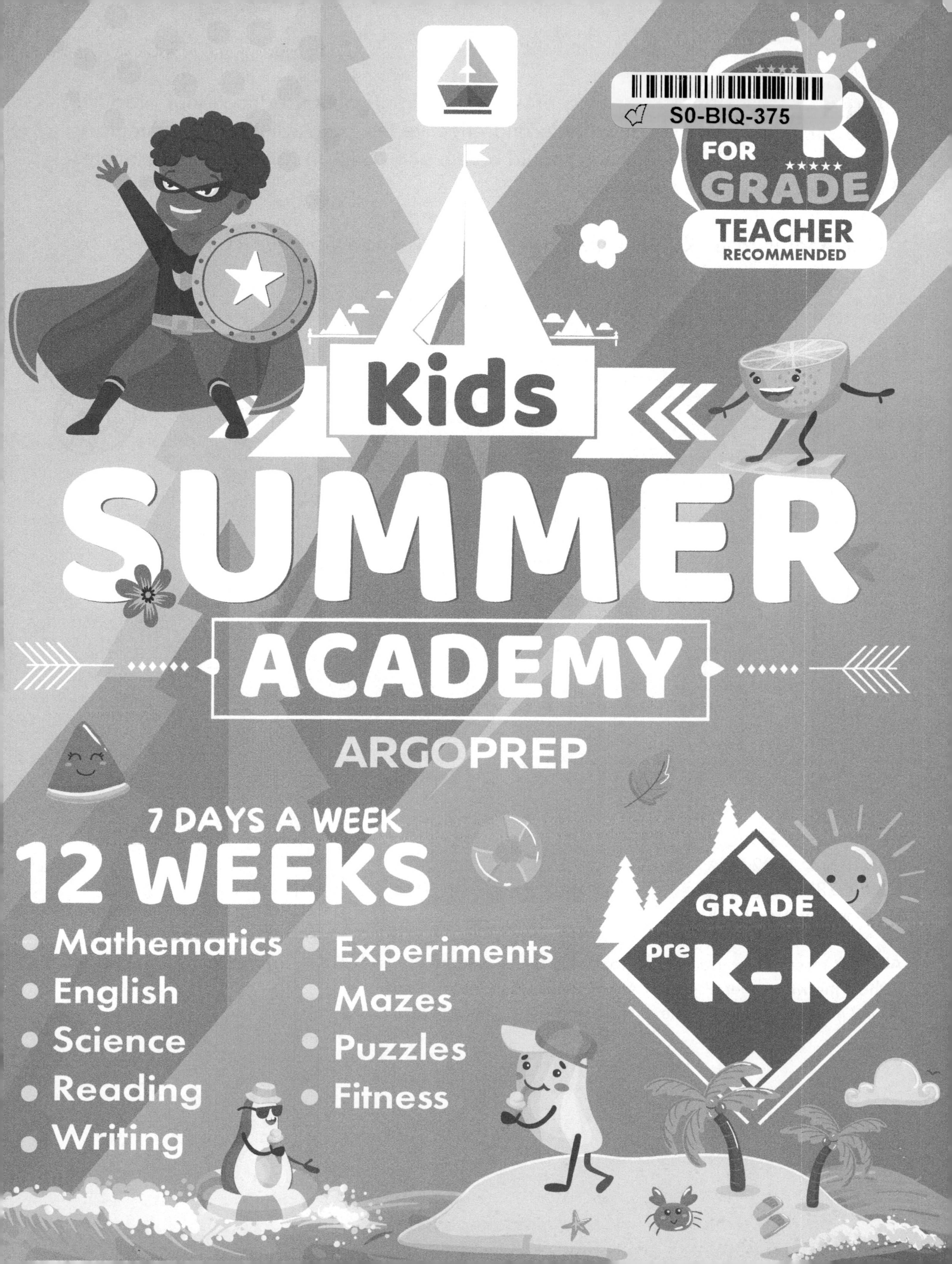

FOR K GRADE

TEACHER RECOMMENDED

Kids SUMMER ACADEMY

ARGOPREP

7 DAYS A WEEK

12 WEEKS

- Mathematics
- English
- Science
- Reading
- Writing
- Experiments
- Mazes
- Puzzles
- Fitness

GRADE pre K-K

ArgoPrep is one of the leading providers of supplemental educational products and services. We offer affordable and effective test prep solutions to educators, parents and students. Learning should be fun and easy! To access more resources visit us at www.argoprep.com.

Our goal is to make your life easier, so let us know how we can help you by e-mailing us at: info@argoprep.com.

ISBN: 9781951048785
Published by Argo Brothers.

- ArgoPrep is a recipient of the prestigious **Mom's Choice Award**.
- ArgoPrep also received the 2019 **Seal of Approval** from Homeschool.com for our award-winning workbooks.
- ArgoPrep was awarded the 2019 **National Parenting Products Award, Gold Medal Parent's Choice Award** and **the Tillywig Brain Child Award.**

TABLE OF CONTENTS

TABLE OF CONTENTS

TABLE OF CONTENTS

TABLE OF CONTENTS

HOW TO USE THE BOOK

Welcome to **Kids Summer Academy** by ArgoPrep.

This workbook is designed to prepare students over the summer to get ready for **Kindergarten.**
The curriculum has been divided into **twelve weeks** so students can complete this entire workbook over the summer.

Our workbook has been carefully designed and **crafted by licensed teachers** to give students an incredible learning experience.
Students start off the week with English activities followed by Math practice. Throughout the week, students have several fitness activities to complete. Making sure students stay active is just as important as practicing mathematics.
We introduce yoga and other basic fitness activities that any student can complete. Each week includes a science experiment which sparks creativity and allows students to visually understand the concepts. On the last day of each week, students will work on a fun puzzle.

HOW TO WATCH VIDEO EXPLANATIONS

IT IS ABSOLUTELY FREE

Go to **argoprep.com/summerprek**
OR scan the QR Code:

WHAT TO READ OVER THE SUMMER

One of the best ways to increase your reading comprehension level is to read a book for at least 20 minutes a day. We strongly encourage students to read several books throughout the summer. Below you will find a recommended summer reading list that we have compiled for students entering into Kindergarten or simply visit us at: www.argoprep.com/**summerlist**

Author: Joanna Cotler
Title: Sorry (Really Sorry)

Author: Nancy Redd
Title: Bedtime Bonnet

Author: DK
Title: How Do I Feel?

Author: Elissa Haden Guest
Title: Baby Builders

Author: Andrea Pippins
Title: Who Will You Be?

Author: Troy Cummings
Title: I Found A Kitty!

Author: Chris Grabenstein
Title: No More Naps!

Author: DK
Title: Look I'm an Engineer

Author: Deborah Freedman
Title: Carl and the Meaning of Life

Author: Hannah E. Harrison
Title: Friends Stick Together

KIDS SUMMER ACADEMY SERIES

ArgoPrep's **Kids Summer Academy** series helps prevent summer learning loss and gets students ready for their new school year by reinforcing core foundations in math, english and science. Our workbooks also introduce new concepts so students can get a head start and be on top of their game for the new school year!

MYSTICAL NINJA

ADRASTOS THE SUPER WARRIOR

FIRESTORM WARRIOR

WATER FIRE

GREEN POISON

CAPTAIN ARGO

THUNDER WARRIOR

DANCE HERO

RAPID NINJA

CAPTAIN BRAVERY

Pineapple

Give your character a name

____

Write down the special ability or powers your character has and how you will help your community with the powers.

____

____

Great! You are all set. To become an incredible hero, we need to strengthen our skills in **english, math** and **science**. Let's get started.

ARGOPREP

WEEK 1
This week, you'll practice letters, numbers and counting? Do you know your 5 senses? Let's find out!

Uppercase and Lowercase Letters
ENGLISH

Read Together

All 26 letters of the alphabet can be written two different ways - uppercase and lowercase. Uppercase letters are used at the beginning of a sentence and at the beginning of words, like names of people and places. Examples of words with uppercase letters at the beginning include: **New York, Olivia, November and Tuesday.** Lowercase letters are used when uppercase letters are not needed. Look back at the words listed in bold. The first letter of each word is uppercase and all the other letters are lowercase.

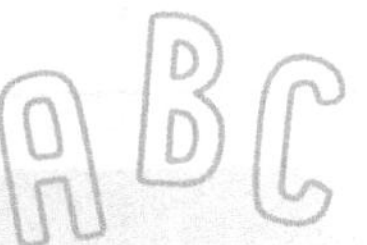

Directions

Practice writing each uppercase and lowercase letter on the lines below. Be sure to write neatly.

For Kids

WEEK 1
DAY 1

Uppercase and Lowercase Letters
ENGLISH

D
d
E
e
F
f
G
g
H
h
I
i
J
j

WEEK 1
DAY 1

Uppercase and Lowercase Letters
ENGLISH

K

k

L

l

M

m

Let's get some fitness in!
Go to page 229 to try some fitness activities.

WEEK 1
DAY 2

Uppercase and Lowercase Letters
ENGLISH

Read Together

Yesterday you were introduced to uppercase and lowercase letters. Remember uppercase letters are used at the beginning of a sentence and at the beginning of words that name specific people and places. All other letters in a word are lowercase letters. Think about the letters in the name Charlie. The first letter is an uppercase letter and the rest of the letters are lowercase letters.

Directions

Practice writing each uppercase and lowercase letter on the lines below. Be sure to write neatly.

For Kids

N

n

O

o

P

p

WEEK 1
DAY 2

Uppercase and Lowercase Letters

ENGLISH

Q

q

R

r

S

s

T

t

U

u

V

v

W

w

Uppercase and Lowercase Letters

ENGLISH

X

x

Y

y

Z

z

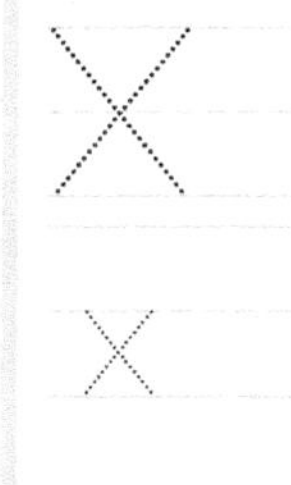

Let's get some fitness in!
Go to page 229 to try some fitness activities.

WEEK 1
DAY 3

Counting to 5
MATHEMATICS

Directions:

Circle the correct number for each of the questions.

Question 1:

Larry the Lobster sees many other creatures in the ocean. How many whales does he see?

1 2 3 4 5

Question 3:

How many starfish does he see?

1 2 3 4 5

Question 2:

How many jellyfish does he see?

1 2 3 4 5

Question 4:

How many seahorses does he see?

1 2 3 4 5

Counting to 5

MATHEMATICS

Question 5:

How many stingrays does he see?

1 2 3 4 5

Question 7:

How many clams does he see?

1 2 3 4 5

Question 6:

How many sea turtles does he see?

1 2 3 4 5

Question 8:

How many octopuses does he see?

1 2 3 4 5

Let's get some fitness in!
Go to page 229 to try some fitness activities.

FITNESS TIME

Counting to 5
MATHEMATICS

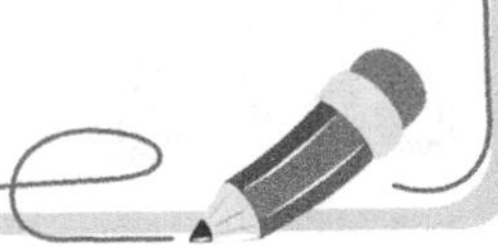

Directions:

Circle the correct number for each of the questions.

Question 1:

Larry the Lobster is playing hide and seek with his friends. How many strands of seaweed is he hiding behind?

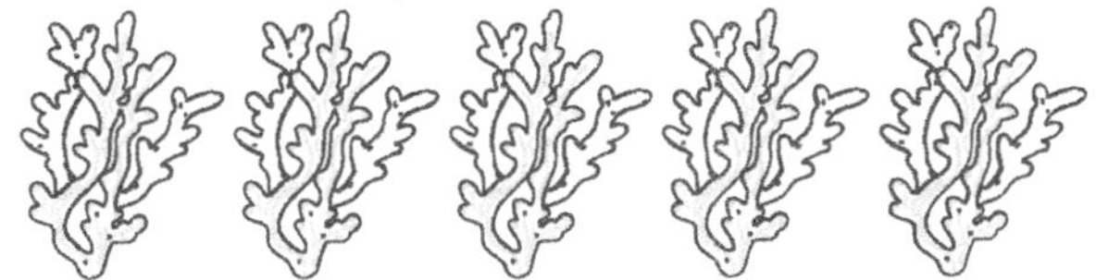

1 2 3 4 5

Question 3:

How many crabs crawl by him?

1 2 3 4 5

Question 2:

How many lobsters are looking for Larry?

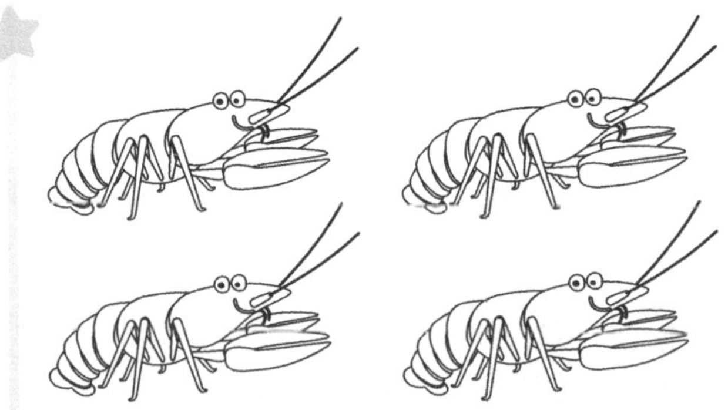

1 2 3 4 5

Question 4:

How many jellyfish float above him?

1 2 3 4 5

WEEK 1 DAY 4

Counting to 5 MATHEMATICS

Question 5:

How many sharks are watching him?

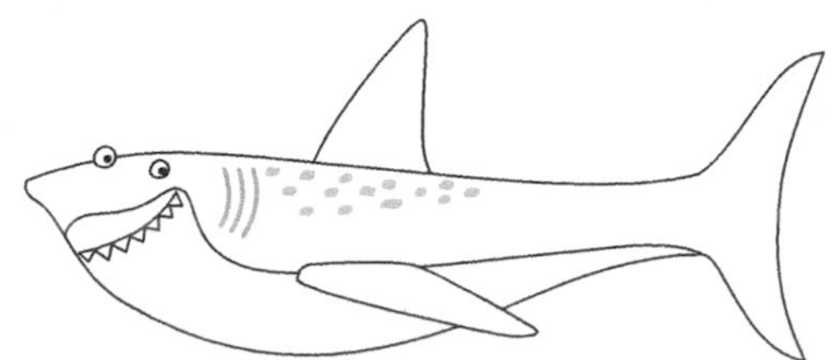

1 2 3 4 5

Question 7:

How many seashells does he count in his hiding spot?

1 2 3 4 5

2+2=4

Question 6:

How many bubbles does he see in the water?

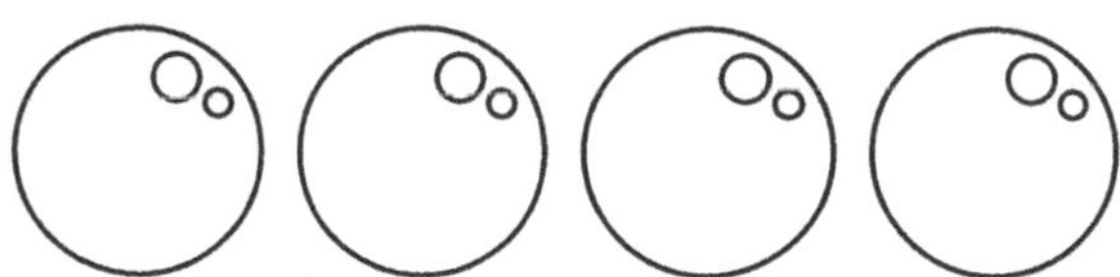

1 2 3 4 5

Question 8:

How many dolphins swim by him?

1 2 3 4 5

Let's get some fitness in!
Go to page 229 to try some fitness activities.

FITNESS TIME

WEEK 1 DAY 5

Counting to 5
MATHEMATICS

Directions:

Circle the correct number for each of the questions.

Question 1:

Larry the Lobster likes to collect shells. How many striped shells does he have?

1 2 3 4 5

Question 2:

How many spotted shells does he have?

1 2 3 4 5

Question 3:

How many small shells does he have?

1 2 3 4 5

Question 4:

How many big shells does he have?

1 2 3 4 5

Counting to 5
MATHEMATICS

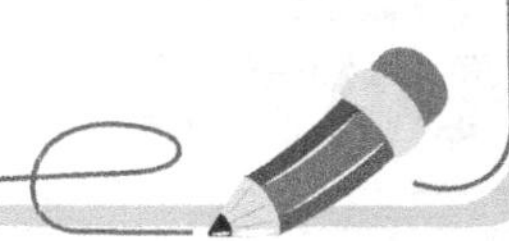

Question 5:

How many round seashells does he have?

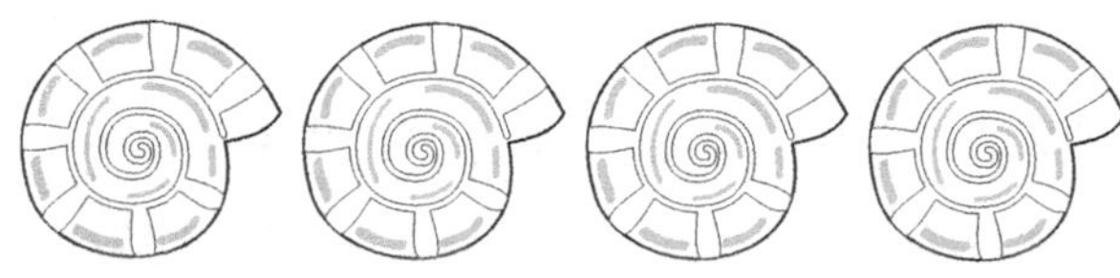

1 2 3 4 5

Question 6:

How many spiral seashells does he have?

1 2 3 4 5

Question 7:

How many cone-shaped shells does he have?

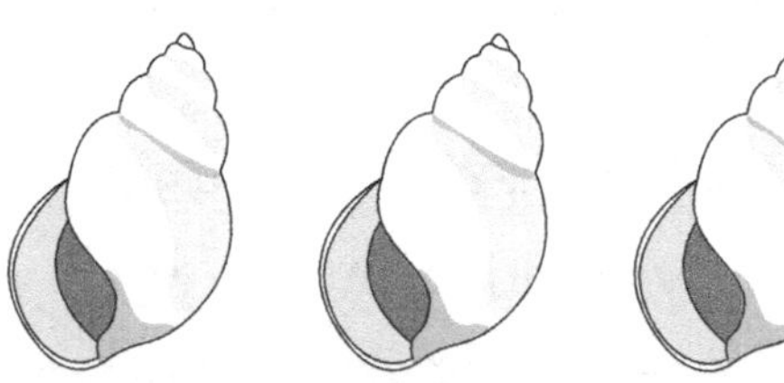

1 2 3 4 5

Question 8:

How many fan-shaped shells does he have?

1 2 3 4 5

Let's get some fitness in!
Go to page 229 to try some fitness activities.

Our Five Senses
EXPERIMENT

Read Together

All living things have five senses that help us to understand what is happening in the world around us. Our five senses are **sight, hearing, touch, taste and smell.**

Think about how you use your five senses. You might explore a new animal by looking at it with your eyes and carefully touching it with your hands. Maybe you smell a new food with your nose before tasting it with your mouth. Or perhaps you listen to the sounds you hear around you to make sense of where you are.

Our five senses are very important in helping us to know what is going on in our environment.

Directions

For each picture below, decide how you can best learn about that object. Circle the senses that would be most helpful to you.

For Kids

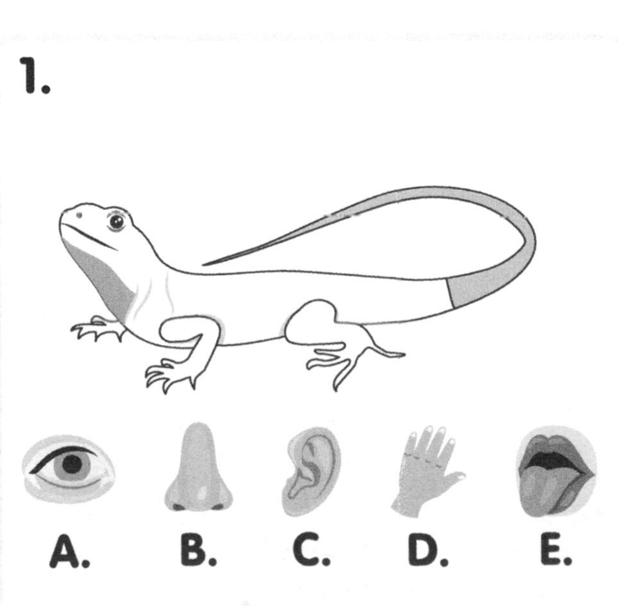

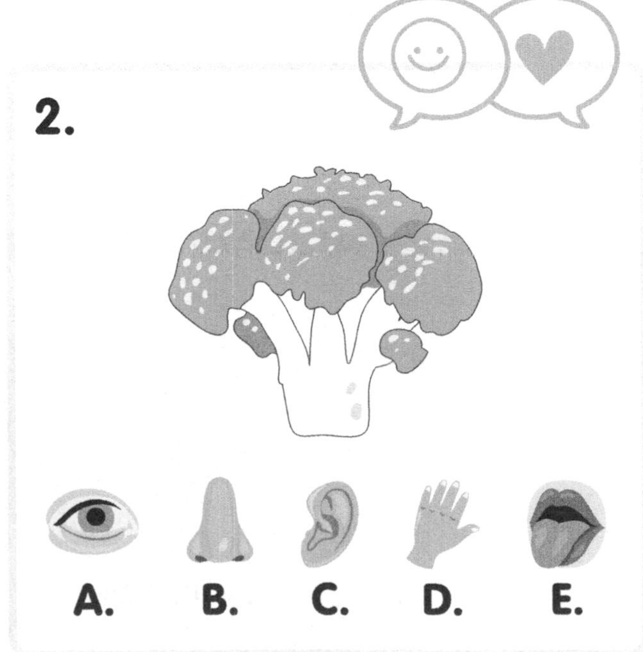

3.

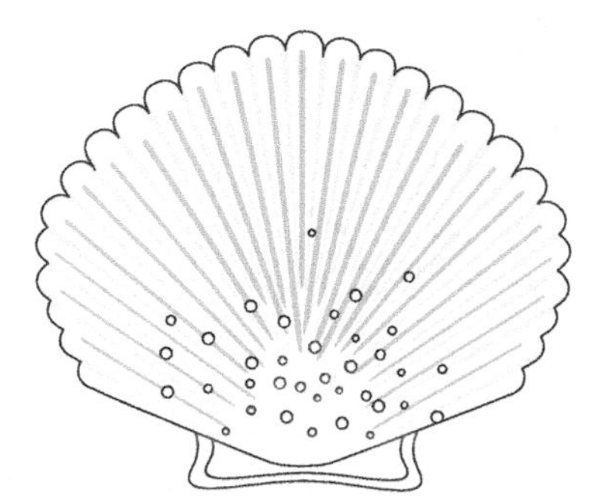

  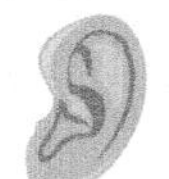  

A. B. C. D. E.

5.

 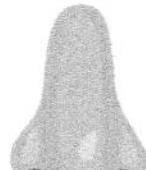   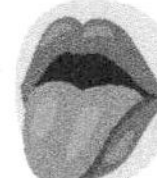

A. B. C. D. E.

4.

  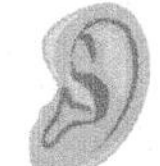   

A. B. C. D. E.

6.

 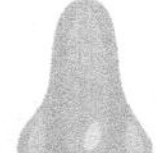 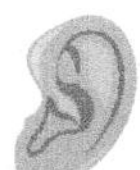  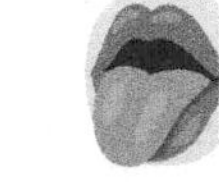

A. B. C. D. E.

Let's get some fitness in!
Go to page 229 to try some fitness activities.

WEEK 1
DAY 7

MAZE

Help John to catch up to the jet ski.

WEEK 2
It's rhyme time! Let's learn about words that rhyme. Be a math detective and find the missing numbers.
ARGOPREP

Read Together

Rhyming words are words that have the same middle and ending sounds but begin with different letters. Sometimes we call these **word families.** For instance, the words **cat** and **bat** belong to the -at word family. Both words end with -at but begin with different letters. Say cat and bat aloud. They probably sound similar. Can you think of other words in the -at word family?

Directions

For each word family listed below, write **5** rhyming words that belong in that family.

For Kids

-it	-all

Rhyming Words
ENGLISH

-et	-am

-ot	-ug

Directions

Look at the pictures below. For each picture, say its name aloud. Then, choose the rhyming word for that picture.

For Kids

1.

A. Log
B. House
C. Shoe
D. Horse

2.

A. Boot
B. Rain
C. Violin
D. Ran

3.

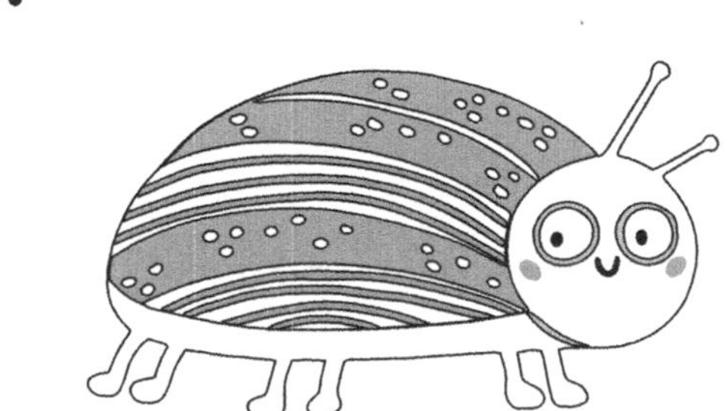

A. Car
B. Bag
C. Rug
D. Sit

4.

A. Toy
B. Toe
C. Big
D. Dog

5.

A. Slide
B. Ring
C. Zoo
D. Queen

7.

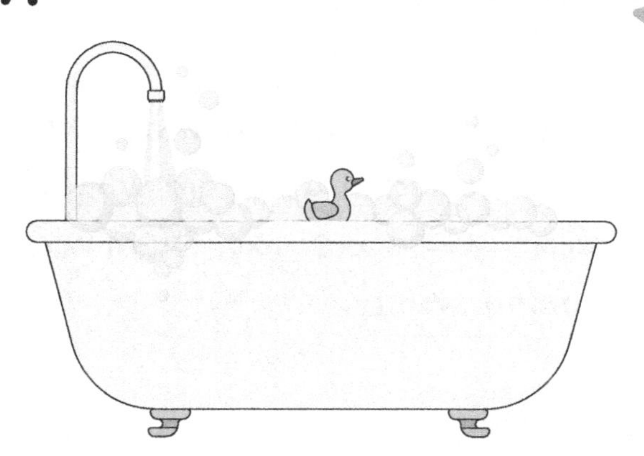

A. Rug
B. Sit
C. Cub
D. Man

6.

A. Mall
B. Mill
C. Silk
D. Sat

8.

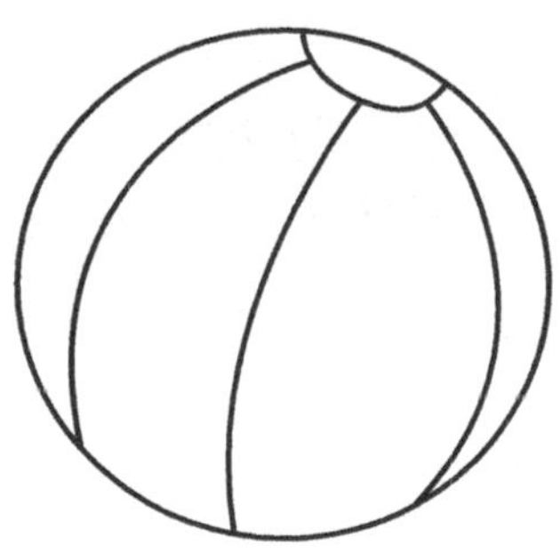

A. Saw
B. Cot
C. Bat
D. Call

Let's get some fitness in!
Go to page 229 to try some fitness activities.

Read Together

Remember rhyming words are words that have the same middle and ending sounds but begin with different letters. Rhyming words sound similar when we say them aloud. Cot, rot and lot are examples of rhyming words.

Directions

Look at each picture. Say the word aloud. Then say or write a word that rhymes with the picture.

For Kids

1.

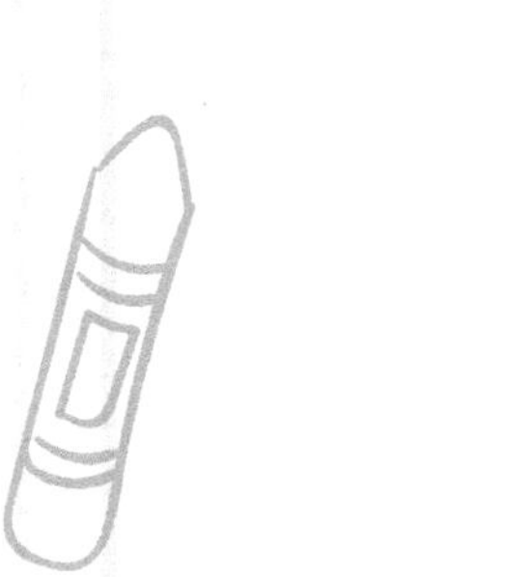

....

3.

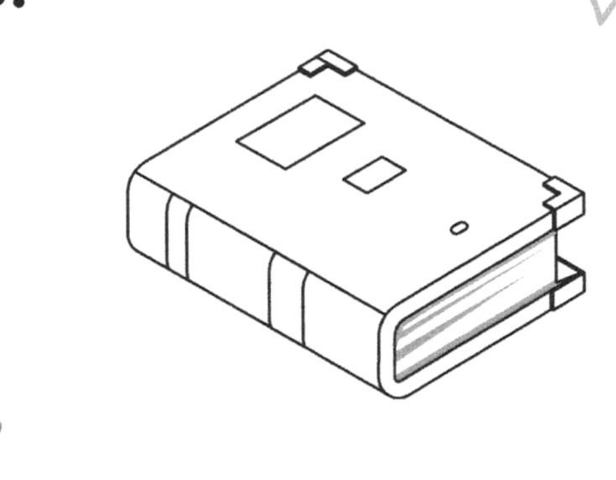

....

2.

....

4.

....

5.

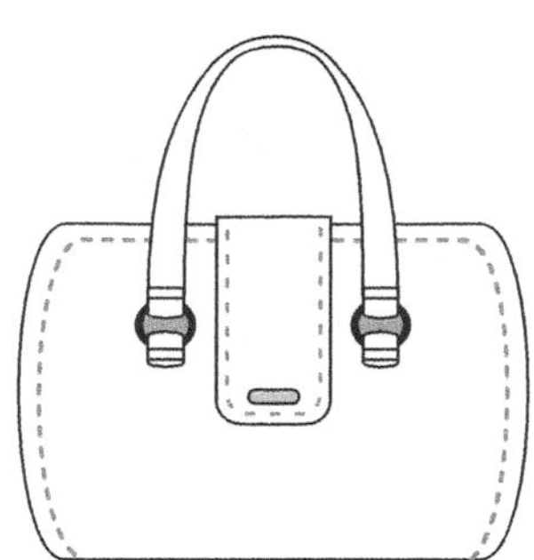

....

8.

....

6.

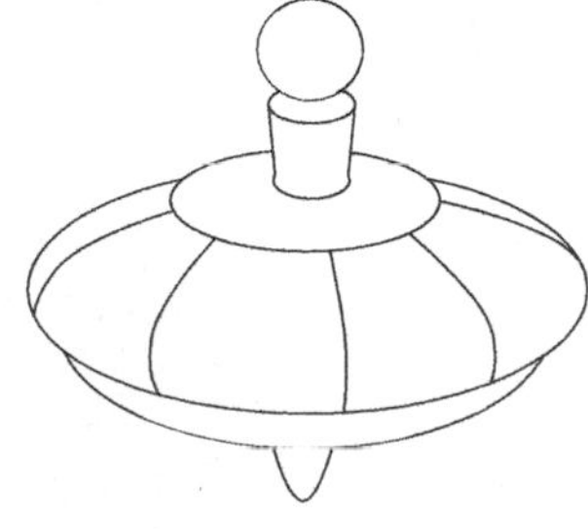

....

9.

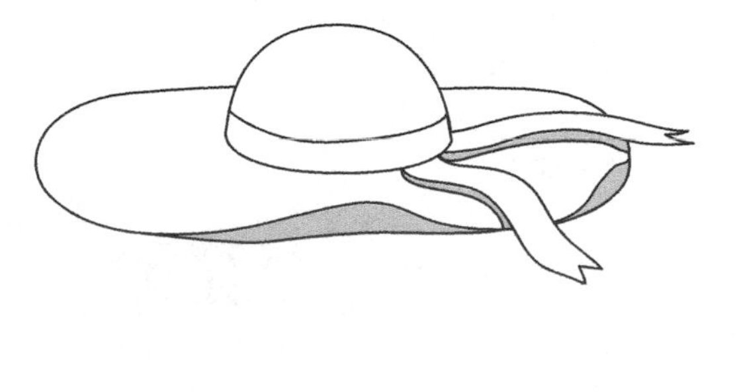

....

7.

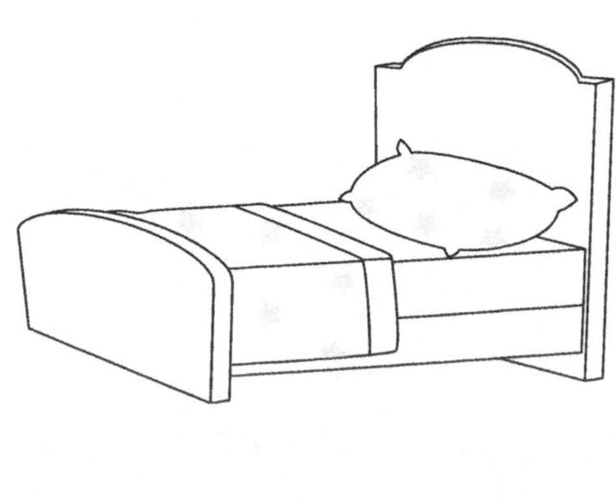

....

10.

....

WEEK 2 DAY 2

Rhyming Words
ENGLISH

Directions

In each box, look at the pictures. Read the name of each picture aloud. Decide which word and picture does not rhyme with the others. Put an X on that picture.

For Kids

1.

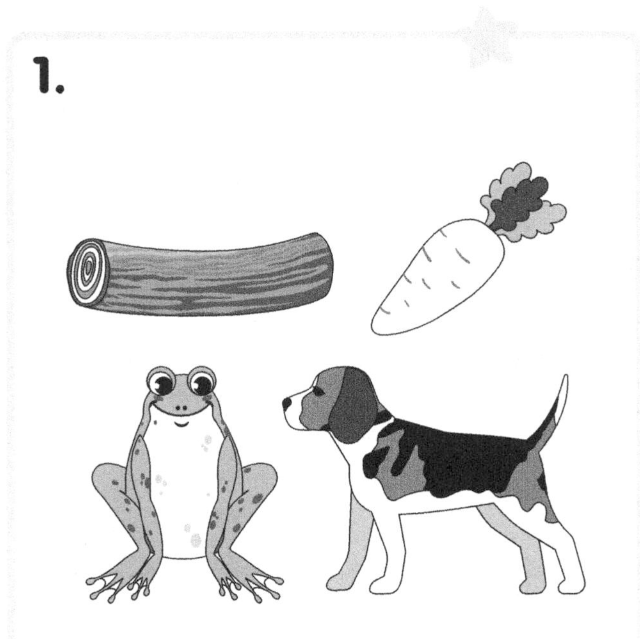

3.

2.

4.

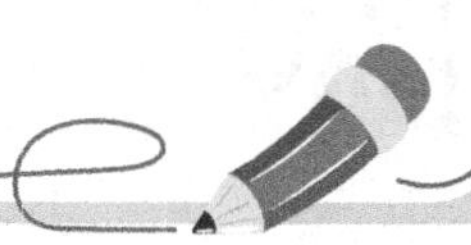

5.

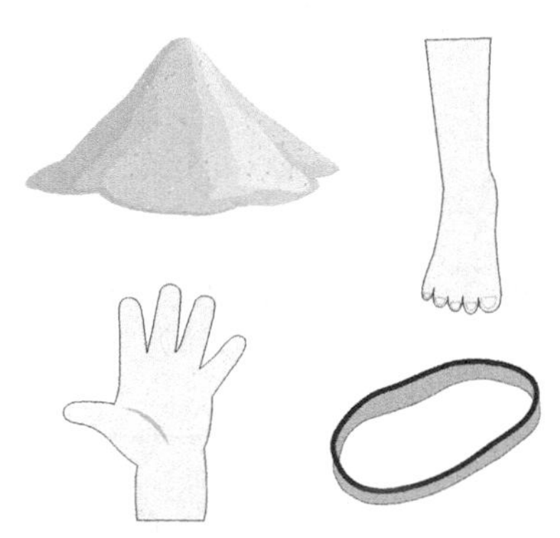

8.

6.

9.

7.

10.

Let's get some fitness in!
Go to page 229 to try some fitness activities.

FITNESS TIME

Directions:

Write in the missing number for each of the questions.

Question 1:

Tom the Turtle works in a bakery near the beach. He counts the sprinkled donuts one by one.

1 2 3 4 ___

Question 2:

Tom the Turtle counts the vanilla cupcakes one by one.

1 2 3 ___ 5

Question 3:

Tom the Turtle counts the sugar cookies one by one.

1 2 ___ 4 5

Question 4:

Tom the Turtle counts the strawberry tarts one by one.

1 ___ 3 4 5

Writing in the Missing Number in a Sequence

MATHEMATICS

Question 5:

Tom the Turtle counts the lemon cakes one by one.

__ 2 3 4 5

Question 7:

Tom the Turtle counts the blueberry muffins one by one.

1 2 __ 4 5

Question 6:

Tom the Turtle counts the chocolate brownies one by one.

1 __ 3 4 5

Question 8:

Tom the Turtle counts the peanut butter cookies one by one.

1 2 3 4 __

Let's get some fitness in!
Go to page 229 to try some fitness activities.

WEEK 2
DAY 4

Writing in the Missing Number in a Sequence

MATHEMATICS

Directions:

Write in the missing number for each of the questions.

Question 1:

Tom the Turtle uses lots of baking tools! He counts his wooden spoons one by one.

1 ___ 3 4 5

Question 2:

Tom the Turtle counts his rolling pins one by one.

1 2 3 ___ 5

Question 3:

Tom the Turtle counts his measuring cups one by one.

1 2 3 4 ___

Question 4:

Tom the Turtle counts his measuring spoons one by one.

1 2 ___ 4 5

Question 5:

Tom the Turtle counts his spatulas one by one.

1 2 3 __ 5

Question 7:

Tom the Turtle counts his big mixing bowls one by one.

__ 2 3 4 5

Question 6:

Tom the Turtle counts his small mixing bowls one by one.

1 __ 3 4 5

Question 8:

Tom the Turtle counts his oven mitts one by one.

1 __ 3 4 5

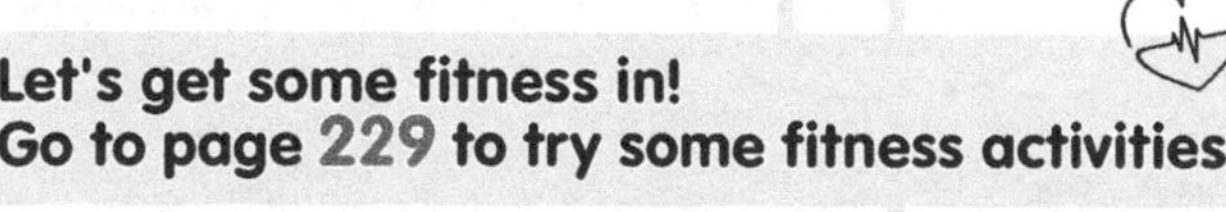

Let's get some fitness in!
Go to page 229 to try some fitness activities.

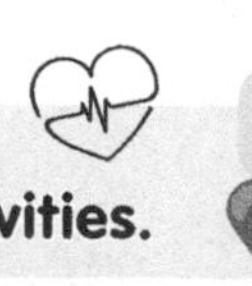

FITNESS TIME

Writing in the Missing Number in a Sequence

MATHEMATICS

Directions:

Write in the missing number for each of the questions.

Question 1:

Tom the Turtle likes to bake pies! He counts the apple pies in the oven.

__ 2 3 4 5

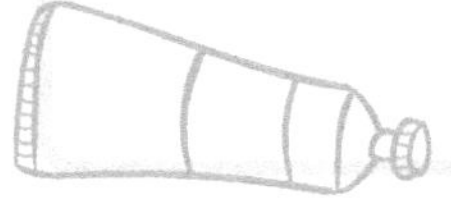

Question 2:

Tom the Turtle counts the cherry pies in the oven.

1 __ 3 4 5

Question 3:

Tom the Turtle counts the blueberry pies in the oven.

1 2 __ 4 5

Question 4:

Tom the Turtle counts the pecan pies in the oven.

1 2 3 __ 5

Writing in the Missing Number in a Sequence

MATHEMATICS

Question 5:

Tom the Turtle counts the blackberry pies in the oven.

1 2 3 4 ___

Question 7:

Tom the Turtle counts the raspberry pies in the oven.

1 ___ 3 4 5

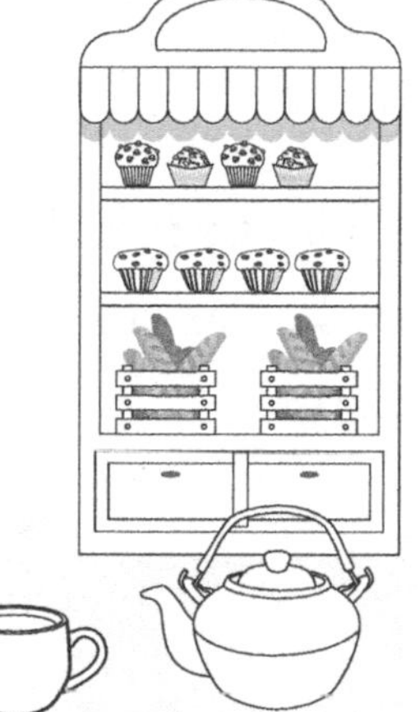

Question 6:

Tom the Turtle counts the peach pies in the oven.

1 2 3 ___ 5

Question 8:

Tom the Turtle counts the pumpkin pies in the oven.

___ 2 3 4 5

Let's get some fitness in!
Go to page 229 to try some fitness activities.

FITNESS TIME

WEEK 2 DAY 6

Classifying Objects by Size

EXPERIMENT

Read Together

All objects can be sorted in many different ways. We can group things by size, shape, weight, color or type.

Today you are going to practice sorting objects by size. **Size** means how big or small something is. For example, a house is big and a caterpillar is small.

Think about the objects you see around you. Are they big or small?

Directions

For each picture below, think about the size of the object. Decide if it is big or small. Circle the picture that best matches the size of the object in the picture.

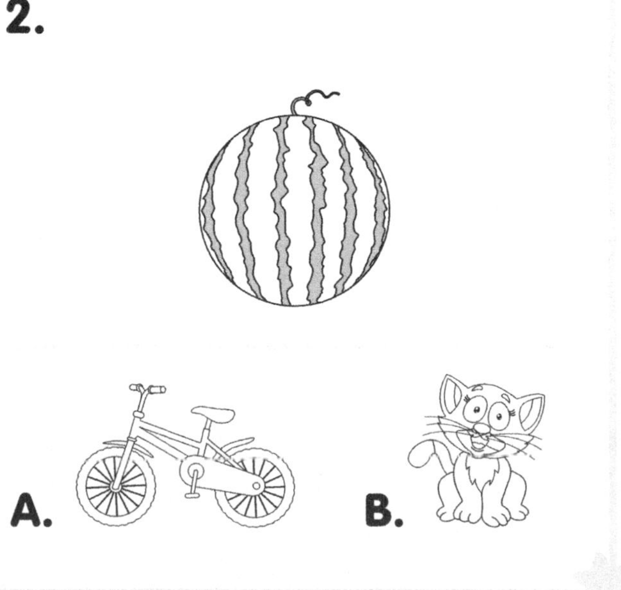

WEEK 2
DAY 6

Classifying Objects by Size

EXPERIMENT

3.

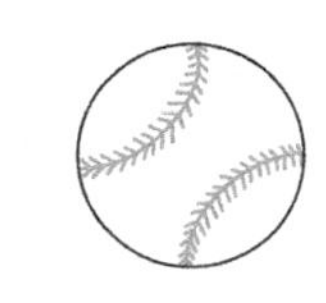

A.  **B.** 

4.

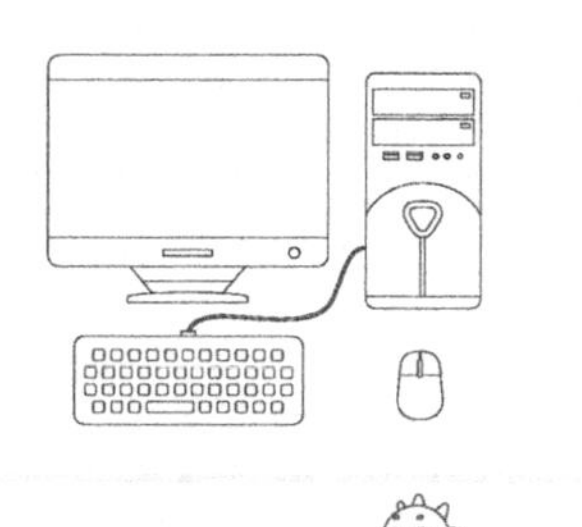

A.  **B.**

5.

A.  **B.** 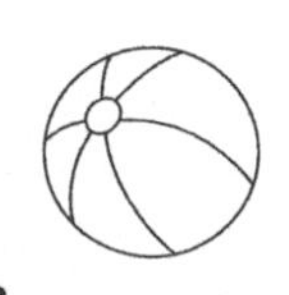

6.

7.

8.

A.  **B.** 

Let's get some fitness in!
Go to page 229 to try some fitness activities.

WEEK 2
DAY 7

MAZE

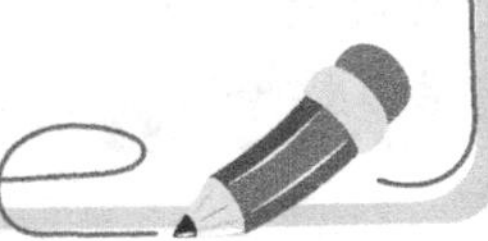

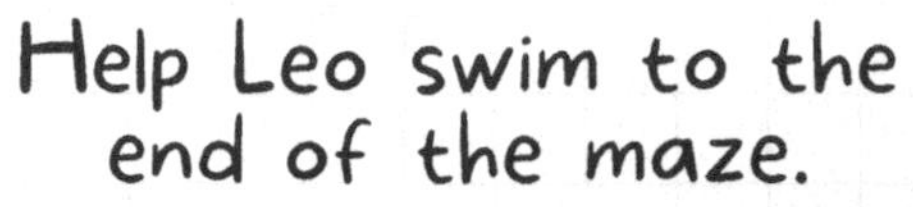

Help Leo swim to the end of the maze.

WEEK 3
Do you know what a syllable is? You'll learn all about these word sounds this week. You can add and sort pictures, too!
ARGOPREP

Read Together

A **syllable** is a part of a word that has sounds in it. All words have at least one syllable. Some words have two, three, four or more syllables. Each syllable usually has one vowel sound in it. Vowels are the letters a, e, i, o and u.

We can figure out how many syllables are in a word by counting or clapping out the "beats" in the word. Sometimes it is helpful to put your hand under your chin and feel when your mouth opens and closes as you say a word aloud.

Think about the word **elephant.** The word elephant has 3 beats in it. They are separated like this: e - le - phant. This means the word elephant has 3 syllables. Practice clapping the syllables in this word.

Directions

Look at the pictures below. For each picture, say its name aloud and clap out the syllables. Circle the correct number of syllables in the word.

For Kids

1.

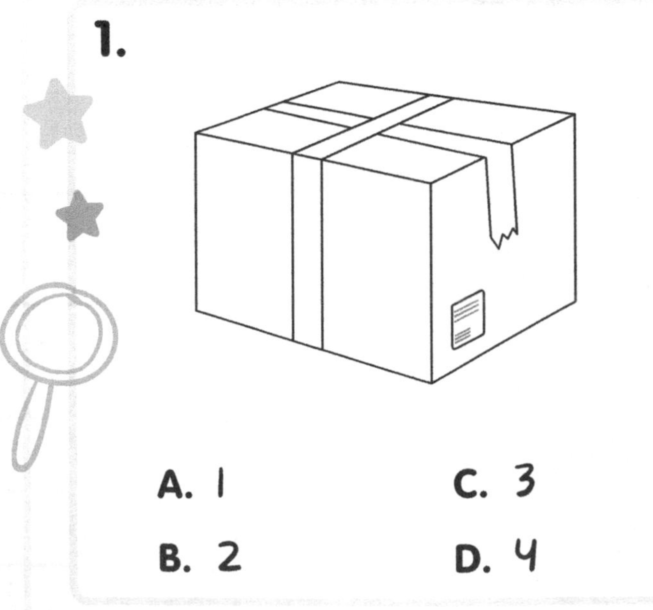

A. 1
B. 2
C. 3
D. 4

2.

A. 1
B. 2
C. 3
D. 4

3.

A. 1
C. 3
B. 2
D. 4

6.

A. 1
C. 3
B. 2
D. 4

4.

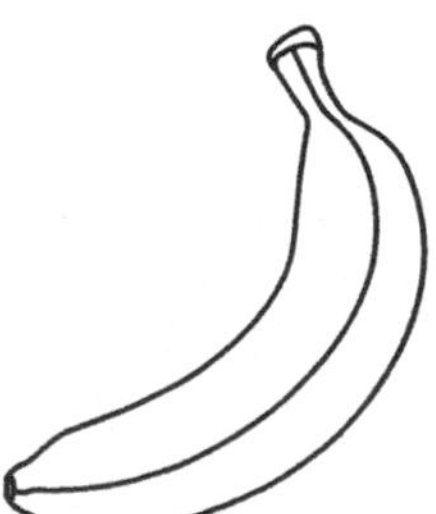

A. 1
C. 3
B. 2
D. 4

7.

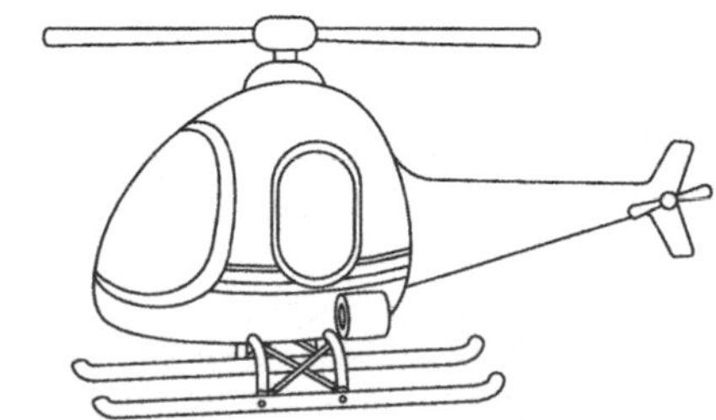

A. 1
C. 3
B. 2
D. 4

5.

A. 1
C. 3
B. 2
D. 4

8.

A. 1
C. 3
B. 2
D. 4

Directions

Look at the pictures below. For each picture, say its name aloud and clap out the syllables. Then, write the correct number of syllables on the line.

For Kids

1.

....

2.

....

3.

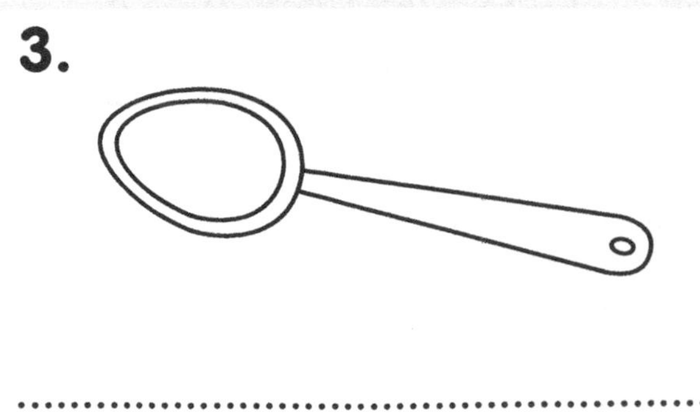

....

4.

....

5.

....

6.

....

7.

....

8.

....

9.

....

10.

....

11.

....

12.

....

Let's get some fitness in!
Go to page 229 to try some fitness activities.

Read Together

Remember all words have beats, or syllables, in them. There may be one syllable or many. Most syllables have a vowel sound in them. Clapping our hands is a good way to figure out how many syllables are in a word.

The word notebook has 2 syllables. They are separated like this: note - book.

Directions

On the tables below, write as many words as you can think of that have 1, 2, 3 and 4 syllables.

For Kids

1 syllable words	2 syllable words
Example: *dog*	***Example:*** *puppy*

Syllables
ENGLISH

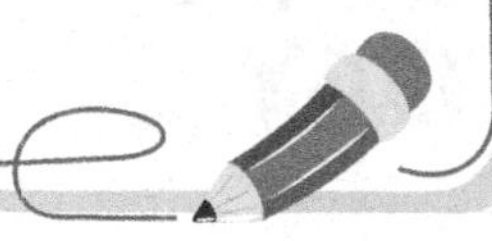

3 syllable words	4 syllable words
Example: thunderstorm	*Example:* watermelon

WEEK 3 DAY 2

Syllables
ENGLISH

Directions

Look at the pictures in each box below. For each picture, say its name aloud and clap out the syllables. Decide which word has the correct number of syllables. Circle that picture.

For Kids

1. Which word has 2 syllables?

3. Which word has 3 syllables?

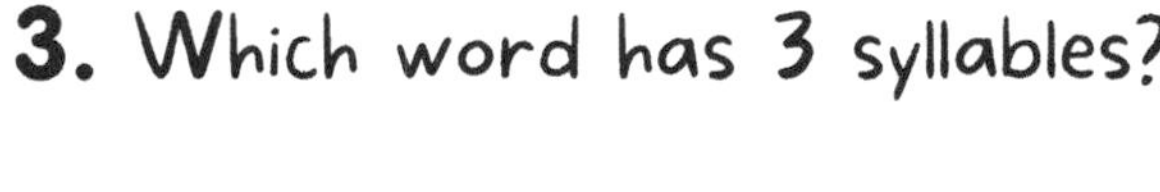

2. Which word has 1 syllable?

4. Which word has 1 syllable?

5. Which word has 4 syllables?

7. Which word has 2 syllables?

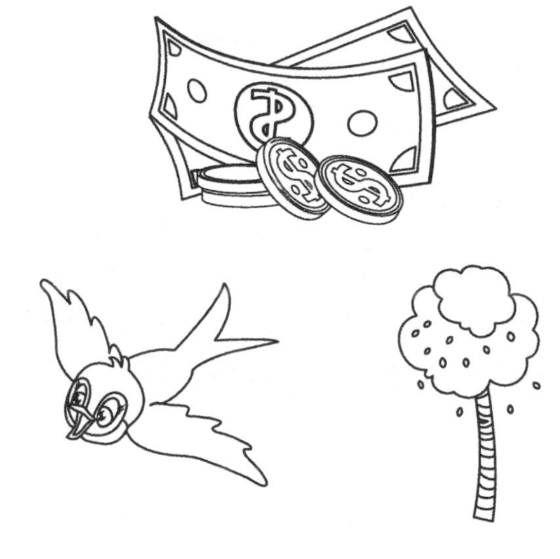

6. Which word has 3 syllables?

8. Which word has 4 syllables?

Let's get some fitness in!
Go to page 229 to try some fitness activities.

WEEK 3 DAY 3

Simple Addition with Pictures
MATHEMATICS

Directions

Fill in the sum for each of the questions.

For Kids

Question 1:

Shelley the Shark is enjoying a summer barbecue. How many hamburgers did she eat?

Question 2:

Shelley the Shark is thirsty! How many glasses of lemonade did she drink?

Question 3:

Shelley the Shark scoops out ice cream into two bowls. How many scoops of ice cream does she have?

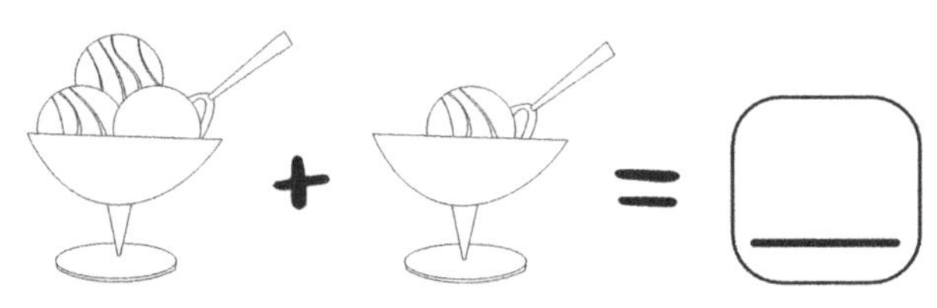

Question 4:

Shelley the Shark is grilling hot dogs. How many hot dogs is she grilling?

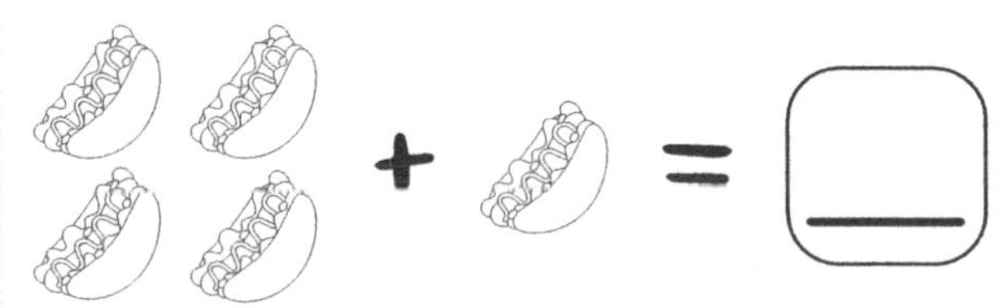

Simple Addition with Pictures

MATHEMATICS

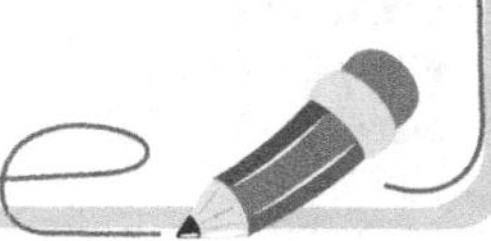

Question 5:

Shelley the Shark gathers up some beach balls. How many beach balls does she have?

+ = ___

Question 7:

Shelley the Shark sets out bottles of ketchup for the barbecue. How many bottles of ketchup are there?

+ = ___

Question 6:

Shelley the Shark is spreading beach towels out on the sand. How many beach towels does she have?

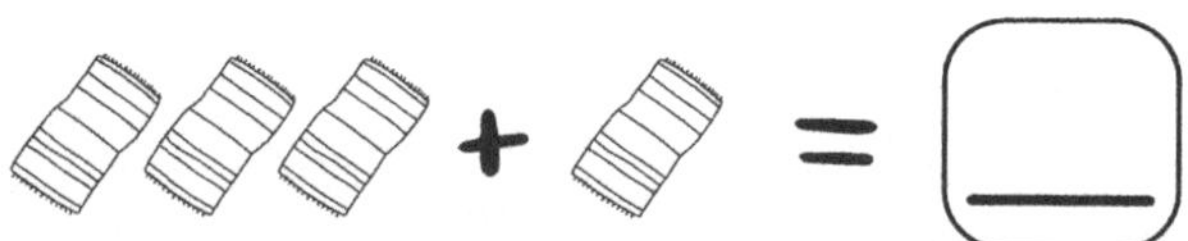

+ = ___

Question 8:

Shelley the Shark sets out bottles of mustard for the barbecue. How many bottles of mustard are there?

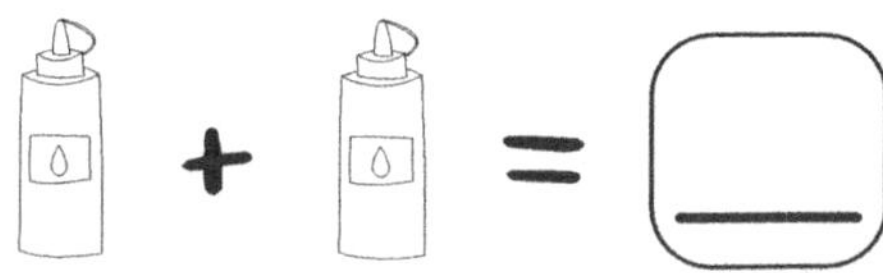

+ = ___

Let's get some fitness in!
Go to page 229 to try some fitness activities.

FITNESS TIME

WEEK 3
DAY 4

Simple Addition with Pictures
MATHEMATICS

Directions

Fill in the sum for each of the questions.

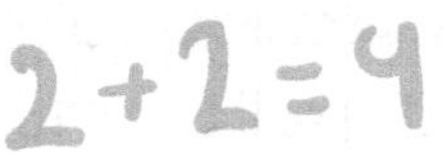

For Kids

Question 1:

Shelley the Shark loves to build sandcastles. How many sand shovels does she have?

+ = ___

Question 2:

Shelley the Shark has several sand buckets. How many sand buckets does she have?

Question 3:

Shelley the Shark likes to build towers on her sandcastles. How many towers are on her sandcastle?

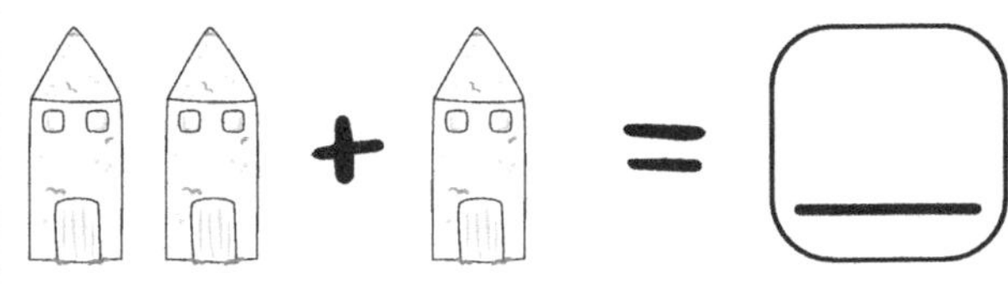

Question 4:

Shelley the Shark collects seashells to decorate her sandcastle. How many seashells does she have?

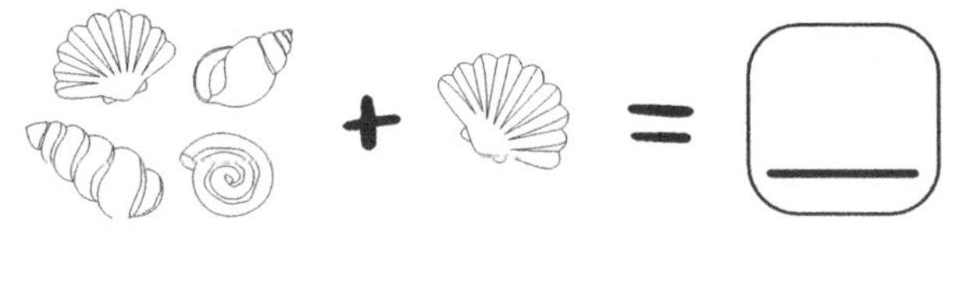

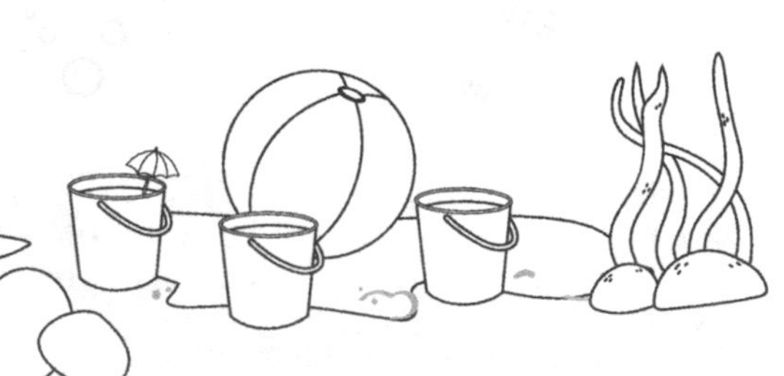

Question 5:

Shelley the Shark likes to decorate her sandcastle with flags. How many flags does she have?

+ = ___

Question 7:

Shelley the Shark needs a lot of water to build her sandcastle. How many buckets of water does she have?

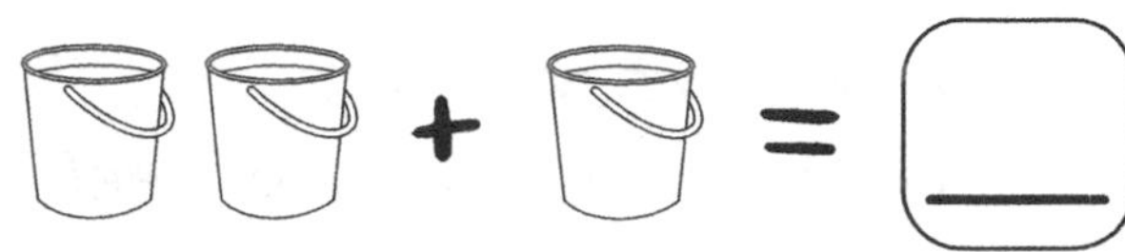

Question 6:

Shelley the Shark finds stones to decorate her sandcastle. How many stones does she find?

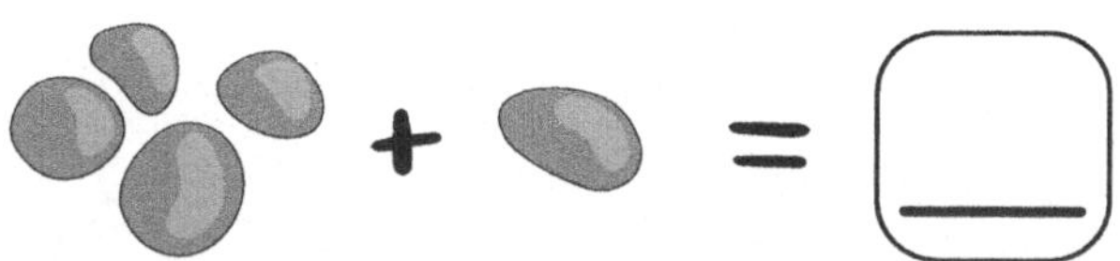

Question 8:

Shelley the Shark has entered several sandcastle contests. How many ribbons has she won?

Let's get some fitness in!
Go to page 229 to try some fitness activities.

FITNESS TIME

WEEK 3
DAY 5

Simple Addition with Pictures
MATHEMATICS

Directions

Fill in the sum for each of the questions.

For Kids

Question 1:

Shelley the Shark spots lots of fishy friends near a coral reef. How many fish does she see?

+ = ___

Question 2:

Shelley the Shark sees crabs playing hide and seek. How many crabs does she see?

+ = ___

Question 3:

Shelley the Shark sees starfish on the sandy ocean floor. How many starfish does she see?

+ = ___

Question 4:

Shelley the Shark sees seahorses bobbing in the water. How many seahorses does she see?

Simple Addition with Pictures
MATHEMATICS

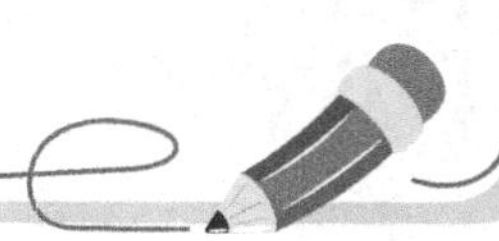

Question 5:

Shelley the Shark sees a family of sea turtles. How many turtles does she see?

Question 7:

Shelley the Shark watches a group of jellyfish drift by. How many jellyfish are there?

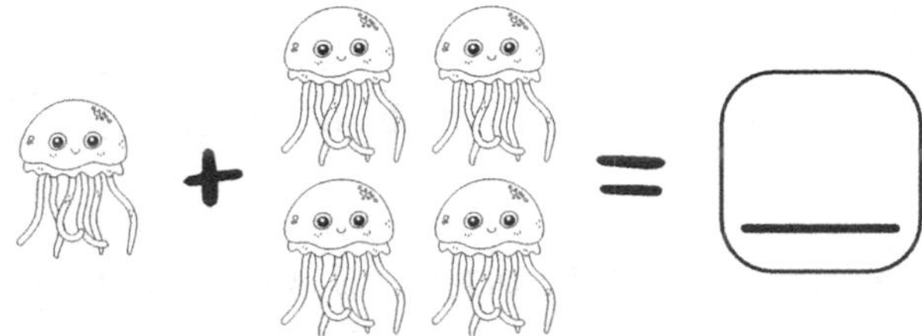

Question 6:

Shelley the Shark takes a close look at some oysters. How many oysters does she see?

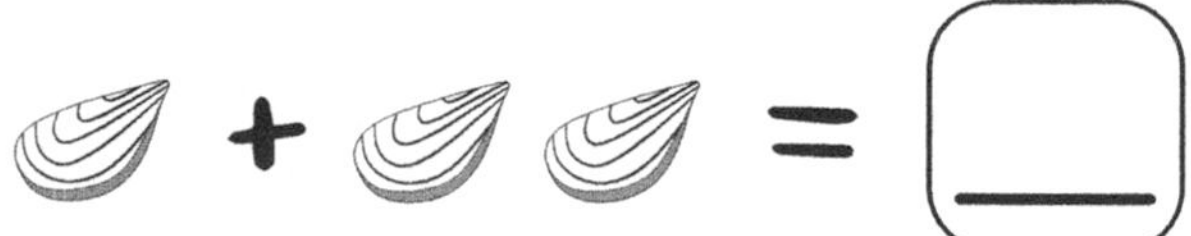

Question 8:

Shelley the Shark is happy to see her whale friends. How many whales have come to play?

Let's get some fitness in!
Go to page 229 to try some fitness activities.

WEEK 3
DAY 6

Classifying Objects by Color
EXPERIMENT

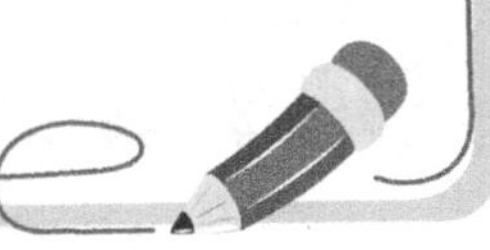

Read Together

All objects can be sorted in many different ways. We can group things by size, shape, weight, color or type.

In a prior lesson, you practiced sorting objects by how big or small they were. Today you are going to practice by identifying objects with their colors. For example, an apple is red and the sun is yellow.

Think about objects you see around you. What colors are they?

Directions

Look at the pictures below and determine what color belongs to that object. Circle the answer that best matches what color the object should be.

For Kids

1.

Banana

A. Red

B. Yellow

C. Pink

2.

Watermellon

A. Blue

B. Yellow

C. Green

Classifying Objects by Color
EXPERIMENT

3.

Strawberry

A. Red
B. Blue
C. Black

4.

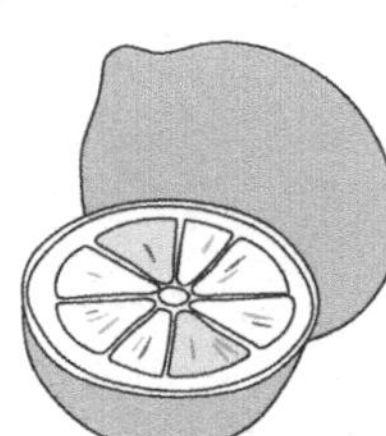

Lemon

A. Blue
B. Green
C. Yellow

5.

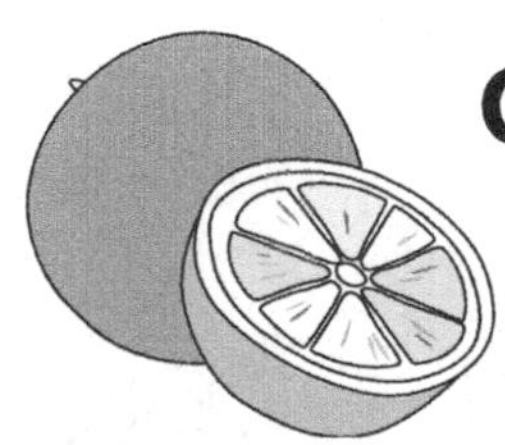

Orange

A. Pink
B. Brown
C. Orange

6.

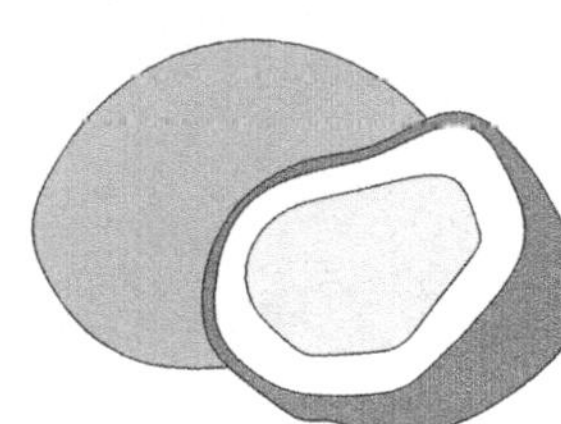

Coconut

A. Black
B. Brown
C. Blue

7.

Pineapple

A. Purple
B. Yellow
C. White

Let's get some fitness in!
Go to page 229 to try some fitness activities.

MAZE

Help the astronaut find Earth.

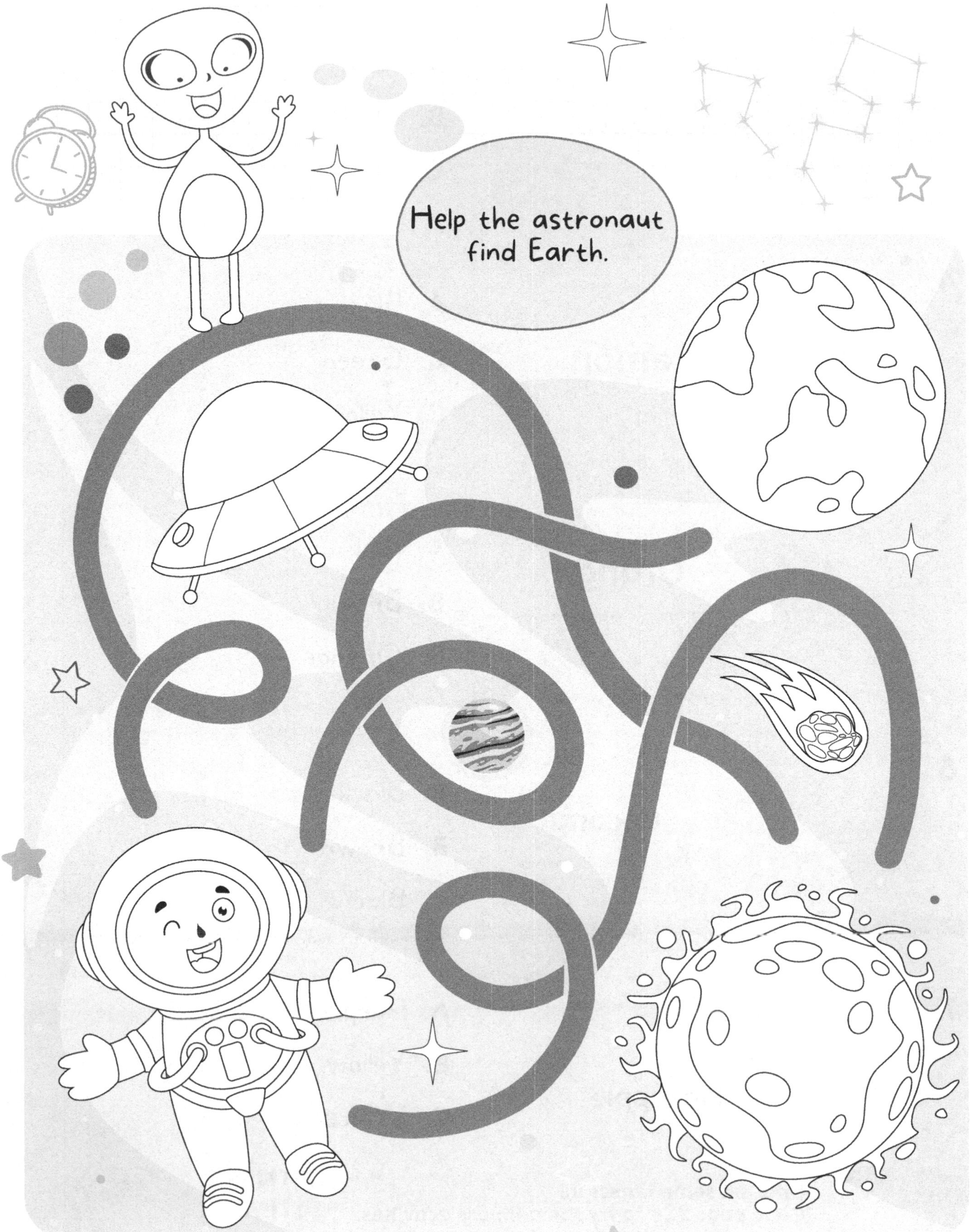

WEEK 4
This week, you'll learn about beginning sounds and simple addition. What happens when you push and pull objects? Let's find out.
ARGOPREP

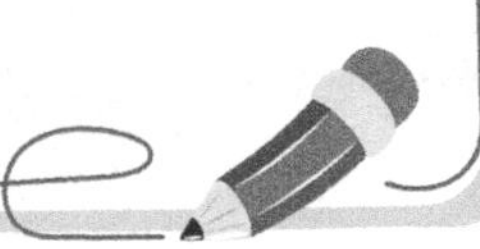

Read Together

Today you are going practice listening to sounds at the beginning of a word. Most simple words have a beginning, middle and ending sound. Usually the middle sound is a vowel - a, e, i, o or u. When we read simple words, we read each sound in the word and then blend them together.

For example, the word cat has three sounds: /c/, /a/ and /t/. We can say each of those sounds on their own. Then, we blend them together to read the entire word - *cat*.

Practice with the following words:

A. Dog
B. Sit
C. Run
D. Bell

Directions

Look at the pictures below. For each picture, say its name aloud and identify the beginning sound in the word. Circle the correct answer.

For Kids

1.

A. S **B.** U **C.** N

2.

A. N **B.** A **C.** M

3.

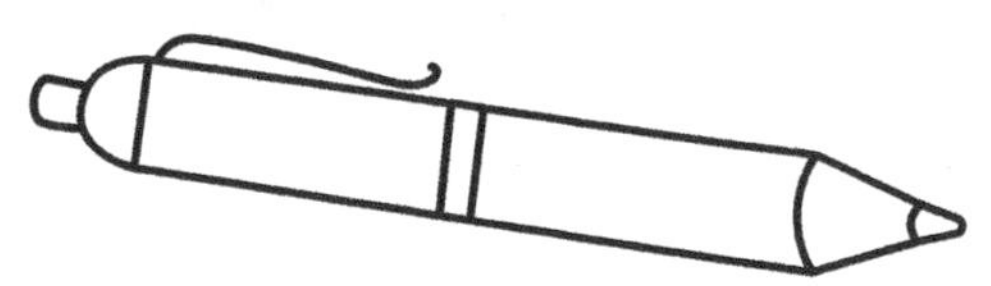

A. E **B.** P **C.** N

6.

A. U **B.** G **C.** B

4.

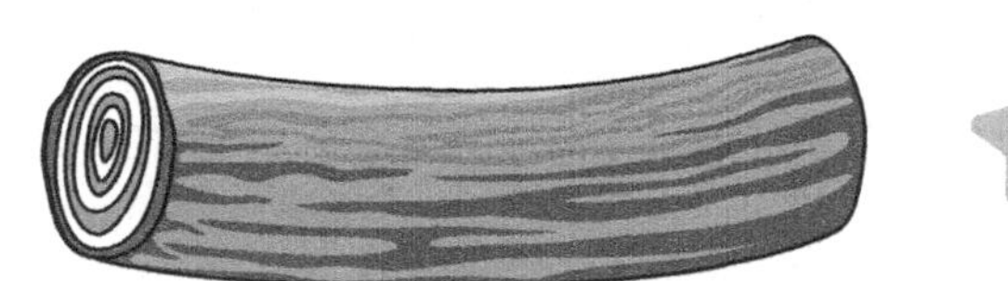

A. G **B.** L **C.** O

7.

A. B **B.** L **C.** A

5.

A. H **B.** N **C.** E

8.

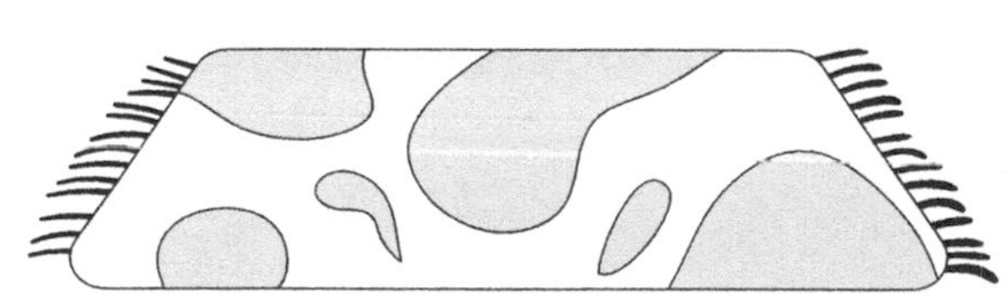

A. U **B.** R **C.** G

WEEK 4 DAY 1

Beginning Sounds
ENGLISH

Directions

Look at the pictures below. For each picture, say its name aloud and identify the beginning sound in the word. Write the correct beginning sound on the line.

For Kids

1.

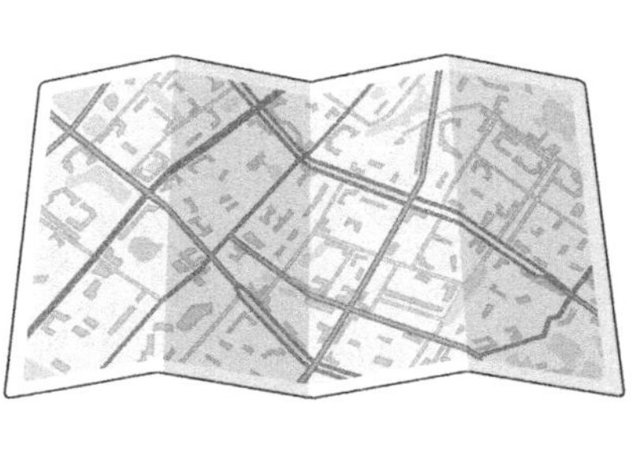

....

4.

....

2.

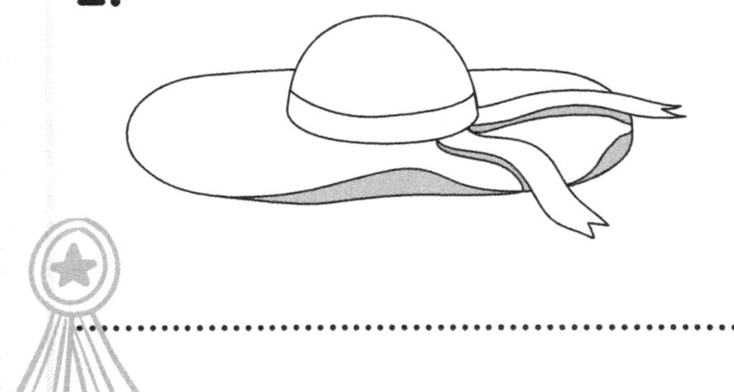

....

5.

....

3.

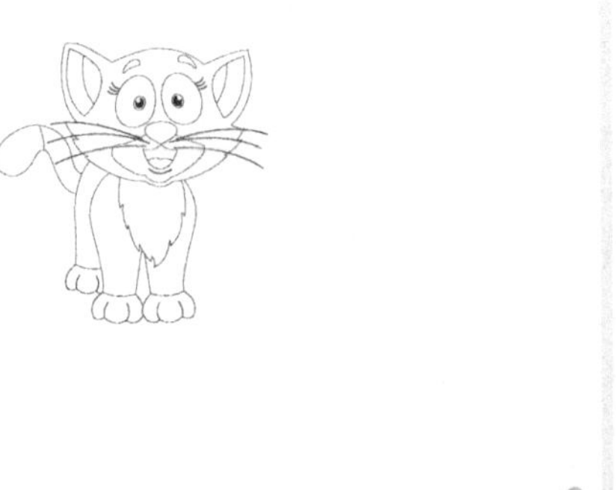

....

6.

....

7.

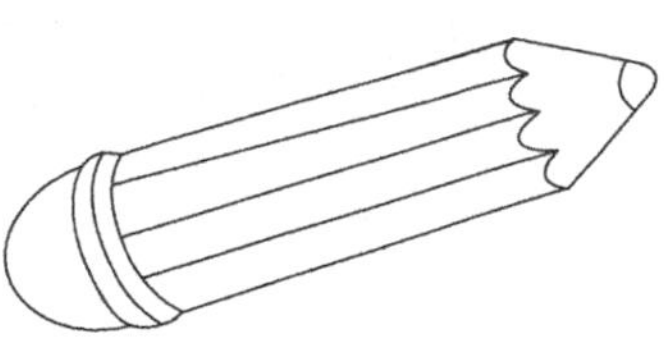

....

10.

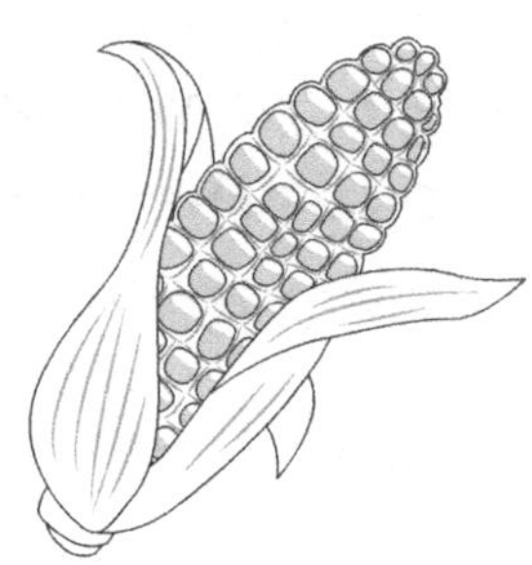

....

8.

....

11.

....

9.

....

12.

....

Let's get some fitness in!
Go to page 229 to try some fitness activities.

Beginning Sounds
ENGLISH

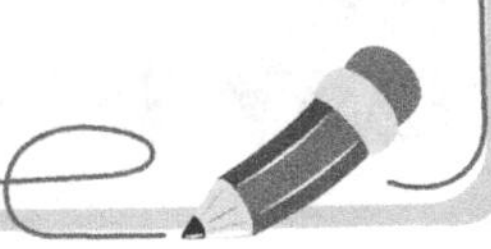

Read Together

Remember simple words have a beginning, middle and ending sound. We can read these sounds on their own and then blend them together to read the whole word.

For example, the word fed has three sounds: /f/, /e/ and /d/. We can say each of those sounds on their own. Then we blend them together to read the entire word - *fed*.

Practice with the following words:

A. Nun

B. Fit

C. Ran

D. Cot

Directions

Look at the beginning sounds in the tables below. Write a few words that begin with each sound.

For Kids

Beginning Sound - /s/	Beginning Sound - /b/
Example: sun	***Example:*** bat

Beginning Sounds
ENGLISH

Beginning Sound - /s/	Beginning Sound - /b/

Beginning Sound - /t/	Beginning Sound - /h/
Example: *tip*	***Example:*** *ham*

WEEK 4
DAY 2

Beginning Sounds
ENGLISH

Directions

Look at the pictures in each box below. For each picture, say its name aloud and identify the beginning sound in the word. Decide which picture has the correct beginning sound. Circle that picture.

For Kids

1. Which word has the beginning sound /m/?

3. Which word has the beginning sound /v/?

2. Which word has the beginning sound /r/?

4. Which word has the beginning sound /h/?

Beginning Sounds
ENGLISH

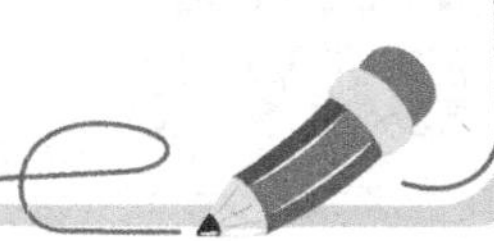

5. Which word has the beginning sound /g/?

7. Which word has the beginning sound /n/?

6. Which word has the beginning sound /d/?

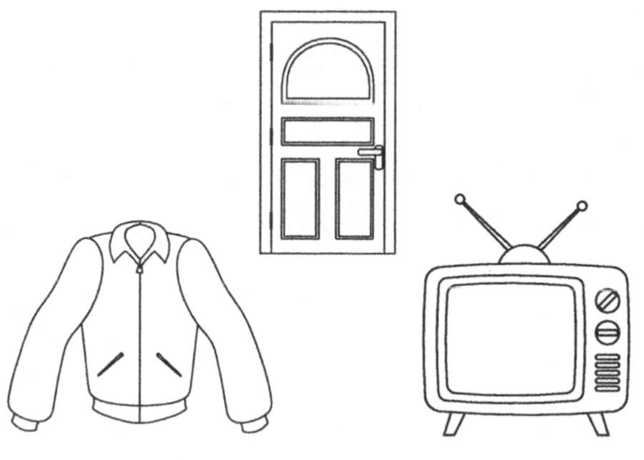

8. Which word has the beginning sound /f/?

Let's get some fitness in!
Go to page 229 to try some fitness activities.

WEEK 4
DAY 3

Simple Addition with Numerals
MATHEMATICS

Directions:

Fill in the sum for each of the questions.

Question 1:

Ollie the Octopus is filling up a treasure chest! He has 1 small coin and 1 big coin. How many coins does he have?

$1 + 1 =$ ___

Question 3:

Ollie the Octopus has 3 diamonds and 1 emerald. How many gems does he have?

$3 + 1 =$ ___

Question 2:

Ollie the Octopus has 2 pearl necklaces and 1 diamond necklace. How many necklaces does he have?

$2 + 1 =$ ___

Question 4:

Ollie the Octopus has 4 big rings and 1 small ring. How many rings does he have?

$4 + 1 =$ ___

Simple Addition with Numerals
MATHEMATICS

Question 5:

Ollie the Octopus has 1 small sparkly cup and 2 big sparkly cups. How many sparkly cups does he have?

1 + 2 = ___

Question 7:

Ollie the Octopus has 1 big crown and 3 small crowns. How many crowns does he have?

1 + 3 = ___

Question 6:

Ollie the Octopus has 1 small treasure map and 1 big treasure map. How many treasure maps does he have?

1 + 1 = ___

Question 8:

Ollie the Octopus has 2 locks on one side and 1 lock on the other side. How many locks are on his treasure chest?

2 + 1 = ___

Let's get some fitness in!
Go to page 229 to try some fitness activities.

FITNESS TIME

Simple Addition with Numerals
MATHEMATICS

Directions:

Fill in the sum for each of the questions.

Question 1:

Ollie the Octopus finds a pirate ship. He sees 2 big sails and 1 small sail. How many sails does he see?

$2 + 1 =$ ____

Question 3:

Ollie the Octopus sees 2 large pirate flags and 1 small pirate flag. How many pirate flags does he see?

$2 + 1 =$ ____

Question 2:

Ollie the Octopus sees 2 portholes on one side and 2 portholes on the other side. How many portholes does he see?

$2 + 2 =$ ____

Question 4:

Ollie the Octopus sees 1 tall mast and 3 short masts. How many masts does he see?

$1 + 3 =$ ____

WEEK 4
DAY 4

Simple Addition with Numerals
MATHEMATICS

Question 5:

Ollie the Octopus sees 1 empty treasure chest and 1 full treasure chest. How many treasure chests does he see?

$1 + 1 =$ ____

Question 7:

Ollie the Octopus sees 3 small parrots and 1 big parrot. How many parrots does he see?

$3 + 1 =$ ____

Question 6:

Ollie the Octopus sees 3 short pirates and 2 tall pirates. How many pirates does he see?

$3 + 2 =$ ____

Question 8:

Ollie the Octopus sees 1 large ship anchor and 1 small ship anchor. How many ship anchors does he see?

$1 + 1 =$ ____

Let's get some fitness in!
Go to page 229 to try some fitness activities.

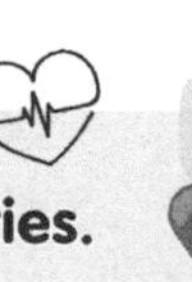

WEEK 4 DAY 5

Simple Addition with Numerals
MATHEMATICS

Directions:

Fill in the sum for each of the questions.

Question 1:

Ollie the Octopus spots a lot of things in the ocean. He sees 2 baby sea turtles and 1 daddy sea turtle. How many turtles does he see?

$2 + 1 = $ ____

Question 3:

Ollie the Octopus sees 1 large lobster and 2 small lobsters. How many lobsters does he see?

$1 + 2 = $ ____

Question 2:

Ollie the Octopus sees 3 small starfish and 1 big starfish. How many starfish does he see?

$3 + 1 = $ ____

Question 4:

Ollie the Octopus sees 1 oyster with a pearl and 1 oyster without a pearl. How many oysters does he see?

$1 + 1 = $ ____

WEEK 5
Let's learn more about letter sounds and simple addition! We'll explore fun facts about the Sun, too!
ARGOPREP

Vowel Sounds
ENGLISH

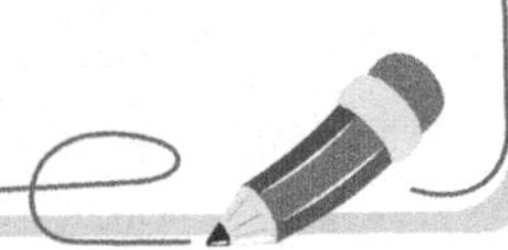

Read Together

Today you are going to practice listening to sounds in the middle of words. Most simple words have a beginning, middle and ending sound. Usually the middle sound is a vowel - a, e, i, o or u. When we read simple words, we read each sound in the word and then blend them together.

For example, the word bit has three sounds: /b/, /i/ and /t/. We can say each of those sounds on their own. Then we blend them together to read the entire word - *bit.*

Practice with the following words:

A. Fat
B. Bed
C. Hog
D. Sum

Directions

Look at the pictures below. For each picture, say its name aloud and identify the middle sound in the word. Circle the correct answer.

For Kids

1.

A. A **B.** E **C.** I **D.** O **E.** U

2.

A. A **B.** E **C.** I **D.** O **E.** U

3.

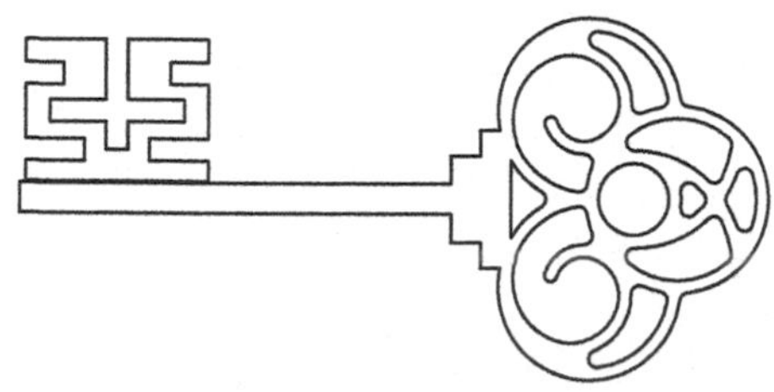

A. A **B.** E **C.** I **D.** O **E.** U

5.

A. A **B.** E **C.** I **D.** O **E.** U

4.

A. A **B.** E **C.** I **D.** O **E.** U

6.

A. A **B.** E **C.** I **D.** O **E.** U

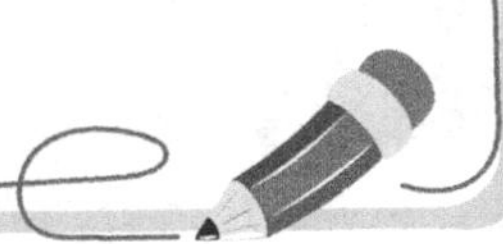

Directions

Look at the pictures below. For each picture, say its name aloud and identify the middle sound in the word. Write the correct middle sound on the line.

For Kids

1.

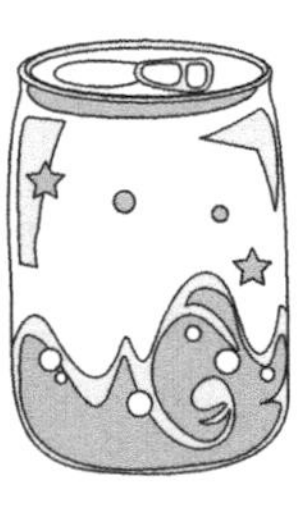

....

4.

....

2.

....

5.

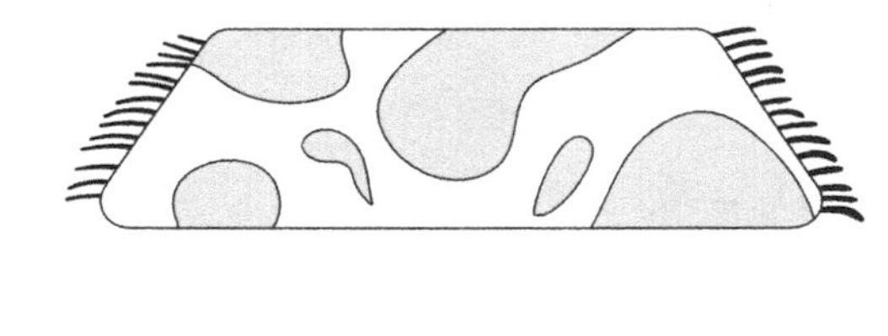

....

3.

....

6.

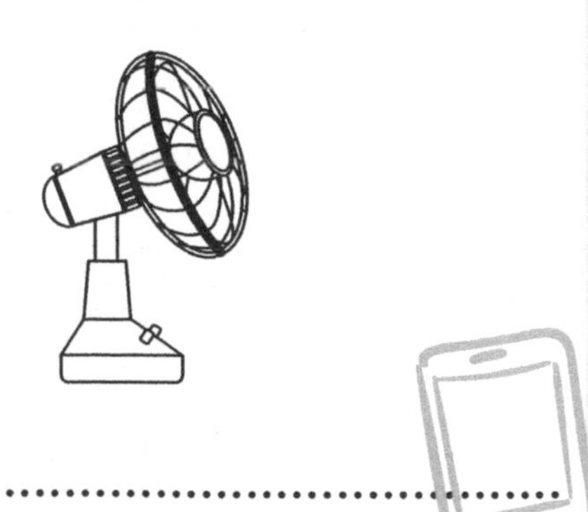

....

7.

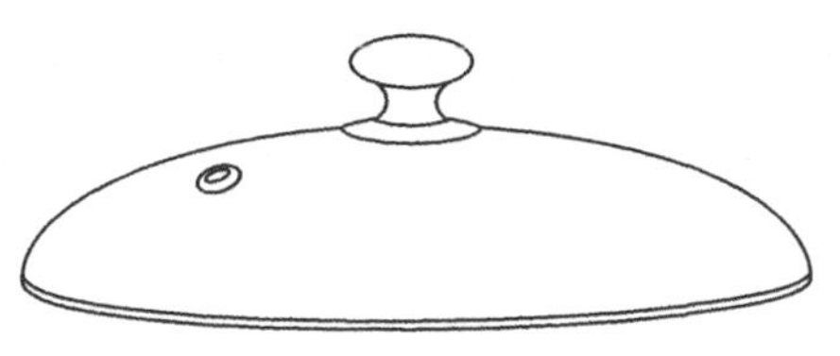

....

10.

....

8.

....

11.

....

9.

....

12.

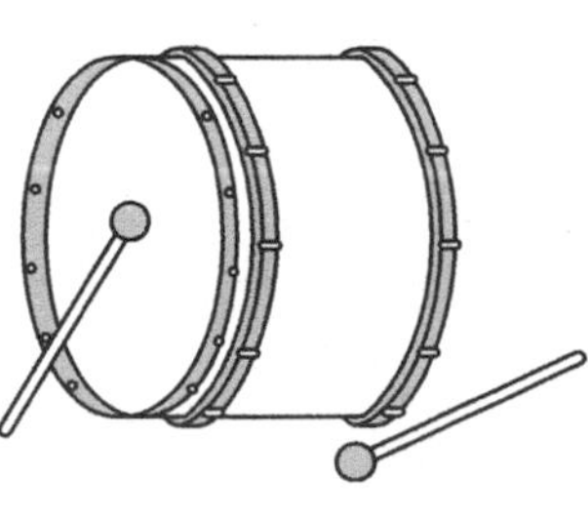

....

Let's get some fitness in!
Go to page 229 to try some fitness activities.

WEEK 5 DAY 2

Middle Sounds
ENGLISH

Read Together

Remember simple words have a beginning, middle and ending sound. We can read these sounds on their own and then blend them together to read the whole word.

For example, the word cut has three sounds: /c/, /u/ and /t/. We can say each of those sounds on their own. Then we blend them together to read the entire word - *cut*.

Practice with the following words:

A. Sat **B.** Led **C.** Bid **D.** Hot

Directions

Look at the middle sounds in the tables below. Write a few words that have each middle sound.

For Kids

Middle Sound - /a/	Middle Sound - /e/
Example: *cat*	***Example:*** *bed*

Middle Sounds
ENGLISH

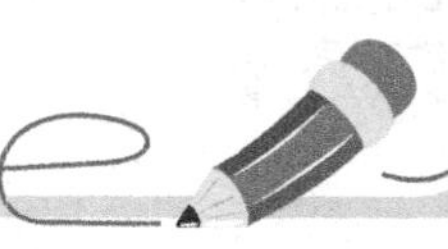

Middle Sound - /i/	Middle Sound - /o/
Example: *tip*	***Example:*** *hot*

Middle Sound - /u/	
Example: *tub*	

Middle Sounds
ENGLISH

Directions

Look at the pictures in each box below. For each picture, say its name aloud and identify the middle sound in the word. Decide which word has the correct middle sound. Circle that picture.

For Kids

1. Which word has the middle sound /a/?

3. Which word has the middle sound /i/?

2. Which word has the middle sound /e/?

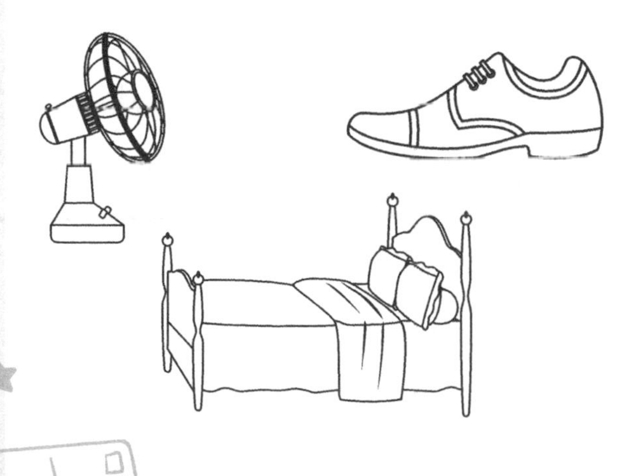

4. Which word has the middle sound /o/?

5. Which word has the middle sound /u/?

7. Which word has the middle sound /e/?

6. Which word has the middle sound /a/?

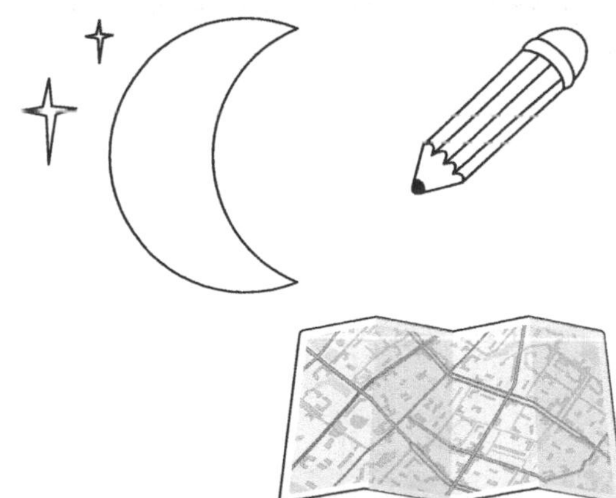

8. Which word has the middle sound /u/?

Let's get some fitness in!
Go to page 229 to try some fitness activities.

WEEK 5
DAY 3

Simple Addition with a Missing Number
MATHEMATICS

Directions:

Fill in the missing number to make the number sentence true.

Question 1:

Carl the Crab finds a sunken pirate ship he wants to repair. He needs 2 hammers. He has 1 hammer. How many more does he need?

1 + ___ = 2

Question 2:

Carl the Crab needs 3 nails to repair his pirate ship. He has 1 nail. How many more does he need?

1 + ___ = 3

Question 3:

Carl the Crab needs 4 wooden boards to repair his pirate ship. He has 1 wooden board. How many more does he need?

1 + ___ = 4

Question 4:

Carl the Crab needs 5 saws to repair his pirate ship. He has 1 saw. How many more does he need?

1 + ___ = 5

Simple Addition with a Missing Number

MATHEMATICS

Question 5:

Carl the Crab needs 3 tape measures to repair his pirate ship. He has 2 tape measures. How many more does he need?

$2 + \_\_\_ = 3$

Question 7:

Carl the Crab needs 5 screws to repair his pirate ship. He has 4 screws. How many more does he need?

$4 + \_\_\_ = 5$

Question 6:

Carl the Crab needs 4 screwdrivers to repair his pirate ship. He has 3 screwdrivers. How many more does he need?

$3 + \_\_\_ = 4$

Question 8:

Carl the Crab wants to put 2 sails on his pirate ship. He has 1 sail. How many more does he need?

$1 + \_\_\_ = 2$

Let's get some fitness in!
Go to page 229 to try some fitness activities.

WEEK 5 DAY 4

Simple Addition with a Missing Number
MATHEMATICS

Directions:

Fill in the missing number to make the number sentence true.

Question 1:

Carl the Crab is gathering up some supplies for his pirate crew. He needs 5 spy glasses. He has 3 spy glasses. How many more does he need?

$3 + \_\_\_ = 5$

Question 2:

Carl the Crab needs 4 eye patches for his pirate crew. He has 2 eye patches. How many more does he need?

$2 + \_\_\_ = 4$

Question 3:

Carl the Crab needs 3 peg legs for his pirate crew. He has 1 peg leg. How many more does he need?

$1 + \_\_\_ = 3$

Question 4:

Carl the Crab needs 4 pirate flags for his pirate crew. He has 1 pirate flag. How many more does he need?

$1 + \_\_\_ = 4$

Simple Addition with a Missing Number
MATHEMATICS

Question 5:

Carl the Crab needs 2 parrots for his pirate crew. He has 1 parrot. How many more does he need?

1 + ___ = 2

Question 7:

Carl the Crab needs 5 soup bowls for his pirate crew. He has 1 soup bowl. How many more does he need?

1 + ___ = 5

Question 6:

Carl the Crab needs 5 bandanas for his pirate crew. He has 3 bandanas. How many more does he need?

3 + ___ = 5

Question 8:

Carl the Crab needs 5 soup spoons for his pirate crew. He has 2 soup spoons. How many more does he need?

2 + ___ = 5

Let's get some fitness in!
Go to page 229 to try some fitness activities.

WEEK 5
DAY 5

Simple Addition with a Missing Number
MATHEMATICS

Directions:

Fill in the missing number to make the number sentence true.

Question 1:

Carl the Crab wants to cook a vegetable soup for his pirate ship crew. He needs 5 potatoes. He has 2 potatoes. How many more does he need?

$2 + \_\_\_ = 5$

Question 2:

Carl the Crab needs 4 carrots. He has 2 carrots. How many more does he need?

$2 + \_\_\_ = 4$

Question 3:

Carl the Crab needs 3 sticks of celery. He has 2 sticks of celery. How many more does he need?

$2 + \_\_\_ = 3$

Question 4:

Carl the Crab needs 4 onions. He has 3 onions. How many more does he need?

$3 + \_\_\_ = 4$

Simple Addition with a Missing Number
MATHEMATICS

Question 5:

Carl the Crab needs 2 cups of green beans. He has 1 cup of green beans. How many more cups does he need?

1 + ___ = 2

Question 7:

Carl the Crab needs 3 zucchinis. He has 1 zucchini. How many more does he need?

1 + ___ = 3

Question 6:

Carl the Crab needs 5 tomatoes. He has 4 tomatoes. How many more does he need?

4 + ___ = 5

Question 8:

Carl the Crab needs 5 cups of water. He has 3 cups of water. How many more cups does he need?

3 + ___ = 5

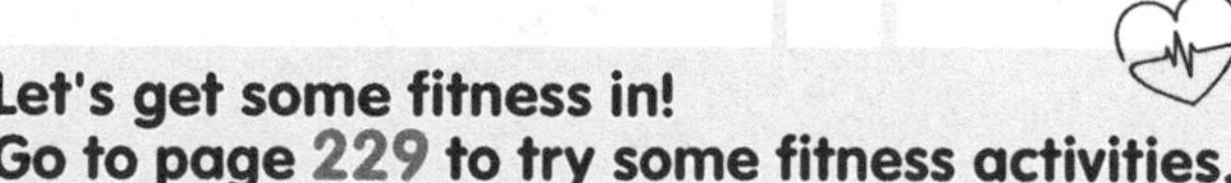

Let's get some fitness in!
Go to page 229 to try some fitness activities.

WEEK 5
DAY 6

The Sun
EXPERIMENTS

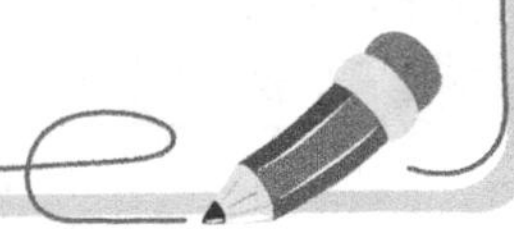

Read Together

The Sun is a star. It is a large ball made of gas. The Sun is over 4 billion years old. It is the largest object in our solar system!

The Sun is very important because it provides light and heat to all living things on the planet Earth. Without the Sun, living things like plants and animals would not be able to survive.

Directions

For each question below, look at the pictures and decide which object needs the Sun in order to grow or survive. Circle the correct answer.

For Kids

1.

3.

2.

4.

Hello

5.

8.

6.

9.

7.

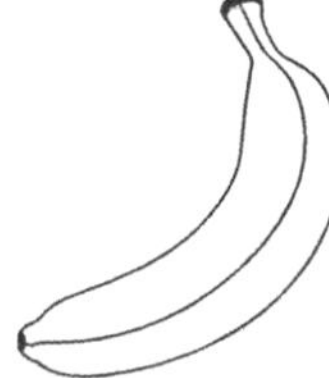

10.

Let's get some fitness in!
Go to page 229 to try some fitness activities.

WEEK 5
DAY 7

MAZE

Find the correct shadow.

1	a
2	b
3	c
4	d
5	e

WEEK 6
Do you know what a noun is? This week, you'll learn about them. Let's explore shapes and learn about the sky, too!
1
2
3
4
ARGOPREP

WEEK 6 DAY 1

Nouns
ENGLISH

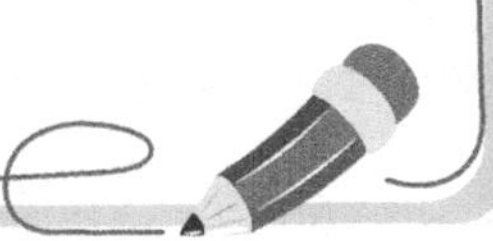

Read Together

There are many different types of words. Today you are going to learn about nouns. A **noun** is a word that names a person, place or thing. Read the table below for examples of nouns.

Person	Place	Thing
teacher	school	couch
kid	park	leopard
Joe	New York	scissors

Directions

Read the words below. For each word, decide whether or not it is a noun. Circle the correct answer.

For Kids

1. **Sad**

   A. Noun

   B. Not a noun

2. **Pants**

   A. Noun

   B. Not a noun

3. **Phone**

   A. Noun

   B. Not a noun

4. **Swimming**

   A. Noun

   B. Not a noun

5.
Elephant

A. Noun

B. Not a noun

8.
Cold

A. Noun

B. Not a noun

6.
Backpack

A. Noun

B. Not a noun

9.
Horse

A. Noun

B. Not a noun

7.
Excited

A. Noun

B. Not a noun

10.
Loud

A. Noun

B. Not a noun

Nouns
ENGLISH

Directions

Look at the pictures below. For each picture, say its name aloud and identify whether it is **a person**, **a place** or **a thing**. Write the correct word on the line.

For Kids

1.

....

4.

....

2.

....

5.

....

3.

....

6.

....

7.

....

10.

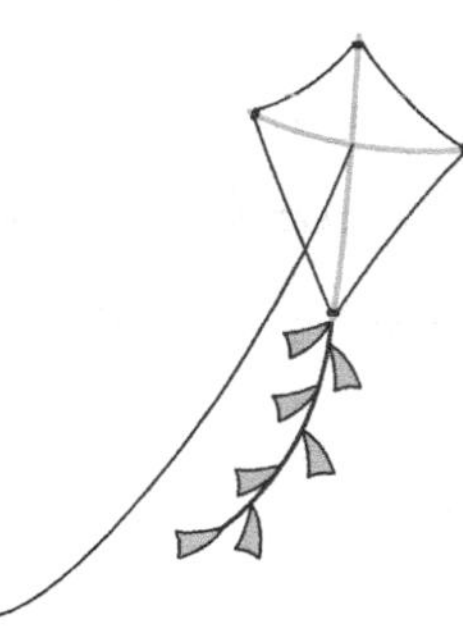

....

8.

....

11.

....

9.

....

12.

....

Let's get some fitness in!
Go to page 229 to try some fitness activities.

Nouns
ENGLISH

Read Together

Remember a noun is a word that is a person, place or thing. There are many nouns. A few examples include: doctor, veterinarian, zoo, office building, panda and centipede.

Directions

On the tables below, write as many nouns as you can think of that are people, places and things.

For Kids

Person	Place
Example: *zookeeper*	***Example:*** *church*

Thing

Example: bathtub

WEEK 6 DAY 2

Nouns ENGLISH

Directions

Look at the pictures in each box below. For each picture, say its name aloud and decide whether the nouns are all people, places or things. Think of another noun that would fit in with the first three. Write the word or draw a picture in the space provided.

For Kids

1.

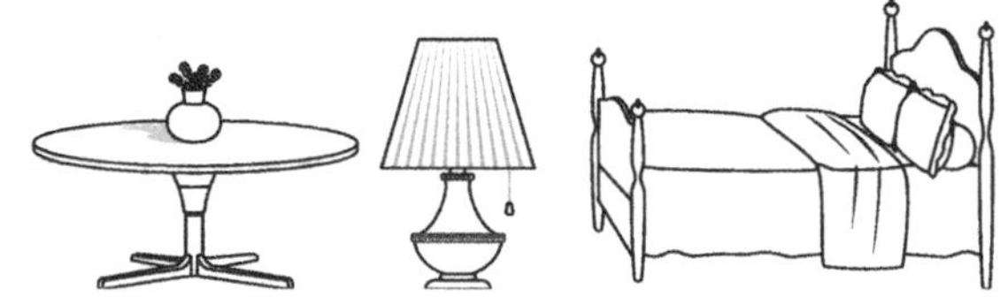

....

2.

....

3.

....

4.

....

5.

....

8.

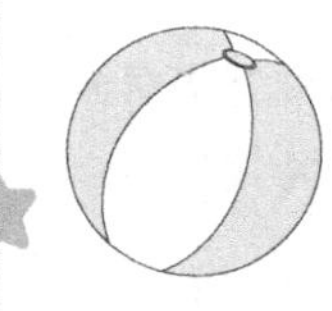
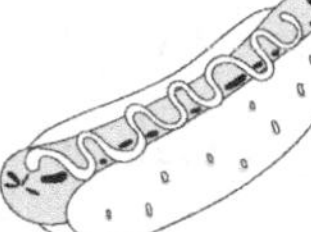

....

6.

....

9.

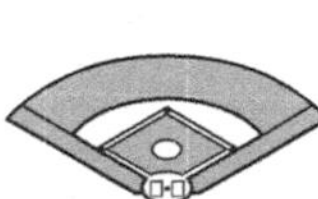

....

7.

....

10.

....

Let's get some fitness in!
Go to page 229 to try some fitness activities.

Question 1:

Sandy the Starfish likes to draw shapes in the sand. Which shape is a circle? Draw an "X" over it.

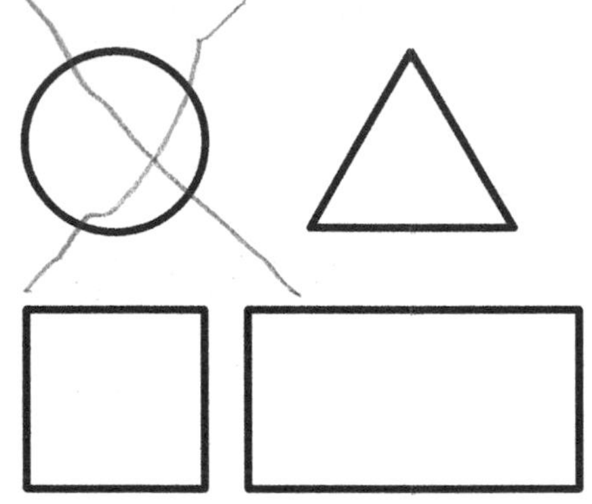

Question 3:

Which shape is a triangle? Draw an "X" over it.

Question 2:

Which shape is a square? Draw an "X" over it.

Question 4:

Which shape is a rectangle? Draw an "X" over it.

Question 5:

Which shape is a triangle? Color it in.

Question 7:

Which shape is a rectangle? Color it in.

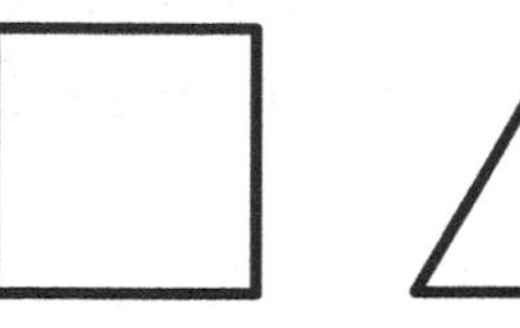

Question 6:

Which shape is a square? Color it in.

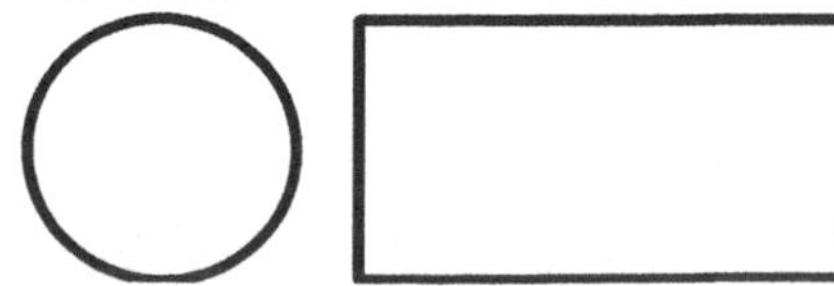

Question 8:

Which shape is a circle? Color it in.

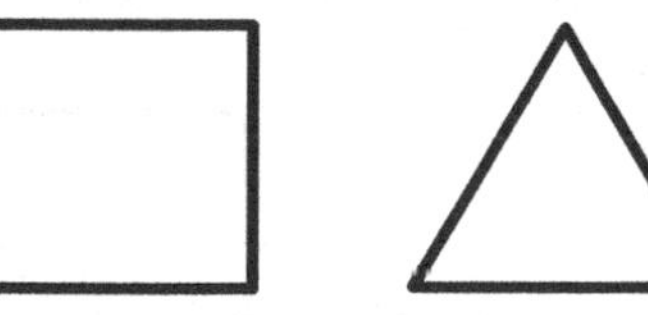

Let's get some fitness in!
Go to page 229 to try some fitness activities.

Question 1:

Sandy the Starfish looks up at the night sky and imagines drawing shapes using the stars. Which shape is a square? Draw an "X" over it.

Question 2:

Which shape is a rectangle? Draw a line around it.

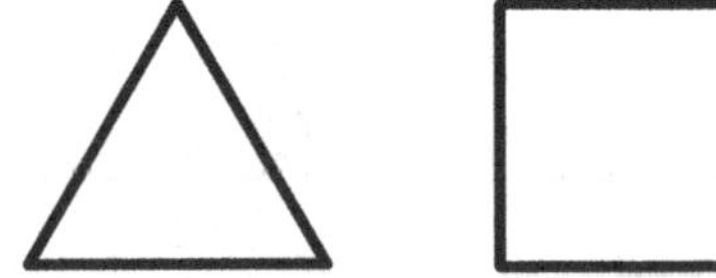

Question 3:

Which shape is a circle? Draw a line around it.

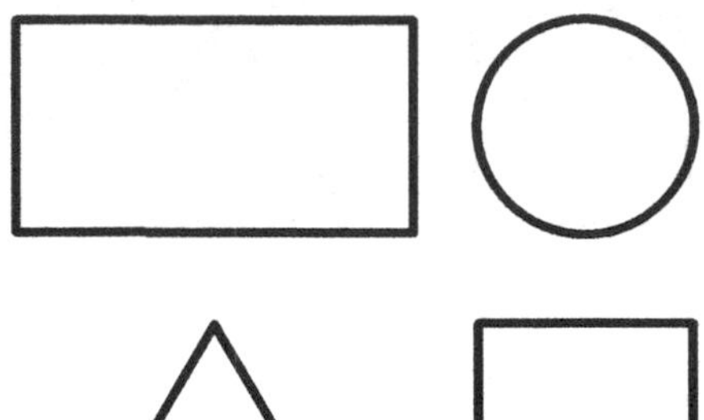

Question 4:

Which shape is a triangle? Draw a line around it.

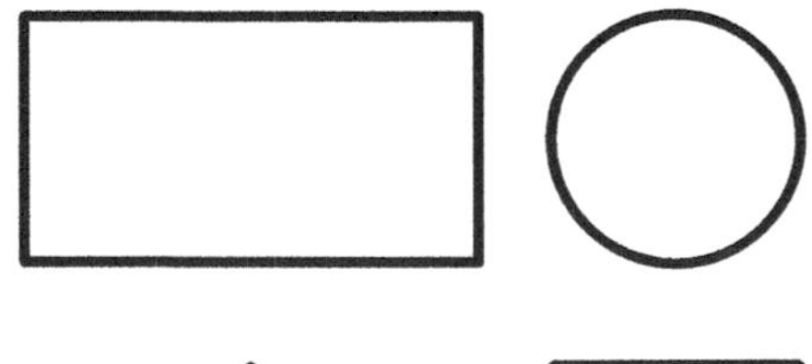

Simple Shapes
MATHEMATICS

Question 5:

Which shape is a rectangle? Color it in.

Question 7:

Which shape is a triangle? Color it in.

Question 6:

Which shape is a circle? Color it in.

Question 8:

Which shape is a square? Color it in.

Let's get some fitness in!
Go to page 229 to try some fitness activities.

Question 1:

Sandy the Starfish spots different shaped stones on the ocean floor. Which shape is a triangle? Draw an "X" over it.

Question 3:

Which shape is a circle? Draw an "X" over it.

2+2=4

Question 2:

Which shape is a square? Draw an "X" over it.

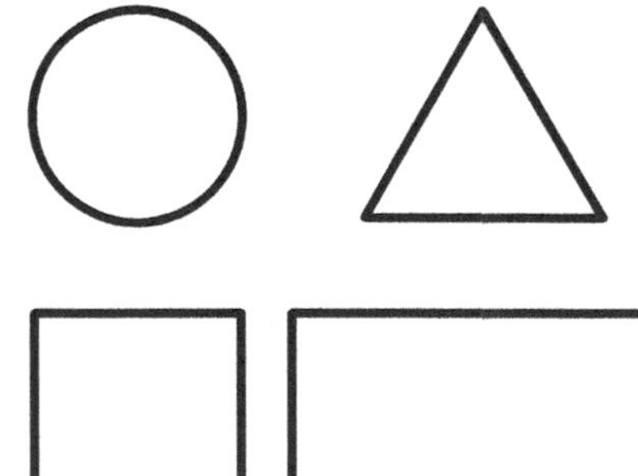

Question 4:

Which shape is a rectangle? Draw an "X" over it.

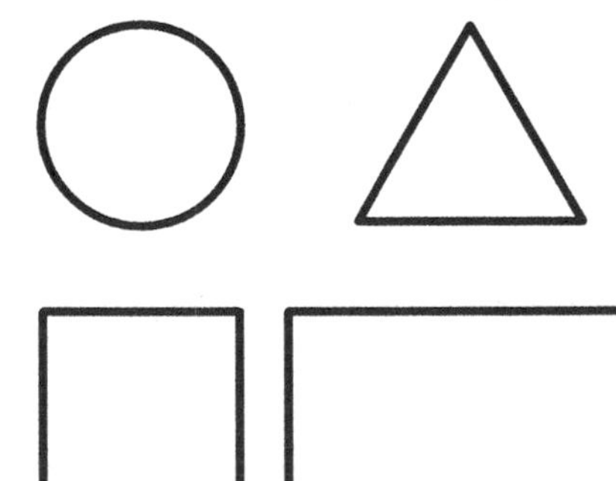

Question 5:

Which shape is a square? Color it in.

Question 7:

Which shape is a circle? Color it in.

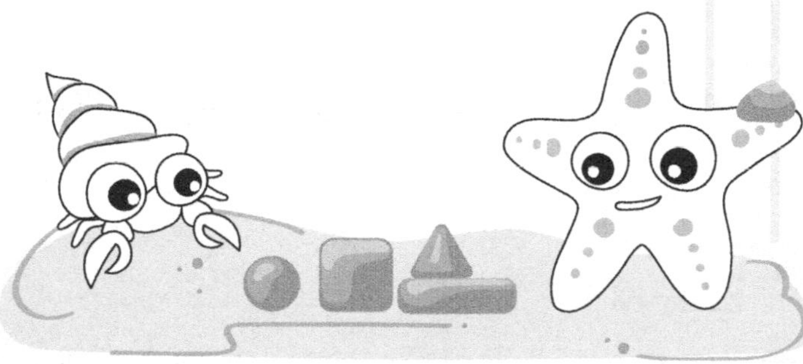

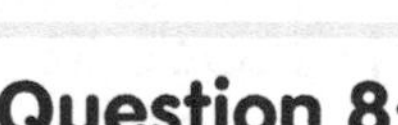

Question 6:

Which shape is a triangle? Color it in.

Question 8:

Which shape is a rectangle? Color it in.

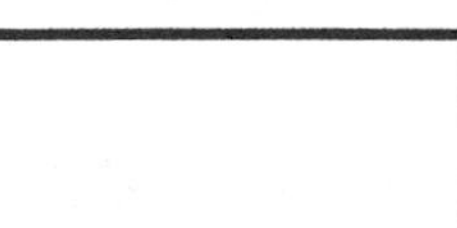

Let's get some fitness in!
Go to page 229 to try some fitness activities.

WEEK 6 DAY 6

The Day and Night Sky EXPERIMENTS

Read Together

In the daytime, the sky looks different than it does at night. Besides the sky looking bright during the day and dark at night, different objects can be seen in the sky at different times.

During the day, we are able to see the Sun, clouds, birds and airplanes in the sky. Some of these objects are not in the night sky or are much harder to see.

At night, we are able to see the moon and stars, the lights of airplanes flying overhead, and possibly clouds.

What are some other objects you might see in the day or night sky?

Directions

For each picture below, decide if the object can be seen only during the day, only at night, or both. Circle the correct answer.

For Kids

1.

A. Day sky
B. Night sky
C. Both

2.

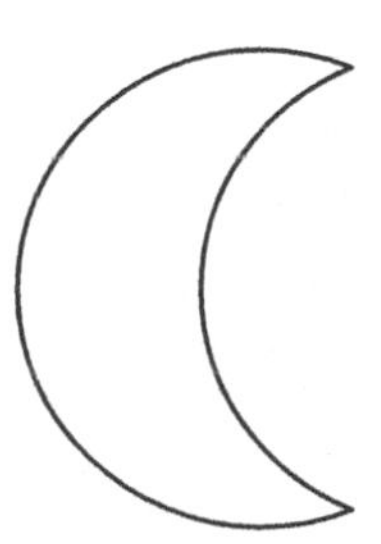

A. Day sky
B. Night sky
C. Both

3.

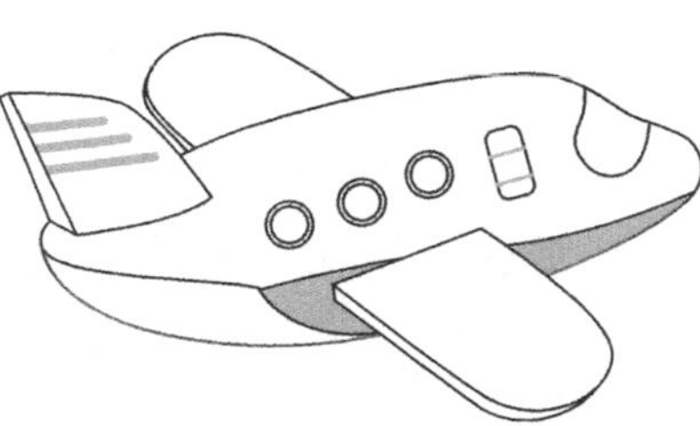

A. Day sky
B. Night sky
C. Both

6.

A. Day sky
B. Night sky
C. Both

4.

A. Day sky
B. Night sky
C. Both

7.

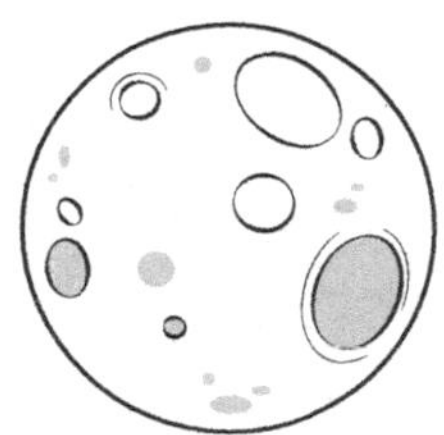

A. Day sky
B. Night sky
C. Both

5.

A. Day sky
B. Night sky
C. Both

8.

A. Day sky
B. Night sky
C. Both

Let's get some fitness in!
Go to page 229 to try some fitness activities.

FITNESS TIME

MAZE

Help little pirate Jack catch a big fish.

WEEK 7
Get ready to learn about verbs, comparing groups and different types of weather! Let's get started!
ARGOPREP

WEEK 7 DAY 1

Verbs
ENGLISH

Read Together

There are many different types of words. Last week, you learned that a noun is a person, place or thing. Today you are going to learn about verbs. A **verb** is a word that shows action. If you can act out the word, it is probably a verb. Read the table below for examples of verbs.

swimming	walking	singing
shouting	twirling	racing

Directions

Read the words below. For each word, decide whether or not it is a verb. Circle the correct answer.

For Kids

1. run

A. Verb

B. Not a verb

2. paint

A. Verb

B. Not a verb

3. snowflake

A. Verb

B. Not a verb

4. blanket

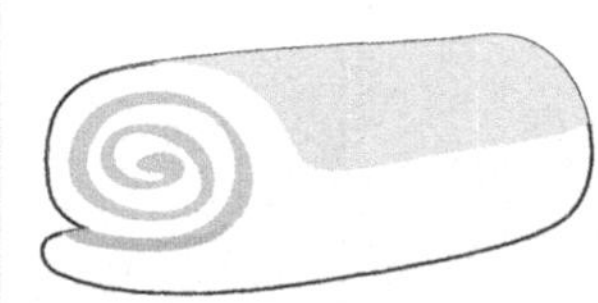

A. Verb

B. Not a verb

5. sloth

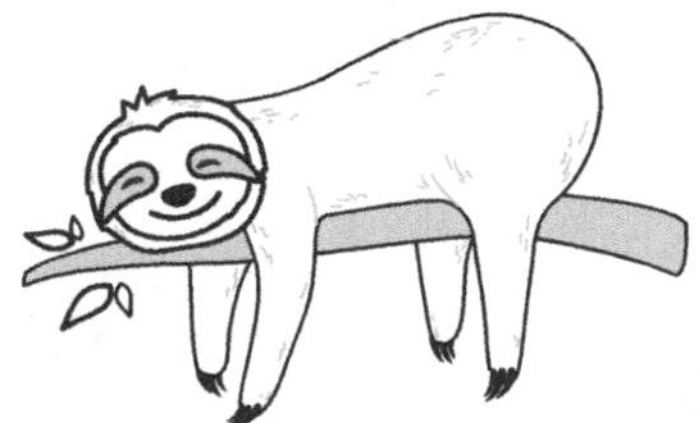

A. Verb

B. Not a verb

6. dance

A. Verb

B. Not a verb

7. cry

A. Verb

B. Not a verb

8. paper

A. Verb

B. Not a verb

9. eat

A. Verb

B. Not a verb

10. light

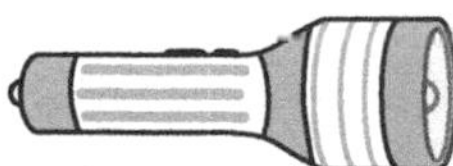

A. Verb

B. Not a verb

WEEK 7
DAY 1

Verbs
ENGLISH

Directions

Read the words below. For each word, identify whether it is a verb or not. Write yes or no on the line.

For Kids

1. Singing

....

4. Write

....

2. Happy

....

5. Dolphin

....

3. Drink

....

6. Drive

....

7. Sit

....

10. Climb

....

8. Door

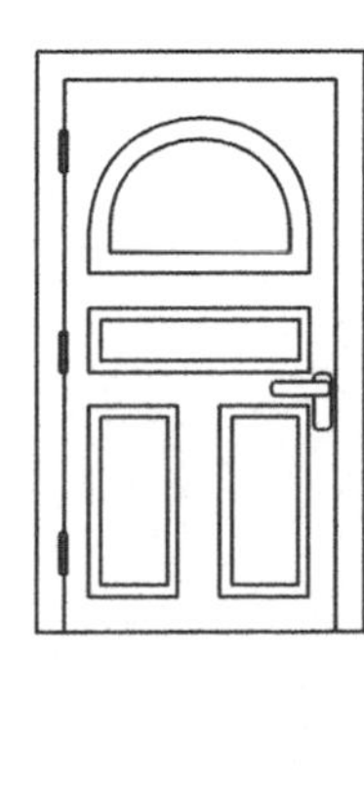

....

11. Draw

....

9. Clothes

....

12. Book

....

Let's get some fitness in!
Go to page 229 to try some fitness activities.

FITNESS TIME

Verbs
ENGLISH

Read Together

Remember a verb is an action word. There are many verbs. A few examples include: jumping, sitting, sleeping and yelling.

Directions

On the table below, write as many verbs as you can think of.

For Kids

Verbs	

Verbs	

Directions

Look at the pictures in each box below. For each picture, say its name aloud and decide whether or not it is a verb. Put an **X** through the picture that does **not** show a verb.

For Kids

1.

3.

2.

4.

5.

8.

6.

9.

7.

10.

Let's get some fitness in!
Go to page 229 to try some fitness activities.

Comparing Groups of Objects
MATHEMATICS

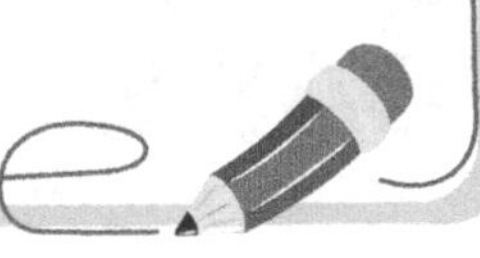

Directions:

Draw a circle around the correct group.

Question 1:

Wally the Whale watches groups of creatures while swimming through the ocean. Which group of manta rays is bigger?

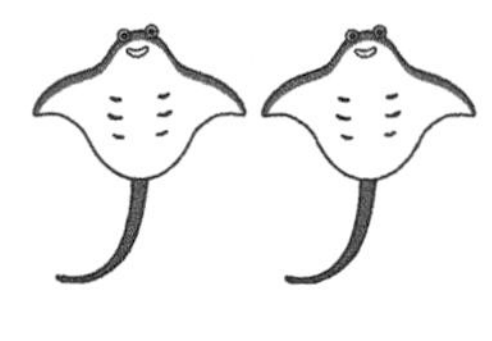

Question 2:

Which group of eels is bigger?

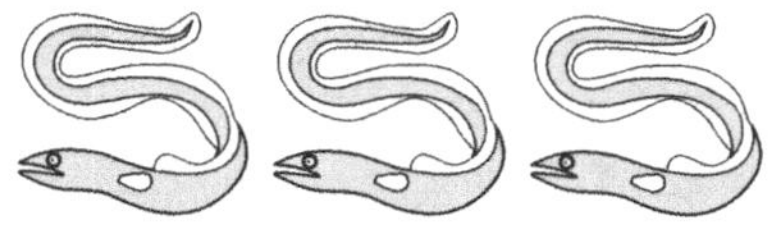

Question 3:

Which group of jellyfish is bigger?

Question 4:

Which group of striped fish is bigger?

Comparing Groups of Objects
MATHEMATICS

Question 5:

Which group of spotted fish is bigger?

Question 6:

Which group of dolphins is bigger?

Question 7:

Which group of sharks is bigger?

Question 8:

Which group of whales is bigger?

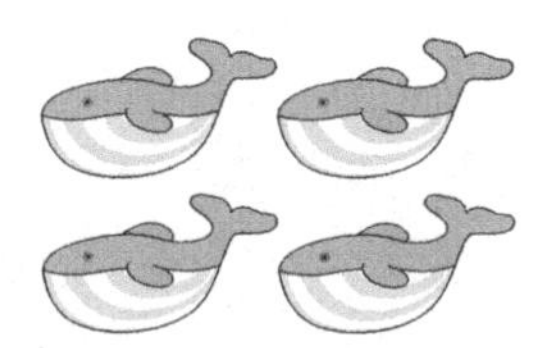
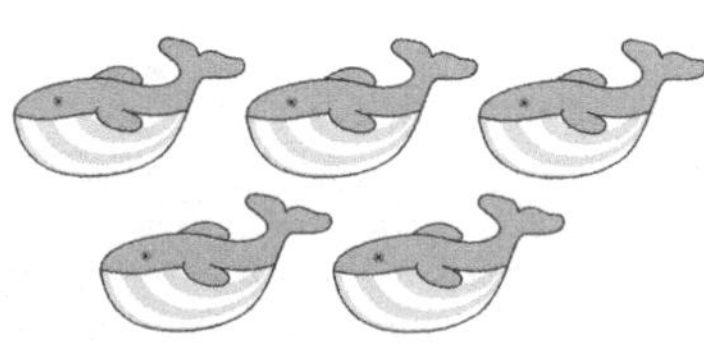

Let's get some fitness in!
Go to page 229 to try some fitness activities.

WEEK 7 DAY 4

Comparing Groups of Objects
MATHEMATICS

Directions:

Draw a circle around the correct group.

Question 1:

Wally the Whale sees groups of things on the beach. Which group of beach balls is smaller?

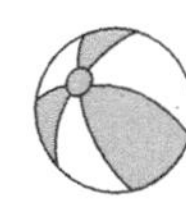
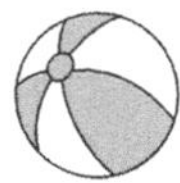
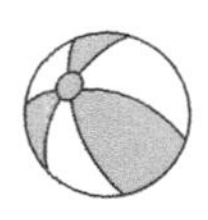
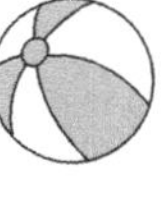
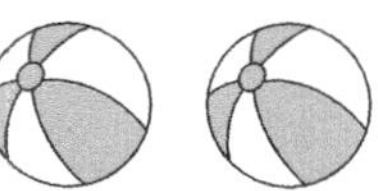

Question 3:

Which group of sand buckets is smaller?

Question 2:

Which group of beach umbrellas is smaller?

Question 4:

Which group of sand shovels is smaller?

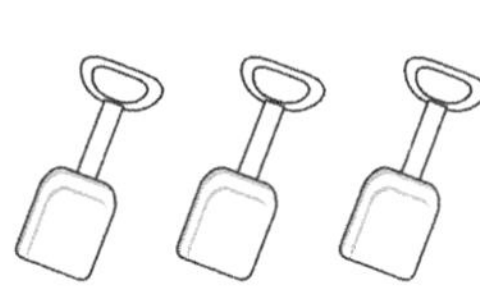

Question 5:

Which group of sandcastles is smaller?

Question 7:

Which group of surfboards is smaller?

Question 6:

Which group of beach towels is smaller?

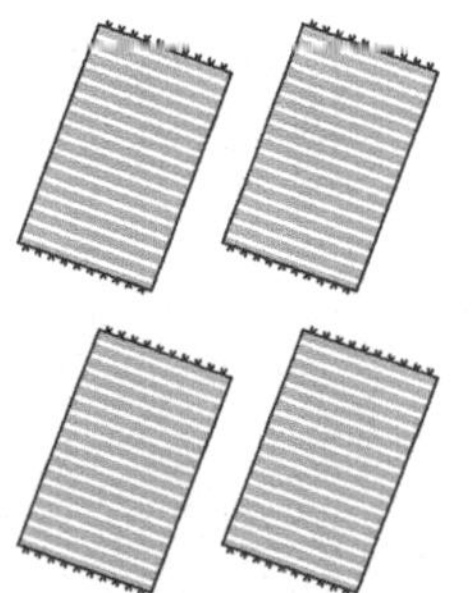

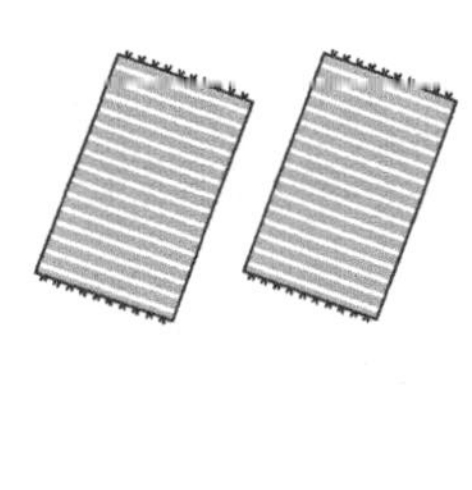

Question 8:

Which group of kids is smaller?

Let's get some fitness in!
Go to page 229 to try some fitness activities.

WEEK 7 DAY 5

Comparing Groups of Objects
MATHEMATICS

Directions:

Draw a circle around the correct group.

Question 1:

Wally the Whale sees groups of things on the ocean's sandy floor. Which group of lobsters is bigger?

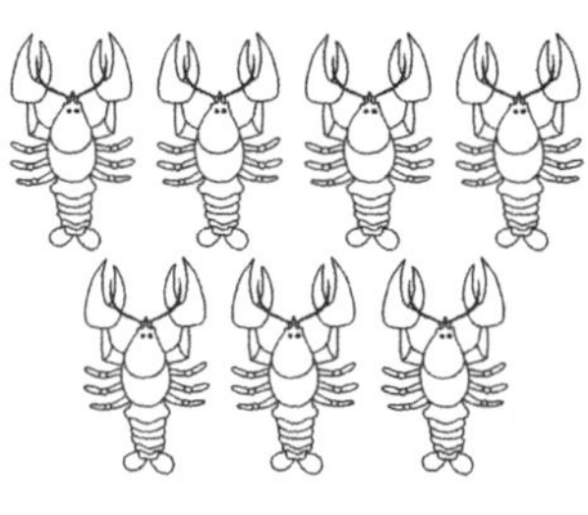

Question 2:

Which group of crabs is smaller?

Question 3:

Which group of seashells is bigger?

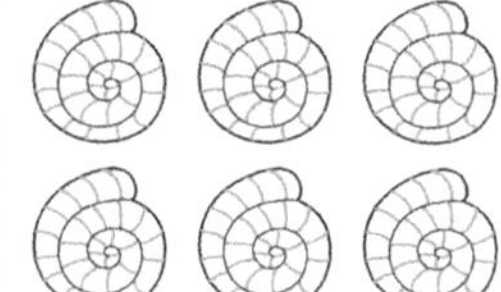

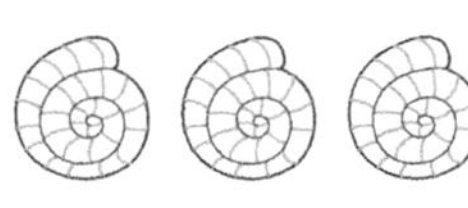

Question 4:

Which group of seaweed strands is smaller?

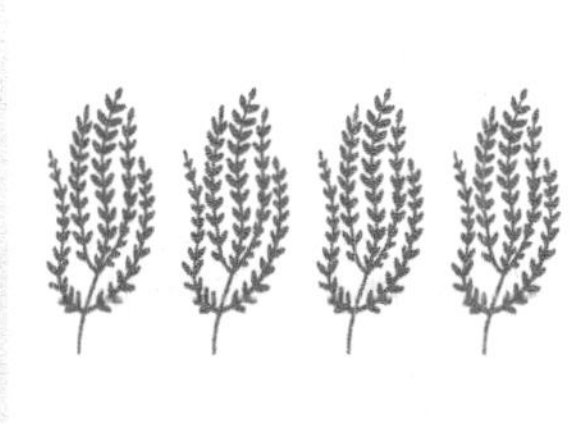

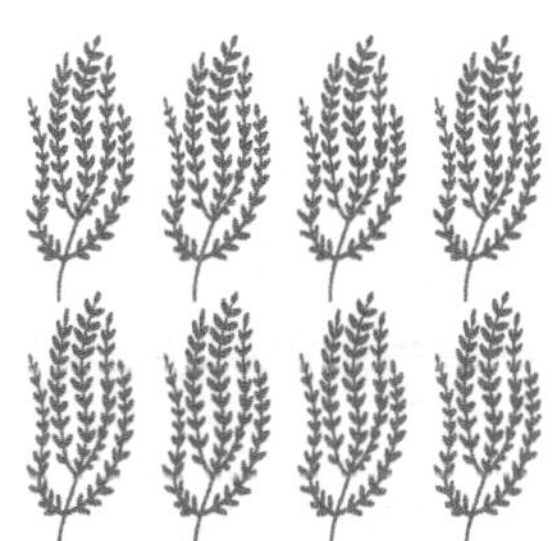

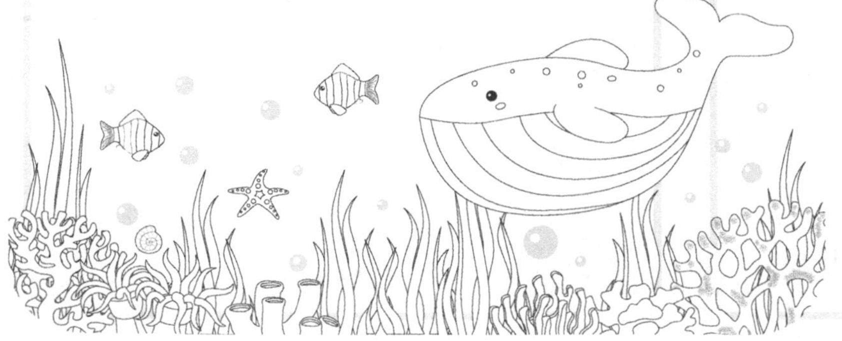

Comparing Groups of Objects
MATHEMATICS

Question 5:

Which group of starfish is bigger?

Question 7:

Which group of shrimp are bigger?

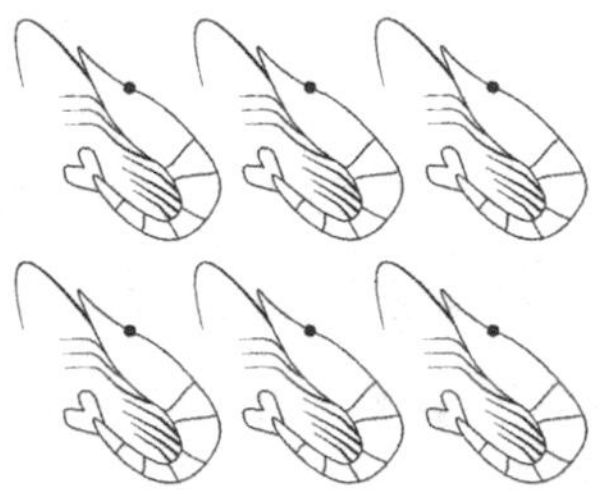

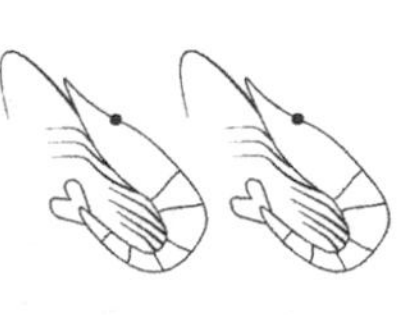

Question 6:

Which group of coral reef rocks is smaller?

Question 8:

Which group of treasure chests is smaller?

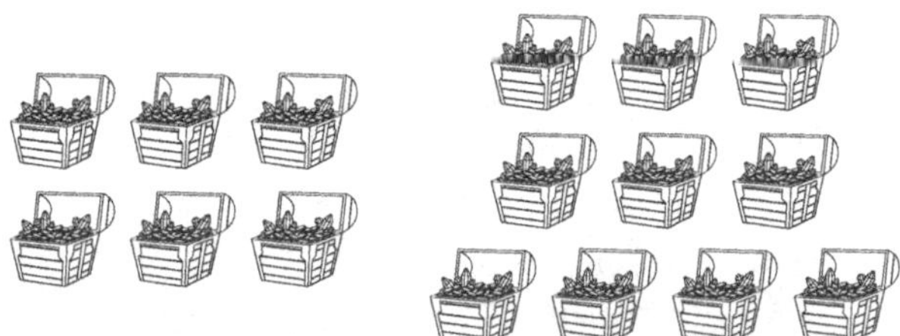

Let's get some fitness in!
Go to page 229 to try some fitness activities.

Weather
EXPERIMENTS

Read Together

Weather describes the sky and air outside. It tells you how it looks and feels outside. The weather might be warm or cold. The sky may be sunny or dark.

There are many different types of weather, such as rain, snow, sleet and sun. We use words like sunny, cloudy, rainy and snowy to describe what the weather is like in our area.

The weather can be very different, depending on where you live. Some areas of our country stay sunny and warm throughout the entire year. Other areas get a lot of snow in the winter.

What is the weather like where you live?

Directions

For each picture below, describe the weather shown by circling the correct answer.

For Kids

1.

A. Sunny
B. Cloudy
C. Snowy
D. Rainy
E. Windy

2.

A. Sunny
B. Cloudy
C. Snowy
D. Rainy
E. Windy

Weather
EXPERIMENTS

3.

A. Sunny
B. Cloudy
C. Snowy
D. Rainy
E. Windy

4.

A. Sunny
B. Cloudy
C. Snowy
D. Rainy
E. Windy

5.

A. Sunny
B. Cloudy
C. Snowy
D. Rainy
E. Windy

6. What is the weather like today where you live?

A. Sunny
B. Cloudy
C. Snowy
D. Rainy
E. Windy

Let's get some fitness in!
Go to page 229 to try some fitness activities.

MAZE

Find the treasure!

WEEK 8
This week, you'll learn about plural nouns and comparing objects. What's the difference between plants and animals? Let's find out!
ARGOPREP

WEEK 8
DAY 1

Plural Nouns
ENGLISH

Read Together

Over the past couple of weeks, you have learned about nouns and verbs. Today, you are going to learn about plural nouns. Remember a **noun** is a word that names a person, place or thing. **Plural** means more than one so a plural noun means that there is more than one person, place or thing. We usually make a noun plural by adding -s or -es to the end of the word. Read the table below for examples of plural nouns.

Person	Place	Thing
teachers	schools	horses
boys	farms	rocks
workers	churches	bottles

Directions

Read the words below. For each word, decide whether the noun is plural or not. Circle the correct answer.

For Kids

1. Bushes

A. Plural noun

B. Not a plural noun

2. Vase

A. Plural noun

B. Not a plural noun

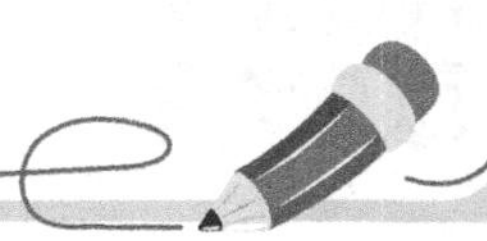

3. Plate

A. Plural noun

B. Not a plural noun

4. Barns

A. Plural noun

B. Not a plural noun

5. Babysitter

A. Plural noun

B. Not a plural noun

6. Girls

A. Plural noun

B. Not a plural noun

7. Theaters

A. Plural noun

B. Not a plural noun

8. Sloth

A. Plural noun

B. Not a plural noun

9. Bedrooms

A. Plural noun

B. Not a plural noun

10. Waitresses

A. Plural noun

B. Not a plural noun

Plural Nouns
ENGLISH

Directions

Look at the pictures below. For each picture, say its name aloud and identify whether it is a **plural noun** or not. Write yes or no on the line.

For Kids

1.

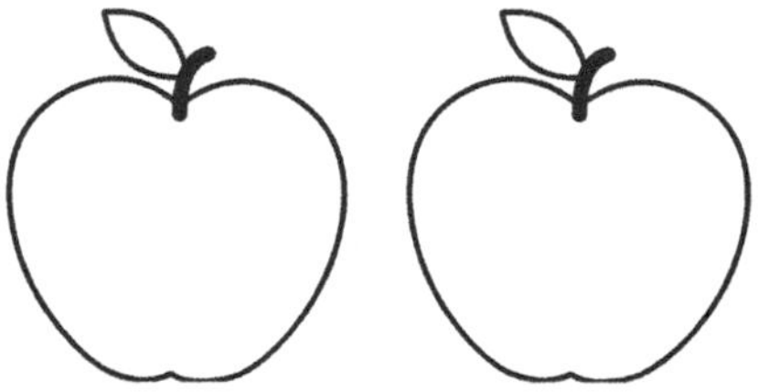

....

2.

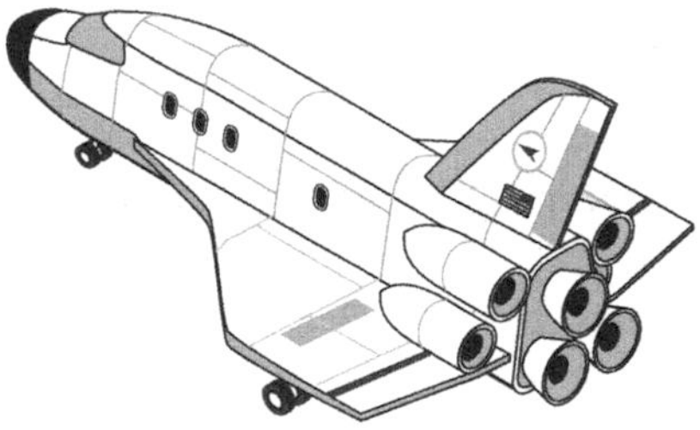

....

3.

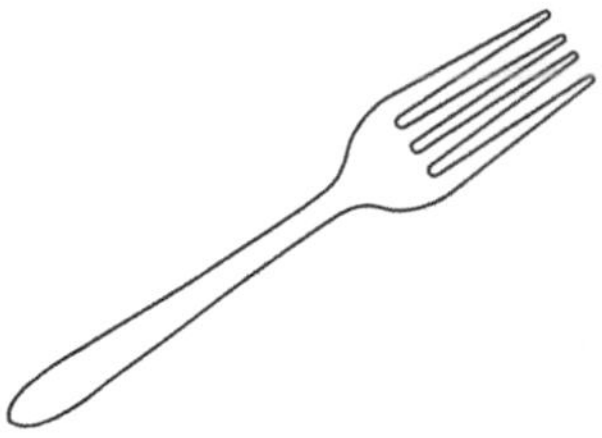

....

4.

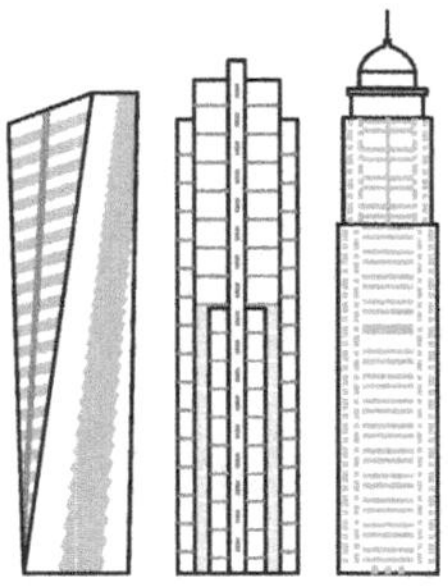

....

5.

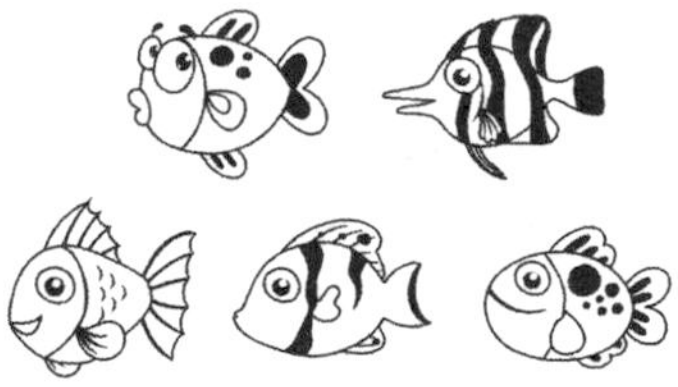

....

6.

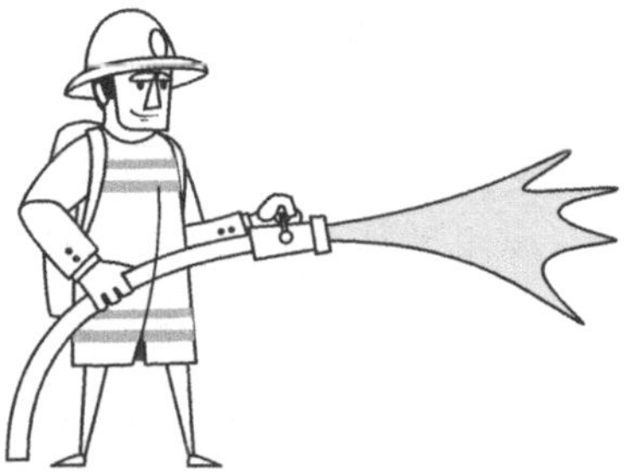

....

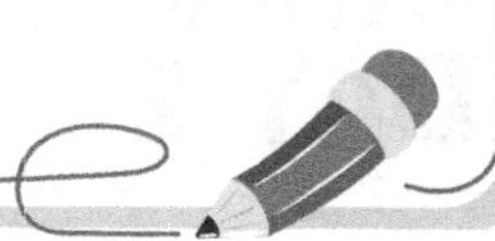

7.

....

10.

....

8.

....

11.

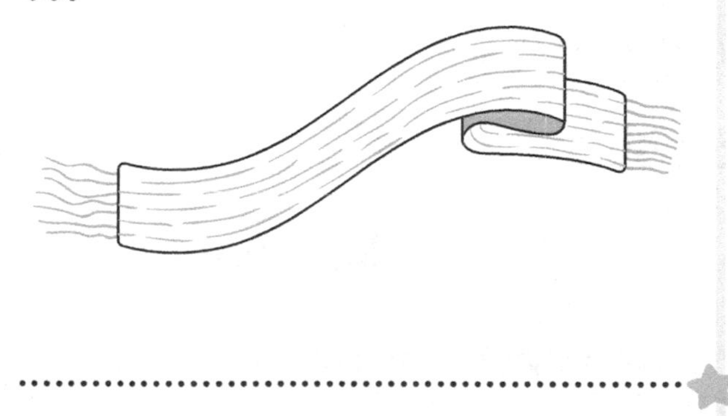

....

9.

....

12.

....

Let's get some fitness in!
Go to page 229 to try some fitness activities.

WEEK 8
DAY 2

Plural Nouns
ENGLISH

Read Together

Remember a noun is a word that is a person, place or thing. A plural noun names more than one person, place or thing. A few examples of plural nouns include: farmers, stores, cats, socks and rectangles.

Directions

On the tables below, have an adult help you read each noun on the left. On the right, rewrite the noun as a plural noun or just say the plural noun aloud. Remember to add an **s** to the noun to make it plural.

For Kids

Singular Noun	Plural Noun
Example: *zookeeper*	***Example:*** *zookeepers*
dog	
tree	
mask	
flower	
lake	
truck	

Plural Nouns
ENGLISH

Singular Noun	Plural Noun
pear	
cup	
bag	
ant	
stair	
hen	
oval	
moon	
doll	
pencil	

BISON

WEEK 8
DAY 2

Plural Nouns
ENGLISH

Directions

Look at each set of pictures below. Say each word aloud. Think about which picture shows a plural noun. Circle the correct answer.

For Kids

1.

3.

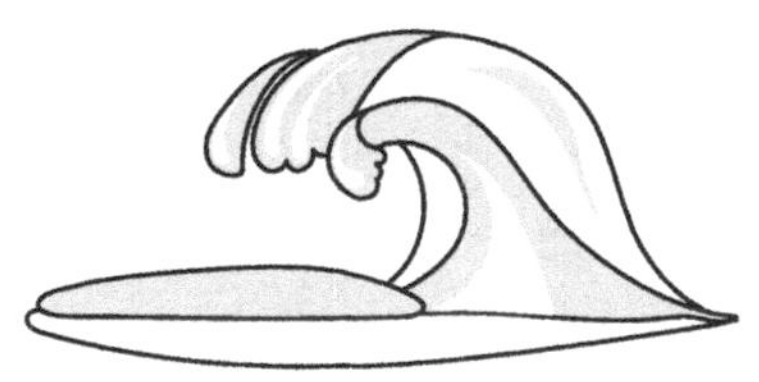

2.

4.

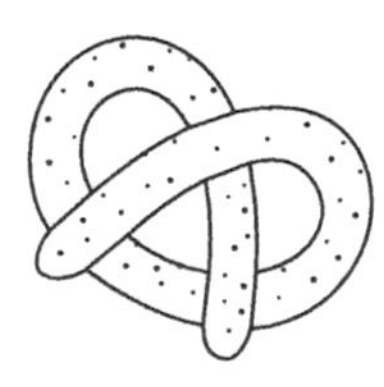

Plural Nouns
ENGLISH

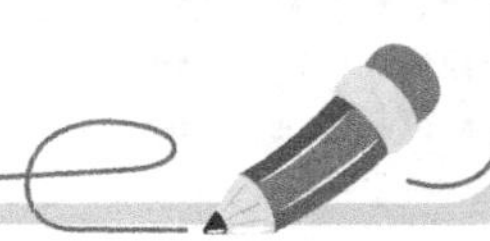

5.

8.

6.

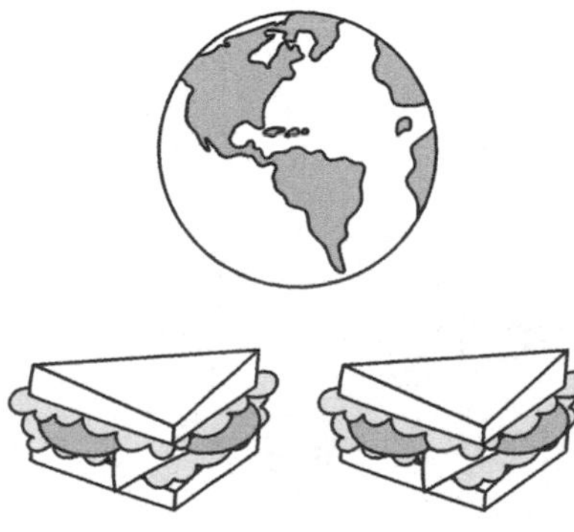

9.

7.

10.

Let's get some fitness in!
Go to page 229 to try some fitness activities.

FITNESS TIME

Directions:

Draw a circle around the correct object.

Question 1:

Eddie the Eel likes to compare the size of things. Which treasure chest is larger?

Question 3:

Which seashell is larger?

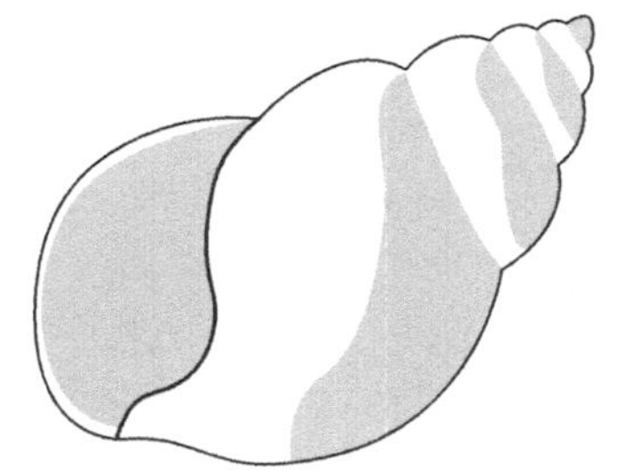

Question 2:

Which sand bucket is larger?

Question 4:

Which fish is larger?

Comparing Large to Small
MATHEMATICS

Question 5:

Which sandcastle is smaller?

Question 7:

Which starfish is smaller?

Question 6:

Which clump of coral is smaller?

Question 8:

Which pirate ship anchor is smaller?

Let's get some fitness in!
Go to page 229 to try some fitness activities.

WEEK 8 DAY 4

Comparing Long to Short and Tall to Short
MATHEMATICS

Directions:

Draw a circle around the correct object.

Question 1:

Eddie the Eel likes to compare the length of things. Which fish is longer?

Question 3:

Which beach towel is shorter?

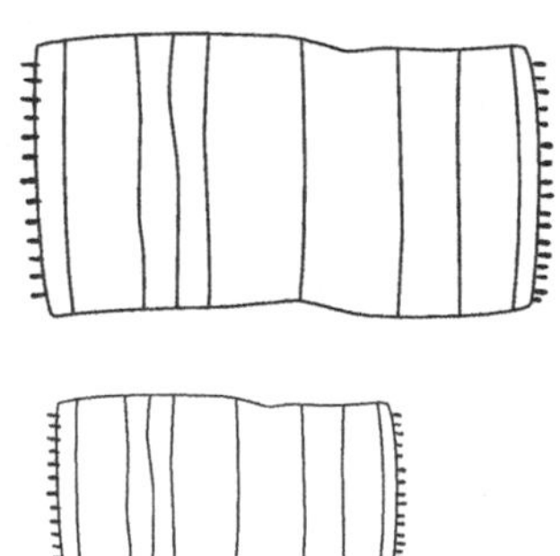

Question 2:

Which shark is longer?

Question 4:

Which eel is longer?

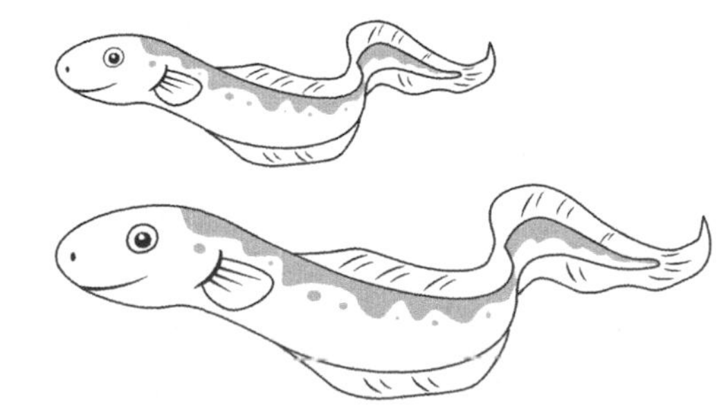

Comparing Long to Short and Tall to Short

MATHEMATICS

Question 5:

Which clump of seaweed is shorter?

Question 7:

Which beach umbrella is taller?

Question 6:

Which palm tree is taller?

Question 8:

Which kid on the beach is shorter?

Let's get some fitness in!
Go to page 229 to try some fitness activities.

Comparing Full to Empty
MATHEMATICS

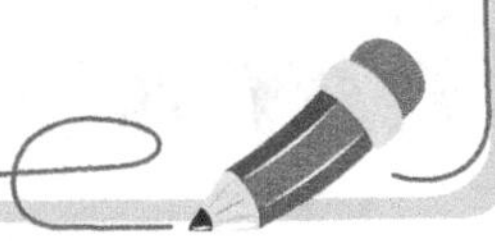

Directions:

Draw a circle around the correct object.

Question 1:

Eddie the Eel likes to check if things are empty or full. Which treasure chest is full of gold?

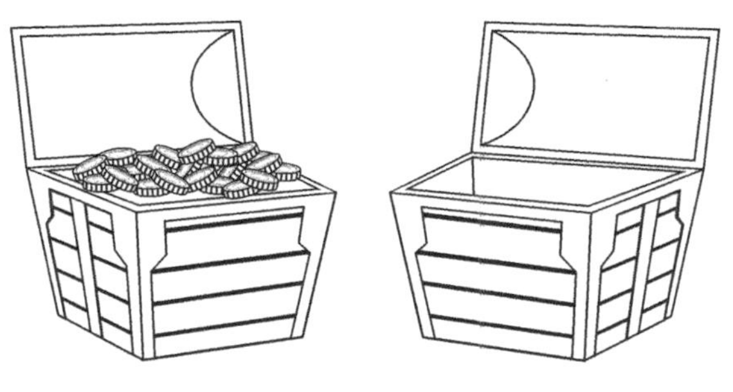

Question 3:

Which sand bucket is full of sand?

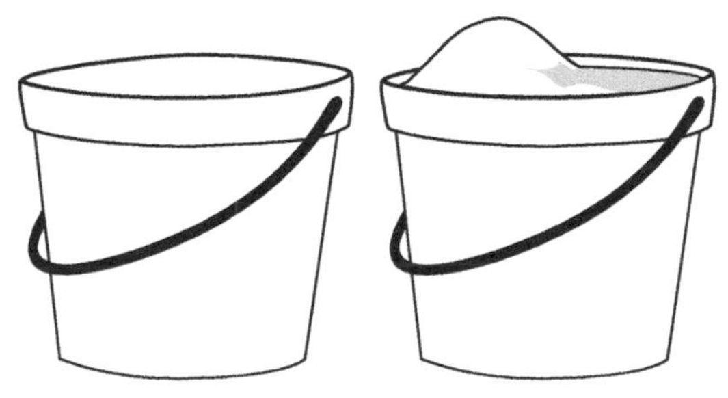

Question 2:

Which sand bucket is full of water?

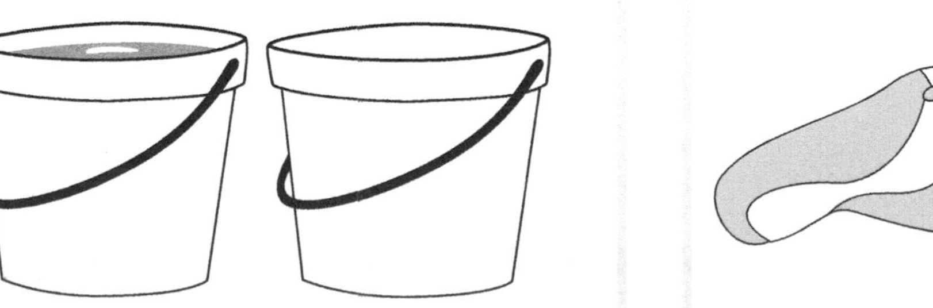

Question 4:

Which beach ball is full of air?

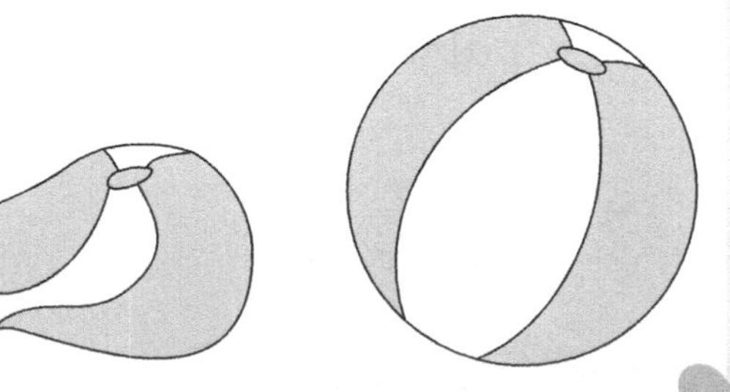

Comparing Full to Empty
MATHEMATICS

Question 5:

Which beach cooler is full of ice?

Question 7:

Which soda bottle is empty?

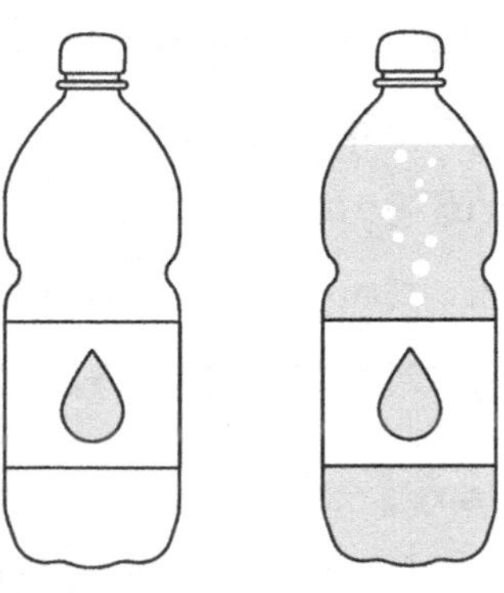

Question 8:

Which beach is empty?

Question 6:

Which glass is empty?

Let's get some fitness in!
Go to page 229 to try some fitness activities.

Plants and Animals
EXPERIMENTS

Read Together

Plants and animals are living things. **Plants** grow from the ground and make their own food. There are many different types of plants, including trees, flowers, grass and bushes. **Animals** are a different type of living thing. They feed themselves by eating plants or other animals. There are also many different types of animals, including bears, birds, dogs, elephants and frogs.

Plants and animals both need food and water to live. Plants also need sunshine and healthy soil to grow.

Directions

For each picture below, decide whether it is a plant or animal. Circle the correct answer.

For Kids

1.

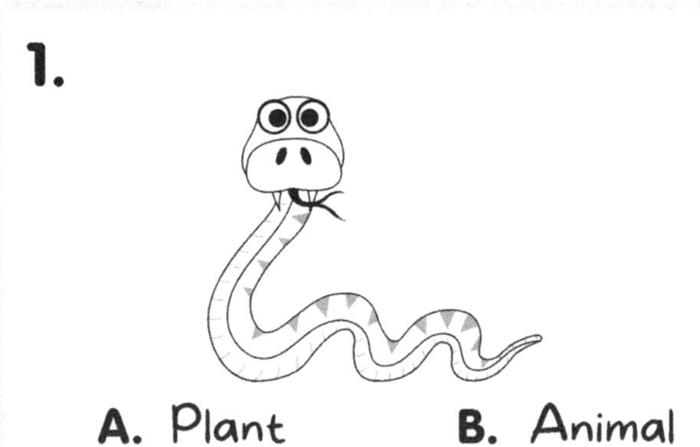

A. Plant **B.** Animal

2.

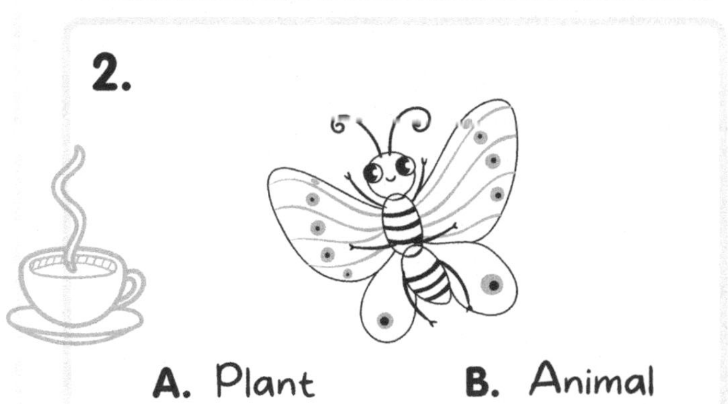

A. Plant **B.** Animal

3.

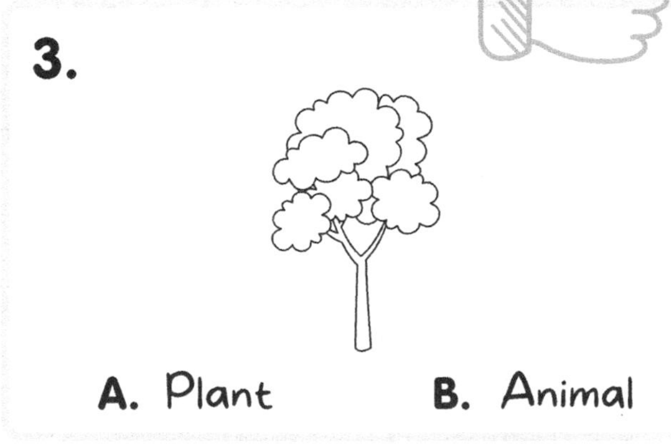

A. Plant **B.** Animal

4.

A. Plant **B.** Animal

Plants and Animals

EXPERIMENTS

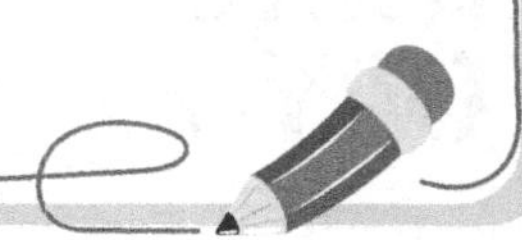

5.

A. Plant **B.** Animal

6.

A. Plant **B.** Animal

7.

A. Plant **B.** Animal

8.

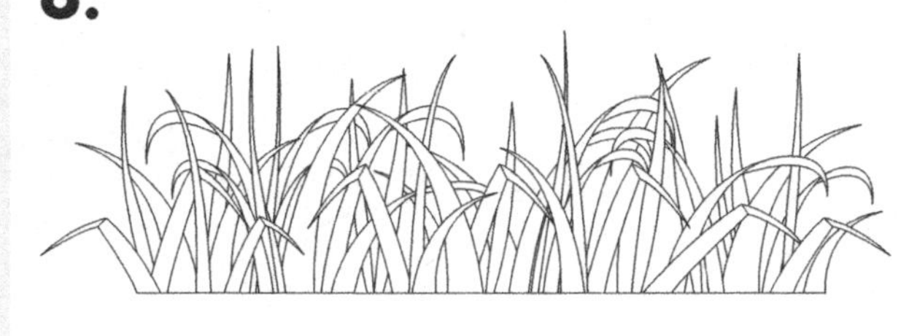

A. Plant **B.** Animal

9.

A. Plant **B.** Animal

10.

A. Plant **B.** Animal

Let's get some fitness in!
Go to page 229 to try some fitness activities.

MAZE

Think about who lives in each egg and mark it with a number, then write the correct number of the egg in the blank to which it rolls.

☐ Lizard ☐ Chick ☐ Duck

☐ Snake ☐ Turtle

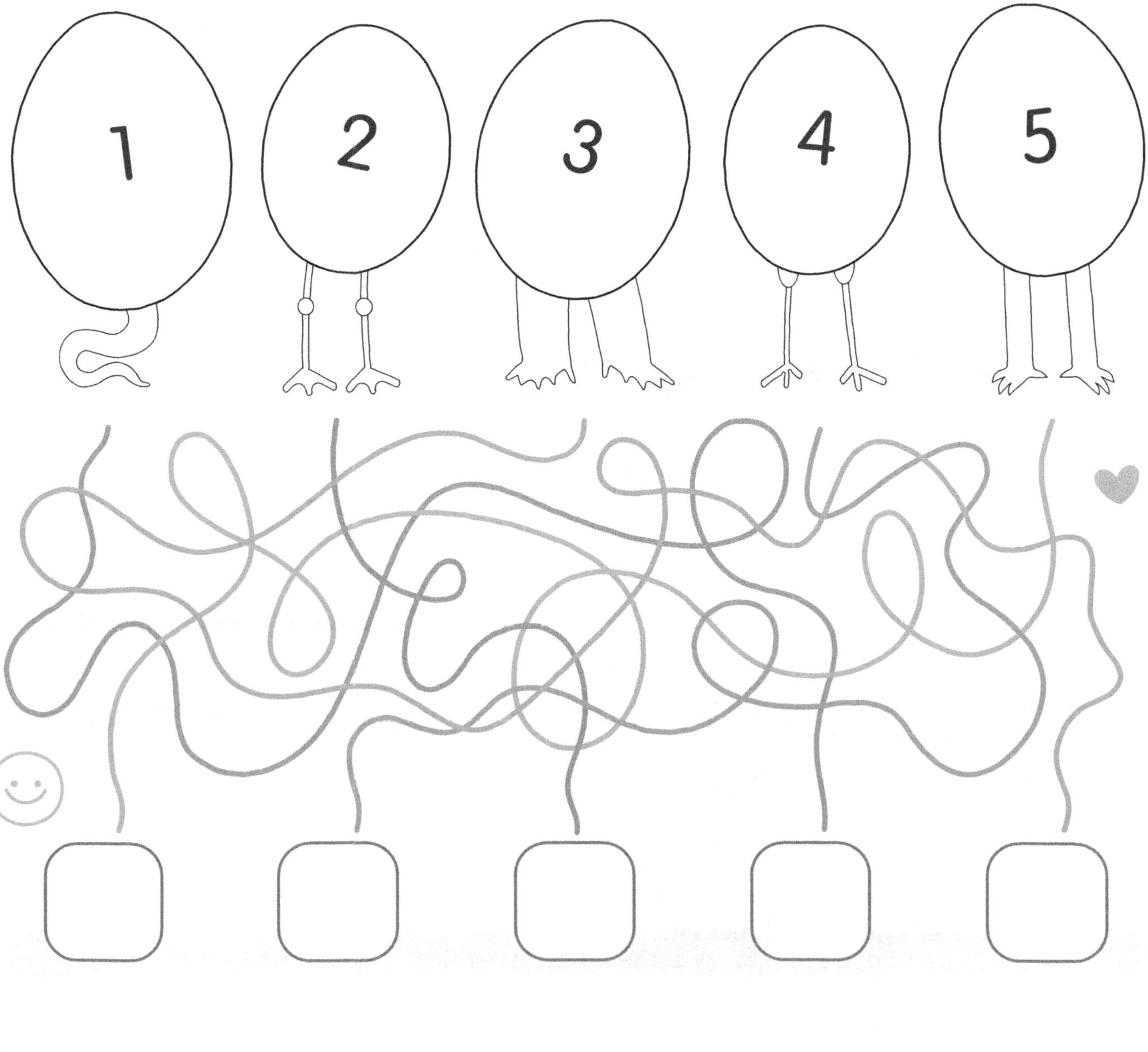

1 2 3 4 5

☐ ☐ ☐ ☐ ☐

WEEK 9
You can use special words to ask questions. Let's learn about them! You'll subtract with pictures and learn more about plants, too.
ARGOPREP

WEEK 9 DAY 1

Question Words
ENGLISH

Read Together

We ask **questions** when we want to know more about something. Question sentences begin with question words such as **who, what, why, when, where** and **how** and end with a question mark. A question mark is a symbol that looks like this: **?**. Read the sample question sentences below. Notice the question word and question mark in bold in each sentence.

1. **What** is your name**?**
2. **Where** are you going**?**
3. **When** do we leave**?**

Directions

Have an adult help you read the sentences below. For each sentence, decide whether or not it is a question. Circle the correct answer.

For Kids

1. That is a dog.

A. Question sentence

B. Not a question sentence

2. What time is it?

A. Question sentence

B. Not a question sentence

WEEK 9
DAY 1

Question Words
ENGLISH

3. How are you?

A. Question sentence

B. Not a question sentence

4. Who is that?

A. Question sentence

B. Not a question sentence

5. The leaf is red.

A. Question sentence

B. Not a question sentence

6. I ran to the store.

A. Question sentence

B. Not a question sentence

7. When will you go?

A. Question sentence

B. Not a question sentence

8. He is 8 years old.

A. Question sentence

B. Not a question sentence

9. Why did she say that?

A. Question sentence

B. Not a question sentence

10. The tree is tall.

A. Question sentence

B. Not a question sentence

WEEK 9
DAY 1

Question Words
ENGLISH

Directions

Have an adult help you read the question sentences below. In each sentence, circle the question word and write a question mark at the end.

For Kids

1. When does school end

2. Who is the teacher

3. What time is it

4. Where did she go

5. Why did you leave

6. How does that work

7. Who is talking

8. What is your favorite food

9. When do you go to bed

10. Where is the zoo

11. Why did she do that

12. How did they do that

Let's get some fitness in!
Go to page 229 to try some fitness activities.

WEEK 9 DAY 2

Question Words
ENGLISH

Read Together

Remember that questions help us learn about something. Questions begin with question words such as **who, what, when, where, why** and **how** and end with a question mark.

Directions

On the tables below, have an adult help you read each question word. Then, write or say aloud 3 question sentences using each word.

For Kids

Who	What

Question Words
ENGLISH

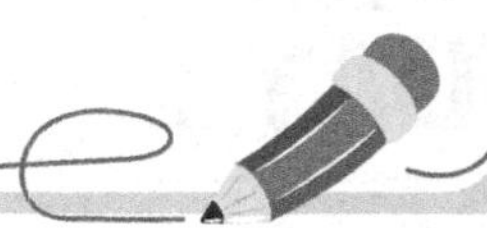

When	Where

Why	How

Hello

Directions

Have an adult help you read each sentence below. Decide which missing question word best completes each sentence. Circle the correct answer.

For Kids

1. .... will the weather be like on Saturday?

A. Who
B. What
C. When
D. Where
E. Why
F. How

2. .... don't you like to eat broccoli?

A. Who
B. What
C. When
D. Where
E. Why
F. How

Question Words
ENGLISH

1. .... will take me to the dentist?

A. Who
B. What
C. When
D. Where
E. Why
F. How

3. .... will the movie begin?

A. Who
B. What
C. When
D. Where
E. Why
F. How

2. .... is the library book?

A. Who
B. What
C. When
D. Where
E. Why
F. How

4. .... did all the boxes fit in the car?

A. Who
B. What
C. When
D. Where
E. Why
F. How

Let's get some fitness in!
Go to page 229 to try some fitness activities.

FITNESS TIME

WEEK 9 DAY 3

Simple Subtraction with Pictures

MATHEMATICS

Directions:

Fill in the missing sum.

2+2=4

Question 1:

Sasha the Seahorse is a little bit clumsy. She was carrying 3 seashells but dropped one. Cross out 1 seashell. How many are left?

....

Question 3:

She was carrying 2 sand buckets but dropped one. Cross out 1 sand bucket. How many are left?

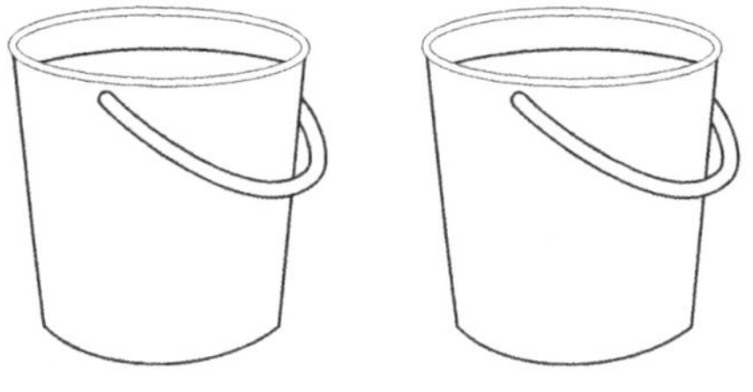

....

Question 2:

She was carrying 4 sand shovels but dropped one. Cross out 1 sand shovel. How many are left?

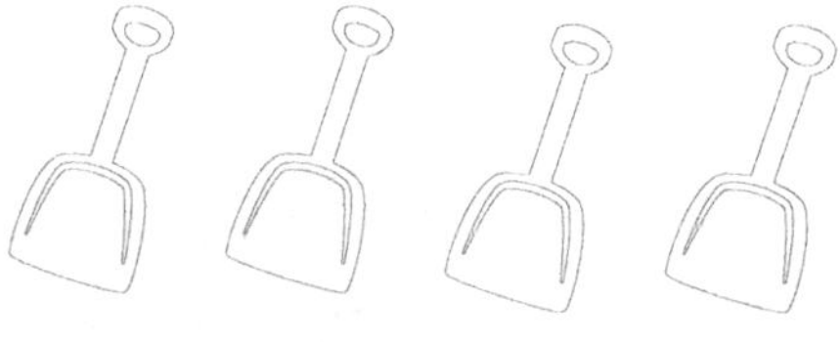

....

Question 4:

She was carrying 5 starfish but dropped one. Cross out 1 starfish. How many are left?

....

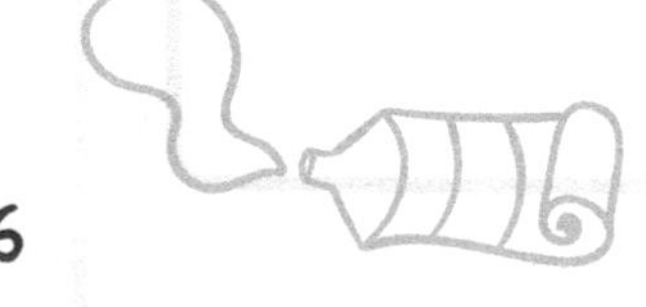

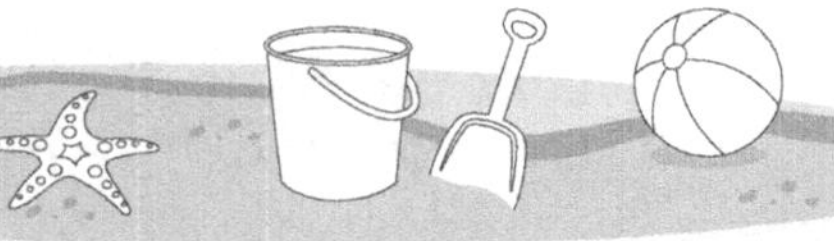

Simple Subtraction with Pictures

MATHEMATICS

Question 5:

She was carrying 3 bottles of sunscreen but dropped one. Cross out 1 bottle of sunscreen. How many are left?

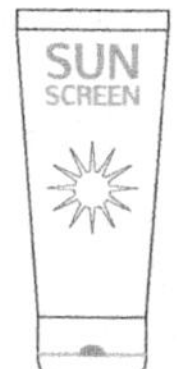

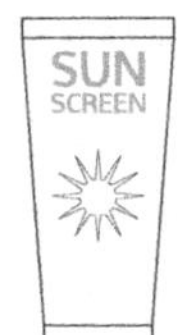

....

Question 7:

She was carrying 3 beach balls but dropped one. Cross out 1 beach ball. How many are left?

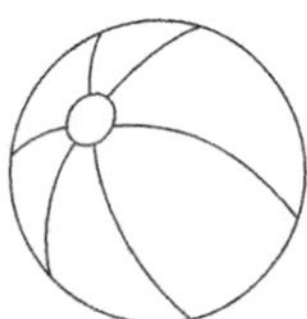
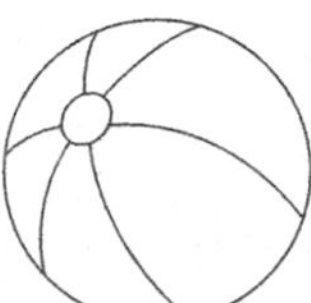
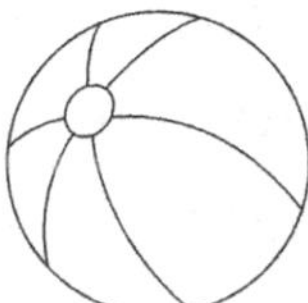

....

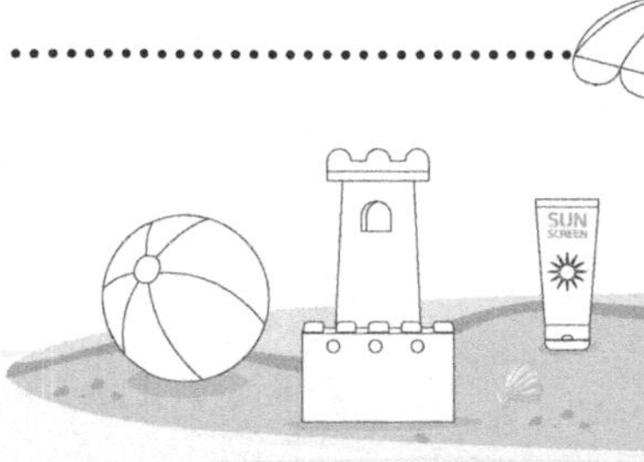
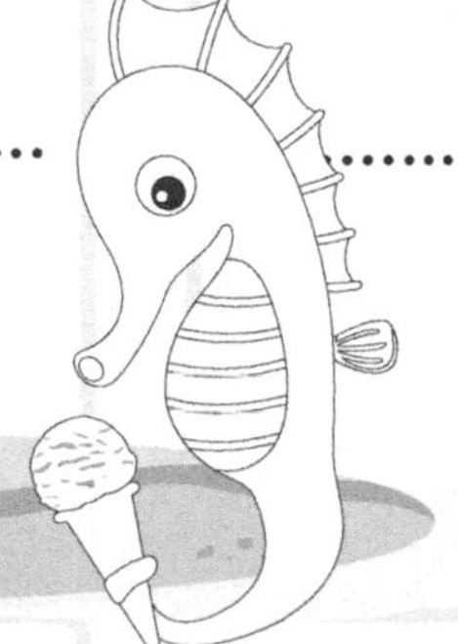

Question 6:

She was carrying 2 beach towels but dropped one. Cross out 1 beach towel. How many are left?

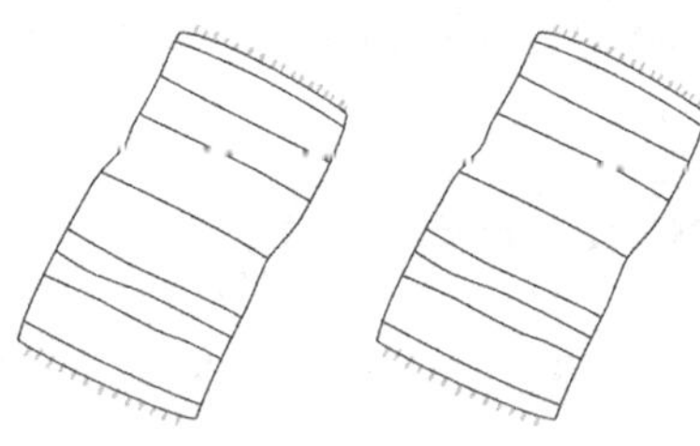

....

Question 8:

She was had 4 scoops of ice cream on a cone, but one scoop dropped off. Cross out 1 scoop. How many are left?

....

Let's get some fitness in!
Go to page 229 to try some fitness activities.

Simple Subtraction with Pictures
MATHEMATICS

Directions:

Fill in the missing sum.

Question 1:

Sasha the Seahorse has been building things in the sand, but the waves keep washing things away. She built 3 castles out of sand. The waves washed one away, so cross 1 castle out. How many are left?

....

Question 2:

She built 4 towers out of sand. The waves washed one away, so cross 1 tower out. How many are left?

....

Question 3:

She built 2 fish sculptures out of sand. The waves washed one away, so cross 1 fish out. How many are left?

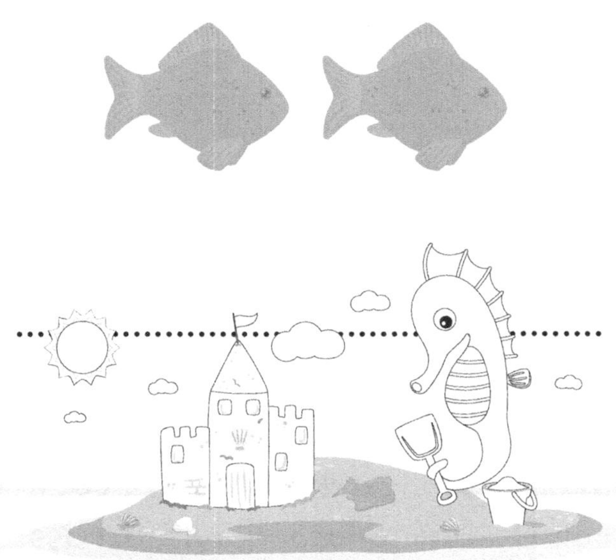

....

Question 4:

She built 4 mermaids out of sand. The waves washed one away, so cross 1 mermaid out. How many are left?

....

Simple Subtraction with Pictures
MATHEMATICS

Question 5:

She built 3 dragons out of sand. The waves washed one away, so cross 1 dragon out. How many are left?

....

Question 7:

She built 5 royal crowns out of sand. The waves washed one away, so cross 1 crown out. How many are left?

....

Question 6:

She built 2 horses out of sand. The waves washed one away, so cross 1 horse out. How many are left?

....

Question 8:

She built 1 queen out of sand. The waves washed it away, so cross it out. How many are left?

....

Let's get some fitness in!
Go to page 229 to try some fitness activities.

Simple Subtraction with Pictures
MATHEMATICS

Directions:

Fill in the missing sum.

Question 1:

Sasha the Seahorse is really hungry at the beach barbecue. There were 5 bags of potato chips. She ate three of them, so cross 3 out. How many are left?

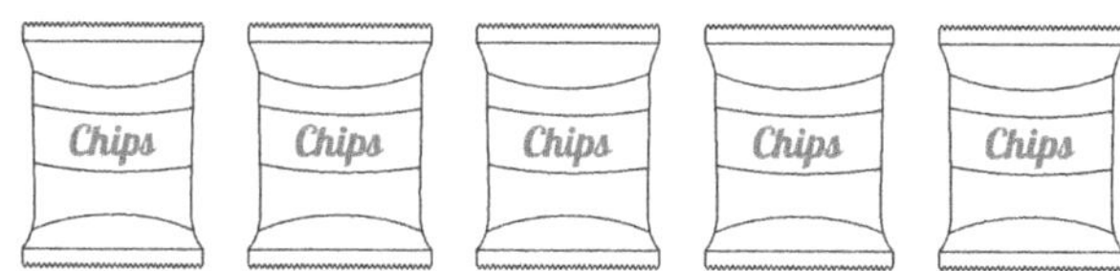

....

Question 2:

There were 5 hamburgers. She ate two of them, so cross 2 out. How many are left?

....

Question 3:

There were 5 hot dogs. She ate four of them, so cross 4 out. How many are left?

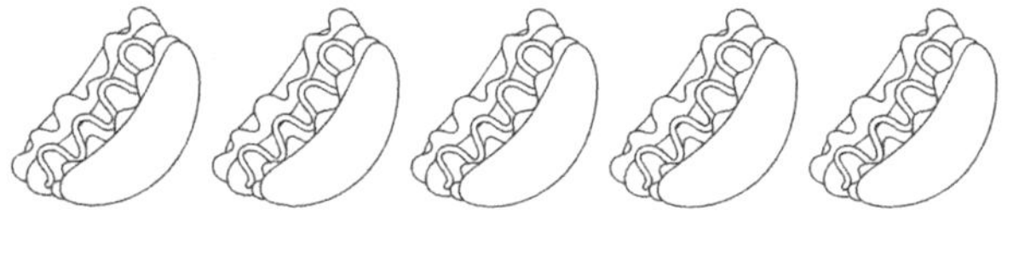

....

Question 4:

There were 5 glasses of lemonade. She drank one of them, so cross 1 out. How many are left?

....

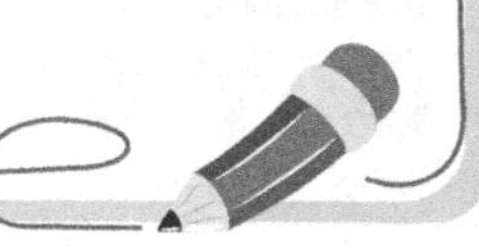

Question 5:

There were 5 chocolate ice cream bars. She ate three of them, so cross 3 out. How many are left?

....

Question 7:

There were 5 apples. She ate four of them, so cross 4 out. How many are left?

....

Question 6:

There were 5 lime popsicles. She ate two of them, so cross 2 out. How many are left?

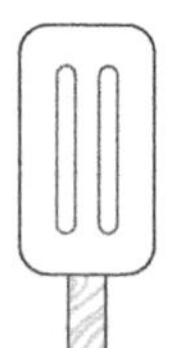 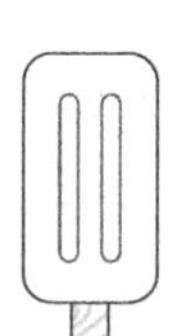 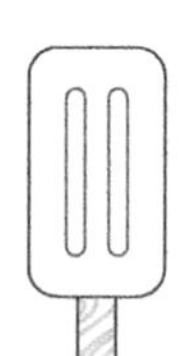 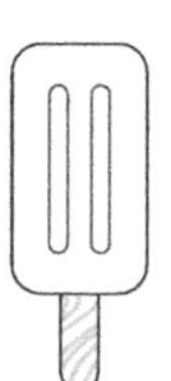 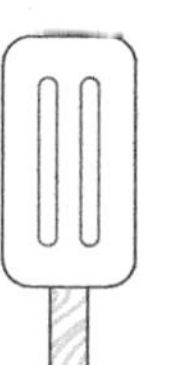

....

Question 8:

There were 5 oranges. She ate one of them, so cross 1 out. How many are left?

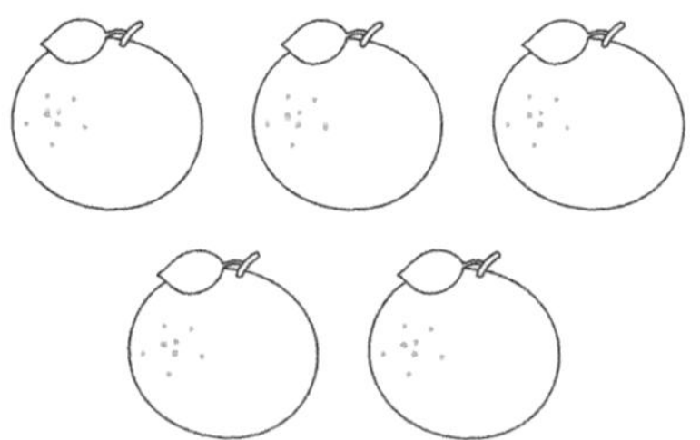

....

Let's get some fitness in!
Go to page 229 to try some fitness activities.

WEEK 9 DAY 6

Classifying Plants EXPERIMENTS

Read Together

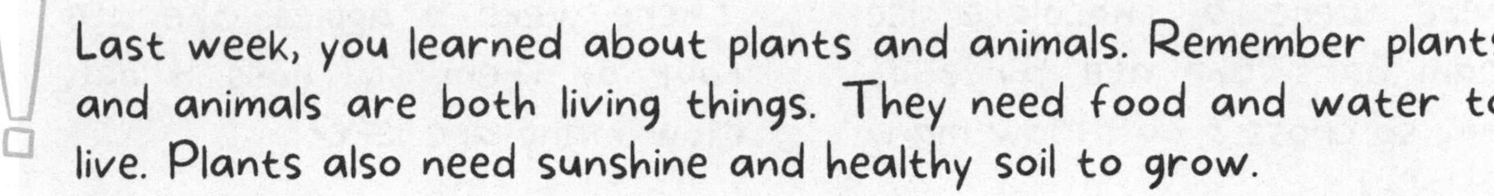

Last week, you learned about plants and animals. Remember plants and animals are both living things. They need food and water to live. Plants also need sunshine and healthy soil to grow.

Plants come in many different shapes and sizes. Some are large trees with tall trunks and leaves. Others are small flowers with a stem and petals. Some plants are vegetables that grow under the ground.

Today you are going to practice sorting plants into categories. A category is a group of things that are the same in some way.

Directions

Look at the pictures below. For each picture, think about which category the plant belongs in. Match the picture to the correct category on the table on the next page and write the letter in the table.

For Kids

Picture Bank

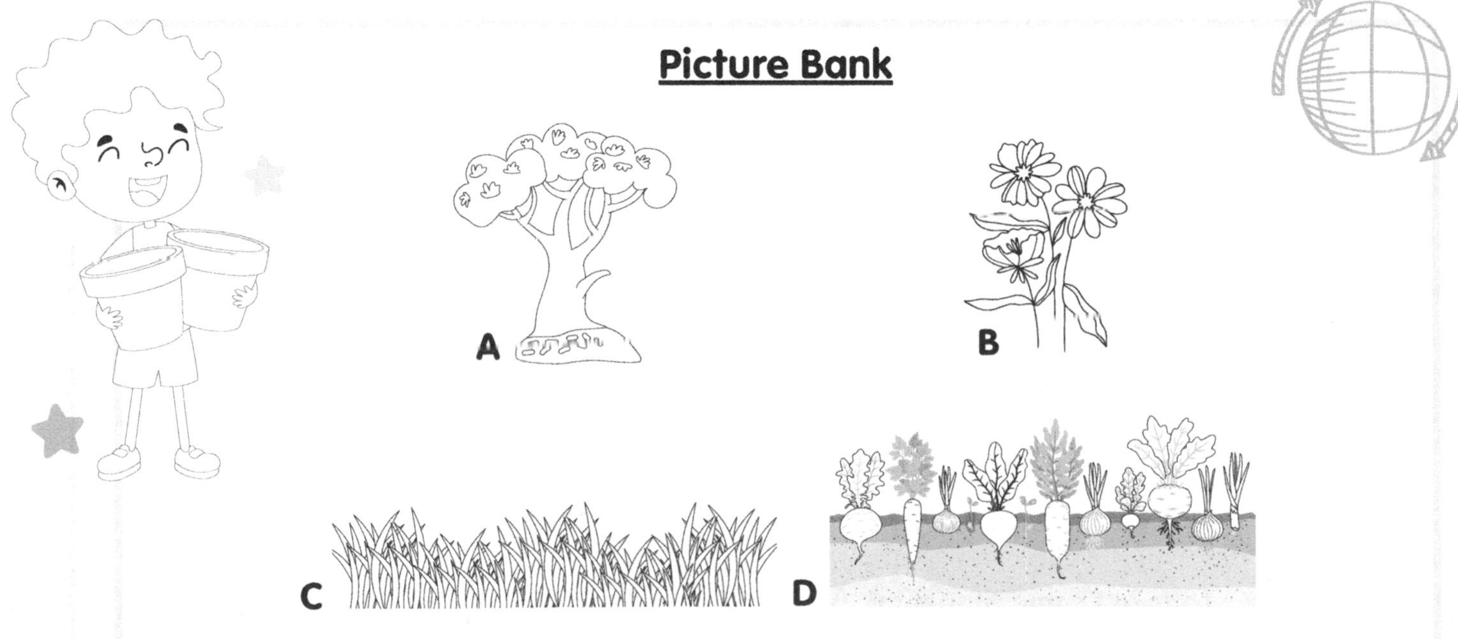

Classifying Plants
EXPERIMENTS

Flower	Grass

Vegetables	Tree

Can you think of other plants that fit into each of the categories above? Draw a picture or write their names in the boxes above.

Let's get some fitness in!
Go to page 229 to try some fitness activities.

FITNESS TIME

MAZE

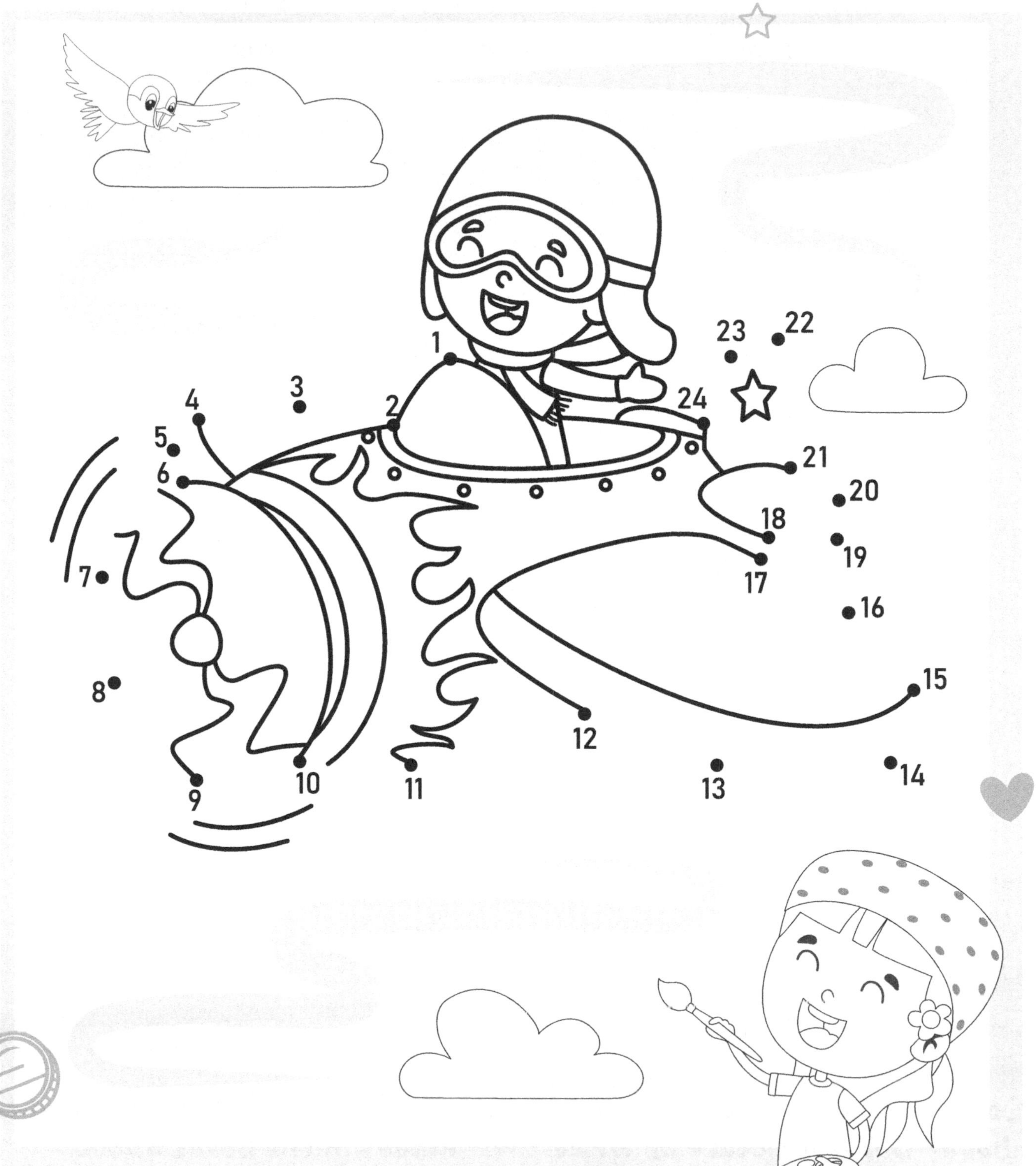

1 2 3 4 5 6 7 8 9 10 11 12 13 14 15 16 17 18 19 20 21 22 23 24

Connect the dots with a line in order of the numbers. Then color the picture.

WEEK 10
Do you know what position words are? These words tell you where something is. Let's learn about position words, subtraction and animals!
ARGOPREP

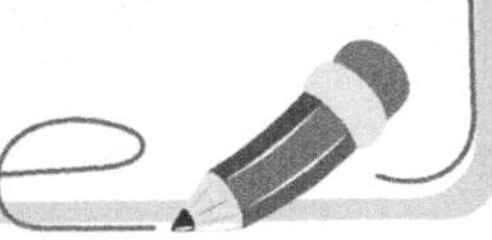

Read Together

Position words tell us where things are. Think about your favorite toy. Where can you find it? Is it under your bed or inside your toy box? Words such as over, under, in front of, near or next to are position words.

Remember you learned about nouns a few weeks ago. A noun is a person, place or thing. Position words help us describe where these things are located. Read the sample sentence below.

My house is next to the big brick church.

In the sentence above, **house** is a noun and **next to** are the position words that tell us where the house is.

Directions

Read the words below. For each word, decide whether it is a position word or not. Circle the correct answer.

1. Left

A. Position word

B. Not a position word

2. Above

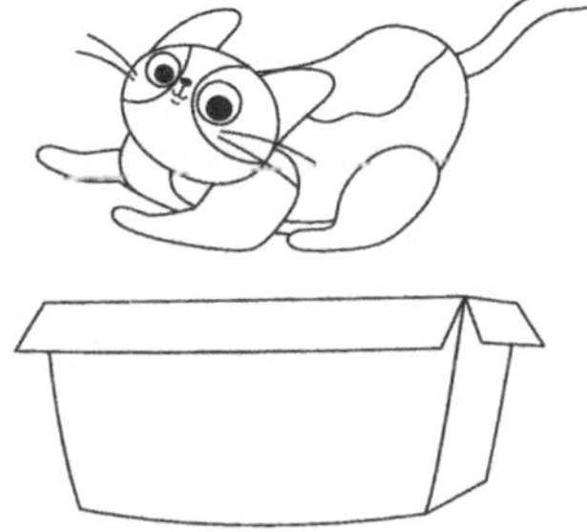

A. Position word

B. Not a position word

3. Table

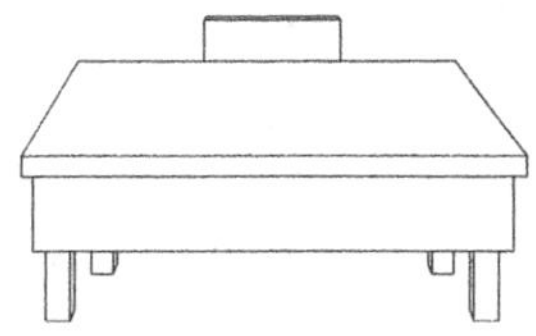

A. Position word
B. Not a position word

4. Garden

A. Position word
B. Not a position word

5. Underneath

A. Position word
B. Not a position word

6. Market

A. Position word
B. Not a position word

7. Below

A. Position word
B. Not a position word

8. Beside

A. Position word
B. Not a position word

9. Baseball

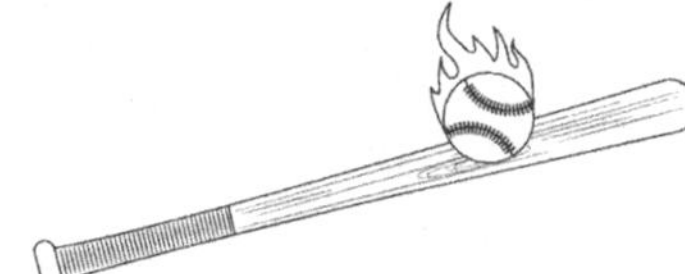

A. Position word
B. Not a position word

10. Right

A. Position word
B. Not a position word

WEEK 10
DAY 1

Position Words
ENGLISH

Directions

Have an adult help you read the sentences below. Complete each sentence with a position word that makes sense.

For Kids

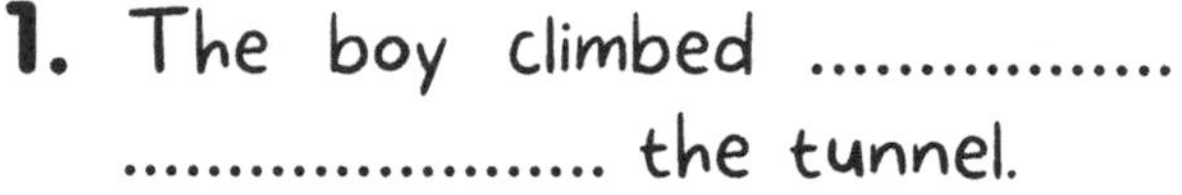

1. The boy climbed .... the tunnel.

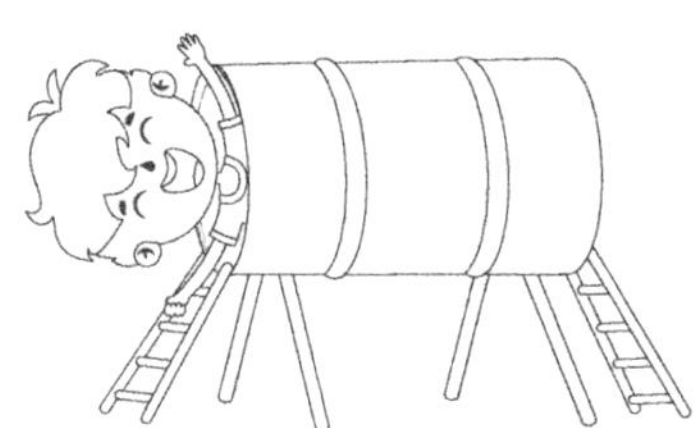

4. I watched dad walk .... the stairs.

2. The playground is .... the school.

5. Mom drove the car .... the bridge.

3. She rode her bike .... the hill.

6. The little boy stood .... the table.

WEEK 10
DAY 1

Position Words
ENGLISH

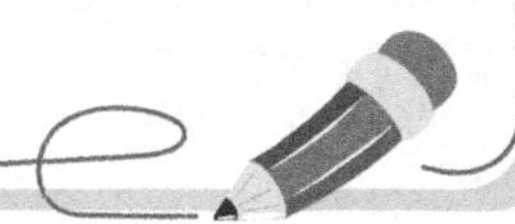

7. The desk is to the .... of the pencil.

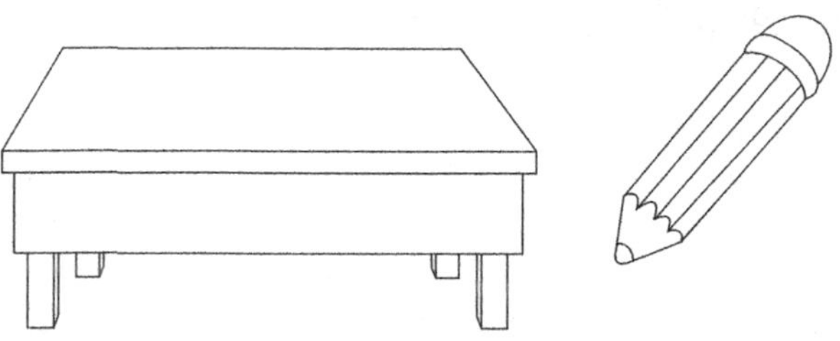

10. All the clothes were hung up .... the closet.

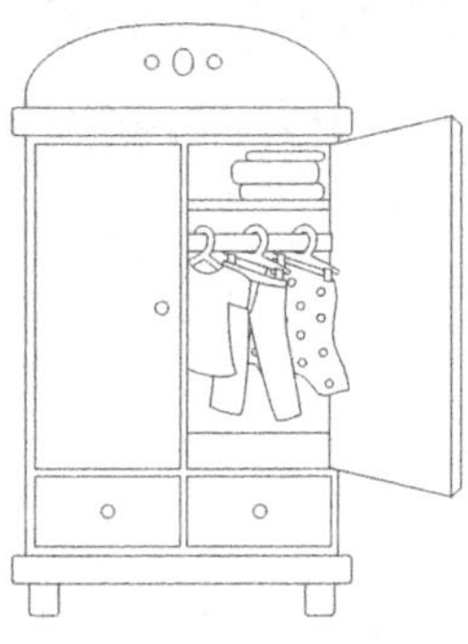

8. The ball flew .... the fence at recess.

11. The red book is to the .... of the blue book.

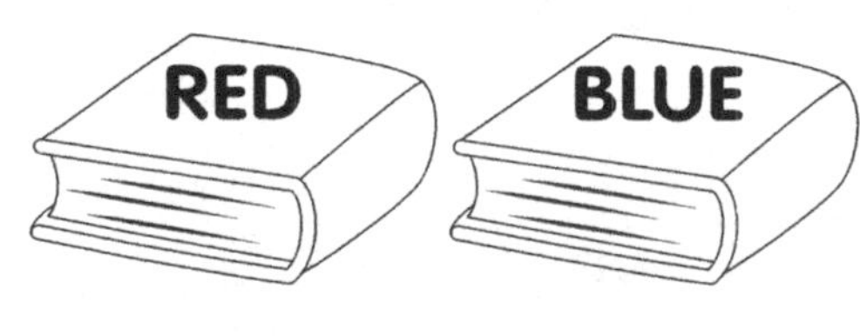

9. The little girl got scared so she hid .... her bed.

12. My best friend stands .... me in line.

Let's get some fitness in!
Go to page 229 to try some fitness activities.

WEEK 10 DAY 2

Position Words
ENGLISH

Read Together

Remember that position words tell us where something is. A few examples of position words include: up, down, over and under.

Directions

On the tables below, have an adult help you read each position word given on the left. On the right, write or say aloud a sentence that uses that position word.

For Kids

Position Word	Sentence
up	
down	
over	
under	

Position Words
ENGLISH

Position Word	Sentence
across	
around	
left	
right	
above	
below	
through	

WEEK 10
DAY 2

Position Words
ENGLISH

Directions

Look at the pictures in each row below. For each picture, have an adult help you read the sentence. Choose the position word that best completes each sentence. Circle the correct answer.

For Kids

1.

The caterpillar is crawling .... the apple.

A. around

B. through

C. over

D. to the left

2.

The dog is .... the box.

A. outside

B. inside

C. on top of

D. below

3.

The teacher is .... the chalkboard.

A. in front of

B. under

C. above

D. inside

4.

The cookies are .... the plate.

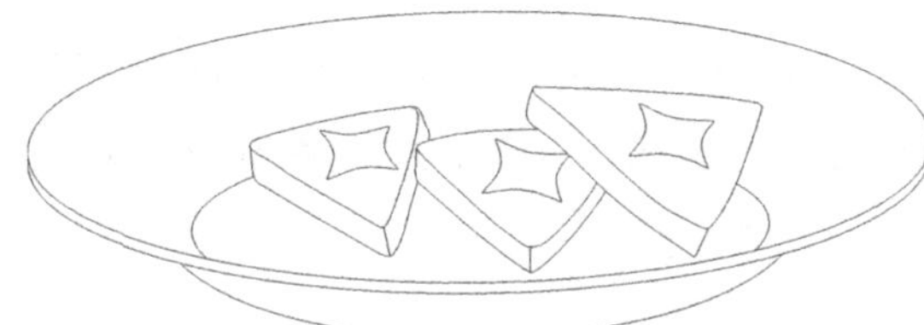

A. below

B. to the left

C. on

D. above

5.

The deer is .... of the trees.

A. above

B. through

C. underneath

D. to the right

Let's get some fitness in!
Go to page 229 to try some fitness activities.

Simple Subtraction with Numerals
MATHEMATICS

Question 1:

Daphne the Dolphin has a hard time keeping track of her things. She had 5 beach balls but lost 1 beach ball. How many does she have left?

$5 - 1 = \square$

Question 2:

She had 4 seashells but lost one of them. How many does she have left?

$4 - 1 = \square$

Question 3:

She had 3 sparkly rocks but lost one of them. How many does she have left?

$3 - 1 = \square$

Question 4:

She had 2 beach towels but lost one of them. How many does she have left?

$2 - 1 = \square$

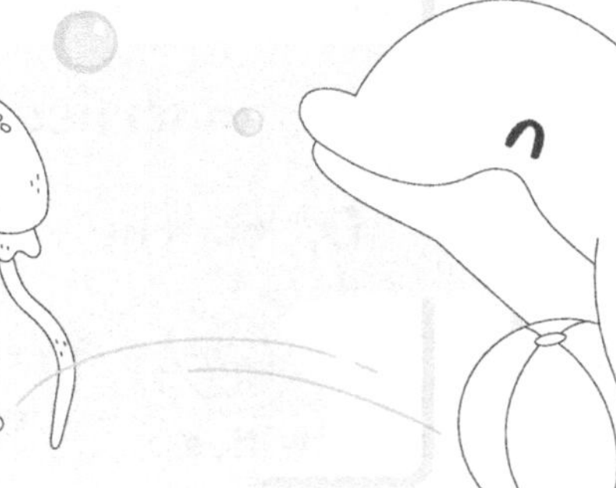

Simple Subtraction with Numerals
MATHEMATICS

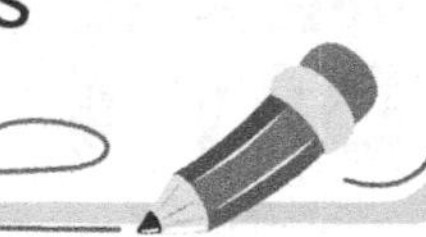

Question 5:

She had 4 sand shovels but lost one of them. How many does she have left?

4 − 1 = ☐

Question 7:

She had 4 seashells but lost one of them. How many does she have left?

4 − 1 = ☐

Question 6:

She had 2 sand buckets but lost one of them. How many does she have left?

2 − 1 = ☐

Question 8:

She had 5 swimsuits but lost one of them. How many does she have left?

5 − 1 = ☐

Let's get some fitness in!
Go to page 229 to try some fitness activities.

FITNESS TIME

Simple Subtraction with Numerals

MATHEMATICS

Directions:

Fill in the missing sum.

Question 1:

Daphne the Dolphin is packing for a beach vacation. She has 5 beach towels but can only pack 3 of them. How many does she have to leave home?

$5 - 3 = \square$

Question 2:

She has 5 paddleboards but can only pack 1 of them. How many does she have to leave home?

$5 - 1 = \square$

Question 3:

She has 5 beach balls but can only pack 2 of them. How many does she have to leave home?

$5 - 2 = \square$

Question 4:

She has 5 swimsuits but can only pack 4 of them. How many does she have to leave home?

$5 - 4 = \square$

WEEK 10
DAY 4

Simple Subtraction with Numerals
MATHEMATICS

Question 5:

She has 5 sand shovels but can only pack 3 of them. How many does she have to leave home?

$5 - 3 = \square$

Question 6:

She has 5 inner tubes but can only pack 1 of them. How many does she have to leave home?

$5 - 1 = \square$

Question 7:

She has 5 sun hats but can only pack 4 of them. How many does she have to leave home?

$5 - 4 = \square$

Question 8:

She has 5 bottles of sunscreen and packs them all. How many does she have to leave home?

$5 - 5 = \square$

Let's get some fitness in!
Go to page 229 to try some fitness activities.

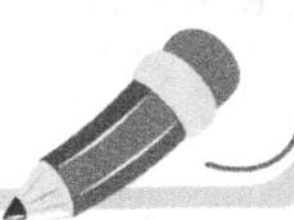

Directions:

Fill in the missing sum.

Question 1:

Daphne the Dolphin is watching groups of creatures in the sea. She sees 10 lobsters, but 1 lobster crawls away. How many are left?

$10 - 1 = \square$

Question 2:

She sees 9 crabs, but 1 crab crawls away. How many are left?

$9 - 1 = \square$

Question 3:

She sees 8 starfish, but 1 starfish moves away. How many are left?

$8 - 1 = \square$

Question 4:

She sees 7 spotted fish, but 1 spotted fish swims away. How many are left?

$7 - 1 = \square$

Simple Subtraction with Numerals

MATHEMATICS

Question 5:

She sees 6 striped fish, but 1 striped fish swims away. How many are left?

$6 - 1 = \square$

Question 7:

She sees 4 sharks, but 1 shark swims away. How many are left?

$4 - 1 = \square$

Question 6:

She sees 5 eels, but 1 eel swims away. How many are left?

$5 - 1 = \square$

Question 8:

She sees 3 whales, but 1 whale swims away. How many are left?

$3 - 1 = \square$

Let's get some fitness in!
Go to page 229 to try some fitness activities.

FITNESS TIME

Classifying Animals
EXPERIMENTS

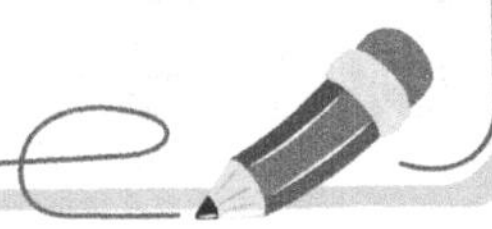

Read Together

A couple of weeks ago, you learned about plants and animals. Remember plants and animals are both living things. They need food and water to survive.

Animals come in many different shapes and sizes. Some are large and have fur like bears and wolves. Others are small and have scaly skin like frogs and lizards. Some animals have feathers and can fly like birds.

Today you are going to practice sorting animals into categories. A category is a group of items that are the same in some way.

Directions

Look at the pictures below. For each picture, decide which category the animal belongs in. Match the picture to the correct category on the table on the next page and write the letter in the table.

For Kids

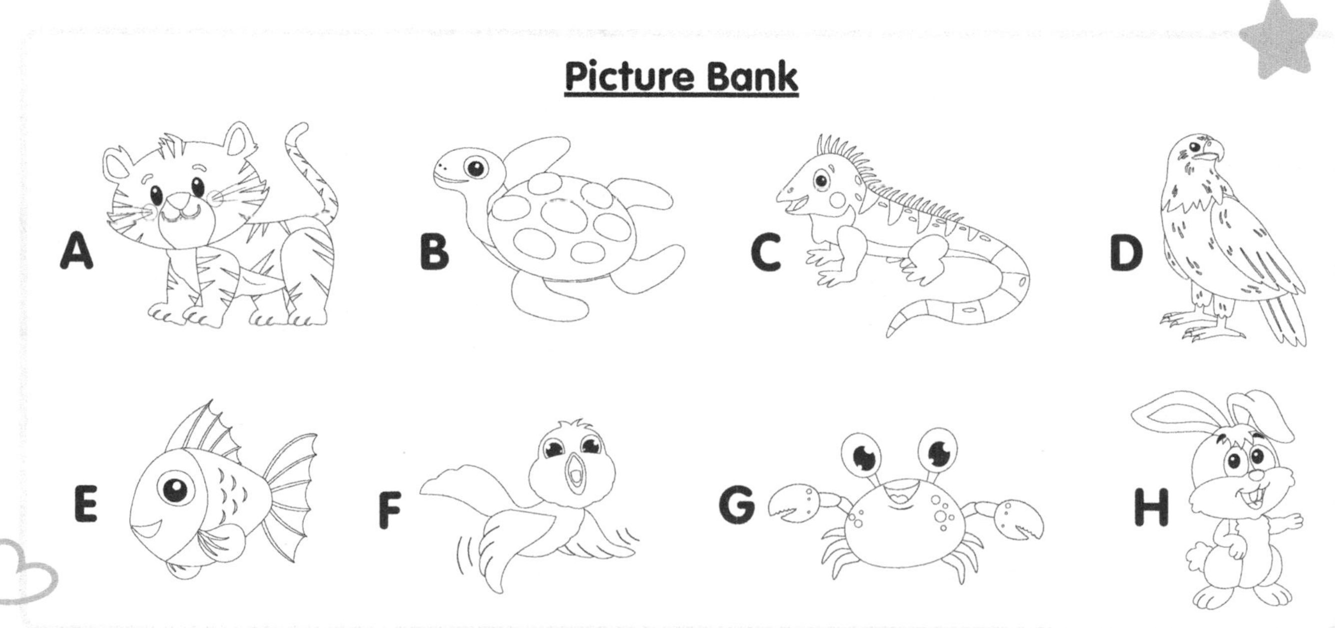

Classifying Animals
EXPERIMENTS

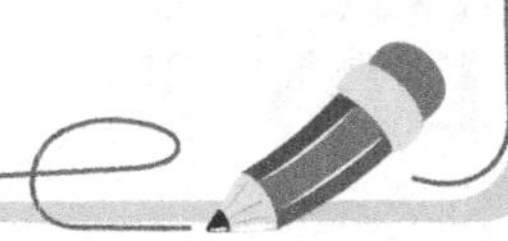

Animals with Fur	Animals with Feathers

Animals with Scaly Skin	Animals with Shells

Can you think of other animals that fit into each of the categories above? Draw a picture or write their names in the boxes above.

Let's get some fitness in!
Go to page 229 to try some fitness activities.

MAZE

Sam is upset because his kitten got lost. Help Sam find his pet.

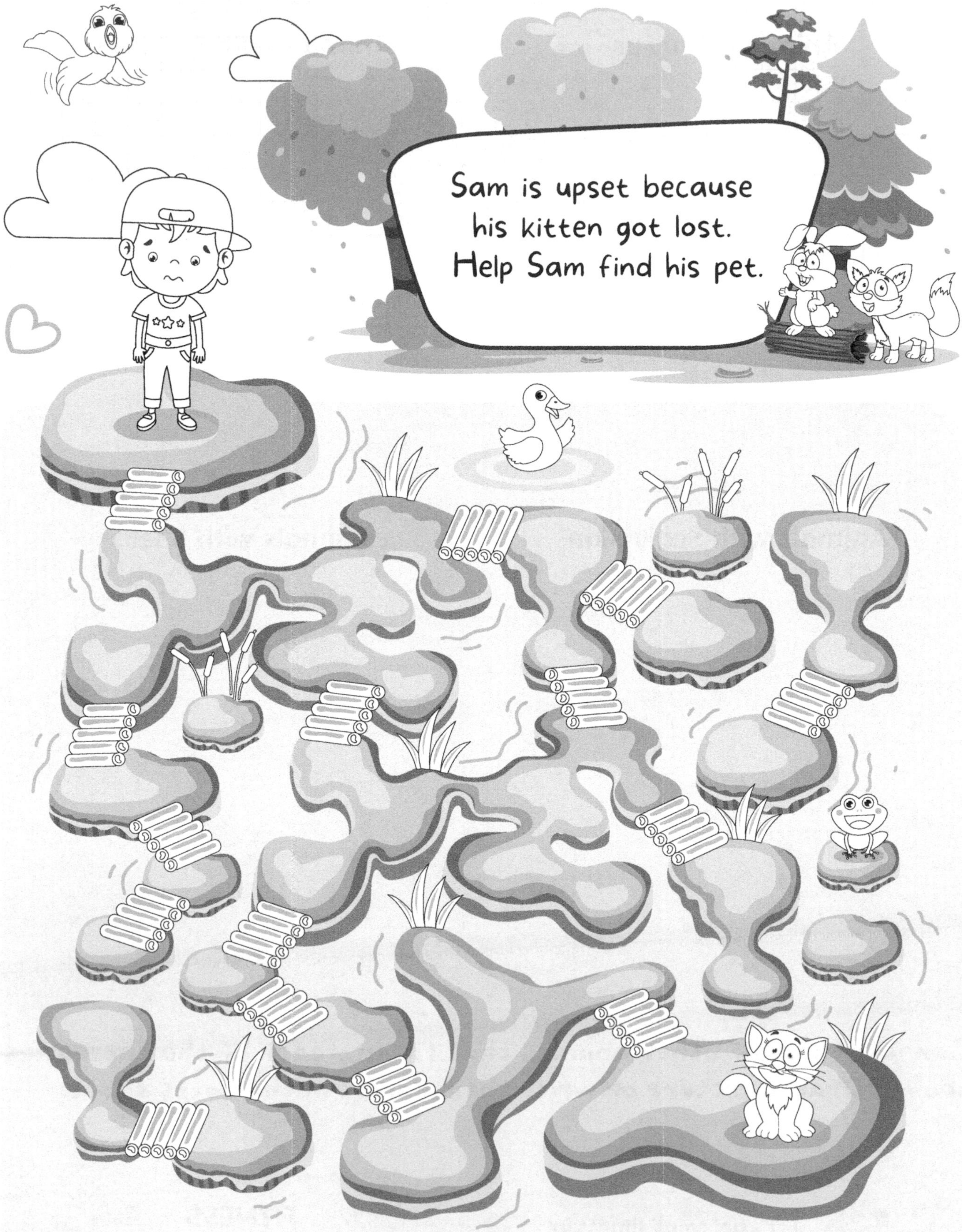

WEEK 11
Get ready to explore punctuation marks and groups of 10! You'll learn more about plants this week, too.
ARGOPREP

WEEK 11 DAY 1

Punctuation Marks
ENGLISH

Read Together

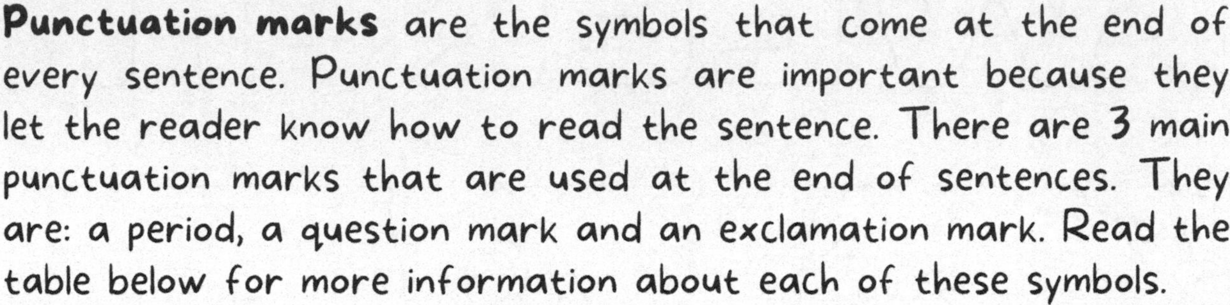

Punctuation marks are the symbols that come at the end of every sentence. Punctuation marks are important because they let the reader know how to read the sentence. There are 3 main punctuation marks that are used at the end of sentences. They are: a period, a question mark and an exclamation mark. Read the table below for more information about each of these symbols.

Punctuation Mark	When It's Used	What It Looks Like	Example Sentence
Period	When someone is stating something or giving a command	.	Please go pick up your toys.
Question mark	When someone is asking a question	?	What would you like to do today?
Exclamation mark	When someone is saying something with excitement	!	Tomorrow is my birthday!

Directions

Have an adult help you read each sentence below. For each sentence, decide whether or not the correct punctuation mark is used. Circle the correct answer. Try your best!

WEEK 11 DAY 1

Punctuation Marks
ENGLISH

For Kids

1. It's time to go to the party.

A. Correct **B.** Incorrect

2. What time is it?

A. Correct **B.** Incorrect

3. Go get dressed.

A. Correct **B.** Incorrect

4. I am not feeling well today?

A. Correct **B.** Incorrect

5. When will it be dinnertime!

A. Correct **B.** Incorrect

6. I am so excited to see grandma!

A. Correct **B.** Incorrect

7. How many more days until the weekend.

A. Correct **B.** Incorrect

WEEK 11 DAY 1

Punctuation Marks

ENGLISH

Directions

Have an adult help you read the sentences below. Complete each sentence with the correct punctuation mark.

For Kids

1. That puppy is so cute

4. Today is Wednesday

2. Close the door

5. Who was that knocking on the door

3. When will we leave on vacation

6. It's snowing outside

7. My favorite color is purple

10. Do you know where my yellow shirt is

8. I love baseball

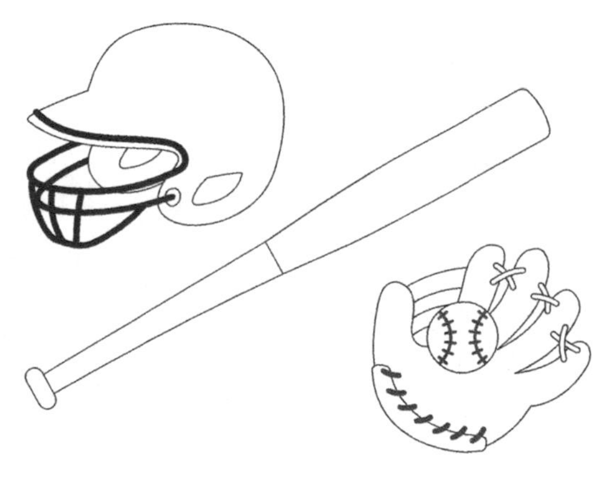

11. That party was so fun

9. What are we having for lunch

12. Put the books away on the shelf

Let's get some fitness in!
Go to page 229 to try some fitness activities.

WEEK 11 DAY 2

Punctuation Marks
ENGLISH

Read Together

Remember that a punctuation mark is a symbol used at the end of a sentence. It tells you how to read a sentence. The 3 main punctuation marks are a period, a question mark and an exclamation mark.

Directions

On the tables below, write or say aloud a sentence that uses the given punctuation mark.

For Kids

Punctuation Mark	Sentence
.	
?	
!	

Punctuation Marks
ENGLISH

Punctuation Mark	Punctuation Mark
.	
?	
!	
.	
?	
!	

WEEK 11 DAY 2

Punctuation Marks
ENGLISH

Directions

Have an adult help you read each sentence below. Decide which punctuation mark belongs at the end of the sentence. Circle the correct answer.

For Kids

1. Horses like to eat apples

A. Period

B. Question mark

C. Exclamation mark

2. That kitten is the cutest thing I've ever seen

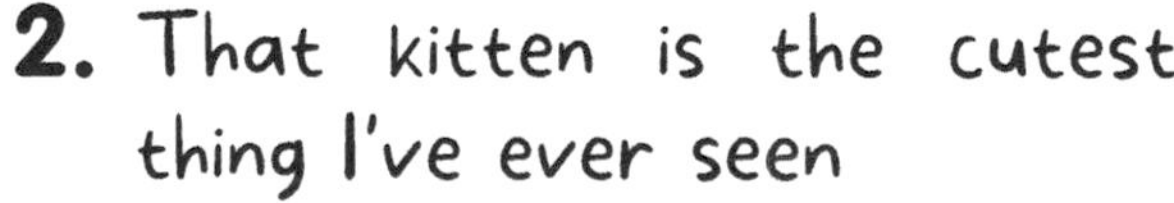

A. Period

B. Question mark

C. Exclamation mark

3. My teacher is named Mrs. Smith

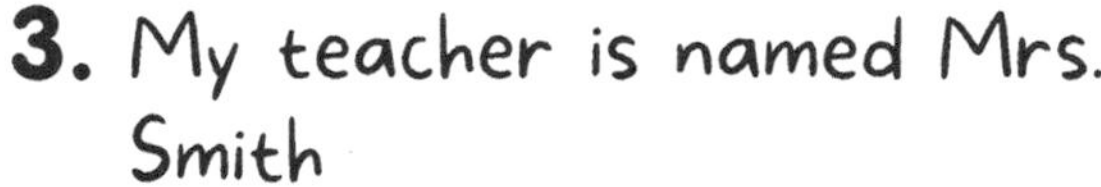

A. Period

B. Question mark

C. Exclamation mark

4. What kind of brownies should we make

A. Period

B. Question mark

C. Exclamation mark

Punctuation Marks
ENGLISH

5. I can't wait for the weekend

A. Period
B. Question mark
C. Exclamation mark

6. How long until we get there

A. Period
B. Question mark
C. Exclamation mark

7. Put your plate in the dishwasher

A. Period
B. Question mark
C. Exclamation mark

8. I love my new dollhouse

A. Period
B. Question mark
C. Exclamation mark

9. Be careful on the ice

A. Period
B. Question mark
C. Exclamation mark

10. Are you ready to go

A. Period
B. Question mark
C. Exclamation mark

Let's get some fitness in!
Go to page 229 to try some fitness activities.

FITNESS TIME

Circling a Number of Objects up to 10

MATHEMATICS

Question 1:

Clarence the Stingray is having a birthday party on the beach! Circle **3** balloons.

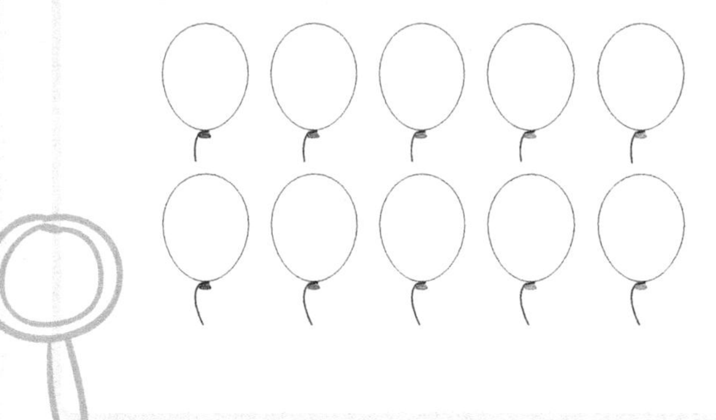

Question 3:

Circle **5** party hats.

Question 2:

Circle **4** party headbands.

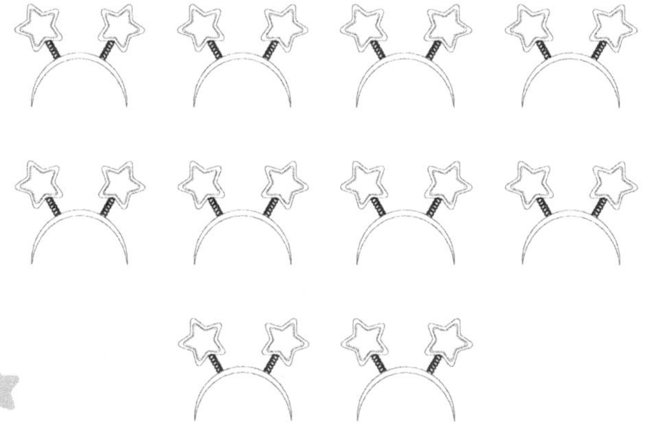

Question 4:

Circle **6** treat bags.

Circling a Number of Objects up to 10

MATHEMATICS

Question 5:

Circle 7 birthday presents.

Question 7:

Circle 9 streamers.

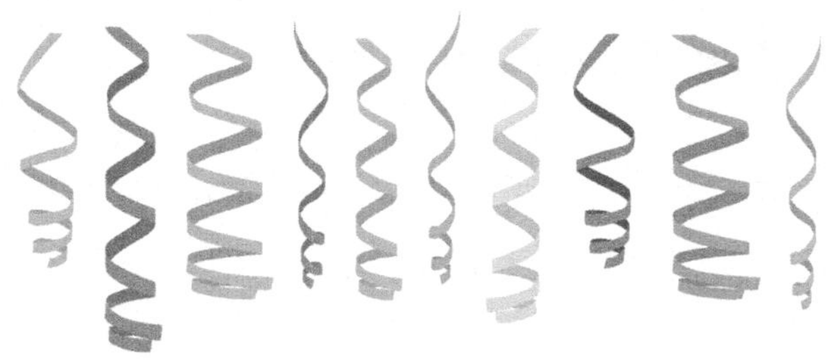

Question 6:

Circle 8 bags of confetti.

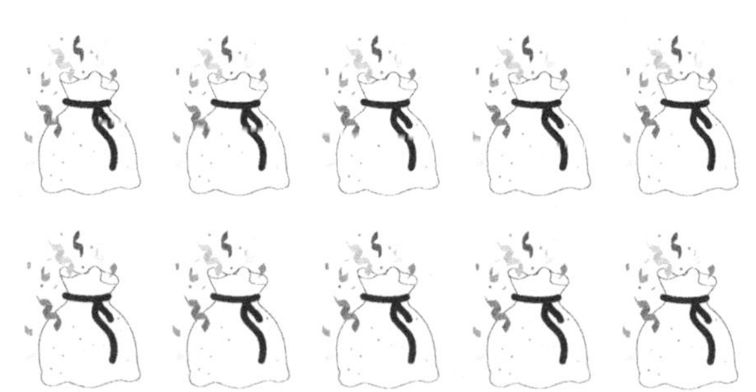

Question 8:

Circle 10 crabs at the birthday party.

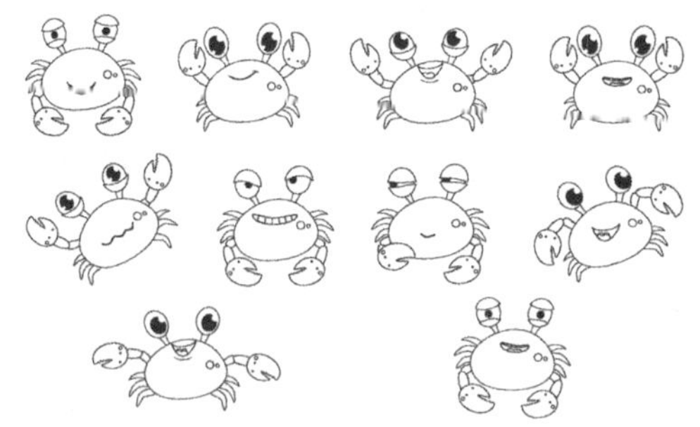

Let's get some fitness in!
Go to page 229 to try some fitness activities.

Circling a Number of Objects up to 10
MATHEMATICS

Question 1:

Clarence the Stingray wants to make his own birthday cake. Circle **2** cups of flour.

Question 3:

Circle **4** eggs.

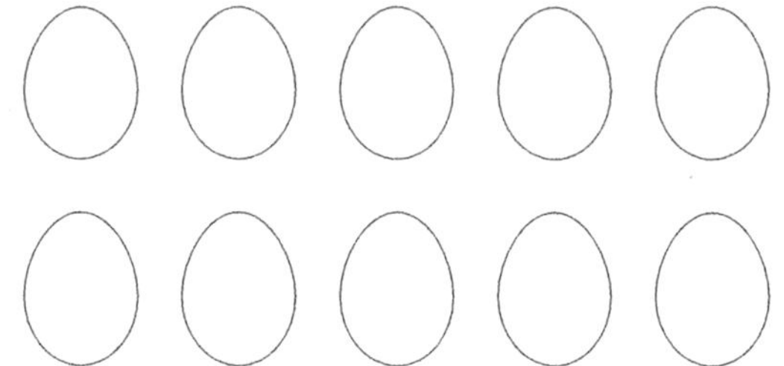

Question 2:

Circle **3** cups of sugar.

Question 4:

Circle **5** cubes of butter.

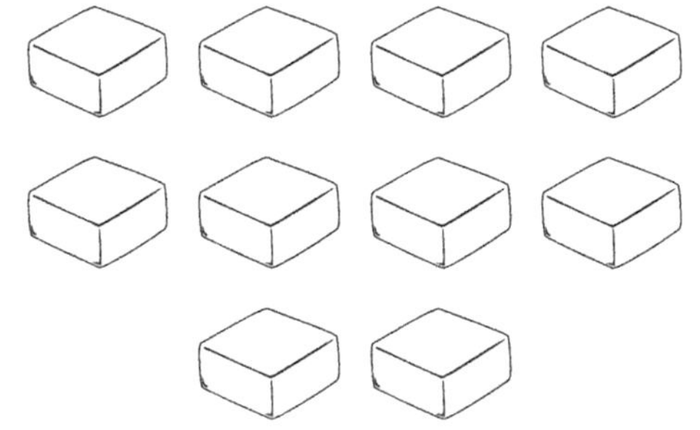

Circling a Number of Objects up to 10

MATHEMATICS

Question 5:

Circle **6** bars of chocolate.

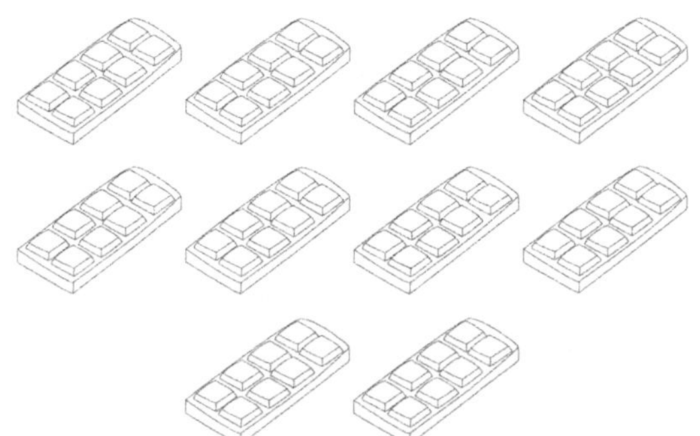

Question 7:

Circle **8** bowls of frosting.

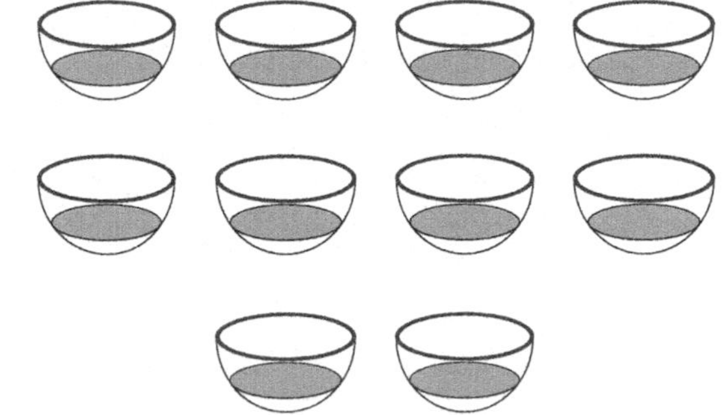

Question 6:

Circle **7** mixing bowls.

Question 8:

Circle **5** birthday candles.

Let's get some fitness in!
Go to page 229 to try some fitness activities.

WEEK 11 DAY 5

Circling a Number of Objects up to 10

MATHEMATICS

Question 1:

Clarence the Stingray and his friends plan to have fun on the beach! Circle 10 beach balls.

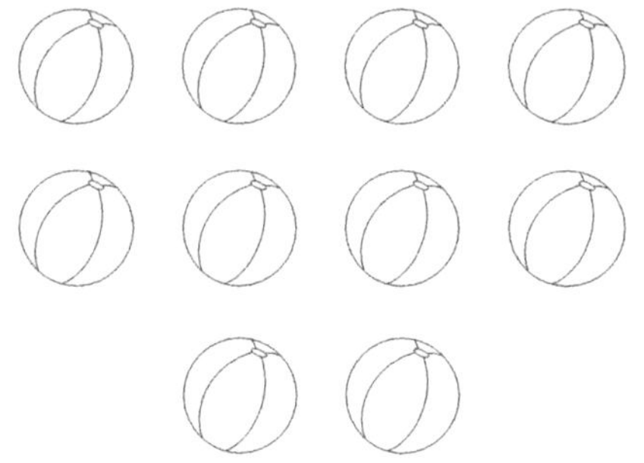

Question 2:

Circle 9 sand shovels.

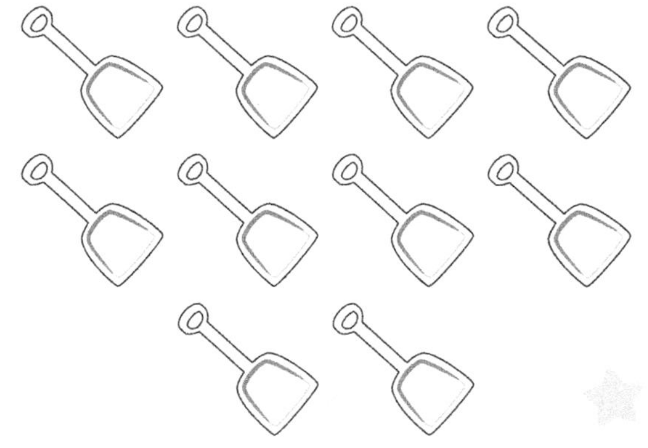

Question 3:

Circle 8 sand buckets.

Question 4:

Circle 7 beach umbrellas.

Circling a Number of Objects up to 10

MATHEMATICS

Question 5:

Circle **6** pairs of sunglasses.

Question 7:

Circle **4** inner tubes.

Question 6:

Circle **5** bags of seashells.

Question 8:

Circle **3** bottles of sunscreen.

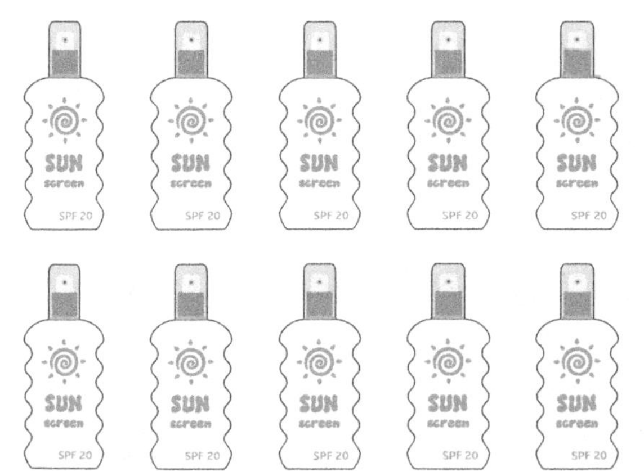

Let's get some fitness in!
Go to page 229 to try some fitness activities.

FITNESS TIME

Plant Needs
EXPERIMENTS

Read Together

You have learned about plants and animals in past lessons. You know that plants and animals are both living things. They need different things in order to survive.

All plants have many things they need in order to grow. These things include: sunlight, air, water, space to grow and healthy soil. If plants don't get enough of these things, they will not survive.

Directions

Look at the pictures in the picture bank below. For each picture, decide if that item is something plants need in order to live. Match the picture to the correct category on the table below and write the letter in the space provided.

For Kids

Picture Bank

A  B  C  D

MILK

E  F  G  H

WEEK 11 DAY 6

Plant Needs
EXPERIMENTS

Plants Need This to Grow	Plants Do Not Need This to Grow

Can you think of other things that fit into each of the categories above? Draw a picture or write their names in the boxes above.

Let's get some fitness in!
Go to page 229 to try some fitness activities.

PUZZLE

Find the correct face for each creature and write its number in the empty blank.

1

2

3

4

5

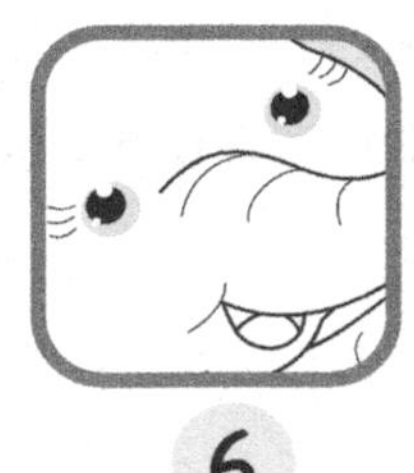

6

7

8

9

WEEK 12
Let's sort, count and match!
We'll compare objects and
learn more about animals, too!
ARGOPREP

Sorting Common Objects
ENGLISH

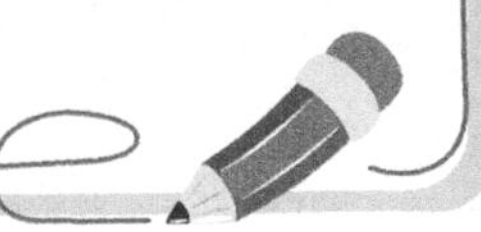

Read Together

To **sort** means to separate things into groups. Each item in the group has something in common. This means they are all the same in some way. For example, we can sort items into groups by color, shape or size.

Imagine you had a handful of jelly beans. They could be grouped according to their color. A pile of rocks could be sorted by their size - small, medium, or large. A container of building blocks could be separated by shape.

What other objects can you think of that can be sorted?

Directions

Look at the pictures below. Decide which item does not belong in the group. Put an x through that picture.

For Kids

1.

2.

3.

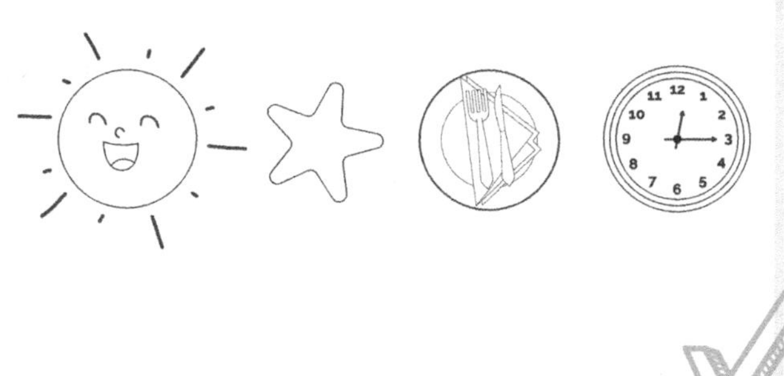

4.

5.

C 3 8 9

6.

7.

8.

9.

WEEK 12 DAY 1

Sorting Common Objects
ENGLISH

Directions

Look at the groups of pictures below. Think about what each set of pictures has in common. Draw a picture or say aloud an object that would fit into the group.

For Kids

1.

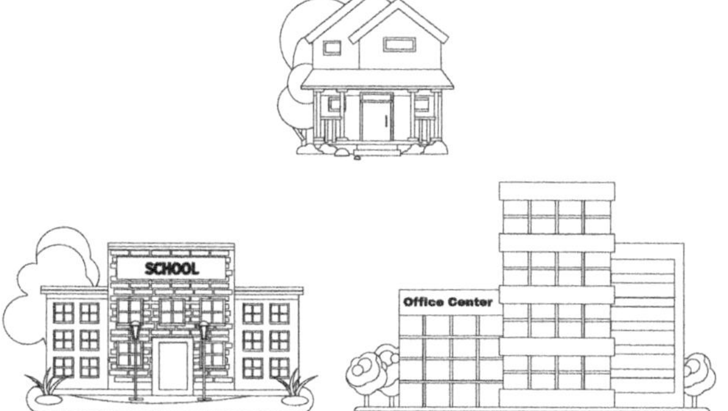

3.

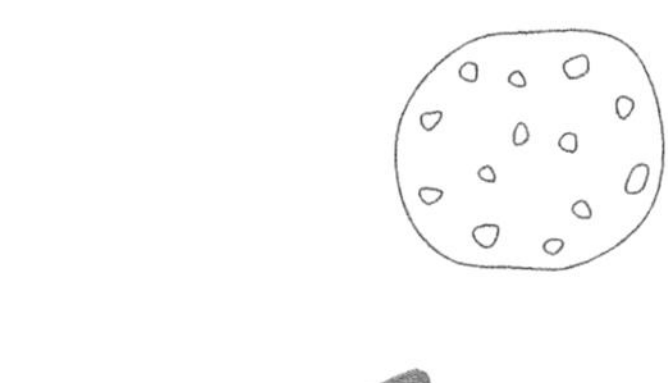

2.

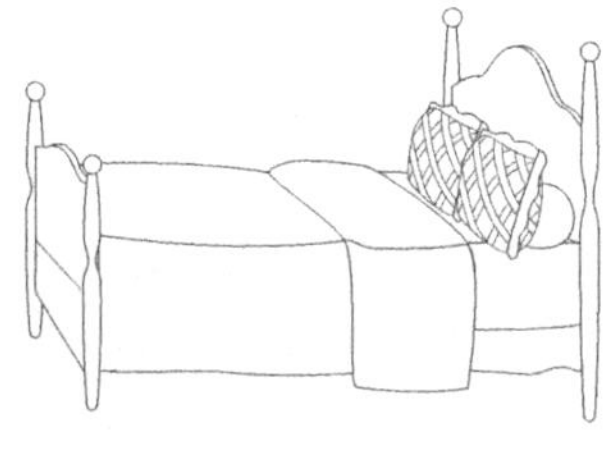

4.

R

D G

5.

8.

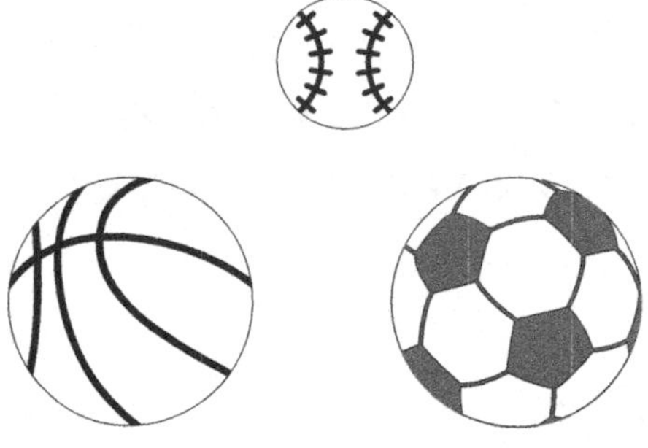

6.

9.

7.

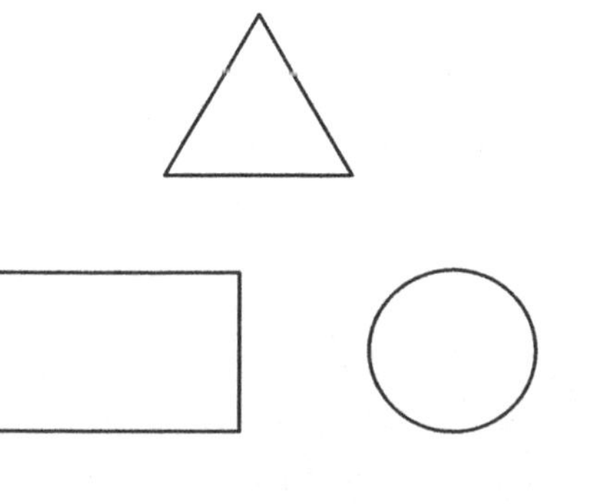

10.

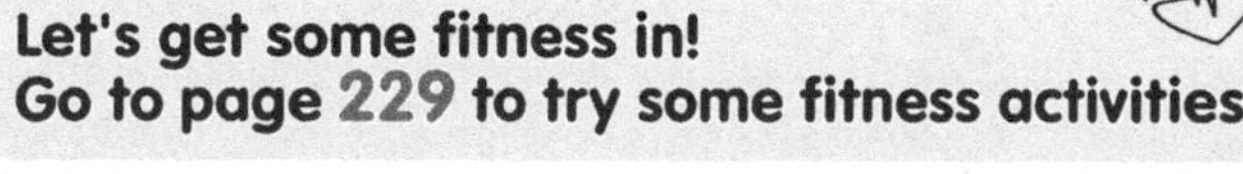

Let's get some fitness in!
Go to page 229 to try some fitness activities.

FITNESS TIME

Sorting Common Objects
ENGLISH

Read Together

Remember that objects can be sorted by what they have in common. This could be size, shape, category or color. For example, a pile of crayons could be grouped by color or size.

Directions

On the table below, write or say aloud objects that could be sorted by each characteristic.

For Kids

Size	Shape

WEEK 12
DAY 2

Sorting Common Objects
ENGLISH

Color	Category

W L
O F

WEEK 12
DAY 2

Sorting Common Objects
ENGLISH

Directions

Look at the groups of pictures below. Think about what each set of pictures has in common. Write or say aloud what they have in common.

For Kids

1.

3.

2.

4.

Sorting Common Objects
ENGLISH

5.

8.

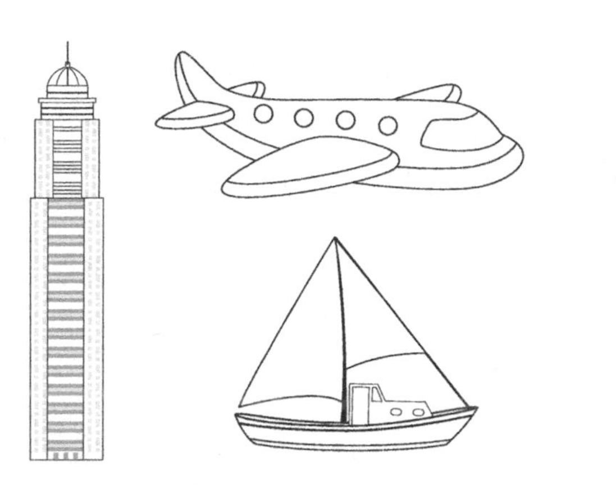

6.

9.

7.

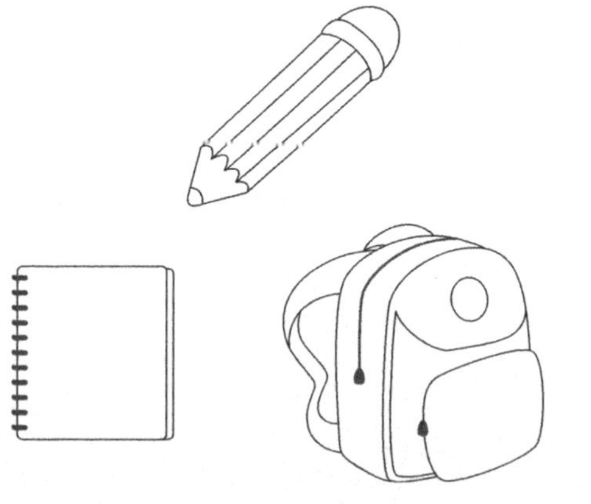

10.

Let's get some fitness in!
Go to page 229 to try some fitness activities.

WEEK 12 DAY 3

Matching a Number to a Group
MATHEMATICS

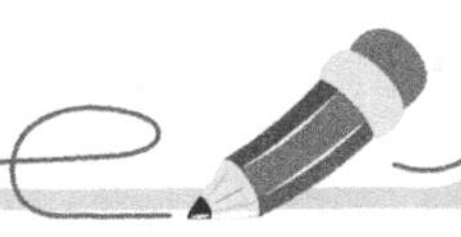

Directions:

Circle the correct number.

Question 1:

Jenny the Jellyfish is ready for school! How many lunch boxes does she have?

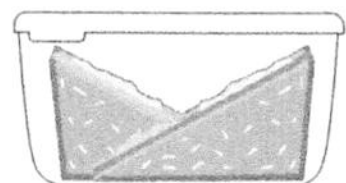 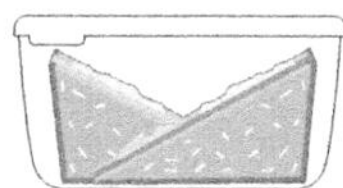 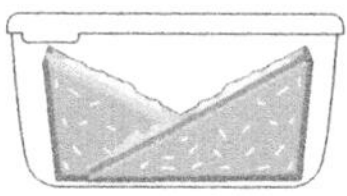

1 2 3 4 5 6 7 8 9 10

Question 3:

How many books does she have?

1 2 3 4 5 6 7 8 9 10

Question 2:

How many pairs of scissors does she have?

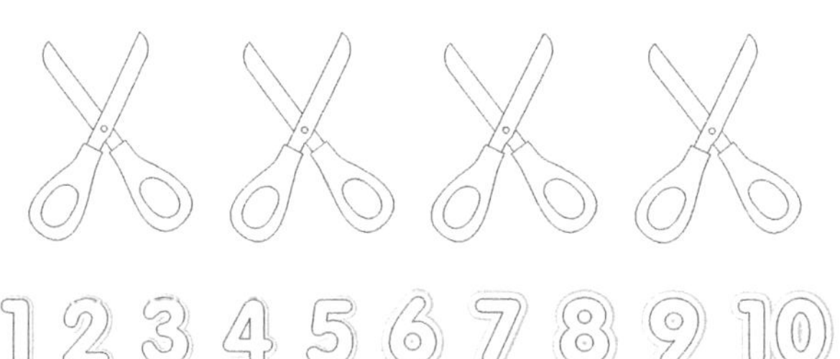

1 2 3 4 5 6 7 8 9 10

Question 4:

How many crayons does she have?

1 2 3 4 5 6 7 8 9 10

Matching a Number to a Group

MATHEMATICS

Question 5:

How many pencils does she have?

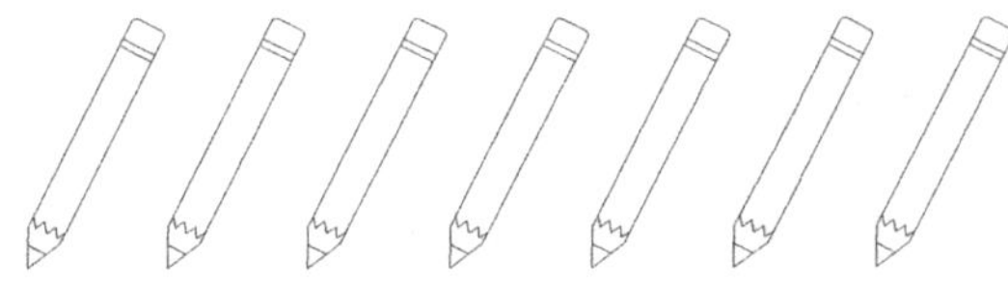

1 2 3 4 5 6 7 8 9 10

Question 7:

How many erasers does she have?

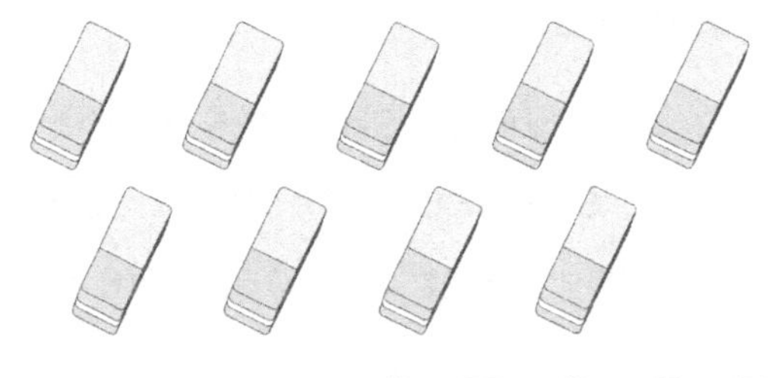

1 2 3 4 5 6 7 8 9 10

Question 6:

How many markers does she have?

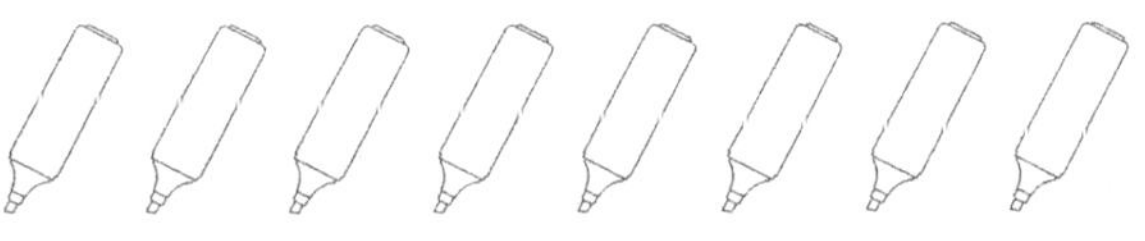

1 2 3 4 5 6 7 8 9 10

Question 8:

How many seashells does Jenny have for show-and-tell?

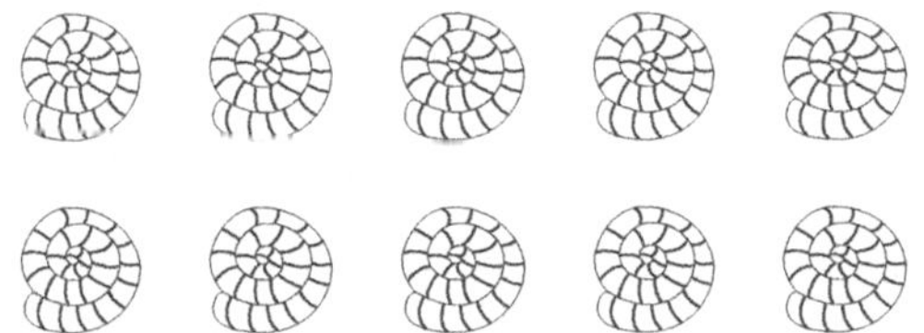

1 2 3 4 5 6 7 8 9 10

Let's get some fitness in!
Go to page 229 to try some fitness activities.

WEEK 12 DAY 4

Matching a Number to a Group
MATHEMATICS

Directions:

Circle the correct number.

Question 1:

Jenny the Jellyfish sees a lot of other creatures at her school. How many sharks does she see?

1 2 3 4 5 6 7 8 9 10

Question 2:

How many seahorses does she see?

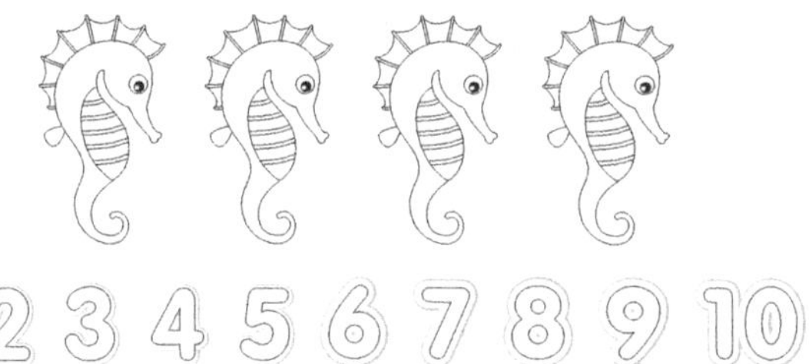

1 2 3 4 5 6 7 8 9 10

Question 3:

How many sea turtles does she see?

1 2 3 4 5 6 7 8 9 10

Question 4:

How many starfish does she see?

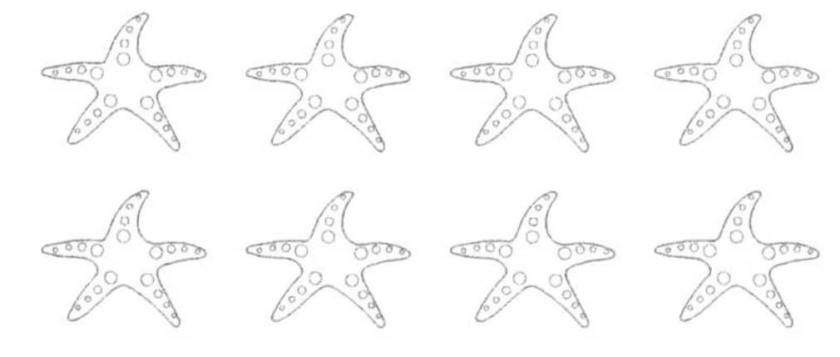

1 2 3 4 5 6 7 8 9 10

Matching a Number to a Group
MATHEMATICS

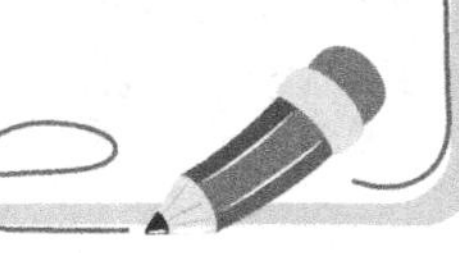

Question 5:

How many fish does she see?

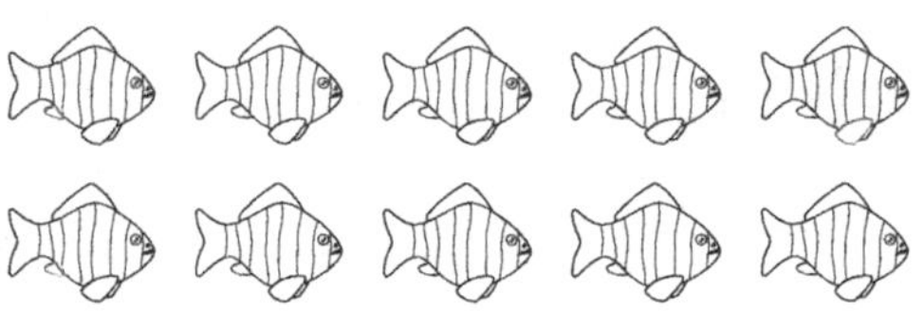

1 2 3 4 5 6 7 8 9 10

Question 7:

How many crabs does she see?

1 2 3 4 5 6 7 8 9 10

Question 6:

How many lobsters does she see?

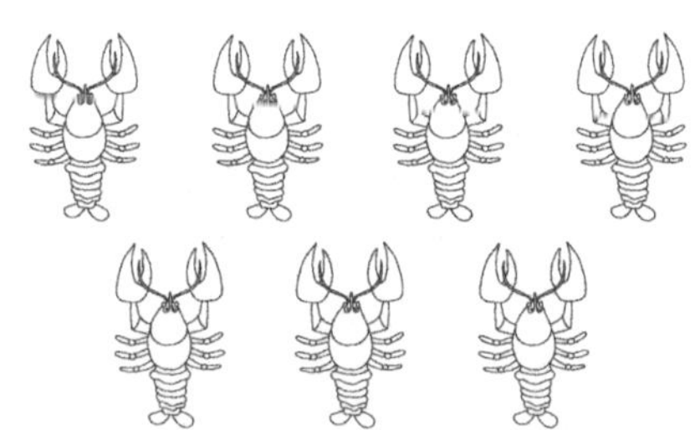

1 2 3 4 5 6 7 8 9 10

Question 8:

How many whales does she see?

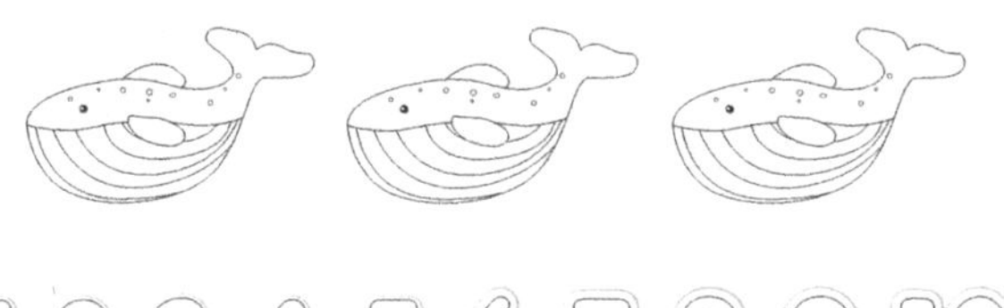

1 2 3 4 5 6 7 8 9 10

Let's get some fitness in!
Go to page 229 to try some fitness activities.

WEEK 12 DAY 5

Matching a Number to a Group
MATHEMATICS

Directions:

Circle the correct number.

Question 1:

Jenny the Jellyfish loves the undersea playground. How many swings are there?

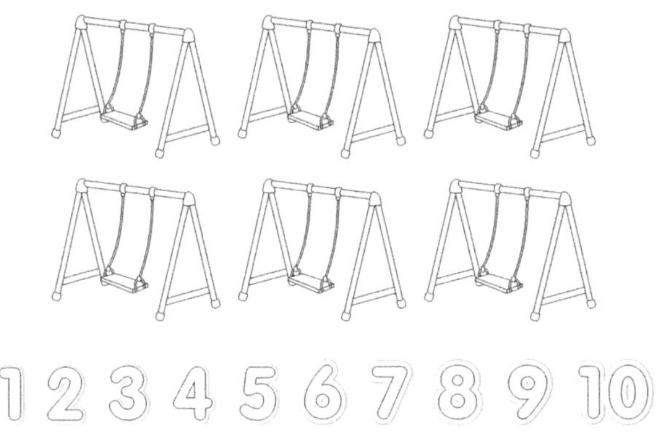

1 2 3 4 5 6 7 8 9 10

Question 2:

How many slides are there?

1 2 3 4 5 6 7 8 9 10

Question 3:

How many teeter-totters are there?

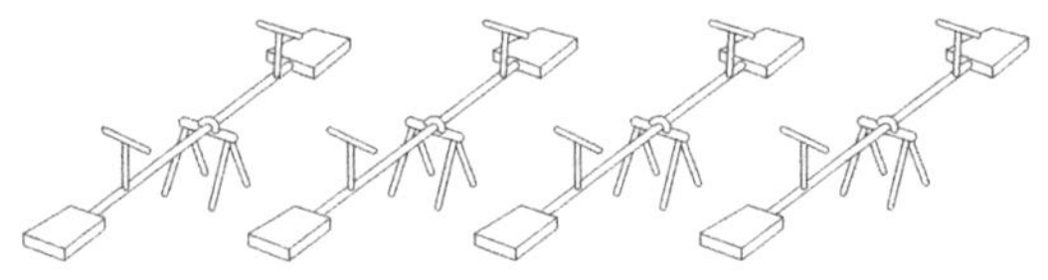

1 2 3 4 5 6 7 8 9 10

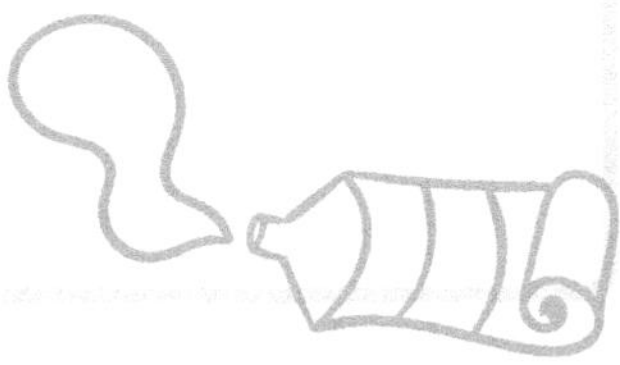

Question 4:

How many basketball hoops are there?

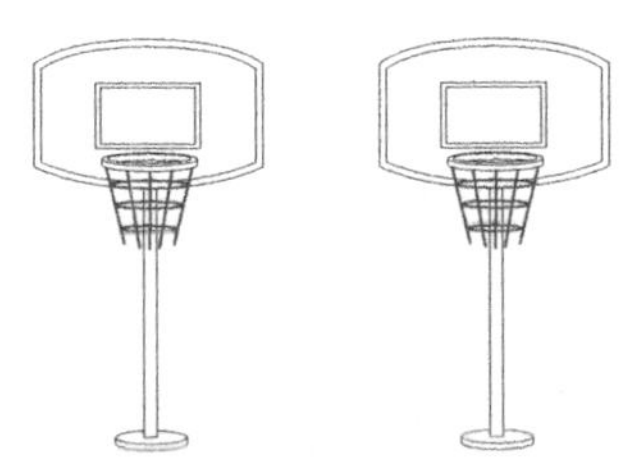

1 2 3 4 5 6 7 8 9 10

Matching a Number to a Group

MATHEMATICS

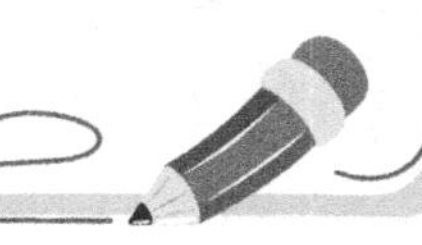

Question 5:

How many balls are there?

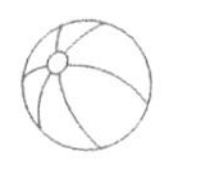 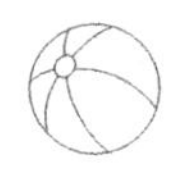 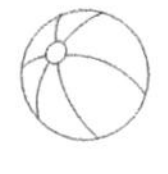 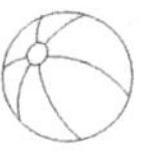

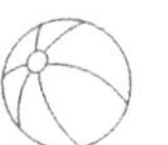 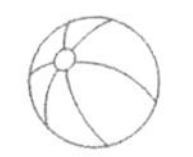 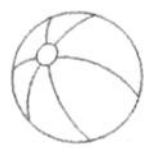

Question 7:

How many sand boxes are there?

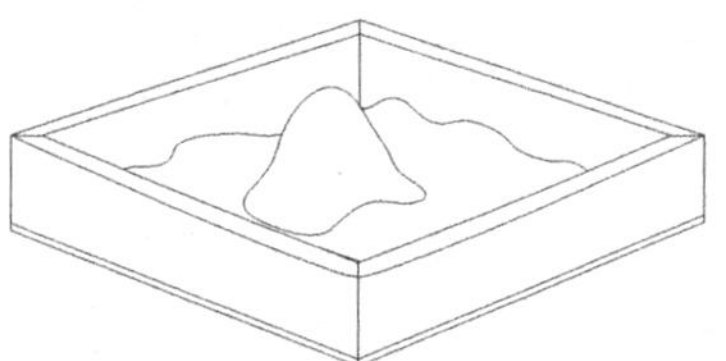

1 2 3 4 5 6 7 8 9 10

Question 6:

How many jump ropes are there?

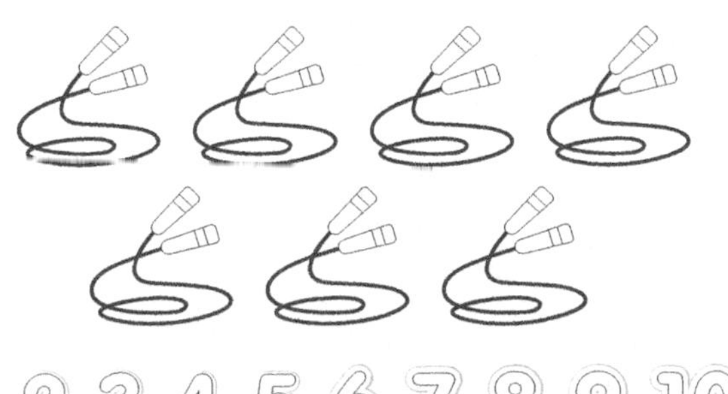

1 2 3 4 5 6 7 8 9 10

Question 8:

How many playground benches are there?

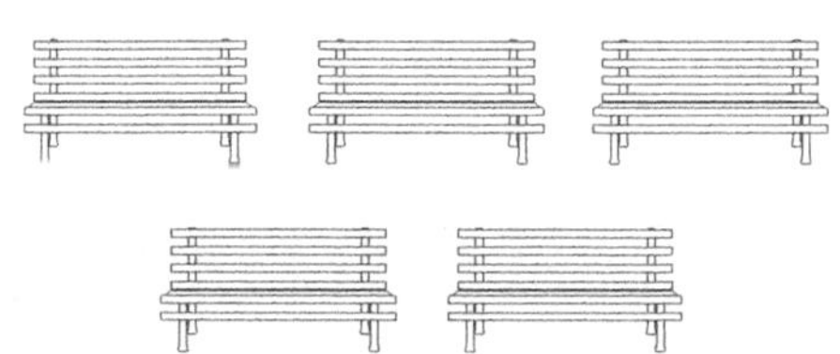

1 2 3 4 5 6 7 8 9 10

Let's get some fitness in!
Go to page 229 to try some fitness activities.

WEEK 12 DAY 6

Animal Needs EXPERIMENTS

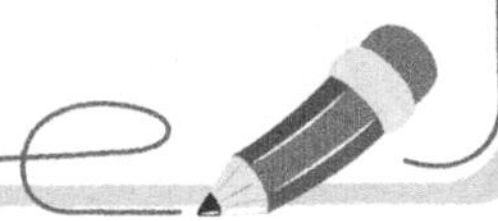

Read Together

You have learned about plants and animals in past lessons. You know that plants and animals are both living things. They need different things in order to live.

All animals have many things they need in order to grow and live. These things include: air, water, food, shelter and space. If animals don't get enough of these things, they will not survive.

Directions

Look at the pictures in the picture bank below. For each picture, decide if that item is something animals need in order to live. Match the picture to the correct category on the table below and write the letter in the space provided.

For Kids

WEEK 12 DAY 6

Animal Needs
EXPERIMENTS

Animals Need This to Survive	Animals Do Not Need This to Survive

Can you think of other things that fit into each of the categories above? Draw a picture or write their names in the boxes above.

Let's get some fitness in!
Go to page 229 to try some fitness activities.

WEEK 12 DAY 7 PUZZLE

These animals are riding on a lift in the mountains. Whose shadow can you see in the window of each cabin? Connect with a line.

FITNESS
TIME
ARGOPREP

FITNESS TIME

exercises complex one

1 - **Abs:** 2 times

2 - **Lunges:** 2 times to each leg.
Note: Use your body weight or books as weight to do leg lunges.

3 - **Plank:** 3 sec.

4 - **Run**: 10m
Note: Run **5** meters to one side and **5** meters back to the starting position.

> Please be aware of your environment and be safe at all times.
> If you cannot do an exercise, just try your best.

exercises complex two

1 - **High Plank:** 3 sec.

3 - **Waist Hooping:** 4 times. Note: if you do not have a hoop, pretend you have an imaginary hoop and rotate your hips 10 times.

2 - **Chair:** 3 sec.
Note: sit on an imaginary chair while keeping your back straight.

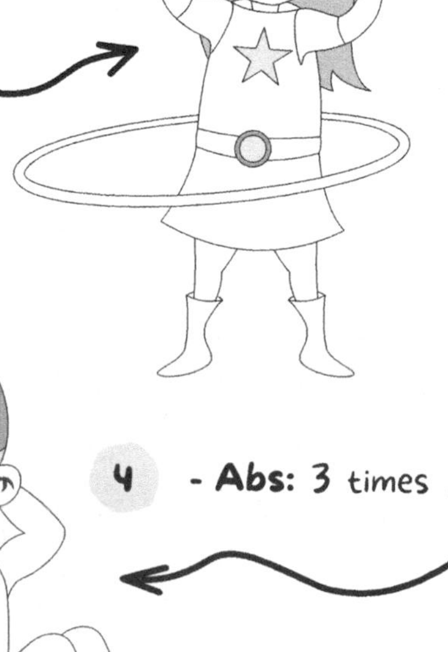

4 - **Abs:** 3 times

FITNESS TIME

exercises complex three

1 - **Down Dog:** 5 sec.

2 - **Bend Down:** 10 sec.

3 - **Chair:** 3 sec.

4 - **Child Pose:** 10 sec.

5 - **Shavasana:** as long as you can.
Note: think of happy moments and relax your mind.

"Please be aware of your environment and be safe at all times. If you cannot do an exercise, just try your best."

exercises complex four

1 - **Bend forward:** 5 times
Note: try to touch your feet. Make sure to keep your back straight, and if needed, you can bend your knees.

2 - **Lunges:** 2 times to each leg.
Note: Use your body weight or books as weight to do leg lunges.

3 - **Plank:** 4 sec.

4 - **Abs:** 3 times

Answer Sheets

To see the answer key to the entire workbook, you can easily download the answer key from our website!

*Due to the high request from parents and teachers, we have removed the answer key from the workbook so you do not need to rip out the answer key while students work on the workbook.

Go to **argoprep.com/summerprek**
OR scan the QR Code:

Kids Summer Academy by ArgoPrep: Grade 8-9

Kids Summer Academy by ArgoPrep: Grade 5-6

Kids Summer Academy by ArgoPrep: Grade 4-5

Kids Summer Academy by ArgoPrep: Grade 6-7

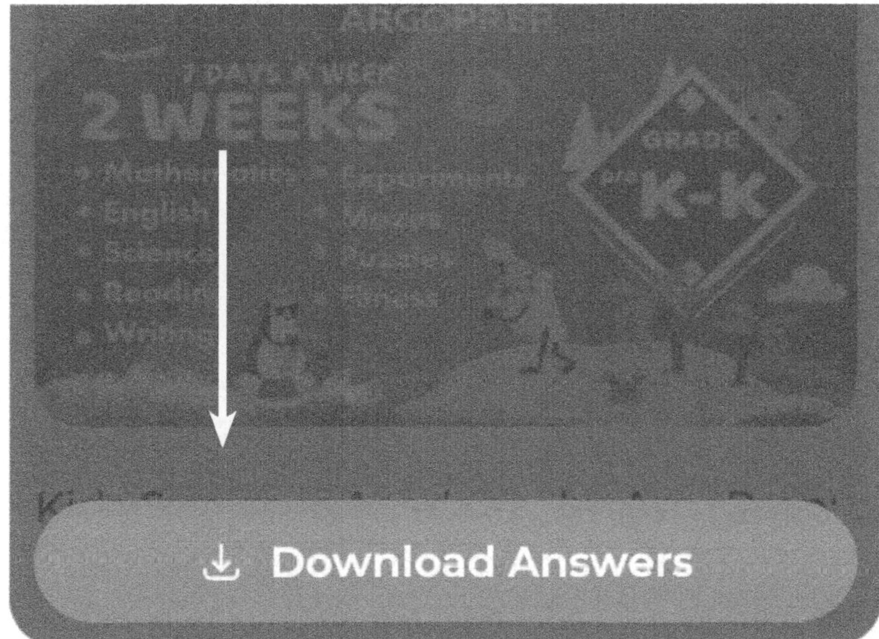

Kids Summer
Grade 8-9

Made in the USA
Las Vegas, NV
07 June 2022